Shitsukan—Understanding and Manipulating Material and Quality Perception

Shin'ya Nishida · Ko Nishino
Editors

Shitsukan—Understanding and Manipulating Material and Quality Perception

Springer

Editors
Shin'ya Nishida
Graduate School of Informatics
Kyoto University
Kyoto, Kyoto, Japan

Ko Nishino
Graduate School of Informatics
Kyoto University
Kyoto, Kyoto, Japan

ISBN 978-981-95-4761-6 ISBN 978-981-95-4762-3 (eBook)
https://doi.org/10.1007/978-981-95-4762-3

This work was supported by Japan Society for the Promotion of Science.

This Springer imprint is published by the registered company Springer Nature Singapore Pte Ltd.
The registered company address is: 152 Beach Road, #21-01/04 Gateway East, Singapore 189721, Singapore

Preface

"Shitsukan," a unique Japanese word, refers to the qualitative, immeasurable attributes pertaining to the materials and quality of objects and scenes. Through the perception of the wide and rich varieties of Shitsukan, humans can gain essential information for daily life, perceive the richness of the world, judge the value of things, and determine appropriate bodily actions. Understanding how to recognize Shitsukan and how to manipulate Shitsukan are thus fundamental research topics for us humans.

This book is a cumulation of our efforts in Shitsukan research mainly centered around three unique interdisciplinary projects in Japan: "Brain and Information Science on Shitsukan" (2010–2014), "Innovative Shitsukan Science and Technology" (2015–2019), and "Analysis and Synthesis of Deep Shitsukan Information in the Real World" (2020–2024). The book provides an overview of what we have achieved through these projects, focusing especially on the last project which aimed at uncovering the deep-level processing of Shitsukan information. The contributors of the book are the core members of this "Deep Shitsukan" project. By reading through this book, readers will gain insight into how humans and machines perceive Shitsukan (psychopysics and computer vision), how the brain processes Shitsukan (neuroscience), and how one can create and modulate Shitsukan (virtual reality, digital art, and industrial engineering).

This book would not have seen the light of day without the help of a large group of people. Our sincere gratitude extends to the authors and publishers, the hundreds of researchers who participated in the three Shitsukan projects, both in their planned research as well as publicly solicited research, and the many others who provided background support to the projects. We also thank MEXT/JSPS KAKENHI Grant Number JP20H05950 for supporting the publication of this book.

Kyoto, Japan

Shin'ya Nishida
Ko Nishino

Contents

Chapter 1
What Is Shitsukan?

Shin'ya Nishida and Ko Nishino

Abstract This brief introductory chapter provides the definition of Shitsukan, the historical background of our Shitsukan projects, and an outline of the following chapters.

Keywords Shitsukan · Perception · Material · Quality

1.1 Shitsukan

"Shitsukan" is a unique Japanese word that does not have a clear English translation. "Shitsu" means quality, and "Kan" stands for sensation. Literally, Shitsukan refers to the sensation of quality, but it means more.

Shitsukan represents the intangible or tangible characteristics of things, matters, and events that determine their impression caused by their underlying material and quality. Through multiple sensory modalities (vision, touch, audition, smell, and taste), we humans can recognize, easily and quickly in some cases, what kind of material an object is made of (e.g., metal or plastic), what kind of quality an object has (e.g., glossy and hard), and what condition an object is in (e.g., dry or fresh).

In addition to such physical material properties, Shitsukan refers to the subjective feelings evoked by objects and events, including comfort or discomfort, pleasant or unpleasant, tasty or disgusting, and luxury or cheap. These feelings include the evaluation of the values of an object and an event. The perceived value can be biological, emotional, aesthetic, or social, and, importantly, it can be either positive or negative. Shitsukan captures that feeling you get when you see a meticulously finished craft work or a rotten apple, when you pick up a dense plank of wood or

S. Nishida (✉) · K. Nishino
Graduate School of Informatics, Kyoto University, Kyoto, Japan
e-mail: nishida.shinya.2x@kyoto-u.ac.jp

K. Nishino
e-mail: nishino.ko.5a@kyoto-u.ac.jp

S. Nishida and K. Nishino (eds.), *Shitsukan—Understanding and Manipulating Material and Quality Perception*, https://doi.org/10.1007/978-981-95-4762-3_1

a light veneer, when walking barefoot on a fine sand beach or a soggy carpet, and when entering a quiet library study or a busy train station hall.

The emotional or value-related feelings, i.e., the emotional Shitsukan, may be obtained through the perception of specific characteristics of the physical material. However, the observers may not notice where the feelings came from. Good or bad Shitsukan is often used to represent the positive or negative sensation, that is hard to describe with words, obtained from an object or an event. Furthermore, such emotional Shitsukan is strongly modulated by the characteristics, preferences, and past experiences of the observer.

In this way, Shitsukan extends well beyond the apparent measurable attributes you find in objects and events, such as their appearance and texture. Shitsukan is inherently multifaceted and qualitative, which makes it hard to even describe, let alone scientifically study. Research on material perception of stuff, a topic extensively studied in the last 20–30 years, only scrapes the surface of the science of Shitsukan perception.

Understanding the mechanisms underlying the perception of Shistukan and manipulating that process to realize a desired Shitsukan in the real world thus inherently requires a multidisciplinary approach. It should naturally span psychology, neuroscience, computer science, virtual reality, medical science, industrial engineering, medicine, art, and likely more disciplines. Shitsukan bridges science and engineering, spanning conventional basic and application research. It touches upon a multitude of sensory modalities, including vision, touch, hearing, taste, smell, and language. Shitsukan research provides an ideal common ground to unite a wide range of research efforts, as you will see in this book.

1.2 Shitsukan Research

Research on Shitsukan has been uniquely developed in Japan through a series of interdisciplinary projects. The foundations were laid between 1998 and 2010, marked by pioneering studies in material perception. During this period, significant discoveries included the identification of image features underlying gloss perception and gloss-selective neurons in the visual cortex.

Building on these foundations, two national research projects were launched in Japan. The first was the Grant-in-Aid for Scientific Research on Innovative Areas titled "Brain and Information Science on Shitsukan" (2010–2014). This project was followed by a second one: "Innovative Shitsukan Science and Technology" (2015–2019). Both projects combined information and computer science, neuroscience, and psychophysics, and adopted a multisensory approach encompassing vision, touch, audition, and language. These efforts contributed to the establishment of "Shitsukan Science," a comprehensive and transdisciplinary field that spans from basic research to application. In terms of scope and interdisciplinarity, this Japanese initiative stands out globally–comparable to efforts such as PRISM and DiViTo in Europe–and has helped establish "Shitsukan" as an internationally recognized word.

Interdisciplinary Shitsukan research carried out in these two projects was further expanded with a third one, namely the Grant-in-Aid for Transformative Research Areas (A) "Analysis and synthesis of deep SHITSUKAN information in the real world (Deep Shitsukan),"(2020–2025). On top of the understanding of surface-level Shitukan, this project aimed at understanding Deep Shitsukan. While surface-level Shitsukan is the computation of Shitukan parameters from image features (in the case of vision), Deep Shitukan includes computing ecological value, triggering affective and emotional responses, and building internal models of the external world that support adaptive interaction with it. Understanding what happens when such perceptual functions deteriorate–and how to intervene–also becomes an important research frontier.

1.3 This Book

This book describes our quest towards defining and excavating this Deep Shitsukan in our real world to advance our understanding of Shitsukan perception at both the computational and experimental levels.

The contributors include human sensory scientists, neuroscientists, computer scientists, virtual reality engineers, medical doctors, and digital artists. They are the core members of the Deep Shistukan project.

This book is organized as follows:

Following this short chapter, Part I introduces how humans and machines perceive Shitsukan.

In Chap. 2, Nishida and Sawayama review the history and future directions of research on human visual material and Shitsukan perception.

In Chap. 3, Nishino provides a comprehensive overview of computational approaches to visual appearance modeling in computer vision.

Chapter 4 outlines Okatani's research on Shitsukan perception from a machine learning perspective.

In Chap. 5, Koumura reviews auditory aspects of Shitsukan perception, presenting studies on estimating material properties from contact sounds and inferring environmental ambience from sound modulations.

Part II introduces diverse studies on the neural processing of Shitsukan.

In Chap. 6, Kamitani, Tanaka, and Horikawa describe their work decoding sensory representations–including Shitsukan–from fMRI signals in humans.

Chapter 7, authored by Komatsu, summarizes his findings from neurophysiological and fMRI studies in monkeys, showing that gloss and other material-related features are processed hierarchically along the ventral pathway.

In Chap. 8, Suzuki, Nakauchi, and Kinzuka investigate inter-individual differences in Shitsukan perception by highlighting research on older adults and brain-damaged people.

Chapter 9 shows work by Minamimoto and Murata on the study of neural mechanisms that underlie the transformation of sensory signals into value-based representations–a key component of deep Shitsukan.

Part III addresses how to control Shitsukan experiences.

Chapter 10 focuses on touch. Kajimoto, Konyo, and Okamoto each introduce recent progress in characterizing tactile material perception in humans and in developing haptic display technologies.

In Chap. 11, Iwai and Itoh introduce recent advances in augmented reality technologies for reproducing Shitsukan with high fidelity.

Chapter 12, by Watanabe, presents technologies for manipulating the appearance of objects and environments through fast, dynamic projection mapping.

In Chap. 13, Nakatani, Kakehi, and Hiura showcase various attempts in digital fabrication aimed at creating novel Shitsukan textures and tactile experiences.

Chapter 14, by Horiuchi and Sakamoto, introduces their approaches to the industrial applications of Shitsukan research.

Finally, in Chap. 15, Ishihara, Nakamoto, Uchiro, Miki, Asano, Taira and Sato present their recent studies on skin Shitsukan in oil paintings using spectral analysis.

We hope this book will assist readers in understanding the progress of our interdisciplinary research on Shitsukan, and in recognizing how placing this unique concept at the core can open up wide-ranging avenues of research.

Part I
Perceiving Shitsukan

Chapter 2
Human Visual Perception of Shitsukan

Shin'ya Nishida and Masataka Sawayama

Abstract Visual estimation of material properties, such as gloss, viscosity, and wetness, is one of the main tasks of human Shitsukan recognition. It is computationally challenging since the image formation involves complex optical interplays of material, geometry, and illumination, and because physical material properties are inherently complex and high-dimensional. It seems difficult for human vision to estimate material characteristics from a single image in a strict inverse-optics way. The hypothesis that human vision heuristically uses image-computable simple features for estimating material properties (e.g., the skewness of the luminance histogram for gloss estimation) was proposed but has been criticized for its ignorance of other relevant stimulus factors (e.g., 3D shape). The complexity of human material computation remains a controversial issue, and the recent success of artificial neural networks in explaining human vision has amplified expectations about the complexity of the underlying neural computation. Here, we argue that specifying relevant image features for material perception still is a useful strategy for an explicit understanding of the human visual computation of material, as long as the study also analyzes the underlying physical mechanism and explains why these features work and when they fail to predict human material perception. Furthermore, for a full understanding of the human material processing, we should investigate how the material affects the perception of the other attributes, such as shape and motion, in addition to how the material perception is affected by the other attributes.

Keywords Human vision · Psychophysics · Gloss · Image statistics · Material perception · Shape perception

---

S. Nishida (✉)
Graduate School of Informatics, Kyoto University, Kyoto, Japan
e-mail: nishida.shinya.2x@kyoto-u.ac.jp

M. Sawayama
Graduate School of Information Science and Technology, Hokkaido University, Sapporo, Hokkaido, Japan
e-mail: masataka_sawayama@ist.hokudai.ac.jp

Prometech CG Research, Tokyo, Japan

S. Nishida and K. Nishino (eds.), *Shitsukan—Understanding and Manipulating Material and Quality Perception*, https://doi.org/10.1007/978-981-95-4762-3_2

2.1 Introduction

We humans have the remarkable ability to recognize, simply by looking, various perceptual properties of objects and events that convey their nature and state. We refer to these properties as Shitsukan in this book. Shitsukan is primarily determined by material properties, including surface optical properties (e.g., glossiness, roughness, transparency, and translucency) and internal mechanical properties (e.g., viscosity, elasticity, and softness). We can visually judge the physical material classes of objects (e.g., metal, glass, and plastic), the condition of the surface (e.g., slipperiness, wetness, dirtiness), as well as the emotional, ecological, and aesthetic values of the object, and personal preferences. Shitsukan perception is one of the essential components of our visual experience of realistic natural scenes. At the same time, Shitsukan perception is one of the most challenging research themes in vision science, since it is a highly ill-posed problem of estimating high-dimensional and mutually interacting physical attributes.

2.1.1 Material Perception in Vision Science

The visual system recognizes the external world (distal stimuli) from retinal images (proximal stimuli). Human visual processing begins with the analysis of the retinal image to reveal primary attributes such as color, shape, position, and motion. The subsequent processing binds the processed attributes to compute a coherent visual representation of realistic scenes.

The computational process of estimating the external world from the retinal image is often regarded as inverse optics [1] (or inverse rendering). While forward optics is the process of rendering images of the visual scene from the physical components of the scene, inverse optics is the process of estimating the physical components from the image by inverting the optical rendering process. For example, how the visual system estimates 3D structure from various depth cues, including binocular disparity, motion parallax, and shading, has been investigated as a typical inverse-optics problem.

As demonstrated by successful photo-realistic rendering in computer graphics, the fundamental physical components of natural scenes are geometric structure, pose, lighting, and material. The material determines how the surface reflects or refracts incoming light, and thus is most relevant to the optical aspects of Shitsukan. Material properties include gloss and translucency, in addition to surface albedo and spectral reflectance that determine the lightness and color of the surface. Albedo, spectral reflectance, and gloss are specified by the Bidirectional Reflectance Distribution Function (BRDF), which characterizes how the light reflection changes as a function of incoming light direction and viewing direction. The Bidirectional Scattering Surface Reflectance Distribution Function (BSSRDF) can describe the subsurface scattering effect that produces translucent appearances. While the BRDF and BSSRDF assume that the material properties of a surface are homogeneous, the Bidirectional Texture Function (BTF) can describe the spatial variation of local reflectance functions of spatially inhomogeneous reflections.

One hypothesis about human material perception processing is a rigorous version of the inverse-optics theory that assumes the estimation of the BRDF, BSSRDF, or BTF that is most consistent with the input image. This computation should include estimations of the remaining rendering components of the image, including the surface geometry and the lightfield. In other words, this theory attempts to recover the physical model underlying the image formation entirely.

An alternative hypothesis is a heuristic-based theory that attempts to infer material properties from image features. These image features may not precisely correspond to the physical ground truths of the material properties, but statistically correlate with them in most of the natural environments. Estimating the geometry and illumination of the scene from the image is not necessary.

As we shall see in the following, both theories have supporting arguments and reasonable criticisms. Plausible theories on human material perception lie somewhere between these two extreme hypotheses.

2.2 Gloss Perception

2.2.1 Inverse-Optics Theory

Physics-based inverse rendering is the most reasonable strategy for visual perception if it is computationally feasible. Recent engineering studies have shown some success in inverse rendering of material properties, utilizing complex iterative operations, including forward rendering models [2–4]. Although we humans can also infer various material properties from images, there is some doubt as to whether inverse optics can be implemented in the human visual system in its strict form.

First, solving this task in a rigorous inverse-optics way is computationally challenging, since the surface reflectance characteristics, as represented by the BRDF, BSSRDF, and BTF, are complex and of high dimension. Scene geometry and illumination structure, which inverse-optics approaches should estimate, are also complex and difficult to estimate from an image. Human material (gloss) perception is known to be multidimensional [5], but it is unlikely that human material representations are as complex as the BRDF, BSSRDF, or BTF. The human ability to estimate illumination is limited and is often insensitive to the inconsistency of lighting in a scene [6, 7]. Whereas the human visual system may be able to estimate the dominant direction and spread of illumination from the spatial distribution of the shading pattern [8], there is no evidence that it can recover the entire lightfield of the scene. The effect of surface geometry on lightness perception [9, 10] suggests that our brain can take into account illumination when estimating surface reflectance. However, it may only assume that nearby surface areas with similar surface normal directions share a common illumination (framework) [10], rather than directly computing the illumination, reflectance, surface orientation, and their optical interactions. Finally, the human visual system has a good ability to estimate the shape of an object even from a single image, but the recovered shape representation is not veridical in the 3D Euclidean space [11]. Our brain may only estimate the affine structure or qualitative shape indices [12, 13].

Second, limited perceptual constancy in human material perception is incompatible with the use of a strict inverse-optics computation. If the human visual system can correctly solve the inverse optics to estimate the geometry, lighting, and material of the scene, as long as the image is rendered using the same material parameters, the perceived material should be constant against changes in geometry or illumination. This holds, though not perfectly, for basic properties of surface albedo and body color, which are known as lightness constancy and color constancy [14, 15]. Do humans have perceptual constancy for material properties? The answer is no, at least for gloss, since changes in surface geometry have severe impacts on gloss perception—when the spatial frequency and amplitude of surface modulation change, the apparent gloss magnitude and shininess change [16]. Furthermore, the effect of surface geometry on gloss perception is consistent with the idea that the observers use the similarity in low-level image features (specifically, luminance histogram) to judge the similarity in apparent gloss. While this finding was made under unnatural point light illumination, a later study confirmed a similar effect of surface geometry on material perception under natural illumination [17].

Changes in illumination have minor effects on gloss perception as long as the lightfield is global illumination of natural scenes, but they have significant negative effects when the illumination is unnatural [18]. Unnatural illuminations include a point light source, a uniform illumination, and an environment lighting made from white or pink ($1/f$) noise. Note that these unnatural illuminations are much simpler (with a smaller number of parameters) than the natural scenes. If the human material perception relies on an inverse optics computation, the results would be the opposite: i.e., complex natural illumination should be more difficult and unstable.

2.2.2 Image Statistics Theory

These findings indicate that the human visual system may not correctly solve the inverse optics. Instead, they suggest an alternative theory that the visual system may judge material based on the presence of image features correlated with the material in most natural environments.

For material properties related to surface reflectance, image statistics of the surface image could provide useful information for material recognition in natural environments. The image statistics of most natural scenes have specific characteristics [19]. In light reflection, the surface acts as an image filter. For example, the image reflected on a rough surface is blurred. If the human brain knows the characteristics of natural scene statistics such that an object border should have a sharp edge, by analyzing the image statistics of the reflected image, it can estimate the surface properties as an image filter. Note that the human brain does not need to estimate the details of the actual scene illumination as long as the scene is natural, sharing basic statistics with other scenes. On the other hand, if the environment is unnatural or too simple to estimate the image statistics, this scheme collapses, as demonstrated by [18].

One candidate of image statistics correlated with gloss is the skewness of the luminance histogram, or subband histogram [20, 21]. This hypothesis was inspired by the findings that luminance histogram similarity explains a significant portion of apparent material similarity [16], and the image features correlated with histogram skewness were good predictors of physical gloss in machine vision [22]. Motoyoshi et al. [20] further showed that many object images look glossier when the luminance histogram is skewed positively by a histogram manipulation, while they look less glossy when the luminance histogram is skewed negatively. They also suggested that a simple neural mechanism, as found in early visual processing, may be used to detect the histogram skew information, demonstrating an adaptation effect consistent with this hypothesis.

The idea that gloss perception, which had been believed to reflect a complex perceptual attribute, might be explained by heuristics based on a simple image cue directly computable from the image attracted a wide range of attention to material perception.

2.2.3 Luminance Histogram Manipulation

One may wonder why the manipulation of histogram skewness effectively controls gloss perception. Intuitively speaking, the positively skewed luminance histogram has a long tail extending toward higher intensities. This corresponds to a small number of pixels for highlights with high intensities. As discussed in detail by [23], a theoretically more important point is that the luminance histogram manipulation does not change the luminance order, and thus the spatial structure, of the image. This is because the intensity transformation for the histogram manipulation is tone remapping of the cumulative histogram of the original image to that of the target image. If pixel A is higher in intensity than pixel B in the original image, pixel B will not be higher than pixel A in any histogram-transformed image. As a result, changing the luminance histogram skewness does not affect the direction map of the intensity gradient in the spatial coordinates of the image, while affecting the magnitude (steepness) of the intensity gradient (Fig. 2.1a).

Furthermore, a global tone mapping which increases the steepness of the gradient in the high-intensity range makes the luminance histogram positive, while another which decreases the steepness of the gradient in the high-intensity range makes the luminance histogram negative. This makes the manipulation of luminance histogram skewness similar to the actual physical change of surface gloss (Fig. 2.1b). Assume a dielectric material whose surface can be modeled by the dichromatic reflection model (i.e., shading image produced by diffuse reflection + specular image produced by specular reflection) [24]. Changing the magnitude of the specular component while keeping the shading component will change the gloss strength. This manipulation

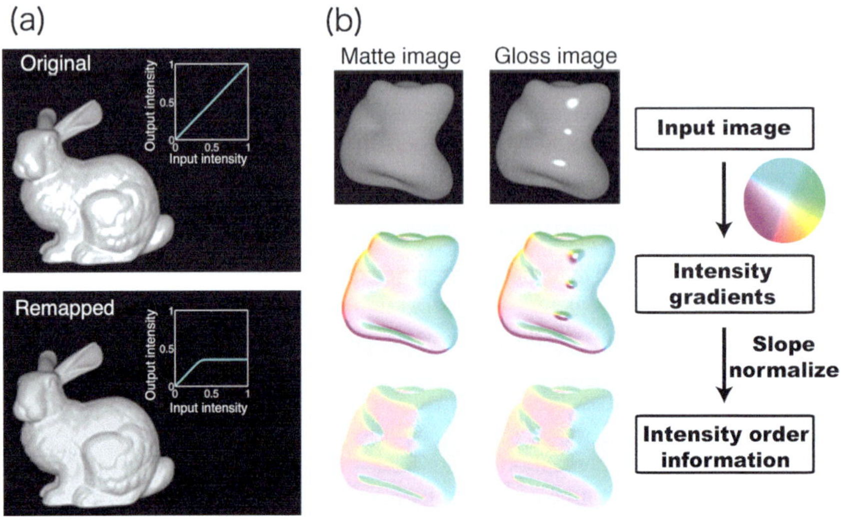

Fig. 2.1 **a** An intensity histogram manipulation through a global tone remapping that decreases the steepness of the gradient at the high-intensity range (as well as the skewness of the intensity histogram) makes a glossy image appear matte. This image operation changes the intensity gradient magnitude map while preserving the intensity gradient order map. **b** Matte and glossy images, rendered with a point light source from the viewing direction, have different intensity gradient magnitudes at highlight areas, but have similar intensity order maps. Adapted from [23]

has a significant impact on the magnitude of the intensity gradient but not much on the spatial structure of the image represented by the direction map of the intensity gradient (or on the isophote, a contour of equal intensity in an image) [25]. The reason the specular image shares the spatial structure with the diffuse-shading image is that both components depend on the incident angle of light (while the specular intensity is additionally affected by the viewing angle). The surface orientations of an area corresponding to a spot highlight are likely to be similar, and thus, the diffuse-shading components are also likely to be uniform. When the specular component is reduced to zero, the diffuse shading pattern revealed under the highlight is smoothly connected with the surrounding diffuse shading. This image change is similar to replacing a bright highlight with a uniform patch in the diffuse shading color of the surrounding area. The spatial structure represented by the direction map of the intensity gradient is not affected by the manipulation of the specular intensity.

In summary, changing the skewness of the luminance histogram in an object image has a similar effect to changing the magnitude of the specular component relative to the diffuse component in the object rendering model. Both change the magnitude of the intensity gradient without changing the structure of the intensity gradient. This is why the luminance histogram skewness is correlated with, and could be an image cue for, the gloss magnitude.

2.2.4 *Limitation of the Image Statistics Theory as an Explanation of Gloss Perception*

According to the analysis described above, changing the skewness of the luminance histogram effectively modulates the apparent gloss when the object material is dielectric one (e.g., plastic) whose surface can be described by the dichromatic reflection model (diffuse + specular reflections). On the other hand, when the surface reflection is pure diffuse (Lambertian) or pure specular (e.g., metallic), the effect of the skewness of the luminance histogram will be limited. Note, however, that the luminance histogram of a smooth metallic surface tends to be positively skewed because it directly reflects the lighting of the natural environment, whose luminance histogram is often positively skewed due to a small number of light sources [26].

Although the skewness of the luminance histogram does not specify spatial information, the spatial information affects gloss perception. When the image does not look like a surface image, such as random noise patterns, luminance histogram manipulation cannot control gloss [20]. In addition, the luminance histogram is also affected by many factors other than surface material, such as albedo change, surface normal direction [27–29], and illumination direction [30]. These factors reduce the correlation between the absolute value of skewness of the luminance histogram and apparent gloss under general conditions [31].

The luminance histogram skewness, an image cue, is not strong enough to predict apparent gloss under any conditions, since it contains an inherent ambiguity. Its theoretical position may be comparable to monocular depth cues, such as size. Human observers can judge the smaller object to be more distant than the larger object, but they do not take this interpretation under conditions where the size change is more likely to be produced by other factors. Likewise, human observers may use the histogram skewness to estimate gloss, but only when other factors cannot explain the histogram skewness. In addition, the human visual system may not directly compute luminance histogram skewness, but instead compute correlated image features, such as the statistics about the steepness of the luminance gradient.

2.2.5 *Intrinsic Image Decomposition in Gloss Processing*

Gloss perception is more than simply judging the intensity and quality of gloss. Before doing so, the visual system must decide whether a specific pattern (e.g., a bright area) is a highlight produced by specular reflection or not. This task is part of intrinsic image decomposition, i.e., separating the image changes into components produced by reflectance changes and geometric changes [32] (Fig. 2.2). The geometric component can be further divided into diffuse shading and specular reflection. To fully understand gloss perception, we must understand how the visual system solves the intrinsic image decomposition.

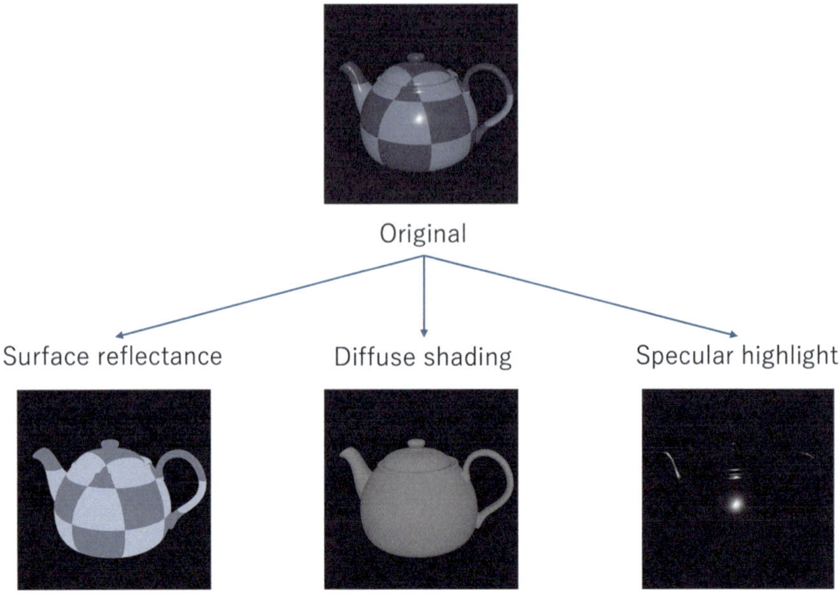

Fig. 2.2 Intrinsic image decomposition of a pod image into a surface reflectance (albedo) image, a diffuse shading image, and a specular highlight image

Most of the limitations of the skewness of the luminance histogram in explaining gloss perception are concerned with intrinsic image decomposition. Shifting or rotating the specular component of the image relative to the remaining image components significantly reduces apparent gloss without changing the luminance histogram [27–29] since this manipulation changes the interpretation of the rotated component from specular highlights to reflectance changes (e.g., white strain). Highlight coverage, contrast, and sharpness are proposed as alternative image cues for gloss perception [33], and shown to be diagnostic also in explaining material class perception [34]. To compute these features, however, the visual system has to first solve the intrinsic image decomposition problem to segment highlight areas. By switching the interpretations from diffuse shading to specular reflection or vice versa, surface geometric changes given by various depth cues can dramatically change apparent gloss without changing the luminance distribution [35–37].

As discussed in **2.3**, the luminance histogram is related to the luminance gradient [23], and the luminance gradient features may play important roles in intrinsic image decomposition. Analyzing the direction map of the luminance gradient, or isophote, is useful for separating reflectance changes from diffuse and specular reflection changes, because the two geometric components are mutually related due to the incident angle dependency, whereas the reflectance changes can occur independently. The covariation of diffuse and specular components in natural object images explains why shifting/rotating the specular component relative to the diffuse shading component makes it appear like reflectance changes [27, 28]. Furthermore, the steepness of the luminance gradient, which is correlated with the skewness of the luminance histogram, is an image feature potentially useful for discriminating diffuse shading and specular highlights. Considering the difference in the surface-angle dependency between diffuse and specular reflections, it is not the absolute value of steepness of the luminance gradient but the steepness of the luminance gradient relative to the steepness of the surface normal orientation change, that discriminates diffuse and specular reflections. There is empirical evidence that the visual system does use surface normal steepness given by a variety of depth cues in this computation [35–38].

In addition to luminance gradient features, the human visual system uses color information to solve the intrinsic image decomposition. When a smooth luminance change is not accompanied by a color change, it is more likely to be produced by a geometric change (diffuse shading) than a reflectance change [39]. The human visual system also uses chromatic information for recognizing specular components in the image [40]. When the color of the diffuse reflectance (body color) and that of specular reflectance (highlight color) are independently manipulated, the object looks naturally glossy when the body and highlights share the same color, either white or a saturated color (e.g., red), or when the body has a saturated color while the highlight is white (Fig. 2.3a-c). On the other hand, the object does not look naturally glossy when the highlight has a saturated color while the body is white or a different saturated color. The highlight portions may look glossy, but the apparently glossy area does not propagate into the remaining body surface (Fig. 2.3d-e). These observations indicate the human visual system realizes the dichromatic reflectance model, i.e., the specular reflection has the color of illumination, while the diffuse reflection reflects and absorbs illumination depending on its spectral characteristic, so that the body color should be included (a component of) the highlight color in the color spectrum (Fig. 2.3f).

Finally, image motion provides powerful cues to the intrinsic image decomposition [41, 42]. Different material components have different dependencies on the surface's normal direction, illumination angle, and viewing angle. As a result, when the object or the viewer moves, the different material components move differently. Based on the motion flow, we can judge whether the internal texture of an object is a surface texture (reflectance change), diffuse shading, specular reflection, or the internal specular reflection of transparent material.

2.2.6 *Processing Architecture of Gloss Perception*

We have seen that human gloss perception is unlikely to be based on a rigorous inverse optics computation, or on a simple computation using image statistics. Then, what is the plausible processing architecture of human gloss processing? More generally, how does the human visual system estimate the material properties together with the shape and other relevant components?

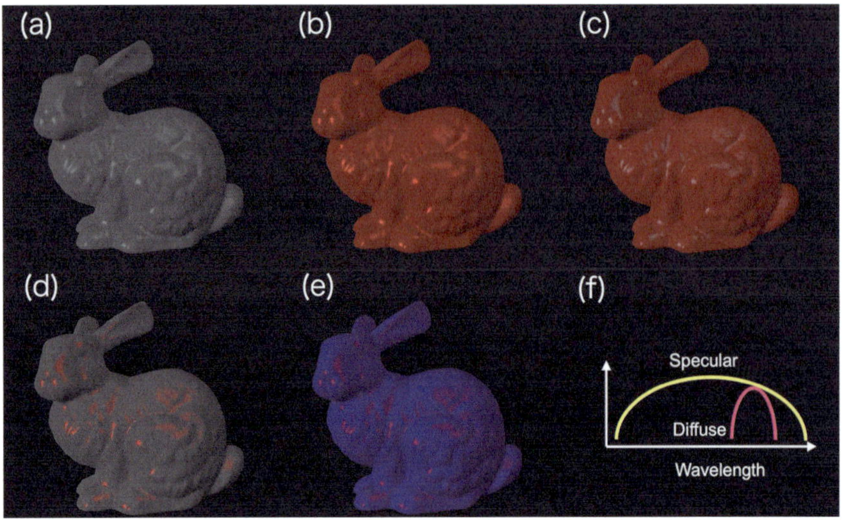

Fig. 2.3 **a** A white body with white highlights, **b** a red body with red highlights, and **c** a red body with white highlights look naturally glossy. On the other hand, **d** a white body with red highlights, and **e** a blue body with red highlights do not look naturally glossy. The latter two violate the physical rule that **f** the body color spectrum should be included in the specular color spectrum

One possible processing architecture is parallel feedforward processing of material and shape. The material estimation pathway extracts gloss-related features from input images and combines them to judge glossiness. Since those features can capture not only image features correlated with gloss magnitude but also various spatial constraints related to gloss, the pathway attempts to solve the intrinsic image decomposition in a feed-forward way. On the other hand, the shape processing pathway estimates shape as independently as possible of the surface material estimation. Stable perception of shape from shading against material changes [43] may be supported by shape perception from the direction map of the intensity gradient (or orientation field), which carries shape information nearly independent of the surface material [23, 25, 44, 45].

Another possible architecture is recurrent processing with a strong interaction between material and shape processing. The material processing uses the output of the depth processing, while the depth processing uses the output of the material processing, to find the best solutions for both. The findings that the depth provided by binocular disparity and motion parallax can affect diffuse-shading/specular-highlight discrimination [35] seem to be consistent with the implementation of a recurrent mechanism in the human visual system. In addition, even if the magnitude of the local luminance gradient, an image correlate of the skewness of the luminance histogram, is used for discriminating diffuse reflection from specular reflection [23], this variable should be normalized by the magnitude of the surface orientation gradient given by the shape processing.

However, solving so-called "egg-and-chicken" problems may take a long time. Simultaneous estimation of mutually dependent material and shape can be helped by good initial guess provided by feedforward pathways, even if the recurrent mechanism further improves the shape-material consistency.

Concerning the performance of the feedforward processing, recent studies suggest that feedforward deep learning networks can learn gloss magnitude estimation by supervised or unsupervised learning in a way somewhat similar to humans [46–48]. However, these networks cannot make accurate predictions about the effects of the (mis)alignment of diffuse shading and specular, at least under the conditions for which they were trained, which did not include the discrimination of highlights from reflectance changes.

Judging spatial (mis)alignment of highlights seems to require considerably complex computation. Online behavioral experiments involving hundreds of participants revealed a larger individual difference in sensitivity to the misalignment of highlights compared to sensitivity to the strength of highlights [49]. Furthermore, a texture synthesis algorithm based on mid-level image statistics [50] cannot reproduce spatially-aligned highlights that look natural for foveal vision [51, 52]; a texture synthesis algorithm based on deep features [53] can generate spatially-aligned highlights, but only when higher-layer representations are used [54]. Intrinsic image decomposition, including discrimination of highlights and albedo changes from spatial distribution, may require highly complex and sophisticated processing, possibly including recurrent computation [55].

Recurrent inference models may include generative networks. The recent success of generative AI in naturalistic image generation and understanding, as well as the advancement of predictive coding ideas in neuroscience [56, 57], has led researchers to seriously consider the idea that an image generation model may play an essential role in human visual processing [58]. Although we believe it unlikely that the human visual system implements a strict physics-based image rendering based on complete internal representations of material, geometry, and lighting, we cannot reject the possibility that some generative models contribute to human gloss and/or other material perception [59].

2.3 Other Material Properties

So far, we have reviewed human gloss perception. This section will discuss how other material properties are perceived.

2.3.1 Translucency

Translucency may be a property of optical material that has been attracting the attention of vision scientists as much as gloss [60] since the development of impressive photo-realistic rending of translucent materials [61]. The physical correlate of translucency is the subsurface scattering of light caused by the material's optical properties, including absorption and scattering coefficients, phase function, and index of refraction. Due to light scattering, the shading patterns of translucent materials are different from those of opaque materials. Typically, the shading contrast is reduced, and the shading pattern can be changed. On the other hand, the specular reflection of the translucent material is nearly the same as that of the opaque material. As a result, the specific relationship between the shading and specular images found with opaque objects is broken with translucent objects. This is how the spatial mismatch between the shading and specular images can be a cue for translucency [62–65]. For instance, the object looks translucent when the shading image is spatially flat, while the specular image indicates a bumpy surface. In other words, translucent materials do not show the correlation in the luminance gradient order structure between shading and specular highlights that holds for opaque materials [23]. This explains why an opaque image can be transformed into a translucent image through a simple image manipulation using a nonlinear tone mapping, which produces an artificial inconsistency between low-intensity (shading) regions and high-intensity (highlight) regions [65]. In addition, the translucency perception depends on the geometry of objects [49, 66, 67]. For example, the relationship between the shading image and surface geometry, as indicated by the occluding contour, could also serve as a cue to transparency [66]. As in the case of gloss perception, material processing is coordinated with shape processing in transparency perception.

Although translucency perception is often studied using analytical approaches similar to those for gloss perception, it presents more difficulties due to the more complex physical properties involved. For instance, even when other optical properties (e.g., the amount of scattering or absorption) are held constant, changes in the phase function, which determines the direction of light scattering, can largely alter the translucency perception [68]. Moreover, the effect of color on translucency is not straightforward; converting images to grayscale can either enhance or reduce the perception of translucency, depending on the material images [69]. Given these analytical difficulties, some recent research has explored data-driven approaches to uncover the image features underlying translucency perception. For example, Liao et al. [70] employed a StyleGAN model to generate synthesized images from a large dataset of translucent images, revealing that latent features corresponding to translucency emerge at intermediate spatial scales relative to the object. Additionally, studies integrating visual and linguistic tasks with large-scale language and image models have demonstrated a close but slightly different relationship between the linguistic categorization of translucency and its visual perception [71].

2.3.2 *Transparency*

Image distortions produced by light refraction produce perceptual cues of transparent materials [72]. Transparent perception is enhanced with dynamic image distortions [73]. Additionally, transparent materials, such as glass, typically exhibit internal specular reflections. As a result of a complex interaction between refraction, reflection, and surface geometry, the internal specular reflections exhibit a characteristic contour structure that can serve as an effective static image cue for transparency [74]. When the object moves, the internal specular reflections behave differently from the standard specular reflection of opaque materials, often moving in opposite directions. This could be a dynamic cue for transparency perception [42].

2.3.3 *Wetness*

Judging surface conditions, such as wet or dry, is also an important function of Shitsukan perception. A wet surface is optically complex because light incident on the surface undergoes subsurface scattering, as in the case of a translucent surface. Despite such complexity, the appearance of surface wetness can be manipulated through simple image transformation—dry surfaces can be visually transformed into wet ones by making the luminance histogram positively skewed, and increasing the saturation of colors of the image [75]. This manipulation was called Wetness Enhancing Transformation (WET). While the luminance histogram manipulation makes the image darker and glossier, the color saturation manipulation can simulate the spectra sharpening effect [76], which is caused by an increase in interactions of light and material due to refraction index matching. The effectiveness of the WET depends on the image, and a critical image feature is the scene color entropy of the image. The WET works well when the number of colors in the scene is large (high color entropy), while not when the number of colors in the scene is small (low color entropy) [75]. Why? High color saturation is an ambiguous cue of surface wetness, as many other factors can also produce saturated colors. The human visual system may use scene color entropy to resolve this ambiguity. Specifically, the modulation of the WET effect by color entropy can be interpreted as an unconscious inference by the visual system: that high color saturation is more likely attributable to a global scene factor (surface wetness) than to an object's intrinsic chromatic property, particularly when more colors in the region of interest are simultaneously saturated.

2.3.4 *Fineness*

The fine microstructures of the surface affect material appearance by changing the BRDF. The geometry on slightly larger scales, the mesostructure of the surface, can also significantly affect material appearance. One example is fineness. We humans can judge the fineness of texture even when the width of each texture component is finer than the spatial resolution of the visual system. An example is textures consisting of hair strings. It is shown that one image cue humans use to judge texture fineness is luminance contrast [77]. The lower the luminance contrast, the finer the hair texture appears. Physically, as each hair string becomes finer, the number of hair strings averaged within the minimum visual angle the visual system can resolve is increased. The more strings are averaged, the less variable the mean (remember the central limit theorem), and the weaker the apparent contrast. It appears that the human visual system unconsciously knows this statistical rule for inferring the fineness of random textures.

2.3.5 Mechanical Material Properties

We humans can visually judge the material and Shitsukan of objects not only with respect to their optical properties, such as gloss and translucency, but also with respect to their mechanical properties, including viscosity, heaviness, and softness.

It has been shown that humans can visually estimate viscosity either from dynamic or static cues. Image speed is one of the effective dynamic cues. Kawabe et al. [78] show that random patch motion, which reproduces the image motion of running liquid while excluding spatial form information, can produce a vivid sensation of liquid. With these stimuli, local image speed is a strong image cue of liquid viscosity. The lower the viscosity, the slower the image motion. This is intuitive, since honey, which has higher viscosity than water, moves more slowly.

On the other hand, a snapshot of liquid includes useful information about viscosity. Humans can often tell whether the liquid is honey or water only from static shape information [79]. Human perception of viscosity magnitude can be explained to some extent by combining various image statistics, including curviness and orientation.

Van Assen et al. [80] rendered various liquid movies to examine the perceived viscosity. They found that mid-level features about 3D distribution, irregularity, rectilinearity, and dynamics of liquid images, estimated from perceptual ratings, provide a more robust estimation of fluid viscosity than simple 2D image statistics.

A more recent study used an artificial neural network to estimate liquid viscosity from videos [81]. Although the network was trained to estimate the ground-truth viscosity, it could replicate the pattern of human errors for both scenes used for training and those not used. *In Silico* analysis of the internal representation suggests that the network uses various image features to estimate the viscosity of the video. However, the network parameters, such as the number of units, significantly alter the neural representation, even when it does not affect the viscosity estimation performance. This suggests one difficulty of using an artificial neural network to estimate the material representations in a biological network.

When a transparent liquid is running, the pattern underneath the water is dynamically deformed due to the refraction of light at the liquid surface. This dynamic deformation also produces the sensation of liquid [73]. Some image cues for perceiving a transparent surface are known, such as the luminance relationship at the

X-junction. However, perceiving a transparent liquid from dynamic deformation is a rare case where a completely transparent material (with no light absorption) is perceived. The pattern of deformation does not have to simulate physically correct liquids to provide observers with a vivid impression of liquids.

2.3.6 Image Naturalness

Shitsukan includes properties that make sensory inputs realistic and natural. Photo-realistic images can be rendered not only by physically simulating forward optics but also by statistically reproducing the probability distribution of natural scenes. Recent generative models are extremely powerful, making it very challenging for humans to distinguish between synthesized images and real images [82]. It has been shown that image similarity between the original natural images and the images distorted in various ways can be predicted by the deep features captured by artificial neural networks [83, 84]. Deep-feature-based models can also predict human sensitivity to detect a few types of image deformations [85]. However, the current models may use a larger number of features than humans do. Finding perceptual metamers is a useful strategy to reveal human-sensitive features.

2.4 Characteristics of Material Processing

2.4.1 Multimodal Integration

Material perception is multimodal. Different modalities are suitable for sensing different aspects of various materials. In general, vision is better at sensing optical properties, while touch and audition are better at sensing mechanical properties. Multisensory experiences may train vision to infer mechanical properties from visual appearance [86]. However, there is a report that visual recognition of non-visual material features (warmness, hardness, heaviness) takes longer processing time than that of visual features (e.g., glossiness, transparency) [87].

Audio-visual signals are integrated with each other in material class judgments [88]. For example, assume there is a visual image of a transparent object that people viewing it would most likely classify as glass. If the object makes a dull sound when it is hit, however, the observers tend to judge the material as soft vinyl rather than hard glass. As is the case with other cross-modal integration [89, 90], this phenomenon could be interpreted as the maximum likelihood estimation of the material category that is most consistent with both visual and auditory inputs. That is, vinyl is chosen since the multiplication of the likelihood of the visual input being vinyl and the likelihood of the auditory signal being vinyl is higher than the multiplication of the audio-visual likelihoods of the other materials, including glass [88].

Note also that this is all about multimodal material category judgment. To the best of our knowledge, accompanied auditory signals induce little changes in the visual appearance, including glossiness and other optical material properties.

2.4.2 *Development of Material Perception*

How does our brain acquire the abilities of various material computations? How does it know which image cues can be used to estimate a particular material property? Is the ability genetically programmed or learned from interactions with the environment?

A report shows that trained visual art experts make more stable judgments of glossiness [91]. In infant development, while 7–8 month-old infants show adult-like gloss perception, younger infants do not [92]. Specifically, 3–4 month-old infants are more sensitive to the shift of highlight position due to a lightfield change than to the presence/absence of highlights due to a surface material change, while 7–8 month-old infants, as well as adults, show the opposite tendency [93]. These findings suggest that individual experience has a significant impact on gloss perception, as in the case of material class perception [86]. However, we should not underestimate the role of innate factors in the development of material perception, particularly that of infants, given the complexity of material perception and its generality across diverse species on Earth. Neural representations for gloss in the monkey cortex have been extensively studied [94], and the humans' ability to judge the freshness of vegetables using luminance histogram cues [95, 96] is shared by chimpanzees [97].

A useful strategy for gaining insight into human material processing is to examine the effects of various factors, including developmental stage, aging, individual differences resulting from medical conditions, culture, country, living environment, and species, among others. To support these investigations, Sawayama et al. have developed a stimulus dataset with the standard data [49]. This type of work will make various types of research ready to start, and make the obtained results directly comparable across studies.

2.4.3 *Interactions with Other Visual Processing*

To fully understand human material perception, we should investigate more intensively how the visual system simultaneously estimates surface material, surface geometry, motion, and lighting from the same natural images and how these attribute computations interact with one another in various environments. Reflectance analysis includes intrinsic image decomposition. Motion analysis includes intrinsic flow decomposition of the image motion into components produced by object's motion, observer's motion, shape change, and optical effects, including reflection and refraction [98].

With this idea in mind, we have been examining the effects of material changes on the perception of motion and shape deformation [99, 100]. When a 3D object moves, its surface texture, diffuse shading, specular highlight, internal specular reflection of transparent material, and occluding contour move differently. Changing material is a challenging image manipulation for estimating the 3D movement and shape change of the object from image motion. Van Assen et al. [99] presented rotating rigid objects of various materials (including matte, glossy, mirror, and transparent) to human observers and found that the perceived rotation speed was overestimated for transparent materials. Van Zuijlen et al. [100] presented rotating non-rigid objects of various materials to the observers and found that the detection threshold of deformation was increased for transparent materials. In both studies, however, the effects of materials were small. In general, the visual system can reliably estimate the 3D motion and deformation of objects despite drastic changes in the image flow due to material changes. This suggests that human vision can estimate various scene parameters robustly under natural environments.

The reason the human visual system achieves material-invariant detection of object deformation [100] may be that it computes the correct object rigid flow for each material type. If the human visual system has a generative model that can predict the future image of a moving object, the deviation from the prediction could serve as a useful cue to identify non-rigid deformation. If the object is glossy, the model will predict how the highlight position and shape should change over time, given that the object is rigid. According to this hypothesis, the deformation detection performance will deteriorate if the object flow is distorted. Nishida et al. [101] tested this by adding perturbations to the lightfield, which was not directly visible to the observers. The results indicate virtually no effect of object flow distortion. This suggests that the human visual system may achieve material-invariant detection of object deformation by wisely ignoring the object flow irrelevant to the task, rather than computing a correct object flow based on, for example, an internal generative prediction model.

In another line of study, we are developing an image-computable model of visual motion estimation that can explain a wide range of human visual motion phenomena with the aid of machine learning [102]. To evaluate the model's performance in predicting human perception of natural movies, we are also developing a data set of human-perceived optical flow for naturalistic scenes [103, 104]. One achievement of this study is to reveal a potential role of materials in the development of visual motion processing. Humans can, although most existing optical flow models cannot, perceive second-order motion—the movement of higher-order features, including spatial or temporal contrast modulations [105, 106]. We hypothesize that the visual system may naturally acquire the ability to perceive second-order motion for estimating the motion of glossy or transparent objects, whose image motion is accompanied by numerous optical noises that do not align consistently with the object's motion. Our model simulation supports the feasibility of this idea [107]. This demonstrates how material perception research can contribute to a broader understanding of human vision.

2.5 Concluding Remark

To understand visual material perception, we have attempted to identify the relevant image cues. We have also attempted to relate the image cues to physical processes underlying the material properties. The latter analysis reveals that the human visual system unconsciously knows the underlying physical rules or ecological optics. It not only explains why the image cue works but also indicates when it should succeed and when it should fail.

We understand the general limitation in explaining human perception using simple image features. As noted in **2.4**, monocular depth cues are as ambiguous as material image cues, working only in specific contexts. While the relative activity of the three types of cones is the sensory origin of color perception, it cannot predict the final color perception due to the modulations by various spatiotemporal context effects. Nevertheless, our understanding of human vision has been advanced by the strategy to investigate the low-level image cues used for the task. This traditional approach will complement the recent machine learning approach that provides a more powerful but less human-interpretable explanation of visual processing.

To estimate surface material from an image, the visual system should evaluate the angle dependency of surface reflectance, as represented with the BRDF, by computing the surface orientation and illumination at each point, or using much simpler heuristics. Although the human visual system can take into account surface geometry in estimating surface reflectance [38], it remains unknown how deep and physically accurate our brain's computation of material and shape is.

Regarding the complexity of the processing, we suspect that the human visual system may change the processing strategy depending on the stimulus condition. It may flexibly employ various strategies to solve the same problem depending on the available information. When many cues are available, our brain can use them as effectively as possible using a rather complex computation. When effective cues are sparse or weak due to image noise, brief exposure, and peripheral viewing [51], our brain may attempt to find the best answer using a simple heuristic. This will lead to the graceful degradation of performance, which has been suggested as a critical characteristic of our visual processing [1].

Acknowledgements This review includes research supported by MEXT/JSPS KAKENHI Grant Numbers JP22135004, JP15H05915, JP20H05957, JP20H00603, and JP24H00721 (to S.N.).

References

1. Marr, D.: Vision: a computational investigation into the human representation and processing of visual information. MIT press (2010)
2. Barron, J.T., Malik, J.: Shape, illumination, and reflectance from shading. IEEE Trans. Pattern Anal. Mach. Intell. **37**(8), 1670–1687 (2014)

3. Enyo, Y., Nishino, K: Diffusion reflectance map: single-image stochastic inverse rendering of illumination and reflectance. In: Proceedings of the IEEE/CVF Conference on Computer Vision and Pattern Recognition, pp. 11873–11883 (2024)
4. Nimier-David, M., Vicini, D., Zeltner, T., Jakob, W.: Mitsuba 2: a retargetable forward and inverse renderer. ACM Trans. Graph. (ToG) **38**(6), 1–17 (2019)
5. Ferwerda, J.A., Pellacini, F., Greenberg, D.P.: Psychophysically based model of surface gloss perception. In: Human Vision and Electronic Imaging VI, vol. 4299, pp. 291–301. SPIE (2001)
6. Farid, H.: Image forensics. Annu. Rev. Vis. Sci. **5**(1), 549–573 (2019)
7. Ostrovsky, Y., Cavanagh, P., Sinha, P.: Perceiving illumination inconsistencies in scenes. Perception **34**(11), 1301–1314 (2005)
8. Koenderink, J.J., Van Doorn, A.J., Pont, S.C.: Perception of illuminance flow in the case of anisotropic rough surfaces. Percept. Psychophys. **69**, 895–903 (2007)
9. Adelson, E.H.: Lightness perception and lightness illusions. In: Gazzaniga, M. (ed.), The New Cognitive Neurosciences, 2nd edn., chapter 24, pp. 339–351. MIT Press, Cambridge, MA (2000)
10. Gilchrist, A.L.: To compute lightness, illumination is not estimated, it is held constant. J. Exp. Psychol. Hum. Percept. Perform. **44**(8), 1258 (2018)
11. Todd, J.T.: The visual perception of 3d shape. Trends Cogn. Sci. **8**(3), 115–121 (2004)
12. Battu, B., Kappers, A.M., Koenderink, J.J.: Ambiguity in pictorial depth. Perception **36**(9), 1290–1304 (2007)
13. Todd, J.T., Oomes, A.H., Koenderink, J.J., Kappers, A.M.: On the affine structure of perceptual space. Psychol. Sci. **12**(3), 191–196 (2001)
14. Foster, D.H.: Color constancy. Vision. Res. **51**(7), 674–700 (2011)
15. Gilchrist, A., Kossyfidis, C., Bonato, F., Agostini, T., Cataliotti, J., Li, X., Spehar, B., Annan, V., Economou, E.: An anchoring theory of lightness perception. Psychol. Rev. **106**(4), 795 (1999)
16. Nishida, S., Shinya, M.: Use of image-based information in judgments of surface-reflectance properties. JOSA A **15**(12), 2951–2965 (1998)
17. Vangorp, P., Laurijssen, J., Dutré, P.: The influence of shape on the perception of material reflectance. In: ACM SIGGRAPH 2007 Papers, SIGGRAPH '07, pp. 77–es, New York, NY, USA, Association for Computing Machinery (2007)
18. Fleming, R.W., Dror, R.O., Adelson, E.H.: Real-world illumination and the perception of surface reflectance properties. J. Vis. **3**(5), 3–3 (2003)
19. Geisler, W.S.: Visual perception and the statistical properties of natural scenes. Annu. Rev. Psychol. **59**(1), 167–192 (2008)
20. Motoyoshi, I., Nishida, S., Sharan, L., Adelson, E.H.: Image statistics and the perception of surface qualities. Nature **447**(7141), 206–209 (2007)
21. Sharan, L., Li, Y., Motoyoshi, I., Nishida, S., Adelson, E.H.: Image statistics for surface reflectance perception. J. Opt. Soc. Am. A **25**(4), 846–865 (2008)
22. Adelson, E.H.: On seeing stuff: the perception of materials by humans and machines. In: Human Vision and Electronic Imaging VI, vol. 4299, pp. 1–12. SPIE (2001)
23. Sawayama, M., Nishida, S.: Material and shape perception based on two types of intensity gradient information. PLoS Comput. Biol. **14**(4), e1006061 (2018)
24. Shafer, S.A.: Using color to separate reflection components. Color. Res. Appl. **10**(4), 210–218 (1985)
25. Fleming, R.W., Torralba, A., Adelson, E.H.: Specular reflections and the perception of shape. J. Vis. **4**(9), 10–10 (2004)
26. Dror, R.O., Willsky, A.S., Adelson, E.H.: Statistical characterization of real-world illumination. J. Vis. **4**(9), 11–11 (2004)
27. Kim, J., Marlow, P., Anderson, B.L.: The perception of gloss depends on highlight congruence with surface shading. J. Vis. **11**(9), 4–4 (2011)
28. Marlow, P., Kim, J., Anderson, B.L.: The role of brightness and orientation congruence in the perception of surface gloss. J. Vis. **11**(9), 16–16 (2011)

29. Todd, J.T., Norman, J.F., Mingolla, E.: Lightness constancy in the presence of specular highlights. Psychol. Sci. **15**(1), 33–39 (2004)
30. Wijntjes, M.W.A., Pont, S.C.: Illusory gloss on lambertian surfaces. J. Vis. **10**(9):13–13 (2010)
31. Chadwick, A.C., Kentridge, R.W.: The perception of gloss: a review. Vision. Res. **109**, 221–235 (2015)
32. Tappen, M.F., Adelson, E.H., Freeman, W.T.: Estimating intrinsic component images using non-linear regression. In 2006 IEEE Computer Society Conference on Computer Vision and Pattern Recognition (CVPR'06), vol. 2, pp. 1992–1999. IEEE (2006)
33. Marlow, P.J., Anderson, B.L.: Generative constraints on image cues for perceived gloss. J. Vis. **13**(14), 2–2 (2013)
34. Schmid, A.C., Barla, P., Doerschner, K.: Material category of visual objects computed from specular image structure. Nat. Hum. Behav. **7**(7), 1152–1169 (2023)
35. Marlow, P.J., Anderson, B.L.: Material properties derived from three-dimensional shape representations. Vision. Res. **115**, 199–208 (2015)
36. Marlow, P.J., Mooney, S.W., Anderson, B.L.: Photogeometric cues to perceived surface shading. Curr. Biol. **29**(2), 306–311 (2019)
37. Marlow, P.J., Todorović, D., Anderson, B.L.: Coupled computations of three-dimensional shape and material. Curr. Biol. **25**(6), R221–R222 (2015)
38. Marlow, P.J., Anderson, B.L.: Interactions between 3d surface shape and material perception. Annu. Rev. Vis. Sci. **10** (2024)
39. Kingdom, F.A.: Color brings relief to human vision. Nat. Neurosci. **6**(6), 641–644 (2003)
40. Nishida, S., Motoyoshi, I., Maruya, K.: Luminance-color interactions in surface gloss perception. J. Vis. **11**(11), 397–397 (2011)
41. Doerschner, K., Fleming, R.W., Yilmaz, O., Schrater, P.R., Hartung, B., Kersten, D.: Visual motion and the perception of surface material. Curr. Biol. **21**(23), 2010–2016 (2011)
42. Tamura, H., Nakauchi, S.: The rotating glass illusion: material appearance is bound to perceived shape and motion. i-Perception **9**(6):2041669518816716 (2018)
43. Khang, B.-G., Koenderink, J.J., Kappers, A.M.: Shape from shading from images rendered with various surface types and light fields. Perception **36**(8), 1191–1213 (2007)
44. Fleming, R.W., Holtmann-Rice, D., Bülthoff, H.H.: Estimation of 3d shape from image orientations. Proc. Natl. Acad. Sci. **108**(51), 20438–20443 (2011)
45. Kunsberg, B., Holtmann-Rice, D., Alexander, E., Cholewiak, S., Fleming, R., Zucker, S.W.: Colour, contours, shading and shape: flow interactions reveal anchor neighbourhoods. Interface Focus **8**(4), 20180019 (2018)
46. Fleming, R.W., Storrs, K.R.: Learning to see stuff. Curr. Opin. Behav. Sci. **30**, 100–108 (2019)
47. Prokott, K.E., Tamura, H., Fleming, R.W.: Gloss perception: searching for a deep neural network that behaves like humans. J. Vis. **21**(12), 14–14 (2021)
48. Storrs, K.R., Anderson, B.L., Fleming, R.W.: Unsupervised learning predicts human perception and misperception of gloss. Nat. Hum. Behav. **5**(10), 1402–1417 (2021)
49. Sawayama, M., Dobashi, Y., Okabe, M., Hosokawa, K., Koumura, T., Saarela, T.P., Olkkonen, M., Nishida, S.: Visual discrimination of optical material properties: a large-scale study. J. Vis. **22**(2), 17–17 (2022)
50. Portilla, J., Simoncelli, E.P.: Texture Modeling and Synthesis Using Joint Statistics of Complex Wavelet Coefficients. In IEEE workshop on statistical and computational theories of vision, Citeseer (1999)
51. Keshvari, S., Wijntjes, M.W.: Peripheral material perception. J. Vis. **24**(4), 13–13 (2024)
52. Wang, Q., Motoyoshi, I., Nishida, S.: Characterization of high-level images features for surface gloss perception. J. Vis. **13**(9), 202–202 (2013)
53. Gatys, L., Ecker, A.S., Bethge, M.: Texture synthesis using convolutional neural networks. Adv. Neural Inf. Process. Syst. **28** (2015)
54. Wallis, T.S., Funke, C.M., Ecker, A.S., Gatys, L.A., Wichmann, F.A., Bethge, M.: A parametric texture model based on deep convolutional features closely matches texture appearance for humans. J. Vis. **17**(12), 5–5 (2017)

55. Adelson, E.H., Pentland, A.P.: The perception of shading and reflectance. Percept. Bayesian Inference **409**, 423 (1996)
56. Huang, Y., Rao, R.P.: Predictive coding. Wiley Interdiscip. Rev.: Cogn. Sci. **2**(5), 580–593 (2011)
57. Lotter, W., Kreiman, G., Cox, D.: A neural network trained for prediction mimics diverse features of biological neurons and perception. Nat. Mach. Intell. **2**(4), 210–219 (2020)
58. Peters, B., DiCarlo, J.J., Gureckis, T., Haefner, R., Isik, L., Tenenbaum, J., Konkle, T., Naselaris,T., Stachenfeld, K., Tavares, Z., et.al.: How does the primate brain combine generative and discriminative computations in vision? ArXiv (2024)
59. Bi, W., Shah, A.D., Wong, K.W., Scholl, B.J., Yildirim, I.: Computational models reveal that intuitive physics underlies visual processing of soft objects. Nat. Commun. **16**(1), 6303 (2025)
60. Fleming, R.W., Bülthoff, H.H.: Low-level image cues in the perception of translucent materials. ACM Trans. Appl. Percept. (TAP) **2**(3), 346–382 (2005)
61. Jensen, H.W., Marschner, S.R., Levoy, M., Hanrahan, P.: A practical model for subsurface light transport. In: Proceedings of the 28th annual conference on Computer graphics and interactive techniques, pp. 511–518 (2001)
62. Kiyokawa, H., Nagai, T., Yamauchi, Y., Kim, J.: The perception of translucency from surface gloss. Vision. Res. **205**, 108140 (2023)
63. Marlow, P.J., Anderson, B.L.: The cospecification of the shape and material properties of light permeable materials. Proc. Natl. Acad. Sci. **118**(14), e2024798118 (2021)
64. Motoyoshi, I.: Highlight-shading relationship as a cue for the perception of translucent and transparent materials. J. Vis. **10**(9), 6–6 (2010)
65. Motoyoshi, I., Nishida, S., Adelson, E.H.: Luminance re-mapping for the control of apparent material. In: Proceedings of the 2nd symposium on Applied perception in graphics and visualization, pp. 165–165 (2005)
66. Marlow, P.J., de Heer, B.P., Anderson, B.L.: The role of self-occluding contours in material perception. Curr. Biol. **33**(12), 2528–2534 (2023)
67. Xiao, B., Zhao, S., Gkioulekas, I., Bi, W., Bala, K.: Effect of geometric sharpness on translucent material perception. J. Vis. **20**(7), 10–10 (2020)
68. Xiao, B., Walter, B., Gkioulekas, I., Zickler, T., Adelson, E., Bala, K.: Looking against the light: How perception of translucency depends on lighting direction. J. Vis. **14**(3), 17–17 (2014)
69. Liao, C., Sawayama, M., Xiao, B.: Crystal or jelly? effect of color on the perception of translucent materials with photographs of real-world objects. J. Vis. **22**(2), 6–6 (2022)
70. Liao, C., Sawayama, M., Xiao, B.: Unsupervised learning reveals interpretable latent representations for translucency perception. PLoS Comput. Biol. **19**(2), e1010878 (2023)
71. Liao, C., Sawayama, M., Xiao, B.: Probing the link between vision and language in material perception using psychophysics and unsupervised learning. PLoS Comput. Biol. **20**(10), e1012481 (2024)
72. Fleming, R.W., Jäkel, F., Maloney, L.T.: Visual perception of thick transparent materials. Psychol. Sci. **22**(6), 812–820 (2011)
73. Kawabe, T., Maruya, K., Nishida, S.: Perceptual transparency from image deformation. Proc. Natl. Acad. Sci. **112**(33), E4620–E4627 (2015)
74. Todd, J.T., Norman, J.F.: Reflections on glass. J. Vis. **19**(4), 26–26 (2019)
75. Sawayama, M., Adelson, E.H., Nishida, S.: Visual wetness perception based on image color statistics. J. Vis. **17**(5), 7–7 (2017)
76. Okawa, H., Shimano, M., Asano, Y., Bise, R., Nishino, K., Sato, I.: Estimation of wetness and color from a single multispectral image. IEEE Trans. Pattern Anal. Mach. Intell. **44**(12), 8740–8753 (2019)
77. Sawayama, M., Nishida, S., Shinya, M.: Human perception of subresolution fineness of dense textures based on image intensity statistics. J. Vis. **17**(4), 8–8 (2017)
78. Kawabe, T., Maruya, K., Fleming, R.W., Nishida, S.: Seeing liquids from visual motion. Vision. Res. **109**, 125–138 (2015)

79. Paulun, V.C., Kawabe, T., Nishida, S., Fleming, R.W.: Seeing liquids from static snapshots. Vision. Res. **115**, 163–174 (2015)
80. Van Assen, J.J.R., Barla, P., Fleming, R.W.: Visual features in the perception of liquids. Curr. Biol. **28**(3), 452–458 (2018)
81. van Assen, J.J.R., Nishida, S., Fleming, R.W.: Visual perception of liquids: insights from deep neural networks. PLoS Comput. Biol. **16**(8), e1008018 (2020)
82. Nightingale, S.J., Farid, H.: AI-synthesized faces are indistinguishable from real faces and more trustworthy. Proc. Natl. Acad. Sci. **119**(8), e2120481119 (2022)
83. Ding, K., Zhong, R., Wang, Z., Yu, Y., Fang, Y.: Adaptive structure and texture similarity metric for image quality assessment and optimization. IEEE Trans. Multimed. (2023)
84. Zhang, R., Isola, P., Efros, A.A., Shechtman, E., Wang, O.: The unreasonable effectiveness of deep features as a perceptual metric. In: Proceedings of the IEEE conference on computer vision and pattern recognition, pp. 586–595 (2018)
85. Zhu, Z., Nishida, S.: The sensitivity to distortions on natural and unnatural images of full-reference image quality assessment models. Master's thesis, Graduate School of Informatics, Kyoto University(2023)
86. Goda, N., Yokoi, I., Tachibana, A., Minamimoto, T., Komatsu, H.: Crossmodal association of visual and haptic material properties of objects in the monkey ventral visual cortex. Curr. Biol. **26**(7), 928–934 (2016)
87. Nagai, T., Matsushima, T., Koida, K., Tani, Y., Kitazaki, M., Nakauchi, S.: Temporal properties of material categorization and material rating: visual vs non-visual material features. Vision. Res. **115**, 259–270 (2015)
88. Fujisaki, W., Goda, N., Motoyoshi, I., Komatsu, H., Nishida, S.: Audiovisual integration in the human perception of materials. J. Vis. **14**(4), 12–12 (2014)
89. Ernst, M.O., Banks, M.S.: Humans integrate visual and haptic information in a statistically optimal fashion. Nature **415**(6870), 429–433 (2002)
90. Massaro, D.W.: From multisensory integration to talking heads and language learning. work **831**, 459–2330 (2004)
91. Tani, Y., Nishijima, R., Nagai, T., Koida, K., Kitazaki, M., Nakauchi, S.: Trained visual art experts make more stable judgments of glossiness. Jpn. J. Psychon. Sci. **36**(1), 17–29 (2017)
92. Yang, J., Otsuka, Y., Kanazawa, S., Yamaguchi, M.K., Motoyoshi, I.: Perception of surface glossiness by infants aged 5 to 8 months. Perception **40**(12), 1491–1502 (2011)
93. Yang, J., Kanazawa, S., Yamaguchi, M.K., Motoyoshi, I.: Pre-constancy vision in infants. Curr. Biol. **25**(24), 3209–3212 (2015)
94. Nishio, A., Goda, N., Komatsu, H.: Neural selectivity and representation of gloss in the monkey inferior temporal cortex. J. Neurosci. **32**(31), 10780–10793 (2012)
95. Arce-Lopera,C., Masuda, T., Kimura, A., Wada, Y., Okajima, K.: Luminance distribution modifies the perceived freshness of strawberries. i-Perception **3**(5):338–355 (2012)
96. Wada, Y., Arce-Lopera, C., Masuda, T., Kimura, A., Dan, I., Goto, S.-I., Tsuzuki, D., Okajima, K.: Influence of luminance distribution on the appetizingly fresh appearance of cabbage. Appetite **54**(2), 363–368 (2010)
97. Imura, T., Masuda, T., Wada, Y., Tomonaga, M., Okajima, K.: Chimpanzees can visually perceive differences in the freshness of foods. Sci. Rep. **6**(1), 34685 (2016)
98. Nishida, S., Kawabe, T., Sawayama, M., Fukiage, T.: Motion perception: from detection to interpretation. Annu. Rev. Vis. Sci. **4**(1), 501–523 (2018)
99. van Assen, J.J.R., Kawabe, T., Nishida, S.: Object motion and flow variance across optical contexts. J. Vis. **20**(11), 458–458 (2020)
100. van Zuijlen, M.J., Yang, Y.-H., Van Assen, J.J.R., Nishida, S.: Optical material properties affect detection of deformation of non-rigid rotating objects, but only slightly. J. Vis. **25**(6), 6–6 (2025)
101. Nishida, S., van Zuijlen, M., Yang, Y.-H., van Assen, J.J.: Can material-robust detection of 3d non-rigid deformation be explained by predictive processing through generative models? J. Vis. **24**(10), 430–430 (2024)

102. Sun, Z., Chen, Y.-J., Yang, Y.-H., Nishida, S.: Modeling human visual motion processing with trainable motion energy sensing and a self-attention network. Adv. Neural Inf. Process. Syst. **36** (2024)
103. Yang, Y.-H., Fukiage, T., Sun, Z., Nishida, S.: Psychophysical measurement of perceived motion flow of naturalistic scenes. Iscience **26**(12) (2023)
104. Yang, Y.-H., Sun, Z., Fukiage, T., Nishida, S.: Huperflow: a comprehensive benchmark for human vs. machine motion estimation comparison. In: Proceedings of the Computer Vision and Pattern Recognition Conference, pp. 22799–22808 (2025)
105. Cavanagh, P., Mather, G.: Motion: the long and short of it. Spat. Vis. **4**(2–3), 103–129 (1989)
106. Chubb, C., Sperling, G.: Drift-balanced random stimuli: a general basis for studying non-fourier motion perception. JOSA A **5**(11), 1986–2007 (1988)
107. Sun, Z., Chen, Y.-J., Yang, Y.-H., Li, Y., Nishida, S.: Machine learning modelling for multi-order human visual motion processing. Nat. Mach. Intell. 1–16 (2025)

Chapter 3
Computational Visual Modeling of Shitsukan

Ko Nishino

Abstract Computational understanding of visual Shitsukan, i.e., understanding the nuanced looks and feels of objects and scenes from their images, is a challenging task that goes to the very heart of computer vision. This chapter reviews the foundations of appearance modeling, the sub-discipline in computer vision centered on the analytical and image-based representations of the radiometric properties of real-world surfaces, namely its geometry, reflectance, and illumination. We particularly focus on the modeling of light reflection at a surface point, the estimation of the radiometric ingredients that participate in it, and also the recognition of the traces of materials that quietly dictate such light interaction, all from images. We then introduce our recent work on each of these fundamental topics of computer vision which collectively advance the frontier of computational visual Shitsukan perception.

Keywords Computer vision · Reflectance modelling · Inverse rendering · Texture modelling · Material recognition

3.1 Visual Appearance Modeling

Computer vision started as an, in retrospect brutal, undergraduate summer project to make computers see [40] as part of a larger quest towards building artificial intelligence. Realizing computational visual perception, at least comparable to the level of humans, turned out to require a much larger and longer expedition by many full-time researchers that continues to this date after more than 60 summers. Computer vision, an independent academic discipline born out of these efforts is still growing with over ten thousand papers submitted to each top international conference, which eloquently speaks to the discipline's success and, simultaneously, the enormity of the challenges left to be tackled.

K. Nishino (✉)
Kyoto University, Kyoto, Japan
e-mail: kon@i.kyoto-u.ac.jp

S. Nishida and K. Nishino (eds.), *Shitsukan—Understanding and Manipulating Material and Quality Perception*, https://doi.org/10.1007/978-981-95-4762-3_3

Fig. 3.1 Real world surfaces exhibit a variety of visual Shitsukan in their appearance. Modeling their image formation (appearance modeling) is essential for visual Shitsukan understanding

In computer vision, understanding real-world appearance, the looks and feels of objects and scenes, from images has always been the central topic of interest. As Fig. 3.1 demonstrates, the visual appearance of real-world surfaces offer rich cues of the Shitsukan. One can easily imagine how the surfaces would look like if we were standing in front of them, how they would change if we moved around them, and even how they would feel when we touch them. The innate desire of humans to accurately understand the rich surrounding visual world by capturing and analyzing it is eloquently inscribed in the wall paintings of ancient caves as early as 40,000 years ago [1]. This drive has produced large strides of progress in our quest for accurately modeling, analyzing, and predicting visual appearance, which has served as the foundation for many research areas in computer vision such as shape reconstruction, motion estimation, and segmentation.

Among such foundational computer vision research, appearance modeling, i.e., the study of deriving representations of the object and scene appearance amenable to efficient image-based analysis, recognition, and synthesis lies at the heart of "physical" understanding of the underlying world. It literally bridges the actual 3D world and its 2D projections in images. In fact, this sub-discipline initially started as "physics-based vision" [52], a name signifying its focus on understanding the physical (radiometric) process underlying our rich visual world.

Understanding of Shitsukan through vision requires this appearance modeling. The Shitsukan of objects and scenes manifest in the way the visual appearance of surfaces are formulated. Many physical ingredients contribute to this instantiation, ranging from the geometric surface structure to the internal material composition. The appearance modeling of these physical ingredients, i.e., reflectance, surface geometry, material composition, etc. all play a concerted role in defining the nuanced visual Shitsukan of our world. Shitsukan, the look and feel that goes well beyond and deeper than what the term "texture" can imply, e.g., from the subtle glint to the deep fuzziness, requires the sound theoretical foundation of appearance modeling.

3.1.1 Reflectance Modeling

Early efforts in physics-based vision centered on analytical modeling of surface reflection—the fundamental radiometric building block underlying the rich Shitsukan of a real-world surface. When light emanating from a source, i.e., illumination, hits object surfaces, it is reflected in various directions in their own strength according to the geometric and radiometric structure of the surface. In addition to the surface local geometry, i.e., the mesoscopic surface geometry within a single pixel, many physical structures dictate this light behavior. These include the global geometry, i.e., the overall structure of the object that can cause self-shadowing and interreflection, and the surface composition including the material construction, finish (e.g., brushed and lackered), and condition (e.g., wet and dirty). When the reflected light energy aligned with the viewing direction is non-zero, we see that surface point. The ratio of the incident light energy to that observed by the viewer is called the reflectance. If we consider all directions as possible viewing directions and also the possible light source directions, the distribution of reflectance in all these directions can be expressed as a four-dimensional function of incoming and outgoing directions. This is called the Bidirectional Reflectance Distribution Function (BRDF) [33]

$$f_r(\mathbf{x}, \mathbf{V}, \mathbf{L}) = \frac{\mathrm{d}L_\mathrm{r}(\mathbf{x}, \mathbf{V})}{\mathrm{d}E(\mathbf{x}, \mathbf{L})}, \tag{3.1}$$

where $\mathbf{x}$ is the surface point of interest, $\mathbf{V}$ is the viewing direction, $\mathbf{L}$ is the incoming light direction, L_r is the reflected radiance, and E is the incoming irradiance (see Fig. 3.2a). Note that the viewing and light source directions are in the local coordinate frame of the surface (i.e.; they are $\mathbf{V}(\mathbf{x})$ and $\mathbf{L}(\mathbf{x})$, which are the corresponding global directions transformed according to the coordinate frame determined by the surface normal at point $\mathbf{x}$).

The radiance of the surface point given the surrounding illumination L_i for a viewing direction $\mathbf{V}$ can then be described with the rendering equation [19]

$$L_r(\mathbf{x}, \mathbf{V}) = \int_\Omega f_r(\mathbf{x}, \mathbf{V}, \mathbf{L}) L_i(\mathbf{x}, \mathbf{L})(\mathbf{N}(\mathbf{x}) \cdot \mathbf{L}) \mathrm{d}\mathbf{L}, \tag{3.2}$$

where Ω is the hemisphere of incoming light directions, and $\mathbf{N}$ is the surface normal at $\mathbf{x}$.

A large body of research has been devoted to the derivation of analytical expressions that faithfully capture the physical light interaction of this abstract BRDF function. Arriving at an expression concise in form that enables efficient parameter estimation has been, and continues to be, one of the central goals of appearance modeling. This reflectance modeling started with the adoption of the Lambert's law to express light reflection by a surface captured in an image. The Lambert's law was originally derived to explain the radiometry in astronomy [21], e.g., for the "appearance modeling" of the lunar surface. It idealizes the reflected radiance to be angularly uniform. That is, the reflected light for a given incident light ray is uniform in all directions

$$f_r(\mathbf{x}, \mathbf{V}, \mathbf{L}) = \rho(\mathbf{x})\mathbf{N}(\mathbf{x}) \cdot \mathbf{L}, \tag{3.3}$$

where $\rho(\mathbf{x})$ and $\mathbf{N}(\mathbf{x})$ are the albedo, the point reflectance, and the surface normal at $\mathbf{x}$, respectively. Note that the Lambertian BRDF model is independent of the viewing direction $\mathbf{V}$. This simplification and its linearity in both the surface normal and the

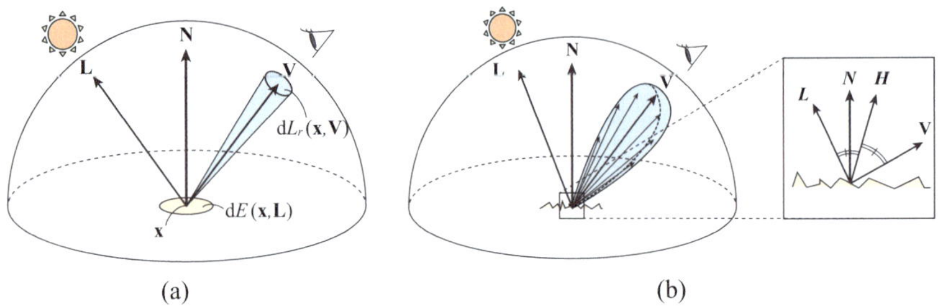

Fig. 3.2 The reflectance at a surface point can be described with the BRDF which expresses the radiance viewed in direction **v** for a unit incident light from direction **L** (**a**). The micro surface geometry within a pixel gives rise to glossiness of specular (surface) reflection which is often modeled with the orientation distribution of the microfacets measured with respect to the half angle **H** of the incident light and the viewing directions (**b**)

light source direction have provided a convenient mathematical footing for many computer vision applications.

Obviously, reflections by real-world surfaces are hardly Lambertian and one would be hard-pressed to find an actual Lambertian surface. Maybe a white piece of paper would be the closest we find in our daily lives. In fact, one can even argue that the Shitsukan of a surface lies exactly in its deviation from Lambertian! Yet most computer vision applications have been built on top of this woefully simplistic approximation of the true reflectance of real-world surfaces due to its mathematical convenience. For instance, the surface normal, i.e., the surface geometry, can be recovered if three observations of the pixel radiance for three distinct light source directions (that sufficiently span the 3D world) are available, which is called photometric stereo [53].

The lack of shininess, the bright layer of dynamically moving reflection as one examines the surface, of objects rendered with Lambertian BRDF is an eyesore for image synthesis. Imagine not having that bright highlight when you are looking at your watch. This in turn speaks to the utter inadequacy of the Lambertian reflection for solving inverse problems.

A large body of research has been proposed to literally add shiny reflection by modeling the BRDF as an affine combination [31] of the matte dull diffuse reflection (f_r^d) and the shiny sharp specular reflection (f_r^s),

$$f_r(\mathbf{x}, \mathbf{V}, \mathbf{L}) = \rho^d(\mathbf{x}) f_r^d(\mathbf{x}, \mathbf{V}, \mathbf{L}) + \rho^s(\mathbf{x}) f_r^s(\mathbf{x}, \mathbf{V}, \mathbf{L})\,, \tag{3.4}$$

scaled by their corresponding contributions ρ^d and ρ^s which are referred to as diffuse and specular albedo, respectively. Most past models use Lambertian Eq. 3.1 as the diffuse reflection

$$f_r^d(\mathbf{x}, \mathbf{V}, \mathbf{L}) = \mathbf{N}(\mathbf{x}) \cdot \mathbf{L}\,. \tag{3.5}$$

Mirror reflection, the light reflected off the surface in the perfect mirror reflection direction [16] can easily be added

$$f_r^s(\mathbf{x}, \mathbf{V}, \mathbf{L}) = \rho^s(\mathbf{x})\delta(\mathbf{V} - \mathbf{R}), \tag{3.6}$$

where **R** is the perfect mirror reflection direction in the local coordinate frame

$$\mathbf{R} = 2(\mathbf{N}(\mathbf{x}) \cdot \mathbf{L})\mathbf{N}(\mathbf{x}) - \mathbf{L}. \tag{3.7}$$

Mirror reflection, however, is hardly visually sufficient. The glossiness found on many real-world surfaces, e.g., the glint of the highlight regions that deform as one moves around a wooden table which is essential for its unique Shitsukan, cannot be captured with just Lambertian plus mirror reflection. What is needed is a principled way to model the spread of the specular reflection around the perfect mirror reflection direction. A physically-based interpretation for this is to explain the spread of mirror reflection with the mesoscopic surface geometry, the finite microgeometry within a surface area projected into a single pixel. The view frustum of a single pixel indeed spans a surface region of certain size which covers complex mesoscopic geometry which is on average flat with a surface normal computed at the pixel-level.

Torrance and Sparrow [51] modeled this mesoscopic structure as a collection of oriented mirrored microfacets. That is, the surface is modeled as a collection of tiny mirror shards that are independently oriented in different directions. As depicted in Fig. 3.2b, perfect mirror reflection by each of these microfacets gives rise to specular reflection that is spread around the dominant orientation of them. Torrance and Sparrow [51] assumed that these shard orientations are independently and identically distributed with a Gaussian distribution

$$f_r^s(\mathbf{V}, \mathbf{L}) = \rho_s \frac{D(\mathbf{V}, \mathbf{L})G(\mathbf{V}, \mathbf{L})F(\mathbf{V}, \mathbf{L})}{4(\mathbf{N} \cdot \mathbf{V})(\mathbf{N} \cdot \mathbf{L})}, \tag{3.8}$$

where we are dropping the dependency on **x** for brevity. As Fig. 3.2b depicts, D is the distribution of microfacet orientations which Torrance and Sparrow modeled with a Gaussian distribution with its mean at the global surface normal at the surface point **x**, i.e., the north pole ($\mathbf{N}(\mathbf{x})$) of the local coordinate frame

$$D(\mathbf{V}, \mathbf{L}) = D(\theta_{\mathbf{H}}) = \exp\left[-\left(\frac{\theta_{\mathbf{H}}}{\sigma}\right)^2\right], \tag{3.9}$$

where $\theta_{\mathbf{H}}$ is the polar angle **H** makes with the surface normal **N** and **H** is the halfway vector between the viewing and incoming light direction $\frac{\mathbf{V}+\mathbf{L}}{\|\mathbf{V}+\mathbf{L}\|}$ (see Fig. 3.2b). The standard deviation σ of the Gaussian, in effect, controls the glossiness of the specular reflection. A large variance of the microfacet orientations would cause wider highlights, and a variance close to zero would mean closer to mirror reflection. As such, the standard deviation can be interpreted as the "surface roughness."

The function G is called the geometric attenuation factor which accounts for self-shadowing and masking of microfacets

$$G(\mathbf{V}, \mathbf{L}) = \min\left(1, \frac{2(\mathbf{N}\cdot\mathbf{H})(\mathbf{N}\cdot\mathbf{V})}{\mathbf{V}\cdot\mathbf{H}}, \frac{2(\mathbf{N}\cdot\mathbf{H})(\mathbf{N}\cdot\mathbf{L})}{\mathbf{V}\cdot\mathbf{H}}\right). \tag{3.10}$$

Again, note that the surface normal at the point of interest is the north pole in the local coordinate frame, so that it can be be interpreted as $[0, 0, 1]^\mathsf{T}$ in the expression. Finally, F is the Fresnel reflection.

Various models with the same approach of modeling the distribution of microfacet orientations have followed [11, 32]. Appearance modeling in computer vision, however, somewhat stagnated after this and most applications, even to date, rely on a simple combination of a purely Lambertian reflection and additive specular reflection model often modeled with Phong [41] or Torrance-Sparrow [51]. This largely owes to the outsized role macrogeometry plays in computer vision. The recovery of overall geometric structure has strong precedence over accurate recovery of geometric details, reflectance and illumination, and "non-Lambertian" reflection is treated as a nuisance that needs to be sifted out as outliers. A notable exception in such shape reconstruction applications is where surface normals are directly recovered from the images, e.g., shape-from-shading [16] and photometric stereo [53]. Even in these applications, however, the majority of approaches has been fixated on additive reflection components to Lambertian as the base Lambertian provides seductive linearity for such inverse problems.

Our research on accurate modeling of the underlying reflectance of Shitsukan goes a significant step beyond these past works. Most notably, we unified "diffuse" and "specular" reflection at the very core physical interpretation level of the reflectance model. That is, we introduce the first comprehensive reflectance model that explains both diffuse and specular reflection with the same surface microgeometry. We detail this contribution in Sect. 3.2.1.

3.1.2 Inverse Rendering

We can go a step further beyond modeling and estimating the reflectance of objects to quantify visual Shitsukan. The appearance of the object is determined by the complex non-linear interplay of light with the surface which is determined by the reflectance, illumination, and geometry. We can attempt to quantitatively recover these three fundamental radiometric ingredients of appearance from the observed images. This is often called inverse rendering [27], radiometric decomposition [25], or inverse optics [42]. This amounts to estimating the BRDF f_r, the illumination L_i, and the surface normal $\mathbf{N}$ in Eq. 3.2 from the observed radiance L_r captured as the image irradiance of that point. This is obviously an ill-posed problem.

Early works attempt to better-condition this ill-posed inverse problem by adding observations (e.g., taking many more images) or by making strong assumptions on the physical components (e.g., assuming Lambertian reflection [2]). These methods, however, are fundamentally limited by the accuracy of the reflectance. Among the radiometric ingredients of Shitsukan, namely the BRDF, illumination, and geometry, the BRDF plays a special role in solving this inverse problem as it dictates the interaction of illumination and geometry. This function is inherently nonlinear and high-dimensional, yet for robust estimation of it, its mathematical expression needs to be tractable for inversion, i.e., it can be recovered uniquely. This motivated most past works to adopt, often woefully simplistic, parametric representations so that BRDF estimation can be formulated as a low-dimensional regression problem. This is exactly why most past works have adopted simple linear combinations of Lambertian and microfacet-based specular reflection models (e.g., starting with early works [18, 45] continuing to recent learning-based methods [55]).

Despite its parametric simplicity that makes the regression stable, a linear combination of Lambertian and microfacet BRDF model embodies an unresolvable physical contradiction. The Lambertian model assumes a flat surface with perfectly uniform angular reflectance, while the microfacet specular reflection model assumes a collection of stochastically oriented mirror shards. These two mesoscopic geometric structures cannot coexist! This contradiction is often swept under the rug in the name of mathematical convenience. Surprisingly, the lack of a physically plausible yet parametric BRDF model that can be used to quantify the Shitsukan from images had been missing in the literature. We fill this gap with a newly derived BRDF model that unifies the diffuse and specular reflections with the same microfacets (Sect. 3.2.1). This paves the way for accurate image-based Shitsukan modeling.

Inverse rendering is also fundamentally hampered by its inherent ambiguities. There are two fundamental ambiguities, both of which are caused by the entanglement of illumination and reflectance. The first is with regards to the color. A white illumination and a green reflectance give rise to the same green surface radiance as caused by a green illumination and a white reflectance. In fact, this ambiguity in color encapsulates infinite possibilities as the spectrum is a continuous distribution. Recovering the surface and the illumination colors from the observed color is thus fundamentally ill-posed. This is true for human visual perception, too. Resolving this ambiguity amounts to leveraging what is physically plausible in the real world. In fact, humans do this quite effortlessly, which is called color constancy [14, 39]. Achieving this color constancy in computer vision is a challenge with a body of work tackling it, and the problem boils down to how to model and leverage plausible illumination spectra in the real world.

The other ambiguity lies in the frequency spectra of illumination and reflectance. Light reflection on a surface can be viewed as a convolution in the angular domain [43]. When the light sources are located at distances sufficiently larger than the size of the object, the illumination can be approximated as those of directional sources. This is usually the case for outdoor scenes and for most indoor scenes with daily hand-sized objects. The illumination in such cases can be represented as a unit sphere with radiance distribution on its surface which is referred to as an environment map. Surface reflection can be viewed as convolution on this spherical surface. The reflectance defines the angular kernel in which the weighted integral of the incident illumination is computed. This kernel is not angularly shift-invariant, so it is not strictly speaking convolution, but the analogy is useful.

The key ambiguity lies in the fact that a wider angular kernel (lower-frequency reflectance) with a tighter illumination (higher-frequency illumination) can give rise to the exact same reflected surface radiance as that resulting from a tighter angular kernel (high-frequency reflectance) with a wider illumination (lower-frequency illumination). That is, the same image intensity can be caused by a blurry reflectance and sharp illumination, or a sharp reflectance and blurry illumination. In fact, this ambiguity is again continuous and contains infinite combinations. Recovering the BRDF and the illumination from images entails disentangling this frequency ambiguity. Past works have relied on learned priors in a Bayesian formulation to enforce the disentanglement to be physically plausible [24, 25, 38]. This is, however, not a canonical solution as there are infinite plausible solutions with associated plausibilities. We address this with a novel stochastic inverse rendering formulation that can return sampled combinations of reflectance and illumination in the solution space according to their probabilities. We detail this in Sect. 3.2.2.

If the goal were to simply synthesize the appearance of the surface from a novel view, without regard to its underlying physical quantities and their interaction, we can circumvent the ill-posed inverse problem and transform the appearance by extracting just enough of the gist of the appearance. By formulating this as an end-to-end learning problem with a differentiable formulation of the rendering equation (Eq. 3.2), the internal representation can be learned from sets of images, i.e., input and view-transformed images. Directly learning such representation as a mesh is challenging, as the geometry is sparse in the 3D space, which is inconvenient for end-to-end learning via backpropagation. By representing the geometry as a volume, instead, dense spatial gradients even from image supervision can be extracted. For this reason, volume rendering [28] has been reinvigorated with a neural representation for novel view synthesis, which is referred to as Neural Radiance Fields (NeRF) [30]. Representing and backpropagating through a 3D volume for 2D image synthesis, however, is obviously redundant and inefficient. Gaussian Splatting [20] overcomes this by limiting the volume rendering close to the actual surface by using 3D Gaussians as proxy volumes. Thanks to the significant reduction in computational complexity, Gaussian Splatting is now the de facto scene representation for novel view synthesis.

Novel view synthesis, however, does not provide the foundation for visual Shitsukan understanding. Without explicit quantitative estimation of the radiometric scene ingredients, namely the geometry, illumination, and reflectance and deciphering of their complex interplay, there is no means to truly quantify the look and feel, including the possible material-dependent physical properties (e.g., is it soft or hard), geometric subtleties (e.g., is it rusted or smooth), surface conditions (e.g., is it weathered and patinated), lighting conditions (e.g., is it vivid because of the lighting), and so on. For this, the disentanglement of the complex interplay of light with real-world surfaces from images, remains the key challenge for realizing intelligent visual perception and also to understand the workings of human perception. As such, visual Shitsukan understanding continues to be a key motivation towards the ultimate goal of computer vision.

3.1.3 Texture Modeling

The light interaction at a surface is not limited to a single point. The spatial interaction of light, for instance, the subsurface light transport from the incident to exiting surface points produces nuanced Shitsukan of the surface such as the softness of a baby's cheek. Physically-based modeling of these spatial light behavior as a higher-dimensional function (e.g., 8D or 10D bidirectional surface scattering reflectance distribution function with 3D or 2D position and 2D angular direction for both the incident and exiting lights) [33] quickly becomes intractable. Instead, we may adopt an image-based representation of this underlying complex function. That is, we can represent it with images captured in canonical settings that record these complex spatial light transports. This is often called texture modeling, a term originally introduced to mean representing "texture maps" of a surface mesh model, but entails a lot more including the visual Shitsukan of a surface.

Texture appearance modeling started by extending reflectance modeling, literally expanding the notion of the BRDF to have a 2D spatial span, namely the bidirectional texture function (BTF). Dana et al. [12] represented this BTF as a set of images by capturing the same surface region for different combinations of incident light source and viewing directions. The BTF does not have any mathematical expression per se, and instead is an empirical representation. Image-based texture representations have also been used for novel view synthesis and relighting, for instance, by extracting a low-dimensional embedding space of them to achieve photorealistic interpolation between the observed texture appearance [36]. Dana et al.'s work on BTF, most important, sparked interest in image-based approaches to texture recognition. Similar to image-based object recognition, this entailed extracting meaningful features from a stack of images that capture the same texture and using that to recognize different textures. For this "texture recognition," many datasets and approaches have been proposed [23].

A few works have also tackled the problem of explicitly quantifying physical properties of texture. Oxholm et al. [37] takes advantage of the self-similarity and scale variability to recover texture geometry and use it for recognition. Explicit disentanglement of texture appearance into geometry and its other radiometric ingredients (spatial variation of reflectance and illumination including the complex visibility variations), however, remains challenging. Most works completely sidestep this and model them as a collection of images for recognition and synthesis (i.e., appearance interpolation and extrapolation).

Texture appearance, however, conveys much more than its identification. A marble surface looks different from the furred animal body, not just because of its geometric smoothness, but because of the complex interaction of geometry and radiometry that gives rise to its unique appearance including its characteristic spatial patterns. The richness of the surface appearance is not just in its texture but also in its depth of light interaction within the mesoscopic surface structure, in the ingrained spatial patterns, the surface highlights, etc. In other words, texture appearance tells us much more than the mere sum of its geometry and individual radiometric ingredients. The way these components orchestrate to give rise to the nuanced looks hint at the very composition of the surface itself, the material, and its properties. As part of the quest to characterize Shitsukan from visual appearance, we pioneered image-based material recognition from visual appearance, which we will detail in Sect. 3.2.3.

3.2 Shitsukan Modeling in Computer Vision

Let us now describe three of our representative works in the quest for computational visual Shitsukan understanding. Each of these works bring fundamental advances in reflectance modeling, inverse rendering, and texture modeling, respectively. These works collectively advance the frontier of visual Shitsukan understanding in computer vision.

3.2.1 Fresnel Microfacet Bidirectional Reflectance Distribution Function

As we reviewed in Sect. 3.1.1, modern computer vision has been built on a simplistic affine combination of diffuse and specular reflection for representing the key function underlying surface light interaction, the BRDF. One is called diffuse reflection as the light is physically diffused (i.e., spread). Geometrically, this is the light that penetrates into the "body" of the surface and eventually re-emerges from the same point after scattering. For this, body reflection is a more apt name [31]. Similarly, specular reflection is also called the surface reflection as it is the light that is immediately reflected back into air at the interface of the surface. As we saw, the Lambertian model for the body reflection and the Torrance-Sparrow microfacet model for the surface reflection are widely adopted choices, especially for solving inverse problems, e.g., 3D reconstruction, reflectance estimation, and illumination recovery.

Such a simplistic affine combination of reflection models has three fundamental problems that fatally fetters them. The first problem is that this affine combination is physically not plausible. Lambertian and its extensions (e.g., Oren-Nayar model [32]) assume a single Lambertian microfacet or an oriented distribution of Lambertian microfacets [32]. Specular reflection models, on the other hand, assume mirrored microfacets [51]. There are no such real-world surfaces that can be both Lambertian and mirror microfaceted at the same time. It also means that the recovered parameter values cannot be accurate.

The second problem is that past diffuse reflection models do not actually model the light transport inside the surface body. In other words, they shortcut the internal light transport modeling by assuming an atomic Lambertian reflection at the surface interface, which is physically incorrect. Although the Oren-Nayar model [32] extends the Lambertian model by considering oriented microfacets, it assumes the same microfacet for incident and exiting light. Although this negligence of subsurface light transport may not affect its accuracy for representing mesoscopic and macroscopic radiance (i.e., Bidirectional Texture Function) as demonstrated in [32], it significantly limits its accuracy in describing the radiometry at the microgeometry level (i.e., regular imaging conditions). Modeling the discrepancy in the incident and exiting microfacets as well as the light transport between them becomes essential for accurate description of body reflection.

The third problem is that the estimation of the parameters (i.e., reflectometry) of an affine combination of diffuse and specular reflection models is inherently challenging. Specular reflection is essentially mirror reflection spread according to the variation of microfacet orientations, which means they are either sparse (e.g., sharp highlights on a smooth surface) or weak (e.g., large dim highlights on rough surface). As a result, estimating the specular parameter values while separating its effects from the total radiance becomes challenging, unless one has the luxury of capturing multiple images in different imaging conditions (e.g., [45]).

We derived a novel analytical reflection model that is physically accurate and general but expressed with a compact representation. It remedies all the problems that simple affine combinations of reflection models suffer from. We achieve this by fundamentally unifying the body and surface reflections with the same microgeometry. We model the microgeometry of the surface within a pixel with oriented planar microfacets, each of which is a mirror. By modeling the body and surface reflections by tracing the transmitted and reflected light based on the atomic Fresnel behavior of light for each microfacet and also the transport between them, we successfully arrive at a unified reflection model. We refer to this novel model as the Fresnel Microfacet BRDF (FMBRDF) model.

For the surface reflection, we generalize the Torrance-Sparrow model [51] Eq. 3.8. In the Torrance-Sparrow model, D is a Gaussian and its parameter σ represents the surface roughness. Nishino introduced the use of an exponential power distribution as the basis of his directional statistics BRDF model [34, 35]. Similarly, we [17] model the orientation distribution D with the generalized normal distribution

$$D(\theta_{\mathbf{H}}) \propto \exp\left[-\left(\frac{\theta_{\mathbf{H}}}{\sigma}\right)^{\beta}\right]. \tag{3.11}$$

where the kurtosis of the distribution is controlled by the parameter β in addition to the standard deviation σ.

We now derive the body reflection induced by the exact same surface microgeometry, e.g., a collection of mirror shards. Each pixel subtends a small surface area in which a collection of microfacets reside. We will denote quantities of these microfacets with lower case vectors. We must consider all combinations of incident and outgoing points within the microgeometry of a pixel A_p to model light transport between microfacets. We first focus on a point $\boldsymbol{p}$ on an oriented microfacet of normal $\boldsymbol{n}$ in A_p. The projected radiance of each microfacet $L_{rp}(\boldsymbol{n})$ can be expressed with the project radiance $L_{rp}(\boldsymbol{p};\boldsymbol{n})$ at $\boldsymbol{p}$ as

$$L_{rp}(\boldsymbol{n}) = \frac{1}{|A_{\boldsymbol{n}}|} \int_{A_n} G_m^b(\boldsymbol{p}; \boldsymbol{n}) L_{rp}(\boldsymbol{p}; \boldsymbol{n}) \mathrm{d}A_{\boldsymbol{n}} \,, \tag{3.12}$$

where $G_m^b(\boldsymbol{p}; \boldsymbol{n})$ is a binary masking function at $\boldsymbol{p}$, $A_{\boldsymbol{n}}$ is the region of microfacets oriented to $\boldsymbol{n}$ in A_p, $|\cdot|$ denotes the area of a region, and $\mathrm{d}A_{\boldsymbol{n}}$ is an infinitesimal area in the vicinity of $\boldsymbol{p}$. The area of the microfacet $|A_{\boldsymbol{n}}|$ is

$$|A_{\boldsymbol{n}}| = |A_p| D(\theta_{\boldsymbol{n}}) \mathrm{d}\omega_{\boldsymbol{n}} \,, \tag{3.13}$$

where $\theta_{\boldsymbol{n}}$ is the polar angle the surface normal $\boldsymbol{n}$ makes with the global surface normal $\mathbf{N}$ (*i.e.*, the overall surface normal of a single pixel) which is set as the north pole of the local coordinate frame.

This projected radiance $L_{rp}(\boldsymbol{p}; \boldsymbol{n})$ is defined by

$$L_{rp}(\boldsymbol{p}; \boldsymbol{n}) = \frac{\mathrm{d}\Phi_r(\boldsymbol{p}; \boldsymbol{n})}{(\boldsymbol{n} \cdot \boldsymbol{N}) d A_{\boldsymbol{n}} (\boldsymbol{N} \cdot \boldsymbol{V}) \mathrm{d}\omega_r} \,, \tag{3.14}$$

where $\mathrm{d}\Phi_r(\boldsymbol{p}; \boldsymbol{n})$ is the flux in the viewing direction at point $\boldsymbol{p}$ and $\mathrm{d}\omega_r$ is an infinitesimal solid angle in the viewing direction. The flux $\mathrm{d}\Phi_r(\boldsymbol{p}; \boldsymbol{n})$ is represented with the radiance $L_r(\boldsymbol{p}; \boldsymbol{n})$ in the viewing direction at $\boldsymbol{p}$ as

$$\mathrm{d}\Phi_r(\boldsymbol{p}; \boldsymbol{n}) = L_r(\boldsymbol{p}; \boldsymbol{n}) \cdot (\boldsymbol{n} \cdot \boldsymbol{V}) \mathrm{d}A_{\boldsymbol{n}} \mathrm{d}\omega_r \,. \tag{3.15}$$

The outgoing light $L_r(\boldsymbol{p}; \boldsymbol{n})$ at a point $\boldsymbol{p}$ is the sum of the light transported from other incident points on the microgeometry. We define $\mathrm{d}L_r(\boldsymbol{p}, \boldsymbol{p}_i; \boldsymbol{n}, \boldsymbol{n}_i)$ as the radiance of light transported from an incident point $\boldsymbol{p}_i$ on a microfacet oriented to $\boldsymbol{n}_i$. Assuming that the surface is opaque enough so that no light is transported from outside of the patch A_p, we can express $\mathrm{d}L_r(\boldsymbol{p}; \boldsymbol{n})$ with the radiance transported from other microfacets $\mathrm{d}L_r(\boldsymbol{p}, \boldsymbol{p}_i; \boldsymbol{n}, \boldsymbol{n}_i)$

$$\mathrm{d}L_r(\boldsymbol{p}; \boldsymbol{n}) = \int_{\Omega} \int_{A_{n_i}} \frac{\mathrm{d}L_r(\boldsymbol{p}, \boldsymbol{p}_i; \boldsymbol{n}, \boldsymbol{n}_i)}{\mathrm{d}\omega_{\boldsymbol{n}_i} \mathrm{d}A_{\boldsymbol{n}_i}} \mathrm{d}A_{\boldsymbol{n}_i} \mathrm{d}\omega_{\boldsymbol{n}_i} \,, \tag{3.16}$$

where $\mathrm{d}\omega_{\boldsymbol{n}_i}$ is an infinitesimal solid angle that represents the normal direction $\boldsymbol{n}_i$ of an incident microfacet, $\mathrm{d}A_{\boldsymbol{n}_i}$ is an infinitesimal area in the vicinity of $\boldsymbol{p}_i$, $A_{\boldsymbol{n}_i}$ is the region of microfacets oriented to $\boldsymbol{n}_i$ in A_p. To represent outgoing radiance $\mathrm{d}L_r(\boldsymbol{p}, \boldsymbol{p}_i; \boldsymbol{n}, \boldsymbol{n}_i)$ with the incident flux $\mathrm{d}\Phi_i(\boldsymbol{p}_i; \boldsymbol{n}_i)$ at $\boldsymbol{p}_i$, we define $S(\boldsymbol{p}, \boldsymbol{p}_i; \boldsymbol{n}, \boldsymbol{n}_i)$ as

$$S(\boldsymbol{p}, \boldsymbol{p}_i; \boldsymbol{n}, \boldsymbol{n}_i) = \frac{\mathrm{d}L_r(\boldsymbol{p}, \boldsymbol{p}_i; \boldsymbol{n}, \boldsymbol{n}_i)}{\mathrm{d}\Phi_i(\boldsymbol{p}_i; \boldsymbol{n}_i)} \,. \tag{3.17}$$

where $S(\boldsymbol{p}, \boldsymbol{p}_i; \boldsymbol{n}, \boldsymbol{n}_i)$ defines how much light is transmitted into the surface, transported from $\boldsymbol{p}_i$ to $\boldsymbol{p}$, and re-transmitted into the air

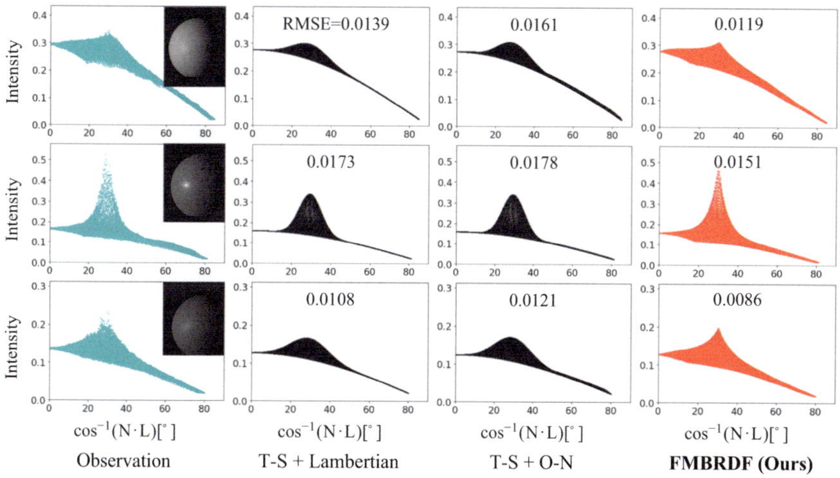

Fig. 3.3 Radiometric accuracy shown with intensity values as a function of the angle between the global surface normal and the light source direction. Each graph shows the fitting results for one of the lighting conditions. The number at the top of the graph is the RMSE. Our FMBRDF model accurately represents both surface and body reflections regardless of the surface roughness and color

$$S(\boldsymbol{p}, \boldsymbol{p}_i; \boldsymbol{n}, \boldsymbol{n}_i) = T(\theta_o) S'(\boldsymbol{p}, \boldsymbol{p}_i; \boldsymbol{n}, \boldsymbol{n}_i) T(\theta_i) \, . \tag{3.18}$$

Here, $T(\theta)$ is the Fresnel transmittance for unpolarized light from the air at incident angle θ, $\theta_i = \cos^{-1}(\boldsymbol{n}_i \cdot \boldsymbol{L})$, $\theta_o = \cos^{-1}(\boldsymbol{n} \cdot \boldsymbol{V})$, and $S'(\boldsymbol{p}, \boldsymbol{p}_i; \boldsymbol{n}, \boldsymbol{n}_i)$ represents scattering and absorption.

We model the masking and shadowing term between the microfacets with a novel correlation function that models the spatial bias of their orientations whose details can be found in [17]. These functions allow us to derive the body reflection by the same microfacets that give rise to the surface reflection as

$$L_b(\boldsymbol{N}, \boldsymbol{L}, \boldsymbol{V}) = \frac{1}{\boldsymbol{N} \cdot \boldsymbol{V}} \int_\Omega \int_\Omega G_m(\boldsymbol{n}) D(\theta_{\boldsymbol{n}}) T(\theta_o) (\boldsymbol{V} \cdot \boldsymbol{n}) \cdot \frac{k_b}{\pi} f(\boldsymbol{n}, \boldsymbol{n}_i) \cdot G_s(\boldsymbol{n}_i) D(\theta_{\boldsymbol{n}_i}) T(\theta_i) (\boldsymbol{L} \cdot \boldsymbol{n}_i) \mathrm{d}\omega_{\boldsymbol{n}} d\omega_{\boldsymbol{n}_i} \cdot E_o \, , \tag{3.19}$$

where G_m and G_s are the average masking and shadowing functions, respectively, and T is the Fresnel transmittance for unpolarized light. In summary, these newly derived expressions allow us to model the light transport between microfacets, which in turn expresses the true body reflection induced by the mirrored-microfacets. In other words, we show in [17], for the first time, that diffuse reflection can fully be expressed with internal light transport of microfacets without the need for the artificial Lambertian assumption.

Although we do not discuss details in this chapter, the Fresnel Microfacet BRDF model also unifies polarimetric properties of light reflection as it is the very atomic light reflection behavior, i.e., the Fresnel reflection and transmission, of the exact same mirrored microfacets. Interested readers are referred to [17] for full details.

We can evaluate the radiometric accuracy of our FMBRDF model by fitting our model and others to images of real surfaces. Figure 3.3 shows the results of our FMBRDF and other radiometric BRDF models on several images taken under different light source directions. These results clearly show that a Gaussian microfacet distribution is hardly appropriate for real-world surfaces. Furthermore, our FMBRDF model can represent observed body reflection more accurately than the Lambertian and Oren-Nayar models.

We quantitatively evaluate the accuracy of the estimated FMBRDF from a polarimetric image by rendering a radiometric image under a novel lighting condition. Figure 3.4 shows rendered images under novel lighting conditions and prediction errors of FMBRDF and other physics-based BRDF models for objects of different colors, surface roughness, and shape. The parameters of the other models and

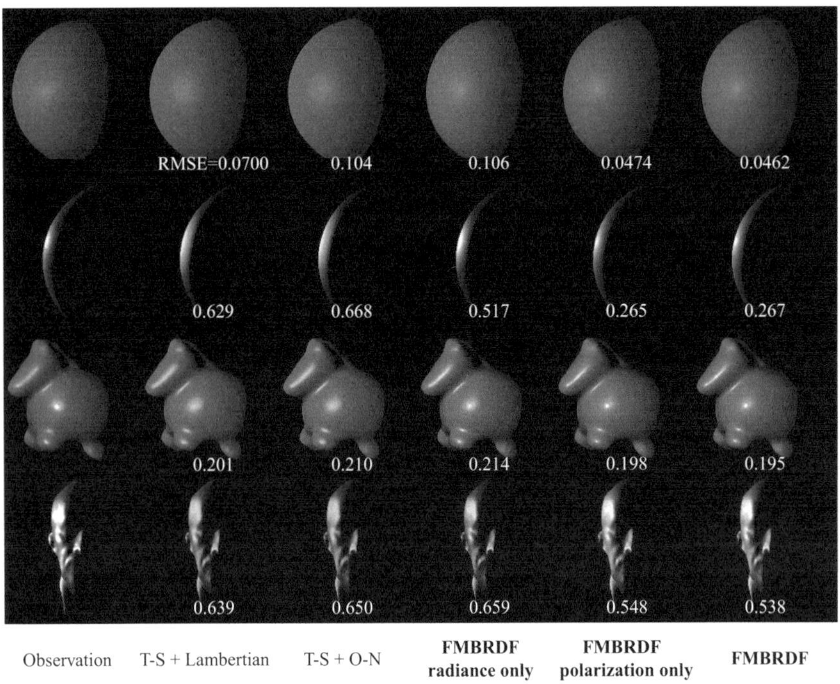

Fig. 3.4 Radiometric renderings using BRDF parameters estimated from single polarimetric images (ours), DoLP images (ours without radiance), and radiometric images (others). The number under the rendered image is the RMSE from the observation. In contrast to BRDFs estimated with only radiance, FMBRDF estimated with radiance and polarization results in accurate radiometric appearance both in surface and body reflection for different surfaces

ours (FMBRDF) "radiance only" are estimated from the observed radiance values. Ours (FMBRDF) "polarization only" is estimated from only the degree of linear polarization values (DoLPs). Radiometric BRDF models, including ours when estimated from observed radiance, fail to accurately predict the surface reflection. In contrast, images rendered with FMBRDF using parameter estimates from polarization are accurate, especially near the highlights regardless of the albedo ratio, roughness, and shape of the object. These results clearly demonstrate the accuracy of polari-radiometric reflectometry and the advantage of FMBRDF which enables it by unifying radiometric and polarimetric reflection modeling.

To the best of our knowledge, FMBRDF is the first reflectance model to seamlessly unify body and surface reflections with the same microgeometry and also describe both its radiometric and polarimetric light reflections in a single model. We believe FMBRDF will provide an invaluable basis for accurate radiometric and polarimetric image analysis and serve as a backbone for a wide range of computer vision applications including visual Shitsukan modeling.

3.2.2 Diffusion Reflectance Map

When the illumination is complex, such as the natural lighting of a real-world environment, estimating the reflectance from the object appearance becomes particularly challenging due to its deep entanglement with the illumination. Even when the surface geometry is known, disentangling the reflectance and illumination from a single image is still ill-posed due to the two key ambiguities in color and frequency (see Sect. 3.1.2).

The frequency ambiguity is particularly troublesome. For past methods, a low-pass reflectance, i.e., closer to Lambertian, causes the illumination estimate to become blurry which can only be used to insert an object in the scene that has lower frequency characteristics than the object used to recover the illumination. The same can be said about relighting using the illumination estimate.

How should we recover the true illumination and reflectance from object appearance? The frequency bound of the object appearance suggests that there is no such thing as a true estimate. Given the object appearance, the illumination must be generated together with the reflectance as only its combined, partial information is encoded in it. Inverse rendering, particularly from a single image, in other words, should be a generative process. In this sense, we aim to establish *generative perception*, a seamless integration of generative modeling in image understanding. As one way to realize this, we argue for *stochastic inverse rendering* in which image formation is explicitly modeled as a stochastic process and its inversion becomes a generative reverse process. Stochasticity needs to be seamlessly integrated into the radiometric disentanglement. We achieve this by first computing a geometry-free representation of the object appearance, the reflectance map, and then estimating the reflectance and illumination from it in a principled stochastic optimization formulation.

The reflected radiance L_r at a surface point $\mathbf{x}$ due to incident directional illumination L_i can be described with the rendering equation [19] as we saw in Eq. 3.2. Estimation of the reflectance (BRDF f_r) and the illumination (L_i) from a single image (L_r at each point in the viewing direction) is challenging even when the surface geometry ($\mathbf{N}$ for every $\mathbf{x}$) is known and the reflectance is homogeneous. The key difficulty stems from the multiplication of the two radiometric ingredients and the integration over the upper hemisphere. These cause frequency attenuation and implicit angular coordinate transform that hamper reflectance and illumination recovery from the object appearance, which past methods tackled with complex non-linear optimization or approximate differentiable rendering.

We can explicitly rotate each local direction into the global coordinate frame and approximate each local integration domain with the hemisphere centered around the viewing direction. This means that, if the surface point $\mathbf{x}$ can be uniquely determined by its surface normal, the surface radiance (i.e., object appearance) can be uniquely defined by $L_r(\mathbf{N})$, the reflectance map [16]

$$L_r(\mathbf{N}) = \int_{\Omega} f_r(\mathbf{V}, \mathbf{L}) L_i(\mathbf{L}))(\mathbf{L} \cdot \mathbf{N}) \mathrm{d}\omega_i \,, \tag{3.20}$$

which is simply rewriting the reflected radiance in the local coordinate frame while assuming orthographic camera projection, i.e., all $\mathbf{V}(\mathbf{x})$ are the same). Different surface points with the same surface normal can have different radiance due to global light transport, such as cast shadows and interreflection. We resolve these when recovering the reflectance map from the image whose details can be found in [13].

Optical image formation adds measurement noise which can be approximated with a zero-mean Gaussian. As such, image formation can be viewed as an additive Gaussian noise process on the reflectance map Eq. 3.20. With the reflectance map, we can formulate single-image reflectance and illumination disentanglement as a geometry-independent stochastic inversion process. This allows us to derive a stochastic inverse rendering approach, a principled inverse rendering approach with stochasticity seamlessly integrated in the estimation process. In particular, we formulate it as generating a reflectance map of a perfect mirror surface from the observed image. This inverse diffusion process is not that of a regular noise to signal, but of a deterministic forward process with stochastic observation noise, similar to heat dissipation [44].

The inverse generative process can be considered as steps taken along the reflectance space towards a perfect mirror. If we employ an analytical reflectance model, this can be considered as a trajectory in its parameter space. We employ the Disney Principled BSDF model [5]

$$\begin{aligned} & f_r(\mathbf{V}, \mathbf{L}; \Psi := \{\boldsymbol{\rho}^d, \rho^s, \alpha, \gamma\}) \\ & \quad = (1-\gamma)\frac{\boldsymbol{\rho}^d}{\pi}(f_r^d(\mathbf{V}, \mathbf{L}) + f_r^r(\mathbf{V}, \mathbf{L}; \alpha)) + f_r^s(\mathbf{V}, \mathbf{L}; \boldsymbol{\rho}^d, \rho^s, \alpha, \gamma)\,, \end{aligned} \tag{3.21}$$

where we use a partial set of its BSDF model parameters for simplicity: $\boldsymbol{\rho}^d$, ρ^s, α and γ, the diffuse color, specular strength, roughness and metallicness, respectively. All of the parameters are normalized to [0, 1].

Figure 3.5 depicts the architecture of Diffusion Reflectance Map Network (DRMNet) which consists of two subnetworks. The first is a diffusion model, IllNet, that learns to invert the forward reflectance map generation process conditioned on the reflectance. The second is a reflectance estimator, RefNet. Input to DRMNet are the observed and current reflectance maps, $L_r^{(K)}$ and $L_r^{(k)}$, respectively.

IllNet estimates the illumination from the observed reflectance map by iteratively generating a reflectance map $L_r^{(k-1)}$ and reflectance parameters one step closer to perfect mirror $f_r^{(k-1)}(\mathbf{V}, \mathbf{L}; \Psi^{(k-1)})$ from the current reflectance map $L_r^{(k)}$ and reflectance parameter estimate $\Psi^{(k)}$. The reflectance estimate of the object is $\Psi^{(K)}$, where K is the maximum time step, i.e., the observation. This recursion traces a trajectory in the reflectance parameter space

$$\Psi^{(k-1)} - \Psi_0 = \eta(\Psi^{(k)} - \Psi_0)\,, \tag{3.22}$$

where η is a constant in (0, 1) that controls the speed towards Ψ_0, i.e., a perfect mirror reflectance [1, 1, 1, 1, 0, 1].

The main parameter that determines the highest frequency of the reflectance is the surface roughness α. When $\alpha = 0$, the surface is perfect mirror reflectance, which we would like to achieve as Ψ_0. If we focus on the surface roughness α, the iterative reverse steps defined in Eq. 3.22 gradually moves it towards 0 and its change $\left|\alpha^{(k-1)} - \alpha^{(k)}\right| = (1-\eta)\alpha^{(k)}$ asymptotically dampens in the process. As these smaller steps in the surface roughness correspond to higher frequencies in the

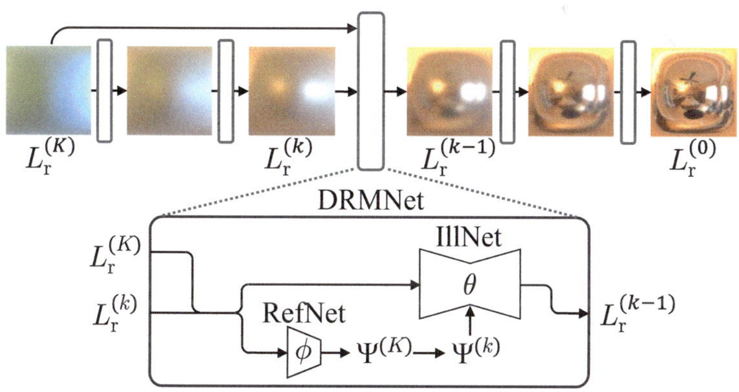

Fig. 3.5 Overall architecture of diffusion reflectance map network (DRMNet). DRMNet consists of two subnetworks, IllNet for stochastic reverse diffusion to recursively transform the observed reflectance map into a reflectance map of a perfect mirror, and RefNet for jointly and iteratively estimating the reflectance

reflectance map, this means, with the uniform steps in Eq. 3.22, the higher the frequencies, the denser the sampled steps. This contributes to robust recovery of the illumination.

This iterative generation, learned as a reverse diffusion process, starts with the observed reflectance map $L_r^{(K)}$ and reflectance parameters $\Psi^{(K)}$ and IllNet is applied recursively until it reaches a reflectance map $L_r^{(0)}$ corresponding to a perfect mirror Ψ_0. In practice, by definition (Eq. 3.22), $\Psi^{(0)}$ only asymptotically reaches Ψ_0. For this, we set K to satisfy $||\Psi^{(0)} - \Psi_0||_2 < \epsilon$ for a small ϵ. At inference time, we do not need to explicitly define K and instead iterate till $\Psi^{(k)}$ reaches $||\Psi^{(k)} - \Psi_0||_2 < \epsilon$ (Fig. 3.6).

RefNet learns to estimate the reflectance parameters of the object in the observed single image: $\Psi^{(K)}$. The reflectance parameter $\Psi^{(k)}$ corresponding to the current reflectance map can be computed from this observed reflectance estimate by

$$\Psi^{(k)} = \eta^{(K-k)}(\Psi^{(K)} - \Psi_0) + \Psi_0\,, \tag{3.23}$$

using the steps taken so far $(K - k)$.

The illumination generation process by IllNet is inherently noisy due to its stochasticity and a direct estimate of the current reflectance parameters $\Psi^{(k)}$ from $L_r^{(k)}$ would be noisy especially as the step size gradually becomes smaller. Instead, by always estimating the observed reflectance and analytically computing the current reflectance, we obtain robust estimates of the current reflectance that are guaranteed to converge. At the same time, this lets RefNet iteratively refine its estimate of the observed object reflectance, i.e., RefNet learns to optimize the object reflectance through its iteration along with IllNet.

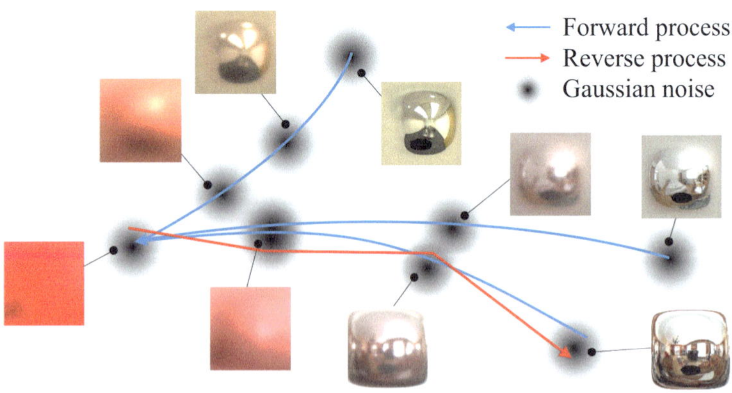

Fig. 3.6 Additive Gaussian observation noise makes each image formation process stochastic, and reflectance attenuates high-frequencies of the illumination whose residues are gradually washed out by the noise. The reverse process is thus necessarily stochastic, effectively generating the lost higher frequency components of the illumination by sampling along learned scores

We can describe the radiometric formulation of an observed reflectance map $L_r^{(K)}$ from the surrounding illumination $L_r^{(0)}$ and the object reflectance $f_r^{(K)}$ as a forward iterative process

$$q(L_r^{(1:K)}|L_r^{(0)}, f_r^{(K)}) = \prod_{k=1}^{K} q(L_r^{(k)}|L_r^{(0)}, f_r^{(K)}) . \tag{3.24}$$

Let us express the reverse process (DRMNet) using IllNet and RefNet parameters, θ and ϕ, respectively,

$$p_\theta(L_r^{(0:K-1)}|L_r^{(K)}) = \prod_{k=1}^{K} p_{\theta,\phi}(L_r^{(k-1)}|L_r^{(k)}) . \tag{3.25}$$

The conditional $p_{\theta,\phi}$ must invert q in Eq. 3.24. Although the forward transition q is deterministic, it cannot be inverted analytically, not just because it is highly non-linear, but also because of the information loss. For this, $p_{\theta,\phi}$ must be a stochastic generative model. In order to make this reverse process stochastic, we must in turn make the forward process q also stochastic while at the same time obeying the deterministic radiometric image formation process.

Similar to [44], we resolve this by adding stochastic perturbations to the deterministic forward process (*i.e.*, the Gaussian observation noise)

$$q(L_r^{(k)}|L_r^{(0)}, f_r^{(K)}) = \mathcal{N}(L_r^{(k)}|L_r(\mathbf{n}; L_i, f_r^{(k)}), \sigma^2\mathbf{I}) , \tag{3.26}$$

where $f_r(k)$ is the reflectance whose parameter $\Psi^{(k)}$ is computed from the observed reflectance estimate $\Psi^{(K)}$ by Eq. 3.23, and σ is the standard deviation of the added noise.

The conditional $p_{\theta,\phi}$ models the reverse process of this stochastic forward radiometric process. Starting from the observed reflectance map, by iteratively reverse transitioning with the conditional $p_{\theta,\phi}$, we can generate one illumination that gives rise to the observed reflectance map for that object reflectance among the infinite possibilities. We model this reverse transition $p_{\theta,\phi}$ with a Gaussian and explicitly condition it on the observed reflectance map (i.e., object appearance) $L_r^{(K)}$

$$p_{\theta,\phi}(L_r^{(k-1)}|L_r^{(k)}, L_r^{(K)}, f_r^{(k)}) = \mathcal{N}(L_r^{(k-1)}|\mu_{\theta,\phi}(L_r^{(k)}, L_r^{(K)}), \delta^2\mathbf{I}) . \tag{3.27}$$

We learn the expectation $\mu_{\theta,\phi}$ of this Gaussian

$$\mu_\theta(L_r^{(k)}, L_r^{(K)}, \Psi_\phi^{(k)}(L_r^{(k)}, L_r^{(K)}, K-k)) ,$$

and set the variance to a constant δ. We further reparameterize $\mu_\theta(L_r^{(k)}, L_r^{(K)}, \Psi_\phi^{(k)}) = L_r^{(k)} + \varepsilon_\theta(L_r^{(k)}, L_r^{(K)}, \Psi_\phi^{(k)})$ to train IllNet from the residuals.

We maximize the evidence lower bound (ELBO) of the marginalized reverse transition $p_{\theta,\phi}(L_r^{(0)}|L_r^{(K)})$ by minimizing the upper bound on the negative log likelihood

$$\mathcal{L}_i = \mathbb{E}_{L_i, f_r, k}|\mu_{\theta,\phi}(\mathbf{n}; L_r^{(k)}, L_r^{(K)}) - L_r(\mathbf{n}; L_i, f_r^{(k)})|_2^2 . \tag{3.28}$$

When training DRMNet, the illumination L_i, reflectance $f_r^{(K)}$, and step k are uniformly sampled from a set of environment maps, reflectance parameter values, and $[1, K]$, respectively. As the reflectance map corresponding to perfect mirror reflection $L_r^{(0)}$ is equivalent to the incident illumination L_i, we can use L_i as the expectation instead of $L_r^{(0)}$.

In addition to the loss on the reflectance map Eq. 3.28, we impose a reflectance loss on the reflectance parameters estimated by RefNet $\Psi_\phi^{(K)}$ using the reflectance parameters corresponding to the forward step and process, Eq. 3.26 $f_r^{(k)}$ and Eq. 3.24 $f_r^{(K)}$, respectively,

$$\mathcal{L}_r = \mathbb{E}_{L_i, f_r, k}\left[|\Psi_\phi^{(k)} - \Psi^{(k)}|_2^2 + |\Psi_\phi^{(K)} - \Psi^{(K)}|_2^2\right] . \tag{3.29}$$

The final loss is $\mathcal{L} = \lambda_i \mathcal{L}_i + \lambda_r \mathcal{L}_r$, where λ_i and λ_r are hyperparameters weighting the ELBO and reflectance losses. IllNet is implemented with a U-Net and RefNet with a simple MLP. Further details can be found in [13].

Figure 3.7 shows qualitative evaluation of the accuracy of illumination and reflectance estimates using the iBRDF synthetic dataset [10]. DRMNet achieves higher accuracy and recovers more natural illumination. Figure 3.7 shows that simply using a diffusion prior [26] (i.e., a generative model of natural illumination as a prior in a Bayesian framework) results in illumination estimates that significantly deviate from the ground truth, as it is a naive noise seeded diffusion model used as an external prior in a classic Bayesian inverse-rendering formulation. As

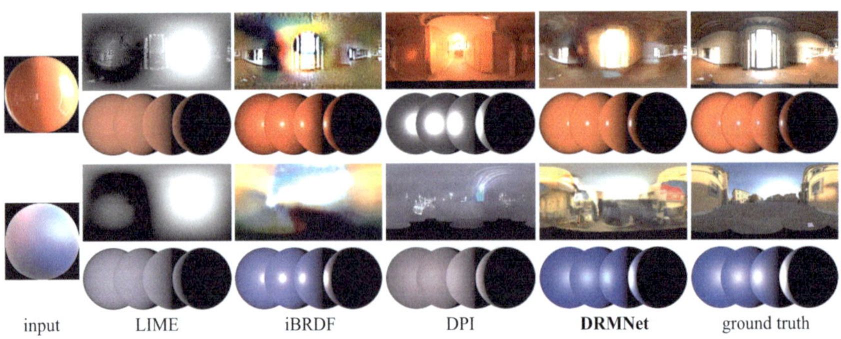

Fig. 3.7 Qualitative results on iBRDF synthetic dataset [10]. For each input, the top row is the illumination estimate shown as a spherical panorama and the bottom row is the reflectance estimate rendered as a sphere under a point source. Compared with past inverse rendering methods that explicitly estimate illumination and reflectance, LIME [29], iBRDF [10], and DPI [26], our method DRMNet recovers more accurate and realistic estimates for both

ground truth reflectance is unknown, we evaluate the accuracy of the reflectance estimate through relighting. Figure 3.8 shows renderings of different objects under the estimated illumination. Since our method explicitly recovers the high frequency spectrum of the illumination, even objects with higher frequency than the one used to recover the illumination can be relit with natural appearance. In other words, our DRMNet successfully retains the Shitsukan of the surrounding environment.

To the best of our knowledge, diffusion reflectance map is the first principled stochastic inverse rendering method, as a prime example of generative perception, that estimates the illumination and reflectance from a single image of an object of known geometry taken under complex natural illumination. By formulating the radiometric disentanglement on the reflectance map and as a recursive inversion of stochastic diffusion but with an underlying deterministic rendering equation, we showed that DRMNet achieves state-of-the-art accuracy and full detailed recovery of surrounding illumination, enabling relighting and replacement of objects with arbitrary reflectance properties. By breaking the fundamental limitations of inverse rendering with a seamlessly integrated generative model, DRMNet opens new possibilities of single-image radiometric understanding and bolsters visual Shitsukan understanding.

Fig. 3.8 Object replacement results on the nLMVS-real dataset. DRMNet produces accurate illumination estimates that enable rendering of detailed object appearance for objects with arbitrary reflectance. The Shitsukan of the illumination is better captured compared with past methods including LIME [29], iBRDF [10], DPI [26], and ALP [54], which demonstrates the accuracy of the recovered illumination by DRMNet

3.2.3 Material Recognition

The visual Shitsukan of a surface also directly hints at its material composition. Different materials exhibit different Shitsukan, which in turn suggests that by recognizing unique visual Shitsukan captured in an image, we can determine the material of the surface. One approach to such image-based material recognition would be to formulate it as a simple pixel-level recognition problem, *i.e.*, a variant of semantic segmentation. This can be cast as fully supervised learning using deep convolutional neural networks. Such an approach, however, would likely implicitly leverage object cues, i.e., that it sees a cup, to determine that its material is ceramic. This could be problematic, especially unless the data can be scaled up, as real-world biases in material compositions of objects would be directly reflected in the recognition. For instance, as the majority of cups captured in web-scraped images are made of ceramic, a wooden cup would hardly be recognized.

We pioneered the use of material properties, not only the visual but also the tactile attributes exhibited by materials for recognizing materials from images [46–48]. In other words, we introduced the recognition of distinct Shitsukan of materials to recognize different materials in images. Examples of material properties include visual properties, such as glossiness or translucency, as well as physical or tactile properties, such as hardness or roughness. The recognition of such material properties is also essential for determining how to act in the real-world. When cleaning a glass cup, for example, we know not to drop it or it will break. Glass is also often smooth, and we grasp it accordingly so it will not slip. In fact, we know how to grasp a plastic cup without crushing it just from sight, without any tactile feedback through our fingers. Such capabilities would be crucial for robots, too.

We refer to such visually-recognizable material properties, in a way the visual Shitsukan itself, as visual material attributes (originally visual material traits [46]). Recognizing visual material attributes in images, however, is particularly challenging. Unlike much prior work in object, face, and scene attribute recognition, material attributes are local properties, as can be seen in Fig. 3.1. While scene, object, and face attributes are typically associated with a characteristic shape and fixed spatial extent, material attributes are not. A car that is "sporty" will have a typically sleek and aerodynamic shape, and if a face has "large eyes," such an attribute is defined by the spatial extent of the eyes relative to the face. If a carpet is "fuzzy," however, the fuzziness is not associated with any characteristic shape or scale, nor is it necessarily a consequence of the object involved (some carpets are not fuzzy). We derived a series of methods for recognizing these visual material attributes and then recognizing the materials themselves based on them. Please refer to [48] for details.

The advent of deep learning opened a new avenue of research for visual recognition. Instead of deriving features that are likely suitable for the recognition task at hand, it now allows us to learn those features directly together with the classifier itself in a single visual information processing pipeline which can be learned end-to-end with backpropagation of gradients computed by the recognition loss. Although this alleviated the need for intermediate representations like visual material attributes for material recognition, which likely now can be learned as an internal representation (although unlikely to be found with semantic structure intact), it inevitably necessitates large amounts of data. Deep neural networks achieve the end-to-end functional approximation of both feature extraction and classification with a composition of linear and non-linear transforms whose parameters grow with every combination. Learning these parameters unsurprisingly requires a large amount of data (but surprisingly not as many as the parameters). This means that to leverage visual Shitsukan to identify the surface materials, a task essential for real-world interaction for computers and humans as we saw, we need large-scale datasets. Closest works only realize image-wise recognition of materials or are primarily of indoor architectural, professional photographs [3, 4]. It is also worth clarifying the distinction of material segmentation from stuff segmentation. "Stuff" [6], in this context, is not a material but rather refers to objects without discernible boundaries (e.g., a road, a representative "stuff," is composed of different materials such as asphalt, paint for markings, and metal for manholes).

We have made significant contributions in deep material recognition. Recognizing surface materials from their visual Shitsukan becomes particularly crucial for real-world interaction as anticipation by sight can potentially play a significant role. A representative example for this would be driving. We effortlessly recognize the materials and their Shitsukan as we drive down the road and react accordingly. If the road changes from asphalt to gravel, we prepare for a slight slip of the tires when we brake. If we see something tumbling off a truck running in front of us, we can immediately determine its softness and decide to overrun it instead of jerking our steering wheel even without recognizing that it is clothes. Recognizing the materials of a road scene for each pixel in a car-mounted video can greatly help autonomous driving systems and advanced driver-assistance systems (ADAS) to make such decisions. We refer to this task of per-pixel material recognition as material segmentation and introduce two novel datasets for road-scene material segmentation.

We introduced a large-scale dataset for RGB road-scene material recognition, which we refer to as KITTI-Materials dataset [7, 8]. We source the images in this dataset from the KITTI raw data [15] so that it is based on a widely accepted dataset whose settings can be reused for new material segmentation research. The dataset consists of 1000 images covering 24 different driving scenes including downtown, campus, residential area, highway, and other city/suburban landscapes captured from a car. We annotated per-pixel material labels of 20 categories by professional paid annotators. All annotations are 1216×320 in resolution, and the raw images are center-cropped to this size beforehand. We have run many baseline methods as well as a novel method for material segmentation on this dataset whose details can be found in [7, 8].

Recognizing materials in regular RGB images, however, remains challenging. Unlike objects which largely exhibit different looks including shape contours and surface textures, different materials often result in similar appearance in regular color images. For instance, a ceramic cup and a plastic cup would have similar global shapes and local surface textures in an image. Some materials don't even have their own defined appearances. For instance, water does not have its own color and metal mostly mirror-reflects, both of which take on the appearance of their surroundings.

Where should we look for reliable visual cues to recognize materials? The surface composition of different materials not just in their spatial distribution but also in their subsurface structure give rise to characteristic radiometric behaviors. For instance, subtle differences in the mesoscopic surface structure change polarization of incident light and variation in subsurface composition result in different absorption of near-infrared (NIR) light. These radiometric features can potentially let us discern different materials robustly. Few works in the past have exploited different imaging modalities in isolation for only material recognition. Recent advances in imaging sensors, most notably the introduction of quad-Bayer CMOS, have brought the opportunity to leverage a variety of imaging modalities in a compact passive setup at low cost, making it particularly suitable for autonomous vehicles and mobile robots.

We introduced the MultiModal Material Segmentation Dataset (MCubeS) [22]. MCubeS captures the visual appearance of various materials found in daily outdoor scenes from a viewpoint on a road, pavement, or sidewalk. At each viewpoint, we capture images with three fundamentally different imaging modalities, RGB, polarization, and near-infrared (NIR). The key challenges lie in systematic image capture with precise spatio-temporal alignment and annotation with pixel-wise material categories.

Surfaces in the real-world made of different materials cause different subsurface compositions and surface structures at the mesoscopic scale. These differences give rise to different behaviors of incident light. Most notably, they alter the radiometric behavior of incident light in its reflection, refraction, and absorption. These differences can often be observed in their polarization properties, i.e., different degree of linear polarization (DoLP) or angle of linear polarization (AoLP), and absorption of NIR light, respectively. For instance, surfaces made of metal specularly reflects light compared with wood which has a more balanced combination of specular and diffuse reflections, which result in differences in observed DoLP and AoLP. Water is transparent in the visible spectrum but absorbs light in the NIR range—water and water-containing surfaces (i.e., foliage) exhibit different shades of intensity in an NIR image.

As shown in Fig. 3.9, MCubeS dataset captures these rich radiometric characteristics of different materials with a camera system consisting of a stereo pair of RGB-polarization (RGB-P) camera and a near-infrared (NIR) camera. The image capture system is also equipped with a LiDAR to assist label propagation. The RGB-P camera is equipped with a quad-Bayer sensor which has a Bayer color filter array over 2×2 block of pixels with four on-chip polarizers of different angles. We mount this custom imaging system on a cart to collect multimodal sequences of real-world scenes from a vantage point similar to a car.

Our MCubeS dataset consists of two distinct types of image sequences. The first type of data consists of sequences of images captured while the imaging system continuously moves forward. These sequences mimic the point of view of a moving vehicle. The second type of sequences is those captured at a single position while

Fig. 3.9 We introduced the first dataset and method for multimodal material segmentation, i.e., per-pixel recognition of materials from multiple imaging modalities. Our dataset captures a scene in RGB, near infra-red (NIR), angle of linear polarization (AoLP), degree of linear polarization (DoLP), each of which encodes the different radiometric characteristics of road-scene materials. Each image is densely annotated with materials

the imaging system pans. Some materials, like water, rarely appear in a road scene. The second type of data helps increase sample images of such materials.

MCubeS dataset consists of 42 scenes of the first type (continuous forward move) sampled at three frames per second. Average length of sequences are 309 s. The raw image sequences consist of 26,650 image sets, from which 424 image sets at almost equal temporal spacing were annotated. We also capture 19 different scenes for the second type of data (fixed location panning). For each scene, eight image sets are captured to cover 360 °C and a total of 76 image sets are annotated from these sequences. The total number of annotated image sets are 500. Each image set of each sequence consists of 5 images: a stereo-pair of RGB and polarization images and an NIR image captured from three distinct viewpoints. As Fig. 3.10 shows, we densely annotate every image with per-pixel material classes. We annotate the left RGB image and propagate the per-pixel labels to other views of the same frame. We recover a dense depth image for the left RGB-P camera by integrating RGB

Fig. 3.10 MCubeS dataset spans a wide range of road scenes (top row), including river sidewalks to railroad tracks, each densely annotated with materials.

stereo and LiDAR 3D points [49]. We use this dense depth image as a proxy to map the pixel-level annotations to the right RGB-P camera and the NIR camera. In this mapping, occluded pixels cannot find the corresponding pixels in the annotated left RGB image. We fill such holes with image inpainting [50].

We define 20 distinct materials by thoroughly examining the data we captured in the MCubeS dataset. MCubeS scenes mainly consist of road scenes and sidewalks whose constituents vary from "stuff" like pavements and roads to objects including bicycles and manholes. Each of these can be made of different materials even for the same instance. For example, pavements can be made of asphalt, concrete, brick, cobblestone, gravel, and sand. We also treat road markings and manholes as made of different materials as they are of special interest in driving scenarios (e.g., they can cause slips when wet). Vehicles are mainly made of metal, rubber, and glass. For people, clothes are made of fabric, while skin and hair are protein which are classes almost exclusive to people. For this, we use human body as the material label for parts other than their clothes. For natural objects, we mainly observe trees and grass as objects in the scene. Considering that wood can appear in sleepers on railroad tracks and fallen leaves may occupy some ground area, we use wood and leaf as material labels (i.e., trees are made of wood and leaves). Another notable material we add is water, which we find in puddles, rivers, and ponds. The "Other" category includes ceramic, plaster, plastic, and sky, which are common but less significant in occurrences or for downstream tasks in a driving scenario.

We also introduced a novel method which we refer to as MCubeSNet based on a convolutional neural network that leverages the semantic segmentation, i.e., what the object is, to recognize the materials, what it is made of, at each pixel. Please see [22] for details. The material segmentation results shown in Fig. 3.11 shows that our method achieves more accurate, detailed segmentation of the materials in the scene thanks to the rich radiometric signals captured in the multiple imaging

Fig. 3.11 Material segmentation results of our method (MCubeSNet) compared with semantic segmentation methods (DeepLab v3+ [9] and DDF [56]). Our method achieves more accurate and detailed segmentation of different materials by fully leveraging their characteristic radiometric properties through multimodal imaging

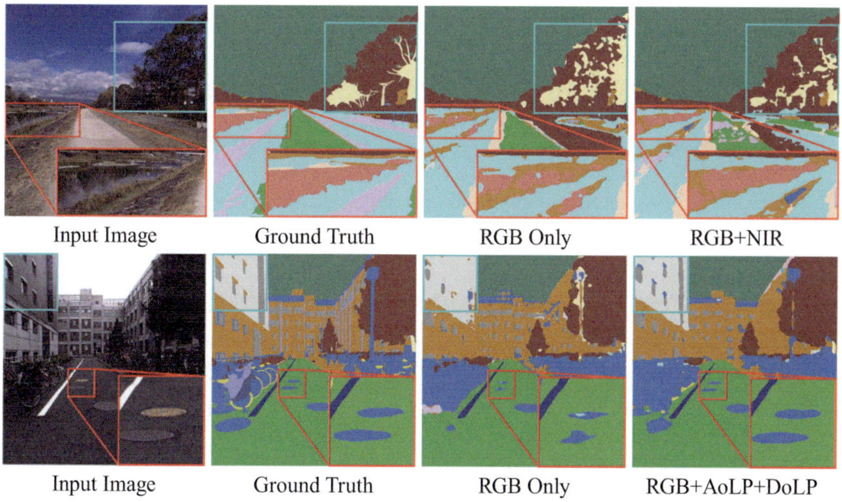

Fig. 3.12 NIR and polarization each add complementary information about the materials. NIR helps recognition of water-rich surfaces (river and leaves), and polarization helps discern metal and dielectrics

modalities. Figure 3.12 demonstrates the effectiveness of the different modalities in capturing key signatures of different materials (i.e., the Shitsukan of surfaces). We believe our work makes an important step forward in material segmentation and opens new avenues of practical use of material information in safety critical applications and makes practical use of computational visual Shitsukan perception in real-world applications.

3.2.4 Conclusion

In this chapter, we reviewed key research works that lay the foundation of computational visual Shitsukan understanding in the areas of reflectance modeling, inverse rendering, and texture modeling. We then discussed our recent research on each of these topics which push the frontier of each of these research areas and collectively cement the grounds for more accurate and richer extraction, representation, and prediction of the Shitsukan in our visual world. We hope to continue building on this foundation towards fully computational understanding of our visual world which will likely also inform studies on human visual perception.

References

1. Aubert, M., Setiawan, P., Oktaviana, A.A., Brumm, A., Sulistyarto, P.H., Saptomo, E.W., Istiawan, B., Ma'rifat, T.A., Wahyuono, V.N., Atmoko, F.T., Zhao, J.X., Huntley, J., Taçon, P.S.C., Howard, D.L., Brand, H.E.A.: Palaeolithic cave art in borneo. Nature **564**(7735), 254–257 (2018)
2. Barron, J.T., Malik, J.: Shape, illumination, and reflectance from shading. IEEE Trans. Pattern Anal. Mach. Intell. **37**(8), 1670–1687 (2015)
3. Bell, S., Upchurch, P., Snavely, N., Bala, K.: OpenSurfaces: a richly annotated catalog of surface appearance. ACM Trans. Graph. **32**(4) (2013)
4. Bell, S., Upchurch, P., Snavely, N., Bala, K.: Material recognition in the wild with the materials in context database. In: IEEE/CVF Conference on Computer Vision and Pattern Recognition (2015)
5. Burley, B.: Physically-based shading at Disney. In: ACM SIGGRAPH (2012)
6. Caesar, H., Uijlings, J., Ferrari, V.: COCO-stuff: thing and stuff classes in context. In: IEEE/CVF Conference on Computer Vision and Pattern Recognition (2018)
7. Cai, S., Wakaki, R., Nobuhara, S., Nishino, K.: RGB road scene material segmentation. In: Asian Conference on Computer Vision (2022)
8. Cai, S., Wakaki, R., Nobuhara, S., Nishino, K.: RGB road scene material segmentation. Image Vis. Comput. **145**, 104970 (2024)
9. Chen, L.-C., Zhu, Y., Papandreou, G., Schroff, F., Adam, H.: Encoder-decoder with atrous separable convolution for semantic image segmentation. In: European Conference on Computer Vision, pp 833–851 (2018)
10. Chen, Z., Nobuhara, S., Nishino, K.: Invertible neural BRDF for object inverse rendering. IEEE Trans. Pattern Anal. Mach. Intell. **44**(12), 9380–9395 (2022)
11. Cook, R.L., Torrance, K.E.: A reflectance model for computer graphics. ACM Trans. Graph. **1**(1), 7–24 (1982)
12. Dana, K.J., van Ginneken, B., Nayar, S.K., Koenderink, J.J.: Reflectance and texture of real-world surfaces. ACM Trans. Graph. **18**(1), 1–34 (1999)
13. Enyo, Y., Nishino, K.: Diffusion reflectance map: single-image stochastic inverse rendering of illumination and reflectance. In: IEEE/CVF Conference on Computer Vision and Pattern Recognition (2024)
14. Foster, D.H.: Color constancy. Vis. Res. **51**(7):674–700 (2011)
15. Geiger, A., Lenz, P., Urtasun, R.: Are we ready for autonomous driving? The KITTI vision benchmark suite. In: IEEE/CVF Conference on Computer Vision and Pattern Recognition, pp. 3354–3361 (2012)
16. Horn, B.K.P.: Robot Vision. The MIT Press (1986)
17. Ichikawa, T., Fukao, Y., Nobuhara, S., Nishino, K.: Fresnel microfacet BRDF: unification of polari-radiometric surface-body reflection. In: IEEE/CVF Conference on Computer Vision and Pattern Recognition (2023)
18. Ikeuchi, K., Sato, K.: Determining reflectance properties of an object using range and brightness images. IEEE Trans. Pattern Anal. Mach. Intell. **13**(11), 1139–1153 (1991)
19. Kajiya, J.T.: The rendering equation. ACM SIGGRAPH **20**(4), 143–150 (1986)
20. Kerbl, B., Kopanas, G., Leimkühler, T., Drettakis, G.: 3D Gaussian splatting for real-time radiance field rendering. ACM Trans. Graph. **42**(4) (2023)
21. Lambert, J.H.: Photometria sive de mensura de gratibus luminis colorum et umbrae. Augsburg (1760)
22. Liang, Y., Wakaki, R., Nobuhara, S., Nishino, K.: Multimodal material segmentation. In: IEEE/CVF Conference on Computer Vision and Pattern Recognition (2022)
23. Liu, L., Chen, J., Fieguth, P., Zhao, G., Chellappa, R., Pietikäinen, M.: From BoW to CNN: two decades of texture representation for texture classification. Int. J. Comput. Vis. **127**(1), 74–109 (2019)
24. Lombardi, S., Nishino, K.: Reflectance and illumination recovery in the wild. IEEE Trans. Pattern Anal. Mach. Intell. (2015)

25. Lombardi, S., Nishino, K.: Radiometric scene decomposition: scene reflectance, illumination, and geometry from RGB-D images. In: International Conference on 3D Vision (2016)
26. Lyu, L., Tewari, A., Habermann, M., Saito, S., Zollhöfer, M., Leimküehler, T., Theobalt, C.: Diffusion posterior illumination for ambiguity-aware inverse rendering. ACM Trans. Graph. **42**(6) (2023)
27. Marschner, S.R.: Inverse Rendering for Computer Graphics. Ph.D. thesis, Faculty of the Graduate School of Cornell University, Ithaca, NY (1998)
28. Max N.: Optical Models for Direct Volume Rendering. IEEE Trans. Visual Comput. Graph. **1**(2), 99–108 (1995)
29. Meka, A., Maximov, M., Zollhoefer, M., Chatterjee, A., Seidel, H.-P., Richardt, C., Theobalt, C.: LIME: live intrinsic material estimation. In: IEEE/CVF Conference on Computer Vision and Pattern Recognition, pp. 6315–6324 (2018)
30. Mildenhall, B., Srinivasan, P.P., Tancik, M., Barron, J.T., Ramamoorthi, R., Ng, R.: NeRF: representing scenes as neural radiance fields for view synthesis. In: European Conference on Computer Vision (2020)
31. Nayar, S.K., Ikeuchi, K., Kanade, T.: Surface reflection: physical and geometrical perspectives. IEEE Trans. Pattern Anal. Mach. Intell. **13**(7), 611–634 (1991)
32. Nayar, S.K., Oren, M.: Generalization of the Lambertian model and implications for machine vision. Int. J. Comput. Vis. **14**, 227–251 (1995)
33. Nicodemus, F.E. , Richmond, J.C., Hsia, J.J., Ginsberg, I.W., Limperis, T.: Geometric Considerations and Nomenclature for Reflectance. National Bureau of Standards (US) (1977)
34. Nishino, K.: Directional statistics BRDF model. In: IEEE/CVF International Conference on Computer Vision, pp. 476–483 (2009)
35. Nishino, K., Lombardi, S.: Directional statistics-based reflectance model for isotropic bidirectional reflectance distribution functions. J. Opt. Soc. Am. **28**(1) (2011)
36. Nishino, K., Sato, Y., Ikeuchi, K.: Eigen-texture method: appearance compression and synthesis based on a 3D model. IEEE Trans. Pattern Anal. Mach. Intell. **23**(11), 1257–1265 (2001)
37. Oxholm, G., Bariya, P., Nishino, K.: The scale of geometric texture. In: European Conference on Computer Vision **I**, 58–71 (2012)
38. Oxholm, G., Nishino, K.: Shape and reflectance estimation in the wild. IEEE Trans. Pattern Anal. Mach. Intell. (2015)
39. Palmer, S.E.:Vision Science: Photons to Phenomenology, 1st edn. The MIT Press (1999)
40. Papert, S.A.: The Summer Vision Project. Technical Report AIM-100, Massachusetts Institute of Technology, Cambridge, MA (1966)
41. Phong, B.T.: Illumination for computer generated pictures. Commun. ACM **18**(6), 311–317 (1975)
42. Poggio, T., Hurlbert, A.: Computational vision as inverse optics: reconstructing spectral reflectances and illuminant. In: Topical Meeting On Signal Recovery and Synthesis II, pp. FD2 (1986)
43. Ramamoorthi, R., Hanrahan, P.: A signal-processing framework for inverse rendering. In: ACM SIGGRAPH, pp. 117–128 (2001)
44. Rissanen, S., Heinonen, M., Solin, A.: Generative modelling with inverse heat dissipation. In: International Conference on Learning Representations (2023)
45. Sato, Y., Wheeler, M.D., Ikeuchi, K.: Object shape and reflectance modeling from observation. In: ACM SIGGRAPH, pp. 379–387 (1997)
46. Schwartz, G., Nishino, K. : Visual material traits: recognizing per-pixel material context. In: IEEE/CVF International Conference on Computer Vision Workshops, pp. 883–890 (2013)
47. Schwartz, G., Nishino, K.: Automatically discovering local visual material attributes. In: IEEE/CVF Conference on Computer Vision and Pattern Recognition, pp. 3565–3573 (2015)
48. Schwartz, G., Nishino, K.: Recognizing material properties from images. IEEE Trans. Pattern Anal. Mach. Intell. **42**(8), 1981–1995 (2020)
49. Shivakumar, S.S., Mohta, K., Pfrommer, B., Kumar, V., Taylor, C.J.: Real time dense depth estimation by fusing stereo with sparse depth measurements. In: International Conference on Robotics and Automation, pp. 6482–6488 (2019)

50. Telea, A.: An image inpainting technique based on the fast marching method. J. Graph. Tools **9**(1), 23–34 (2004)
51. Torrance, K.E., Sparrow, E.M.: Theory for off-specular reflection from roughened surfaces. J. Opt. Soc. Am. **57**(9), 1105–1114 (1967)
52. Wolff, L.B., Shafer, S.A., Healey, G.E.: Physics-Based Vision: Principles and Practice. A K Peters/CRC Press (1993)
53. Woodham, R.J.: Photometric stereo: a reflectance map technique for determining surface orientation from a single view. In: Image Understanding Systems and Industrial Applications, Proceedings of the SPIE 22nd Annual Technical Symposium, vol. 155, pp. 136–143 (1978)
54. Yu, H.-X., Agarwala, S., Herrmann, C., Szeliski, R., Snavely, N., Wu, J., Sun, D.: Accidental light probes. In: IEEE/CVF Conference on Computer Vision and Pattern Recognition, pp. 12521–12530 (2023)
55. Zhang, K., Luan, F., Wang, Q., Bala, K., Snavely, N.: PhySG: inverse rendering with spherical Gaussians for physics-based material editing and relighting. In: IEEE/CVF Conference on Computer Vision and Pattern Recognition (2001)
56. Zhou, J., Jampani, V., Pi, Z., Liu, Q., Yang, M.-H.: Decoupled dynamic filter networks. In: IEEE/CVF Conference on Computer Vision and Pattern Recognition, pp. 6643–6652 (2021)

Chapter 4
Shitsukan at The Intersection of Vision and Language

Takayuki Okatani

Abstract This chapter examines Shitsukan recognition as a key challenge for computer vision and multimodal AI. Unlike object recognition, Shitsukan involves subtle properties—such as glossiness, transparency, and softness—as well as holistic impressions like warmth or atmosphere. We review classical approaches that frame Shitsukan recognition as material classification, multi-label attribute prediction, or ranking-based estimation, noting their limitations in scope and robustness. Recent advances in web-scale image—text mining and contextual captioning broaden recognition beyond predefined categories. With the rise of generative AI, multimodal large language models (MLLMs) trained on massive image—text corpora now achieve remarkable image understanding, often capturing Shitsukan at near-human levels. Yet challenges remain, including generalization beyond training distributions and the absence of embodied experience. We argue that Shitsukan recognition highlights both the potential and the limits of current AI, offering a path toward deeper alignment with human perception.

Keywords Computer vision · Deep learning · Vision and language · Multi-modal AI · Large language model · Generative AI

4.1 Introduction

In this chapter, we discuss the visual recognition of *Shitsukan* from an engineering perspective.[1] The goal of this discussion is to create an image recognition AI that can recognize the Shitsukan of objects in an image in the same way as humans do. In

[1] Although the discussion focuses on a problem in computer vision, it specifically targets methods that do not rely on physics-based vision models, namely, machine learning using samples, with a particular emphasis on deep learning.

T. Okatani (✉)
Graduate School of Information Sciences, Tohoku University, Sendai, Japan
e-mail: okatani@tohoku.ac.jp

RIKEN Center for AIP, Chuo City, Tokyo, Japan

S. Nishida and K. Nishino (eds.), *Shitsukan—Understanding and Manipulating Material and Quality Perception*, https://doi.org/10.1007/978-981-95-4762-3_4

other words, the aim is to develop an AI for Shitsukan image recognition. If this goal is achieved, the technology could have valuable applications in society. Moreover, there is an underlying expectation that, through the pursuit of such AI, we may gain a deeper understanding of how humans recognize Shitsukan.

Although we do not provide a strict definition here, the term *Shitsukan* in this chapter broadly refers to the following. When people view an image of a scene or object, they perceive various elements. For example, they can identify the types of objects present—such as a cup or a dog—the relationships between those objects—such as a cup on a table or containing liquid—the setting—whether it's a kitchen, living room, or outdoor space—and even the time of day—whether it's daytime or nighttime. Shitsukan encompasses all other perceptual aspects of the image that go beyond what can be reliably inferred and clearly expressed in words.

First, there are surface properties of objects, particularly those characteristics that are easily perceived—for example, the glossiness of metal or plastic, or the transparency of glass or gemstones, as well as surface qualities that are better understood through touch than vision, such as coldness, softness, or roughness. In addition to individual objects, people can also sense the "atmosphere" created by the relationship between multiple objects and the lighting in the environment—like a cozy living room with a fireplace, or a bedroom where one can feel the cool air. Shitsukan refers to all of these elements. Its spectrum is broad, ranging from physical characteristics defined by the material and lighting, like glossiness, to aspects rooted in personal preferences, such as aesthetic appeal.

Although the scope of Shitsukan is broad, a common characteristic is its difficulty to express in words. Unlike object categories which can be defined objectively and unambiguously, Shitsukan will be represented by continuous values in the human brain—consider, for example, the varying degrees of glossiness—and often differs between individuals. Consequently, it is challenging to describe in universally understandable, simple terms.

That said, Shitsukan is not confined to individual perception; when one wishes to share it with others—an intrinsic feature of Shitsukan—it must be articulated through language. While this is a difficult task, people often strive to overcome this challenge, sometimes employing elaborate descriptions to convey their perception.[2]

Building on this, the chapter explores the development of AI capable of recognizing Shitsukan as humans do, and how such AI might be built. The discussion follows a chronological overview of the research and achievements of the author's group, extending to the latest breakthroughs in generative AI.

[2] For example, describing wine as, "This white wine features the soft sweetness and refreshing note of ripe pear, with subtle acidity," though this pertains to taste, which is outside the scope of this chapter.

4.2 Formulating Shitsukan Recognition as Image Recognition

In this section, we present solutions for Shitsukan recognition based on fundamental methodologies in image recognition and discuss the associated challenges.

4.2.1 *Problem Formulation*

The most basic approach to problem-solving involves formulating the task as a single input-output function. This method is characterized by strictly defining the input and output formats. For Shitsukan recognition, we consider a function that generates an output x representing the Shitsukan for a given input image I. To address this problem, a prediction model f_θ (where θ denotes the model parameters) is introduced, and predictions based on the input I are made in the form of $x = f_\theta(I)$.

The prediction model f_θ typically leverages deep neural networks, particularly convolutional neural networks (CNNs) [1, 2] or Vision Transformer (ViTs) [3], and is trained on a dataset $\mathcal{D} \equiv (I_i, x_i)$ composed of image pairs and their corresponding ground truth data. In this formulation, the way the output x represents the Shitsukan is of paramount importance. Below, we introduce several methods for addressing this problem.

4.2.1.1 Multi-class Classification

The simplest approach is multi-class classification, where the output x corresponds to one of the N predefined classes. This is a standard image classification problem, in which the input image I is categorized into one of the N known classes. The prediction model f_θ is trained on a dataset consisting of pairs $(I_i, \bar{x}_i)$, where I_i represents the input images and $\bar{x}_i$ the true labels. The difference between the predicted value $\hat{x}_i = f_\theta(I_i)$ and the true label $\bar{x}_i$ is quantified using cross-entropy loss, which is minimized during training.

Although this formulation is not specifically designed for Shitsukan recognition, it is closely related to material classification [6]. In this context, we examined CNN-based approaches and reported their performance [5]. The task is to determine the material composition of an object in an image I—for example, whether a cup is made of glass or a table is made of wood—based on a single input image (Fig. 4.1a).

To evaluate CNN-based approaches for material recognition in practice, we employed the Flickr Material Database (FMD) [4]. FMD includes 10 material classes, such as glass, metal, and paper, with 100 images per class, resulting in a total of 1000 images. However, due to the limited size of this dataset, training deep learning models effectively is challenging. To address this, we developed an Extended FMD (EFMD),

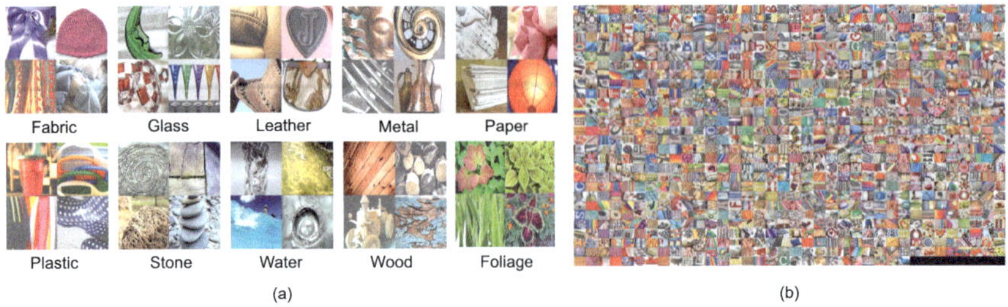

Fig. 4.1 Datasets for material recognition. **a** Flickr Material Database (FMD) [4]. **b** Extended FMD [5]. Only images of the 'Fablic' class are shown

an expanded version of FMD that includes high-quality, diverse images with similar characteristics, resulting in a dataset of 10,000 images. The EFMD dataset was created by collecting approximately 100,000 images through text-based searches on Flickr, which were then curated using Amazon Mechanical Turk.

Our study shows that when EFMD was used as training data and the CNN was evaluated on the FMD test set, the material recognition accuracy for 10 classes reached $84.0 \pm 1.8\%$. This result closely approaches the human accuracy of 84.9% reported in prior research [4] for the same classification task. Other notable studies on material recognition include the work by Bell et al. [7].

This demonstrates that standard deep learning methods can achieve near-human accuracy in material image classification when sufficient training data is available. However, it is important to recognize that this high performance is limited to evaluations on specific datasets. Two significant assumptions are inherent in this approach.

First, the materials to be recognized are confined to a fixed set of 10 classes. This means that materials outside these 10 categories cannot be identified, which differs from human capability. Second, the domain of the input image I, specifically the statistical distribution $p(I)$ followed by images in FMD or EFMD, plays a critical role. The images in FMD and EFMD were selected from photos uploaded to Flickr, and thus, their compositions and photographic intentions share some similarities. As a result, if an input image I significantly differs from these images, classification accuracy may decline sharply. This phenomenon, known as "domain shift," occurs when the statistical distribution of the training data and test data differ considerably, leading to reduced prediction accuracy.

4.2.1.2 Multi-label Classification

In the previously discussed material recognition, the task was to classify an image I into a specific material class. However, the Shitsukan perceived from a single object can be multifaceted such as transparent or glossy. Therefore, it is more natural to formulate Shitsukan recognition as "multi-label classification," where multiple labels are assigned to a single image I, rather than multi-class classification.

Specifically, let us assume there are M "Shitsukan attributes" of interest, such as transparency or glossiness. For each attribute, we express whether it is perceived (presence/absence) or its intensity as a vector $x \in \mathbb{R}^M$. Each element of x can either take a binary value (0 or 1) or a continuous value $x_m \in [0, 1]$, where in the latter case, it can be interpreted as a score representing the degree to which the m-th Shitsukan attribute is relevant. Model training is conducted by learning each attribute (the m-th component of x_i) with a binary classification task and using the training data $\mathcal{D} \equiv (I_i, \bar{x}_i)$. The difference between the predicted value $\hat{x}_i = f_\theta(I_i)$ and the true value $\bar{x}_i$ is measured independently for each component using binary cross-entropy loss, which is then minimized.

The key difference from multi-class classification is that, in multi-label classification, the inference for each component of the output vector x is formally independent. Indeed, in loss computation, the influence of each attribute is handled independently. However, in actual inference, Shitsukan attributes are not independent and are expected to exhibit some dependencies. For instance, there is likely a correlation between glossiness and hardness, as materials that are highly glossy are often not soft.

In our work [8], we investigated how to exploit label dependencies for multi-label classification—a problem that was central prior to the deep learning era. However, with deep learning, these dependencies can be naturally leveraged through the network structure. Specifically, rather than using separate models for each attribute x_m ($m = 1, \ldots, M$), it becomes possible to use a single model f_θ. For example, when constructing the model using a CNN, all layers except the output layer are shared across all attributes. In the simplest case, this means sharing all layers except the output layer. By learning to predict various Shitsukan attributes simultaneously, the feature extraction process of the CNN is expected to naturally leverage the interdependencies between attributes.

4.2.1.3 Learning via Ranking

In the multi-label classification formulation mentioned above, the ground truth label $\bar{x}_i$ in the training data is given as either a binary or a continuous value. For example, when representing the presence or absence of glasses in a facial image I, $\bar{x}_i$ can be expressed as a binary value. However, Shitsukan attributes like glossiness or transparency are not necessarily suited for binary representation (presence/absence). Instead, it is more natural to express the strength of each Shitsukan attribute as a continuous value.

That said, ground truth labels $\bar{x}_i$ for images I_i typically need to be manually annotated. While binary labeling is relatively simple, assigning continuous scores is often more challenging. For instance, if participants are asked to label the degree of transparency on a 5-point scale, their judgment may be difficult, and forcing this task could lead to poor label quality, particularly in terms of inter-annotator consistency.

One method to ensure stable labeling is to use synthetic images generated via computer graphics (CG), where labels can be derived from the synthesis parameters.

Fig. 4.2 Learning to rank Shitsukan attributes. **a** Annotation by ranking image pairs. **b** Sorted results of novel images by predicted strengths of several Shitsukan attributes. Top: 1st to 5th images. Bottom: 496th to 500th images

However, this approach introduces other issues. First, it is difficult to accurately reproduce the complex and diverse surface properties of real objects using CG. Moreover, the relationship between the physical parameters of synthetic images and human perception of Shitsukan may not always be clearly defined.

A technique to alleviate the challenges of manual labeling is to present multiple images and assign relative rankings between them. The simplest method is to present two images, I_α and I_β, and ask participants to label which of the two exhibits a stronger or more relevant Shitsukan attribute [9–11]. This method is known as "relative attributes." For instance, one might label I_α as having a stronger glossiness than I_β. During training, the loss function is designed so that the model f_θ outputs $f_\theta(I_\alpha) > f_\theta(I_\beta)$, and this loss is minimized.

We were the first to apply the relative-attribute ranking approach to Shitsukan recognition [12]; see Fig. 4.2a. Our study focused on surface Shitsukan attributes such as glossiness, transparency, smoothness, and coolness, addressing the features that humans perceive through vision and touch in image recognition. In our work, a support vector machine (SVM) was used as the prediction model f_θ. From the input image I, image features such as SIFT [13] and RGB-based Bag of Visual Words (BoVW) [14] were extracted, and the SVM was used to output scores for each Shitsukan attribute. Different f_θ (SVM parameters) were used for each Shitsukan attribute.

For training and evaluation, we used 500 images from the Flickr Material Database (FMD) [4], a dataset containing images of various materials such as metal, glass, plastic, stone, and wood. For each Shitsukan attribute, participants were asked to label random pairs of images by indicating which image exhibited the attribute more strongly, creating the training and test data. We trained f_θ using ranking from 200 pairs of images for each of the four Shitsukan attributes, and after training, they demonstrated that the model could rank unseen images based on Shitsukan attributes (Fig. 4.2b). The experimental results showed that the rankings based on Shitsukan attributes aligned well with human judgment, confirming the effectiveness of this approach.

Although this method achieves high precision in estimating the strength of four Shitsukan attributes on the FMD, it shares some of the same limitations as the aforementioned material recognition approach. Specifically, it can only handle predefined

Shitsukan attributes and suffers from the "domain shift" problem, where performance degrades when applied to images that are not part of the training data (Fig. 4.3).

4.2.2 Automated Discovery of Diverse Visual Attributes via Web-Scale Mining

When developing AI systems to recognize Shitsukan attributes, selecting the appropriate attributes to target poses a significant challenge. In previous studies—such as material classification and ranking-based strength estimation of Shitsukan attributes—the selection of recognition targets was often arbitrary, determined subjectively by researchers. This raises the question: how many, and what types of (Shitsukan) attributes do humans naturally recognize in everyday life or specialized tasks, such as art evaluation?

We proposed a method for automatically discovering visually recognizable attributes, including Shitsukan attributes, by mining data from online communities [15]. Our approach leverages a pre-trained object recognition CNN, exploiting the property that intermediate layer units respond selectively to various visual concepts. This enables not only the identification of visual concepts but also the automatic construction of recognition models for them. Since many websites feature images paired with descriptive text, the method utilizes these large-scale image—text pairs. Specifically, images are fed into a CNN pre-trained on ImageNet's 1000-class object recognition task, and the activation patterns of intermediate layer units are analyzed. These units are known to correspond to image content, with certain convolutional filters responding selectively to particular visual concepts.

In this framework, the system first extracts a set of images whose associated text contains specific keywords. These images are then passed through the CNN to observe whether certain units activate selectively. If activation occurs, the unit is considered to be responding to the visual concept represented by the keyword. To account for the noise in web data, the importance of these activated units is

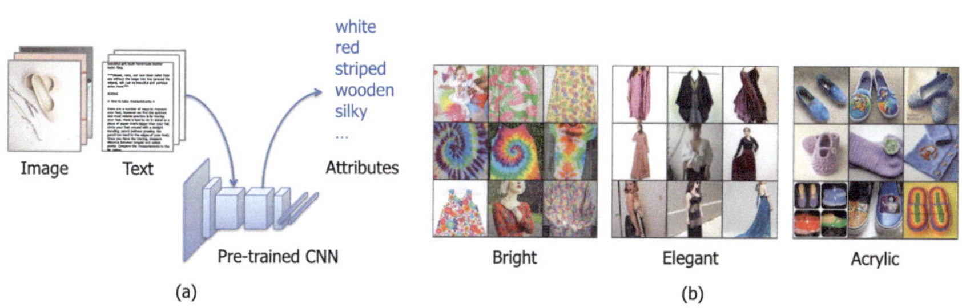

Fig. 4.3 Mining web-scale data to discover visually recognizable concepts [15]. **a** Method illustration. **b** Examples of discovered concepts

measured using the Kullback-Leibler (KL) divergence, which helps identify the units that selectively respond to particular concepts.

To validate this approach, we used two domain-specific datasets: Etsy and Wear. The Etsy dataset was collected from an online marketplace for handmade products, while the Wear dataset was sourced from a social fashion-sharing platform. Both datasets contain images paired with descriptive information, such as product details for Etsy and fashion item descriptions for Wear. Using this data, the method successfully identified visually recognizable attributes, and the corresponding activated units could be directly used as recognition models for these visual attributes.

Traditional image recognition methods required a predefined list of visual concepts to be recognized, followed by the creation of a training dataset based on that list. This approach limited the recognition process to a closed set of concepts—such as material classes or Shitsukan attributes—making it difficult to handle an open set of visual concepts. Additionally, the need for extensive manual annotation posed a significant challenge, especially as the number of recognition targets increased. Another difficulty was adapting to evolving vocabulary over time. For instance, the word “wicked” has shifted from meaning “bad” to “very” in modern slang. This study offers a potential solution to these issues.

4.2.3 Contextual Dependence of Visual Concept Representation

While the methods above enable the automatic extraction of diverse visual concepts from the web, they are often limited to concepts expressed by single words or short phrases. However, Shitsukan perception is context-dependent, and such simplistic approaches may not always be sufficient. For instance, the word “red” in “red apple” and “red hair” is the same, yet the actual color it represents can vary significantly. How can AI handle such contextual dependencies?

To address this, the output x for a given image I must be interpreted as a complete sentence rather than a single word or phrase. This process, known as image captioning [17], involves mapping an image I to a sentence x. While substantial research has been conducted in this area, most studies focus on everyday scenes, emphasizing factual descriptions. Although texture is occasionally addressed, it has not been a primary focus in these efforts.

We tackled the challenge of generating descriptions with a focus on Shitsukan, specifically aiming to create product titles from images in an e-commerce context [16]. The objective was to generate title sentences that accurately represent a wide range of product attributes that buyers find important, with texture playing a central role. In e-commerce, especially on platforms like Etsy, product images often depict a single object, but the titles must convey enough detail to help potential buyers understand and be drawn to the product. This involves describing features such as color, shape, pattern, and material, as well as more abstract concepts. Traditional image captioning methods, which typically focus on describing object relationships and context within images, struggle to capture these subjective and ambiguous attributes effectively.

In the work, we developed a model combining a CNN and an RNN, which was a common architecture at the time, and trained it using product images and their corresponding titles collected from Etsy.

One challenge was the significant amount of noise in the online data. To address this, the proposed method applied linguistic filtering to the noisy Etsy data, extracting high-quality samples suitable for training. Specifically, the Stanford Parser was used for syntactic analysis to identify useful data within the noisy datasets, and approximate duplicate removal techniques were employed to reduce bias, creating a corpus with diverse expressions. Using this cleaned corpus, the model was trained to generate natural language descriptions from images.

Experimental results showed that the model successfully generated natural language expressions, including subjective attribute descriptions, from product images and titles; see Fig. 4.4. To evaluate the model, metrics commonly used in machine translation and automatic summarization—such as BLEU, ROUGE, METEOR, and CIDEr—were used to assess how closely the generated expressions matched human descriptions. The study also demonstrated that incorporating e-commerce-specific metadata and fine-tuning further improved the quality of the generated descriptions.

4.3 Toward Comprehensive Image Understanding

While the aforementioned studies have provided effective solutions within a limited scope, developing a system that can recognize Shitsukan with human-like accuracy remains a significant challenge. A key insight from this body of work is the inherent difficulty of defining Shitsukan recognition as a concrete problem in computer vision or machine learning. Unlike image classification, Shitsukan recognition

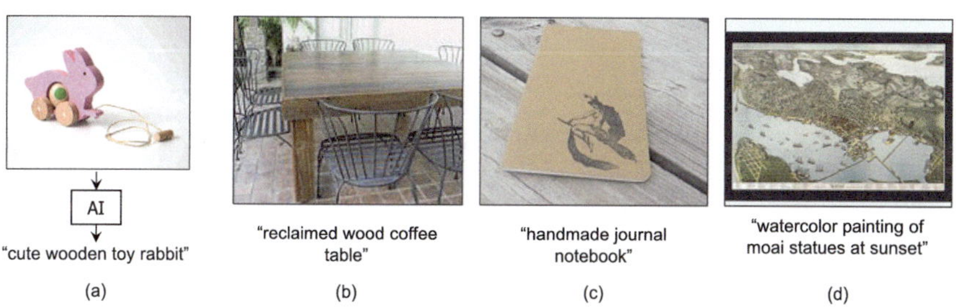

Fig. 4.4 Image description considering visual context: **a** Generating appropriate titles for product images [16]. **b-c** The model generates suitable titles for these images. **d** The model generates an inappropriate title

cannot be easily reduced to a simple input-output function. The concepts to be recognized are often ambiguous, context-dependent, and not easily articulated, making it challenging to define a clear set of recognition targets at the outset.

Given these challenges, it becomes evident that an artificial system designed for Shitsukan recognition must have the ability to "comprehensively understand images," similar to human perception. The following section will discuss the progress made in AI research on image understanding, showing how, while not yet fully achieved, AI with image understanding capabilities has come significantly closer to realization. We will examine the key obstacles encountered, the methods developed to address them, and our contributions to advancing this field.

4.3.1 Formalizing Image Understanding

A fundamental challenge in image understanding is how to appropriately formulate the problem. Several approaches have been explored in the literature (see Fig. 4.5). One approach is image captioning, where the task is to generate a description of the scene in the input image, as shown in Fig. 4.5a. Another approach is Visual Question Answering (VQA), illustrated in Fig. 4.5b. In VQA, given an image I, the task is to answer a question q about the scene or objects in I by producing an answer y [18]. Both the question q and the answer y are expressed in natural language. Visual dialog extends VQA by incorporating multiple rounds of questions and answers. Successfully addressing these tasks indicates progress in understanding the image. Research on these vision and language tasks continues to be an active area in computer vision.

A common challenge identified across many of these studies is determining the necessary computations for solving the problem. In other words, how should the neural network architecture be designed? Much of the research has focused on how to enable effective interactions between the features extracted from both the image and the text within the network. As a result of ongoing experimentation in the field, attention mechanisms have become a focal point for researchers.

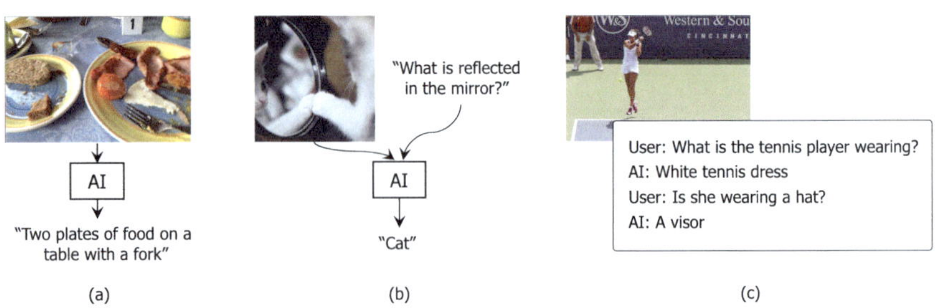

Fig. 4.5 Illustration of various problem settings in image understanding: **a** Image Captioning, **b** Visual Question Answering (VQA), and **c** Visual Dialog

Fig. 4.6 **a** An input image and division into sub-regions. **b** Attention directed to each region of the image in response to the question "What is this animal?" **c** Attention directed in response to the question "Is it cloudy?"

4.3.2 Attention Mechanisms

The attention mechanism is a fundamental component of modern deep neural networks. In particular, the attention mechanism used in the Transformer [19]—originally designed for machine translation but now widely applied to a range of tasks, from language modeling to image recognition—has become a standard approach. Before explaining the Transformer and its attention mechanism, it is helpful to first define what attention entails.

Attention is the process of assigning weights to each element in a set based on its relevance to the current focus or task. For instance, in the context of VQA, the importance of different parts of an image may shift depending on the specific question being asked. In Fig. 4.6 a, what is deemed important in the scene will vary depending on the question posed [20]. Figure 4.6b highlights the region relevant to the question "What animal is this?" (the giraffe), while Fig. 4.6c highlights the region pertinent to the question "Is the sky cloudy?" (the sky).

This process is carried out through the following computation. First, as shown in Fig. 4.6a, the image is divided into small regions, each indexed by $i(= 1, \ldots, N)$. From each region i, we extract an image feature vector $x_i \in \mathbb{R}^D$. Additionally, let us assume that the question is represented as a vector $q \in \mathbb{R}^D$ (referred to as a query). The relevance between the image feature vector x_i of each region and the query q is computed using a function r (commonly the dot product of vectors) as $a_i \sim r(x_i, q)$. These values are then normalized so that the sum across all regions $i = 1, \ldots, N$ equals 1 ($\sum_{i=1}^{N} a_i = 1$).[3] These weights, visualized as intensity variations for each region of the image, are shown in Fig. 4.6.

By using the attention weights a_i, we can selectively extract information from the regions most relevant to the current query q, rather than from the entire image. Specifically, we compute the weighted average of the feature vectors x_i, weighted by a_i, as $\tilde{x} = \sum_{i=1}^{N} a_i x_i$. This $\tilde{x}$ can be considered as a compact representation of the image content that is most relevant to the query q. Once the relevant feature $\tilde{x}$

[3] Usually, the softmax function is used for this.

is selectively extracted in this manner, it becomes much easier to answer specific questions, such as "What is this animal?" or "Is the sky cloudy?"

4.3.3 Transformer

The Transformer incorporates the attention mechanism described earlier as a core operation, along with additional computations [19]. As illustrated in Fig. 4.7a, the network consists of multiple layers (or blocks) stacked sequentially, each with the same structure. The input to each layer is a set of vectors, $X = x_1, \ldots, x_N$, and the output is a set of vectors of the same size, $Y = y_1, \ldots, y_N$. Both x_i and y_i are D-dimensional vectors, and the dimensionality D remains consistent between the input and the output of each layer. Since the network is composed of identical layers, this structure applies to the input and the output of the entire network.

The structure of a single layer, which is shown in Fig. 4.7b, consists of several key components. These include the attention mechanism, known as multi-head attention, and a multi-layer perceptron (MLP). Additionally, layer normalization and residual connections are incorporated, both of which are crucial components. We will explain each of these elements in detail below.

The attention mechanism used in the Transformer is a generalized version of the one described in Sect. 4.3.2. In the basic attention mechanism, the interaction between q and $x_1, \ldots, x_N$ is calculated, and these interactions are used to assign weights to $x_1, \ldots, x_N$, which are then aggregated into a single vector. This mechanism can be extended in two ways: cross-attention and self-attention.

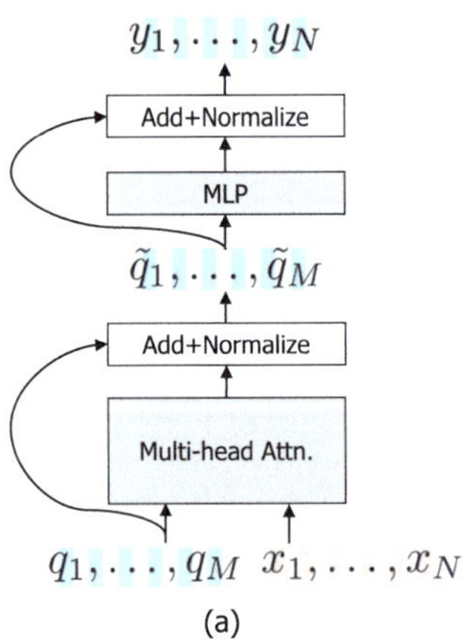

Fig. 4.7 Overview of the architecture of a single transformer layer. **a** Cross attention. **b** Self attention. Mult-head attention mechanism and MLP (multi-layer perceptron) are the main components with learnable parameters. 'Add+Normalize' indicates the addition of vectors followed by the application of layer normalization [19]

In cross-attention, instead of a single query vector q, we consider a set of M query vectors $q_1, \ldots, q_M$. For each query q_j $(j = 1, \ldots, M)$, attention weights a_{ji} $(i = 1, \ldots, N)$ are computed between q_j and $x_1, \ldots, x_N$. These weights are then used to compute the weighted sum $\sum_i a_{ji} x_i$. The result for each query q_j is denoted as $\tilde{q}_j$. After applying attention, we obtain M aggregated feature vectors, $\tilde{q}_1, \ldots, \tilde{q}_M$, corresponding to each query.

In self-attention, the queries are the image feature vectors $x_1, \ldots, x_N$ themselves. In this case, for each query $q = x_j$ $(j = 1, \ldots, N)$, attention weights a_{ji} are calculated between x_j and $x_1, \ldots, x_N$, and the weighted sum $\tilde{x}_j = \sum_i a_{ji} x_i$ is computed. The output of self-attention consists of the same number of vectors, $\tilde{x}_1, \ldots, \tilde{x}_N$, as the input X.

These two forms of attention calculations form the foundation for further extensions. Let's take cross-attention as an example. The process involves calculating the relevance (or similarity) between q_j and x_i, normalizing the attention weights a_{ji} across $i = 1, \ldots, N$ (such that $\sum_i a_{ji} = 1$), and then using these weights to compute the weighted sum $\tilde{q}_j = \sum_i a_{ji} x_i$. The first extension applies linear transformations to the vectors $q_j \leftarrow W_q q_j$, $x_i \leftarrow W_k x_i$, and $x_i \leftarrow W_v x_i$ during the process. The matrices W_q, W_k, and W_v are shared across all vectors in the layer and are learnable parameters. The relevance between q_j and x_i is then determined by their dot product, $q_j^\top x_i$. These linear transformations add flexibility to the attention calculation, which can be optimized during training.

The second extension is called multi-head attention. In this case, the attention weights $a_{j1}, \ldots, a_{jN}$ for each j are calculated in parallel multiple times. As explained in Sect. 4.3.2, the importance weights a_i for each input vector x_i depend on the query q, and the resulting $\tilde{q}_i$ is calculated. Multi-head attention allows this $q \to a_i \to \tilde{q}_i$ process to occur multiple times simultaneously. This approach addresses cases where a single attention distribution is insufficient. Specifically, for each parallel attention calculation, indexed by $h(= 1, \ldots, H)$, one set of attention weights is computed for each head (with different W_q, W_k, and W_v parameters for each head). This results in the calculation of $\tilde{q}_{j1}^{(h)}, \ldots, \tilde{q}_{jN}^{(h)}$ for each head. The parallel results are then combined into a single sequence $\tilde{q}_{j1}, \ldots, \tilde{q}_{jN}$ using another linear transformation, W_o (where $\tilde{q}_{ji} \leftarrow \sum_h \tilde{q}_{ji}^{(h)}$).

The other major component of the basic Transformer layer is the multi-layer perceptron (MLP) (Fig. 4.7). After applying attention, an MLP is applied independently to each vector $\tilde{x}_i$, resulting in $y_i = \text{MLP}(\tilde{x}_i)$ for each $i = 1, \ldots, N$. The independent application of the MLP can be considered a *local* computation, as it models local interactions within each vector x_i[4]. On the other hand, the attention mechanism handles interactions between the input vectors $x_1, \ldots, x_N$ (in the case of self-attention) or between them and the query vectors $q_1, \ldots, q_M$ (in the case of cross-attention). This makes attention a *global* computation, in contrast to the local computations performed by the MLP (Fig. 4.8).

[4] It is important to note that layer normalization is also applied independently to each vector $\tilde{x}_i$.

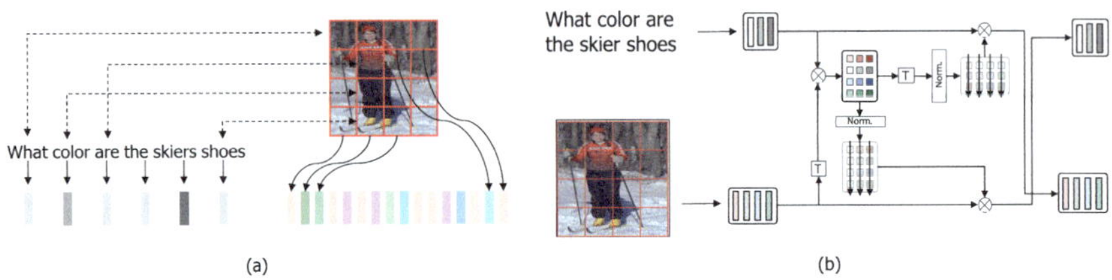

Fig. 4.8 **a** Bi-directional attention between the input text and image. **b** The core architecture of dense co-attention network (DCN) [20]

4.3.4 Applying Attention Mechanisms to VQA

As discussed later, the Transformer has become a crucial architecture in image understanding. While the field has undergone various experiments and iterations, these efforts have largely converged on Multimodal Large Language Models (MLLMs)—extensions of Large Language Models (LLMs) that incorporate image inputs. LLMs can be entirely built using Transformers, and MLLMs are similarly composed almost exclusively of Transformer architectures. However, even before the advent of MLLMs, the application of Transformers to image understanding tasks had already become commonplace. We were the first to apply the Transformer's attention mechanism to Visual Question Answering (VQA) [20].

In our study, since the term "Transformer" was not yet widely used, we referred to the proposed network as the "Dense Co-attention Network (DCN)." This name reflects the fact that DCN is designed to allow the two inputs in VQA—the image and the question text—to interact symmetrically. The network employs the cross-attention mechanism described earlier in the Transformer, applied between the image I and the question text q. Specifically, DCN extracts features $x_1, \ldots, x_N$ from regions of the image I and converts the question text into a sequence of feature vectors $q_1, \ldots, q_M$, based on the words in the question. It then computes cross-attention between the image and text features in both directions, simultaneously.

In this approach, each image region x_i attends to every word in the question q_j, and conversely, each word q_j attends to every image region x_i. This mutual attention (co-attention) mechanism allows for a dense integration of the image and question features, enabling more precise answers to complex questions. Earlier methods had limited fusion between visual and textual information, as they failed to account for interactions between all image regions and all words, making it difficult to fully capture the intricate relationships between images and questions.

In our study, DCN was evaluated using the VQA 1.0 and VQA 2.0 datasets [18]. The results showed that DCN set new benchmarks, outperforming the state-of-the-art methods at the time on both datasets. Furthermore, the proposed attention mechanism was visualized, demonstrating how it accurately focused on the relevant parts of the image and derived the correct answers to the questions. Figure 4.6 provides an example of such an attention map, illustrating how the model's attention aligns with the question and image.

The process from the input image I and question q to the final answer y closely resembles modern MLLMs. First, to extract the region features $X = x_1, \ldots, x_N$ from the input image I, a CNN pre-trained on object recognition is used, with the upper-layer feature map of the CNN serving as X. For the input text, the feature sequence $q_1, \ldots, q_M$ is generated by transforming the word sequence using an LSTM-based embedding method, which was common at the time (in contrast, modern MLLMs use more advanced tokenizers). These image and text features are then passed into a network composed of multiple stacked layers with identical structures, where they interact at each layer. Through these repeated interactions, the final output is produced. While generating the answer y as free-form text was explored, at the time, the task was often simplified into a classification problem by predefining a finite list of possible answers and selecting from that list. In contrast, modern MLLMs, leveraging the full capabilities of LLMs, can generate y as free-form text without such constraints.

The DCN largely incorporates the Transformer's attention mechanism in its basic layers, along with an MLP and residual connections, similar to the Transformer architecture. The overall model is built by stacking multiple of these layers. However, there are notable differences, such as the absence of multi-head attention. In this respect, the later MCAN model is known for applying a more complete Transformer architecture to VQA [21]. We introduced a multitask learning approach for image understanding in a follow-up study [22], where a single DCN was trained jointly on caption retrieval, VQA, and visual grounding.

4.3.5 Improved Feature Extraction from Images

In the previous section on VQA solutions, features were extracted from regularly divided sub-regions of the image I. This approach uses feature maps from the upper layers of a CNN pre-trained on object recognition, with image I as input. This method was one of the most common approaches at the time and remains a mainstream technique today—even in the latest MLLMs, where the core approach is largely unchanged, with a ViT replacing the CNN. However, since image understanding requires capturing a wide range of information within an image, whether this method is truly optimal remains a subject of ongoing debate.

In the previous studies of vision and language tasks, there have been two common approaches to image feature extraction: *grid-based* and *region-based*. Region-based feature extraction involves applying an object detector to the image and independently extracting features from each detected object region. In contrast, grid-based feature extraction uniformly samples features from the entire image using a pre-trained CNN or ViT, as mentioned earlier.

To overcome the limitations of relying on either approach alone, we optimized image feature extraction for captioning [23], combining grid- and region-based representations in a Transformer. Image captioning, which involves generating natural language descriptions of an image's content, requires precise visual feature extraction. In their study, they introduced a novel Transformer architecture, "GRIT" (Grid- and Region-based Image Captioning Transformer), which combines both grid-based and region-based features. This approach enables GRIT to capture more comprehensive visual information, achieving a balance between improved accuracy and efficiency compared to prior methods.

Early research on image understanding often relied on region-based features, where information was extracted from object regions detected by object detectors such as Faster R-CNN [24]. However, this approach faced several challenges. First, region-based features often failed to capture contextual relationships between objects, limiting the model's ability to fully understand the overall meaning of the image. Second, object detectors were prone to errors, such as false detections or missing important objects, which could negatively impact the accuracy of tasks like caption generation. Third, extracting region-based features was computationally expensive, especially when using high-performance object detectors like Faster R-CNN, leading to longer processing times. In contrast, grid-based features are better at capturing relationships and contextual information between objects. Therefore, the key challenge is how to effectively combine these two types of features.

The GRIT architecture is built on the Transformer and enables fully end-to-end training. Traditionally, object detectors and caption generation models were trained separately. However, GRIT utilizes the Deformable DETR object detection model, which eliminates the need for non-maximum suppression (NMS) typically required in CNN-based detectors. This allows for unified training of the entire model, significantly reducing computational costs while maintaining high performance.

For caption generation, GRIT processes region-based and grid-based features in parallel, generating captions through a cross-attention mechanism between the two feature types. Specifically, GRIT employs a parallel cross-attention mechanism that integrates information from both region and grid features, resulting in contextually accurate captions. This design allows GRIT to effectively leverage object-level information from region features and contextual information from grid features, improving both accuracy and efficiency.

In experiments, GRIT demonstrated superior performance compared to previous state-of-the-art methods on the COCO dataset. Moreover, in terms of computational efficiency, GRIT significantly reduced the time required for caption generation compared to traditional region-based methods, achieving both improved performance and reduced computational cost. GRIT shortened the total processing time for generating captions for a single image to about one-tenth of that required by previous methods.

4.4 Sitsukan Recognition by Generative AI

One of the most significant recent topics in AI research and development is generative AI, specifically the advent of large language models (LLMs) and image generation AI. LLMs have enabled advanced applications that were previously impossible, such as natural language-based interactions and complex problem-solving through dialogue. On the other hand, image generation AI has made it possible to freely create images and videos from text. By integrating these and related technologies, multi-modal LLMs (MLLMs) have emerged. MLLMs are now achieving (at least superficially) unprecedented levels of image understanding.

4.4.1 Classical AI Versus Generative AI

The rise of generative AI has greatly transformed the research and development landscape of AI. Before discussing the specifics of this transformation, it is important to review the state of AI prior to this—what we will refer to here as classical AI.

In classical AI, the first step is to determine how the task to be solved can be expressed as a function, followed by the design of input and output formats for that function. Next, a neural network is designed to represent that function, and the parameters are optimized using a set of input-output pairs (pairs of inputs and their corresponding correct outputs), so the network can accurately replicate the function on the given data. Thus, both the network and training data are task-specific, and the task itself is often a narrow representation of a specific aspect of human cognition. For this reason, classical AI has sometimes been referred to as "cognitive automation" rather than "artificial intelligence."

For instance, the research on image recognition, described in Sect. 4.2, is a typical example of classical AI. Likewise, the studies on image understanding prior to generative AI, mentioned in Sect. 4.3, also adhere to classical AI methodologies in that they involve training specialized models on specialized data.

So, how does generative AI differ from classical AI? There are two major differences.

The first difference is the flexibility in defining the problem to be solved. With the advent of LLMs, it has become possible to express problems in natural language through interactions with the user. This contrasts with classical AI, where the expression of a single function is fixed, and the input and output formats are strictly predefined—especially the output, which was typically limited to numerical formats such as class indices.[5]

[5] The image understanding studies mentioned in Sect. 4.3 also dealt with natural language in their inputs and outputs. However, their performance was not high, although they can still be seen as early bridges between classical AI and generative AI.

The second difference lies in the method of learning. While generative AI is still based on deep learning as its core technology, the neural networks at its foundation—often called foundation models—exhibit the following characteristics:

- Training is conducted on a massive scale using large datasets, particularly web data, which are traces of human activity left in the digital space, often referred to as "human digital traces."
- The training conducted is only pretraining, not yet aimed at solving the final task.

Foundation models, in their state immediately after pretraining, are generally not directly usable. The true target task is solved by conducting additional training with the foundation model. However, the amount of data required for this additional training is significantly smaller compared to pretraining, as it mainly involves fine-tuning the foundation model.

Through large-scale pretraining on web data, foundation models acquire the ability to extract useful features from real-world data (including images and language). This capability aids in solving a variety of downstream tasks.[6] Examples of foundation models include LLMs and visual language models (VLMs) like CLIP,[7] all of which share the characteristics described above.

4.4.2 Shared Representation Space for Images and Text

Consider a scenario where we have an image of a scene and a text that describes the same scene. These image and text can be seen as expressing the same concept (i.e., the scene) in two different modalities. Naturally, there should be a strong relationship between them, but how should this relationship be represented? One possible answer is to project both the image and the text into a common space, as illustrated in Fig. 4.9, and to create mappings that relate the two within that shared space.

Typically, an image consists of tens of thousands to millions of pixels, meaning that the amount of information contained in it is very large. However, the portion of the image's information that can be described in text is only a small fraction of that total. As the saying "a picture is worth a thousand words" suggests, text always contains less information than an image. Therefore, it is useful to project an image into a lower-dimensional space that preserves key information using a mapping. It is important to note that the inverse of this mapping is not uniquely determined. Similarly, on the text side, while the information content is not as large as in images, we consider a mapping that extracts the meaning conveyed by the text.

In these mappings for images and text, if we can find a mapping that projects pairs of an image and its corresponding text onto the same point in this common space,

---

[6] The concept of transfer learning and fine-tuning existed in classical AI as well, but web-scale pretraining has resulted in emergent properties that far exceed prior expectations.

[7] In this paper, "VLM" refers to models like CLIP that learn the correspondence between images and language, while "MLLM" refers to models that extend LLMs to handle multi-modal inputs.

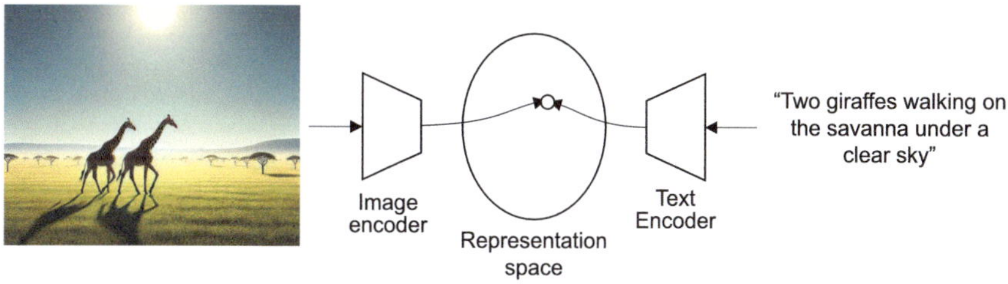

Fig. 4.9 Common representation space for images and text. Vision-language models (VLMs), such as CLIP, establish this shared space, effectively linking the two modalities and enabling cross-modal understanding

while projecting non-corresponding pairs to different points, then it becomes possible to retrieve text that describes the scene by finding texts close to the image within this space (e.g., through search among candidates). Conversely, it also becomes possible to find an image corresponding to a given text.

CLIP, developed by OpenAI [25], realizes two such mappings through deep learning using large-scale data. These two mappings are represented by two neural networks, an image encoder and a text encoder. The image encoder takes an image as input and outputs a vector that compactly represents its content, while the text encoder takes any text as input and outputs a vector that compactly represents its content. Both vectors have the same dimensionality, such as 1024 dimensions.

The two encoders are trained using a method called contrastive learning, utilizing a large number of image-text pairs. Specifically, given N pairs of images and texts, these are broken down into N^2 possible new pairs, where the original pairs are projected as close as possible in the space, and non-corresponding pairs are projected as far apart as possible. The encoders are trained to achieve this.

In the original CLIP model, it was reported that a total of 400 million image-text pairs, crawled from the web, were used for training [25]. Much of this data consists of everyday scenes uploaded by users, accompanied by descriptions, typically shared on social media. Although the CLIP training data has not been made public, an independent project, LAION, has published five billion image-text pairs collected in a similar manner [26].

By learning from a vast and diverse set of image-text pairs from web data, CLIP has demonstrated performance beyond expectations in various applications. Each encoder also functions as a powerful feature extractor on its own, making it usable, for example, in image classification. Additionally, using both encoders, it has been shown that CLIP can generate text describing an image's scene, or perform "zero-shot image classification" by recognizing new object classes without additional training using text templates.

4.4.3 Large Language Models

The technical details of large language models (LLMs) are widely covered in the literature (e.g., [27–30]), so only a brief explanation will be given here.

LLMs are primarily built using Transformers [19] (see Sect. 4.3.3). As mentioned in that section, the Transformer model generally accepts a set of fixed-length vectors as input and outputs a set of vectors of the same length.

To input text data, such as sentences, into a Transformer, an external model called a tokenizer is used [31, 32]. The tokenizer converts text data into a sequence of vectors known as tokens. The tokenizer is trained using a certain amount of text data. As a result, in the case of English, frequently occurring words are typically converted into a single token, while less common words may be split into multiple tokens. For other languages, the tokenizer also segments the text data into tokens consistently.

The Transformer itself lacks a mechanism to distinguish the order of the elements (tokens) in the input and output sets. Therefore, positional encoding vectors [19], representing the position of each token in the original text, are added. This ensures that the position of each token in the original text is preserved, enabling effective language processing.

With these preparations, LLMs are constructed as follows. There are several types of LLMs, distinguished by how the Transformer is applied. The most common type is a decoder-based LLM [28, 33, 34], which, as shown in Fig. 4.10(left), takes a sequence of tokens representing part of a sentence as input and predicts the next token. The predicted token is added to the end of the input sequence, and the process repeats, predicting the subsequent token. Through this autoregressive process, the model can generate text that flows smoothly from the initial part of a sentence.

LLMs are trained to accurately perform the task of predicting the next token. Typically, this training involves two stages, enabling the LLM to function as, for example, a chatbot capable of engaging in human conversation.

The first stage is pre-training, where the model is trained using as much existing text data as possible, obtained from the web and other sources. The task is to predict the next token in a sequence given part of a sentence as input. To achieve this, the

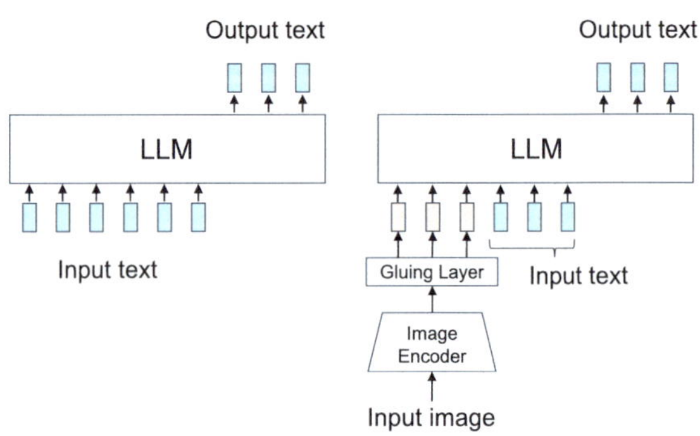

Fig. 4.10 Left: A decoder-based large language model (LLM). Right: Architecture of a multi-modal large language model (MLLM)

model must not only understand the grammar of the language but also accurately grasp the context and make predictions that are both semantically coherent and, in many cases, factually correct. By performing this task on a massive scale using diverse text data, the model develops predictive abilities that apply to a wide range of scenarios. The scale of this training is considered one of the key factors that determine the final performance of the LLM.

In the second stage, the model is fine-tuned to improve its usability for specific tasks, such as engaging in smooth conversations with users. After pre-training, the LLM can accurately predict the next token for a wide variety of text data, but its real-world functionality—such as engaging in fluid dialogue—is often limited. Hence, supervised fine-tuning is employed.

Specifically, the model is trained to correctly respond to specific applications, such as conversation, problem-solving in mathematics, or translation. The required training data is usually created through human annotation. In some cases, multiple types of tasks, such as question-answering or other language tasks, are trained simultaneously. When the model is trained to handle tasks by following instructions in the input, this is called instruction learning [35]. On the other hand, when human evaluations of the model's responses (e.g., ranking multiple outputs) are collected and used to adjust the model's behavior, this is known as alignment [36].

In general, while the first stage of pre-training is large-scale, the second stage of supervised learning is relatively small-scale in comparison. The diverse capabilities (knowledge and skills) of LLMs are primarily acquired during pre-training, while the second stage is mainly for refining and cementing the abilities necessary for specific applications; see [37] for example.

4.4.4 Multi-modal LLM

A Multi-modal LLM (MLLM) is an extension of LLMs that allows the input of non-linguistic modalities such as images[8] [38–42], and it demonstrates excellent capabilities in image understanding. Figure 4.10 (right) shows the structure of a typical MLLM. It consists of an LLM and a separate network called the image encoder, with a network called the gluing layer inserted between them to connect the two [43]. The image encoder functions to extract features from images. MLLMs with this standard architecture can process image-text pairs as input and generate text as output, enabling them to handle a range of tasks related to vision and language, including all image understanding tasks discussed in Sect. 4.3.1.

When constructing MLLMs as described above, both the LLM and the image encoder are usually pre-trained models. For the LLM, a model that has undergone pre-training and supervised fine-tuning, as described in the previous section, is used. For the image encoder, typically the VLM from Sect. 4.4.2, such as the image encoder of a pre-trained CLIP model, is used. The gluing layer inserted between the two has

[8] Here, we consider the most basic MLLM that takes only one image as input in addition to text.

been explored in the field, and reports indicate that a fully connected layer of one to two layers is sufficient [44–46].

The MLLM operates as follows: the input image is converted into a sequence of tokens, comparable to language tokens, by the image encoder and the gluing layer. These image-derived tokens are concatenated with a sequence of tokens derived from the text input, which has been tokenized by a tokenizer, forming a long sequence of tokens that is input to the LLM. The output is generated autoregressively in the usual manner by the LLM and converted back into text.

Simply connecting a pre-trained LLM and image encoder does not result in the desired behavior. The task involving both images and language (e.g., VQA) is learned, including the gluing layer. In this process, supervised data for the task is provided, consisting of an input image, a text input containing task instructions, and the desired textual response, and supervised learning is performed. During training, the newly added gluing layer's parameters are randomly initialized, while the LLM and image encoder start from their pre-trained states and are fine-tuned. Both the LLM and the image encoder leverage the capabilities obtained from their respective pre-training, so only minor adjustments to their weights are typically required. Given the large scale of both models, methods like parameter-efficient fine-tuning (PEFT) [47], such as LORA [48], are often employed to consider computational efficiency.

What tasks or data should be used for the above supervised fine-tuning? Currently, the most effective approach is believed to be visual instruction tuning [41], which extends instruction tuning for LLMs to tasks involving images. Various visual tasks using images as input are provided with task instructions, questions, and the correct answers, and supervised learning is performed as described above.

It has been analyzed [44, 45] what factors influence performance in image understanding tasks. In addition to the basic performance of the LLM, which generally scales with size, the quality and quantity of the training data for visual instruction tuning are reported to be critical factors influencing the final performance.

By leveraging the capabilities of LLMs, acquired through large-scale pre-training and supervised fine-tuning, and the capabilities of image encoders, acquired through learning on large-scale image-text pairs on the web, MLLMs achieve exceptional image understanding abilities through visual instruction tuning. It can be said that their performance far surpasses previous image understanding AI. Figure 4.11 shows the response when providing a scene image to a proprietary state-of-the-art MLLM, OpenAI's GPT-4o [49], and instructing it to describe the scene with attention to Shitsukan. As can be seen, it is able to describe the Shitsukan of the objects in the scene, as well as the overall atmosphere of the scene, with considerable accuracy. Its descriptive ability seems at least on par with humans, and in terms of detail, it appears to surpass the average human level.

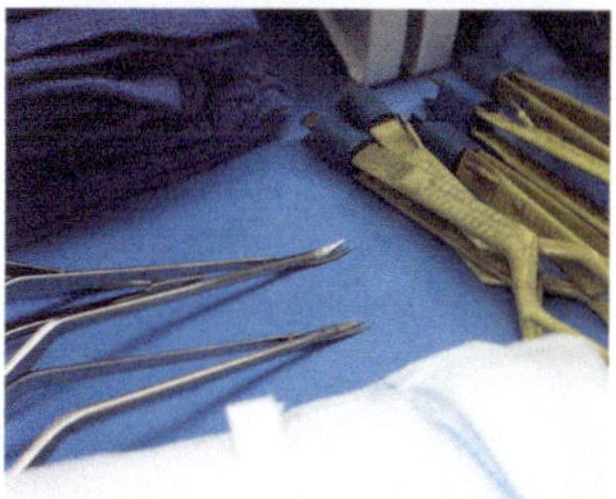

Fig. 4.11 Image captioning results focusing on Shitsukan, generated by GPT-4o (accessed on Oct. 1st 2024)

4.4.5 Image and Video Generation AI

Image captioning involves taking an image as input and generating a natural language description of the scene. The reverse task, generating images from textual descriptions, is called text-to-image synthesis. While this is a key aspect of generative AI, research on this topic predates the rise of generative AI, progressing in parallel with advancements in deep learning. The primary focus of this research has been to synthesize high-quality images—ones that do not appear artificially generated—and to control the content of these images according to specific requirements.

Deep generative models play a central role in image generation. These models include generative adversarial networks (GANs) [50], variational autoencoders (VAEs) [51], normalizing flows [52], and diffusion models [53, 54]. In image generation, the primary goal of these models is to learn the underlying generative distribution of images from a finite set of samples, and then generate new samples (images) that follow this learned distribution. However, rather than directly modeling the probability distribution of the images, many of these models focus on the process of sampling (i.e., generating) new images from that distribution.

Among deep generative models, diffusion models are the most widely employed for text-to-image synthesis. The diffusion models reverse a diffusion process in which noise is gradually added to an image until it becomes complete noise. Starting from a noisy image, diffusion models iteratively remove the noise to generate a natural image. This process of noise removal is typically implemented using deep networks, most commonly U-Net [55].

This denoising capability is learned through training, using a set of images (assumed to be) sampled from the target distribution. The training objective is straightforward: to predict a noise-free image from a noisy version, where the noisy image is created by adding random noise to real images. Since training data can be generated indefinitely from any given image, this process is considered a form of self-supervised learning. Through this approach, the model learns to generate images that follow the same distribution as the training set, a process referred to as unconditional image generation.

Text-to-image synthesis introduces textual input into the generation process, enabling conditional image generation where the images are produced based on the given text. Vision and language models (VLMs), explained in Sect. 4.4.2, play a key role in controlling this process. For example, the text encoder from CLIP is often used directly for the purpose. As mentioned earlier, this text encoder maps the input text into a shared representation space for both images and text. The vector representation (embedding) of the text within this space is then used to guide the image generation process.

More specifically, the denoising network of the unconditional diffusion model is modified to incorporate the text embedding from the input text. This is done by applying an attention mechanism similar to the Transformer. The network is then trained on a dataset of image-text pairs, similar to the training of VLMs. The network's parameters are optimized to remove noise in a way that ensures the generated image matches the description provided by the text. After training, the process begins with a noisy image, and as in the unconditional case, the noise is gradually removed. However, at each step, the denoising process is guided by the content of the input text. This results in the generation of images that correspond to the given text.

Building on this basic approach, several extensions have been developed. These include the latent diffusion models [56], which maps images into a lower-dimensional latent representation space where the diffusion process is carried out; the Diffusion Transformer (DiT) [57], which replaces the U-Net architecture with a Transformer for the denoising process; and text-to-video synthesis [58], which incorporates a time axis into the framework to generate short video sequences.

The technology for generating images and videos has advanced significantly, and its performance continues to improve. However, the foundation of these advancements lies in learning the relationship between images (or videos) and text, with training data playing a crucial role in this process. As a result, the availability and quality of training data largely determine the upper limits of the performance of these technologies.

4.5 Summary and Remaining Challenges

So far, we have explored how AI can be developed to recognize Shitsukan as humans do. We began by outlining the trajectory of the author's group's research, presenting key achievements in chronological order. The following is a brief summary.

In Sect. 4.2, we discussed the formulation of Shitsukan recognition as a standard image recognition task, highlighting the inherent limitations of this approach.

The primary limitation arises from the ambiguity surrounding what the recognition output should be. The concept of Shitsukan is difficult to fully enumerate in a top-down fashion and is highly context-dependent, often resisting concise description. This led to the conclusion that overcoming these challenges requires a more comprehensive approach to image understanding, prompting us to shift towards a broader investigation into image comprehension.

In Sect. 4.3, we introduced the efforts of the author's group in advancing the research of image understanding. We highlighted our studies that incorporated the Transformer into visual question answering [20], explored the multi-task learning of image understanding tasks [22], developed models for high-precision visual dialogue [59], and improved image feature extraction and efficiency in image captioning models [23]. These studies served as a bridge to modern image understanding AI. They also represent important examples of the research conducted in the field at the time, providing a comprehensive view of the area. However, the performance of image understanding AI at that time was still limited and fell far short of human capabilities. This was primarily due to the classical AI approach, which relied on training models with task-specific datasets that were inherently limited in size.

As discussed in Sect. 4.4, this barrier was partially overcome with the advent of generative AI and the introduction of foundation models. A key breakthrough was the ability to integrate web-scale data—referred to as the "human digital trace"—which was not originally intended for AI training, into the learning process. Combined with the massive expansion in model parameters, this enabled large-scale learning on web-scale data. Consequently, image understanding AI, driven by multi-modal large language models (MLLMs), has seen significant performance improvements. For example, in tasks such as image-based question answering, AI now exhibits behavior that, in certain scenarios, approaches or even rivals human-level performance.

So, what challenges remain after the success of MLLMs? Although it is difficult to precisely assess the limitations of MLLMs, it is evident that in the realm of Shitsukan recognition, there are still many tasks that AI struggles with—tasks that humans can easily perform.

First, compared to humans, AI—including MLLMs—significantly lags in its ability to generalize what it has learned. This disparity may arise from fundamental differences in how AI and humans learn. Even in the case of generative AI, the learning framework remains essentially the same as classical AI, differing mainly in scale. It is important to note that humans do not acquire knowledge from the "digital trace" of others on the web. The majority of human abilities are developed through interactions with the physical world in daily life. In contrast, AI learns from a finite set of samples drawn from a vast input space, with its learning concentrated locally around these samples. Although AI can generalize well within the proximity of these points, it often fails when encountering out-of-distribution data [60]. In this regard, AI's robustness to out-of-distribution scenarios is significantly weaker than that of humans.

How can we overcome this limitation of AI? One approach is to improve the current AI learning framework. However, the path to achieving this is still unclear. For example, there has been discussion in the community around the importance of providing AI with a world model [61–63]—a human-like understanding of the world—but concrete steps toward realizing this goal have yet to be defined.

Another approach is to explore how far we can push the current AI learning framework. The author is particularly interested in this direction, focusing on enabling practical engineering applications. This involves identifying the current AI's limitations and investigating how it can still be effectively applied in real-world contexts. We proposed imagination-driven captioning in our study [64], which generates explanations by drawing comparisons to familiar concepts—a common strategy humans use when interpreting images. We also enabled AI to acquire specialized knowledge beyond web-based data in the studies by Kunlamai et al. [65] and Yamane et al. citech4yamane2024deep. Additionally, we explored abductive visual reasoning [67] in the study by Charoenpitaks et al. [68], predicting plausible future scenarios from scenes and explaining them logically.

As mentioned in Sect. 4.1, Shitsukan recognition is characterized by the difficulty of articulating it in words, yet it is motivated by a desire to share these perceptions with others. In the current AI research and development landscape, where LLMs—which inherently rely on language—play a central role, the study of Shitsukan recognition can help identify what is still missing for further progress and offer pathways to bridge those gaps. It is hoped that this chapter will serve as a guide on that journey.

References

1. Krizhevsky, A., Sutskever, I., Hinton, G.E.: Imagenet classification with deep convolutional neural networks. Adv. Neural Inf. Process. Syst. **25** (2012)
2. He, K., Zhang, X., Ren, S., Sun, J.: Deep residual learning for image recognition. In: Proceedings of the IEEE Conference on Computer Vision and Pattern Recognition, pp. 770–778 (2016)
3. Dosovitskiy, A.: An image is worth 16x16 words: transformers for image recognition at scale. arXiv preprint arXiv:2010.11929 (2020)
4. Sharan, L., Liu, C., Rosenholtz, R., Adelson, E.H.: Recognizing materials using perceptually inspired features. Int. J. Comput. Vision **103**, 348–371 (2013)
5. Zhang, Y., Ozay, M., Liu, X., Okatani, T.: Integrating deep features for material recognition. In: 2016 23rd International Conference on Pattern Recognition (ICPR), pp. 3697–3702. IEEE (2016)
6. Sharan, L., Rosenholtz, R., Adelson, E.: Material perception: what can you see in a brief glance? J. Vis. **9**(8), 784–784 (2009)
7. Bell, S., Upchurch, P., Snavely, N., Bala, K.: Material recognition in the wild with the materials in context database. In: Proceedings of the IEEE Conference on Computer Vision and Pattern Recognition, pp. 3479–3487 (2015)
8. Yamaguchi, K., Okatani, T., Sudo, K., Murasaki, K., Taniguchi, Y.: Mix and match: joint model for clothing and attribute recognition. In: BMVC, vol. 1, p. 4 (2015)
9. Parikh, D., Grauman, K.: Relative attributes. In: 2011 International Conference on Computer Vision, pp. 503–510, IEEE (2011)
10. Dong, Y., Huang, C., Liu, W.: RankCNN: When learning to rank encounters the pseudo preference feedback. Comput. Stand. Interfaces **36**(3), 554–562 (2014)
11. Burges, C., Shaked, T., Renshaw, E., Lazier, A., Deeds, M., Hamilton, N., Hullender, G.: Learning to rank using gradient descent. In: Proceedings of the 22nd International Conference on Machine Learning, pp. 89–96 (2005)

12. Abe, T., Okatani, T., Deguchi, K.: Recognizing surface qualities from natural images based on learning to rank. In: Proceedings of the 21st International Conference on Pattern Recognition (ICPR2012), pp. 3712–3715. IEEE (2012)
13. Lowe, D.G.: Distinctive image features from scale-invariant keypoints. Int. J. Comput. Vision **60**, 91–110 (2004)
14. Sivic, Zisserman: Video Google: a text retrieval approach to object matching in videos. In: Proceedings Ninth IEEE International Conference on Computer Vision, pp. 1470–1477. IEEE (2003)
15. Vittayakorn, S., Umeda, T., Murasaki, K., Sudo, K., Okatani, T., Yamaguchi, K.: Automatic attribute discovery with neural activations. In: Computer Vision–ECCV 2016: 14th European Conference, Amsterdam, The Netherlands, 11–14 Oct, Proceedings, Part IV vol. 14, pp. 252–268, Springer (2016)
16. Yashima, T., Okazaki, N., Inui, K., Yamaguchi, K., Okatani, T.: Learning to describe e-commerce images from noisy online data. In: Computer Vision–ACCV 2016: 13th Asian Conference on Computer Vision, Taipei, Taiwan, 20-24 Nov, Revised Selected Papers, Part V vol. 13, pp. 85–100, Springer (2017)
17. Vinyals, O., Toshev, A., Bengio, S., Erhan, D.: Show and tell: a neural image caption generator. In: Proceedings of the IEEE Conference on Computer Vision and Pattern Recognition, pp. 3156–3164 (2015)
18. Antol, S., Agrawal, A., Lu, J., Mitchell, M., Batra, D., Zitnick, C.L., Parikh, D.: Vqa: visual question answering. In: Proceedings of the IEEE International Conference on Computer Vision, pp. 2425–2433 (2015)
19. Vaswani, A.: Attention is all you need. Adv. Neural Inf. Process. Syst. (2017)
20. Nguyen, D.-K., Okatani, T.: Improved fusion of visual and language representations by dense symmetric co-attention for visual question answering. In: Proceedings of the IEEE Conference on Computer Vision and Pattern Recognition, pp. 6087–6096 (2018)
21. Yu, Z., Yu, J., Cui, Y., Tao, D., Tian, Q.: Deep modular co-attention networks for visual question answering. In: Proceedings of the IEEE/CVF Conference on Computer Vision and Pattern Recognition, pp. 6281–6290 (2019)
22. Nguyen, D.-K., Okatani, T.: Multi-task learning of hierarchical vision-language representation. In: Proceedings of the IEEE/CVF Conference on Computer Vision and Pattern Recognition, pp. 10492–10501 (2019)
23. Nguyen, V.-Q., Suganuma, M., Okatani, T.: GRIT: Faster and better image captioning transformer using dual visual features. In: European Conference on Computer Vision, pp. 167–184, Springer (2022)
24. Ren, S., He, K., Girshick, R., Sun, J.: Faster r-cnn: Towards real-time object detection with region proposal networks. IEEE Trans. Pattern Anal. Mach. Intell. **39**(6), 1137–1149 (2016)
25. Radford, A., Kim, J.W., Hallacy, C., Ramesh, A., Goh, G., Agarwal, S., Sastry, G., Askell, A., Mishkin, P., Clark, J., et al.: Learning transferable visual models from natural language supervision. In: International Conference on Machine Learning, pp. 8748–8763, PMLR (2021)
26. Schuhmann, C., Beaumont, R., Vencu, R., Gordon, C., Wightman, R., Cherti, M., Coombes, T., Katta, A., Mullis, C., Wortsman, M., et al.: Laion-5b: an open large-scale dataset for training next generation image-text models. Adv. Neural. Inf. Process. Syst. **35**, 25278–25294 (2022)
27. Bommasani, R., Hudson, D.A., Adeli, E., Altman, R., Arora, S., Arx, S., Bernstein, M.S., Bohg, J., Bosselut, A., Brunskill, E., et al.: On the opportunities and risks of foundation models. Technical Report, Center for Research on Foundation Models (CRFM) (2021)
28. Brown, T.B., Mann, B., Ryder, N., Subbiah, M., Kaplan, J.D., Dhariwal, P., Neelakantan, A., Shyam, P., Sastry, G., Askell, A., et al.: Language models are few-shot learners. In: Advances in Neural Information Processing Systems, vol. 33, pp. 1877–1901 (2020)
29. Kumar, A., Gupta, P., Goel, S., et al.: Large language models: a survey. ACM Comput. Surv. (2024)
30. Laskar, M.T.R., Fakhoury, S., Ghosal, T., Gelbukh, A., Rudzicz, F., Hoque, E.: A systematic survey and critical review on evaluating large language models: challenges, limitations, and recommendations. In: Proceedings of the 2024 Conference on Empirical Methods in Natural Language Processing, pp. 13768–13791 (2024)

31. Sennrich, R., Haddow, B., Birch, A.: Neural machine translation of rare words with subword units. In: Proceedings of the 54th Annual Meeting of the Association for Computational Linguistics (Volume 1: Long Papers), pp. 1715–1725 (2016)
32. Kudo, T., Richardson, J.: Sentencepiece: a simple and language independent subword tokenizer and detokenizer for neural text processing. In: Proceedings of the 2018 Conference on Empirical Methods in Natural Language Processing: System Demonstrations, pp. 66–71 (2018)
33. Radford, A., Narasimhan, K., Salimans, T., Sutskever, I.: Improving language understanding by generative pre-training. In: OpenAI Technical Report (2018)
34. Radford, A., Wu, J., Child, R., Luan, D., Amodei, D., Sutskever, I.: Language models are unsupervised multitask learners. In: OpenAI Technical Report (2019)
35. Wei, J., Bosma, M., Zhao, V.Y., Guu, K., Yu, A.W., Lester, B., Du, N., Dai, A.M., Le, Q.V.: Finetuned language models are zero-shot learners. In: International Conference on Learning Representations (2022)
36. Ouyang, L., Wu, J., Jiang, X., Almeida, D., Wainwright, C., Mishkin, P., Zhang, C., Agarwal, S., Slama, K., Ray, A., et al: Training language models to follow instructions with human feedback. In: Advances in Neural Information Processing Systems, vol. 35, pp. 27730–27744 (2022)
37. Yu, L., Yu, B., Yu, H., Huang, F., Li, Y.: Language models are super mario: absorbing abilities from homologous models as a free lunch. In: Forty-first International Conference on Machine Learning (2024)
38. Alayrac, J.-B., Donahue, J., Luc, P., Miech, A., Barr, I., Hasson, Y., Lenc, K., Mensch, A., Millican, K., Reynolds, M., et al.: Flamingo: a visual language model for few-shot learning. Adv. Neural. Inf. Process. Syst. **35**, 23716–23736 (2022)
39. Li, J., Li, D., Xiong, C., Hoi, S.: Blip: Bootstrapping language-image pre-training for unified vision-language understanding and generation. In: International Conference on Machine Learning, pp. 12888–12900, PMLR (2022)
40. Yang, Z., Li, L., Lin, K., Wang, J., Lin, C.-C., Liu, Z., Wang, L.: The dawn of lmms: preliminary explorations with gpt-4v (ision). Comput. Vis. Pattern Recognit. **9**(1), 1. arXiv preprint arXiv:2309.17421 (2023)
41. Liu, H., Li, C., Wu, Q., Lee, Y.J.: Visual instruction tuning. Adv. Neural Inf. Process. Syst. **36** (2024)
42. Zhu, W., Cao, Q., Xu, H., Wang, Y., Xu, Y., Zhang, Z., Wang, Y., Zhang, Y.: Multimodal large language models: a survey. arXiv preprint arXiv:2306.13549 (2023)
43. Li, J., Li, D., Savarese, S., Hoi, S.C.: Blip-2: Bootstrapping language-image pre-training with frozen image encoders and large language models. In: International Conference on Machine Learning, pp. 19730–19742 (2023)
44. Liu, H., Li, C., Li, Y., Lee, Y.J.: Improved baselines with visual instruction tuning. In: Proceedings of the IEEE/CVF Conference on Computer Vision and Pattern Recognition, pp. 26296–26306 (2024)
45. McKinzie, B., Gan, Z., Fauconnier, J.-P., Dodge, S., Zhang, B., Dufter, P., Shah, D., Du, X., Peng, F., Weers, F., et al.: MM1: Methods, analysis & insights from multimodal LLM pre-training. arXiv preprint arXiv:2403.09611 (2024)
46. Awadalla, A., Liu, H., Chen, X., Alayrac, J.-B., Li, C., Lin, K., Wang, X., Zhou, Y., Caron, M., Holtzman, A., et al: Openflamingo: an open-source framework for training large multimodal models. In: Proceedings of the 37th Conference on Neural Information Processing Systems (NeurIPS), Datasets and Benchmarks Track (2023)
47. Han, Z., Gao, C., Liu, J., Zhang, J., Zhang, S.Q.: Parameter-efficient fine-tuning for large models: a comprehensive survey. Trans. Mach. Learn. Res. (2024)
48. Hu, E.J., Shen, Y., Wallis, P., Allen-Zhu, Z., Li, Y., Wang, S., Wang, L., Chen, W.: Lora: Low-rank adaptation of large language models. In: International Conference on Learning Representations (2021)
49. OpenAI: Gpt-4 technical report. arXiv preprint arXiv:2303.08774 (2023)
50. Goodfellow, I., Pouget-Abadie, J., Mirza, M., Xu, B., Warde-Farley, D., Ozair, S., Courville, A., Bengio, Y.: Generative adversarial networks. Commun. ACM **63**(11), 139–144 (2020)

51. Kingma, D.P.: Auto-encoding variational bayes. arXiv preprint arXiv:1312.6114 (2013)
52. Papamakarios, G., Nalisnick, E., Rezende, D.J., Mohamed, S., Lakshminarayanan, B.: Normalizing flows for probabilistic modeling and inference. J. Mach. Learn. Res. **22**(57), 1–64 (2021)
53. Ho, J., Jain, A., Abbeel, P.: Denoising diffusion probabilistic models. Adv. Neural. Inf. Process. Syst. **33**, 6840–6851 (2020)
54. Song, J., Meng, C., Ermon, S.: Denoising diffusion implicit models. arXiv preprint arXiv:2010.02502 (2020)
55. Ronneberger, O., Fischer, P., Brox, T.: U-net: convolutional networks for biomedical image segmentation. In: Medical Image Computing and Computer-assisted intervention–MICCAI 2015: 18th International Conference, Munich, Germany, 5-9 Oct, Proceedings, Part III vol. 18, pp. 234–241, Springer (2015)
56. Rombach, R., Blattmann, A., Lorenz, D., Esser, P., Ommer, B.: High-resolution image synthesis with latent diffusion models. In: Proceedings of the IEEE/CVF Conference on Computer Vision and Pattern Recognition, pp. 10684–10695 (2022)
57. Peebles, W., Xie, S.: Scalable diffusion models with transformers. In: Proceedings of the IEEE/CVF International Conference on Computer Vision, pp. 4195–4205 (2023)
58. Brooks, T., Peebles, B., Holmes, C., DePue, W., Guo, Y., Jing, L., Schnurr, D., Taylor, J., Luhman, T., Luhman, E., Ng, C., Wang, R., Ramesh, A.: Video generation models as world simulators (2024)
59. Nguyen, V.-Q., Suganuma, M., Okatani, T.: Efficient attention mechanism for visual dialog that can handle all the interactions between multiple inputs. In: Computer Vision–ECCV 2020: 16th European Conference, Glasgow, UK, 23–28 Aug, Proceedings, Part XXIV vol. 16, pp. 223–240, Springer (2020)
60. Chollet, F.: On the measure of intelligence. arXiv preprint arXiv:1911.01547 (2019)
61. Ding, J., Zhang, Y., Shang, Y., Zhang, Y., Zong, Z., Feng, J., Yuan, Y., Su, H., Li, N., Sukiennik, N., et al.: Understanding world or predicting future? a comprehensive survey of world models. ACM Comput. Surv. (2024)
62. DeepMind, G.: Genie 3: a new frontier for World models. https://deepmind.google/discover/blog/genie-3-a-new-frontier-for-world-models/ (2025). Accessed 25 Aug 2025
63. AI, M.: Our new model helps AI think before it acts: V-JEPA 2. https://about.fb.com/news/2025/06/our-new-model-helps-ai-think-before-it-acts/(2025). Accessed: 25 Aug 2025
64. Tran, H.T.T., Okatani, T.: Bright as the sun: In-depth analysis of imagination-driven image captioning. In: Proceedings of the Asian Conference on Computer Vision, pp. 4613–4630 (2022)
65. Kunlamai, T., Yamane, T., Suganuma, M., Chun, P.-J., Okatani, T.: Improving visual question answering for bridge inspection by pre-training with external data of image-text pairs. Comput.-Aided Civ. Infrastruct. Eng. **39**(3), 345–361 (2024)
66. Yamane, T., Chun, P.-J., Dang, J., Okatani, T.: Deep learning-based bridge damage cause estimation from multiple images using visual question answering. Struct. Infrastruct. Eng. 1–14 (2024)
67. Liang, C., Wang, W., Zhou, T., Yang, Y.: Visual abductive reasoning. In: Proceedings of the IEEE/CVF Conference on Computer Vision and Pattern Recognition, pp. 15565–15575 (2022)
68. Charoenpitaks, K., Nguyen, V.-Q., Suganuma, M., Takahashi, M., Niihara, R., Okatani, T.: Exploring the potential of multi-modal AI for driving hazard prediction. IEEE Trans. Intell. Veh. (2024)

Chapter 5
Shitsukan of Sound

Takuya Koumura

Abstract This chapter explores the auditory perception of sound Shitsukan, which differs from the basic contents of sound and includes more abstract, often difficult-to-verbalize qualities, such as material properties, spatial characteristics, and environmental factors including reverberation and ambient noise. I begin by examining how the physical properties of sound sources shape perceived Shitsukan, focusing on studies related to material perception of impact sounds. I then explore various other aspects of Shitsukan, such as the effects of reverberation on material and emotion perception, the perception of silent objects and sound textures, and the experience of a sound source moving closely around the listener's head. These discussions illustrate how sound interacts with physical environments, including the listener's body, to create a perceptual experience. The chapter concludes by considering the potential to quantify more elusive Shitsukan experiences, such as particular emotions evoked by voices and the unique auditory qualities of traditional songs, suggesting that Shitsukan may be key to understanding both modern and traditional cultural expressions of sound.

5.1 What is Sound Shitsukan?

This chapter focuses on the auditory perception of sound Shitsukan. First of all, what exactly is sound Shitsukan? When we hear a sound, we almost instantly gather a wide range of information about its source and the environment [16]. To simplify, we can divide this perceived information into two categories: the contents of the sound and its Shitsukan. The contents can refer to the significant events within the sound and the categories of its sources. For example, we can recognize distinct sounds such as a smartphone dropping and hitting the floor, a cat meowing, or the rain falling (Fig. 5.1). Shitsukan, on the other hand, can refer to more subtle information that is not easily conveyed through a simple form of language. This includes the physical properties of the sound sources and environmental factors. In the examples above,

T. Koumura (✉)
NTT Communication Science Laboratories, Atsugi, Kanagawa, Japan
e-mail: koumura@cycentum.com

S. Nishida and K. Nishino (eds.), *Shitsukan—Understanding and Manipulating Material and Quality Perception*, https://doi.org/10.1007/978-981-95-4762-3_5

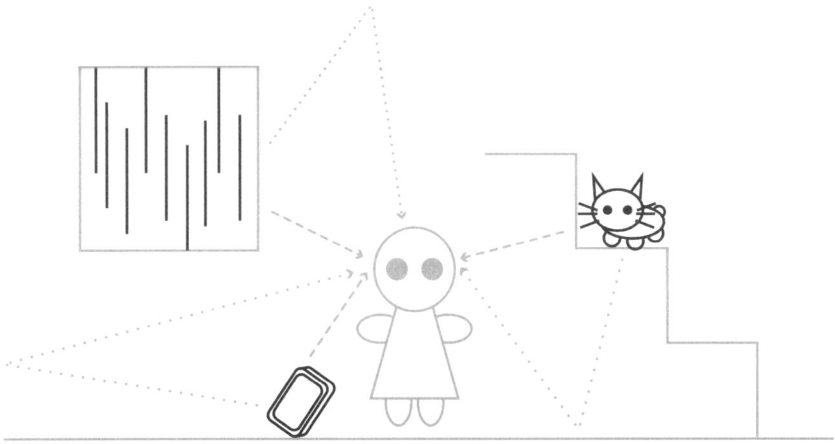

Fig. 5.1 Illustration of sounds in an everyday environment. A person can simultaneously be exposed to and recognize sounds such as a smartphone dropping and hitting the floor, a cat meowing, and rain falling. These sounds can originate from different locations. The sources generate direct sounds, which travel straight from the source to the listener without reflecting off surfaces (illustrated by dashed lines). In addition to direct sounds, sound waves are reflected off surrounding objects, such as walls, floors, and ceilings, creating multiple delayed reflections (illustrated by dotted lines), resulting in reverberation. Furthermore, ambient noise from other sources may be present in the environment, contributing to the overall soundscape (not shown in the illustration)

the physical properties of the sound sources would include details such as the size of the phone, the material of the floor, the location of the cat, and the intensity of the rain. Environmental properties might involve the dimensions of the room, the material of the walls, or ambient noise.

A sound contains information about the physical properties of its source because it is produced by the physical movements or interactions of substances (solid, liquid, or gas). It also carries information about the environment, as the sound is modulated by its surroundings before reaching our ears. This modulation includes factors like reflections from objects (creating reverberation) and the addition of ambient noise. Therefore, to fully understand auditory Shitsukan perception, we must consider both the nature of the sound source and how the environment alters or modulates the sound.

If we apply this speculative distinction between contents and Shitsukan to speech, we can think of speech contents as the verbal information describable in a language, while speech Shitsukan encompasses nonverbal information, such as emotion conveyed through prosody, voice characteristics, and the speaker's identity. Similarly, in music, the content can be the melody, whereas its Shitsukan is the timbre of the instruments. Although nonverbal information in speech and timbre in music has been extensively studied over the years, this chapter seeks to move beyond these classic examples of sound Shitsukan and focus more broadly on everyday sounds. We will explore the Shitsukan of sound sources' materials, the perception of silent objects, environmental modulation, an ensemble of many overlapping sounds, and more abstract Shitsukan that currently lack quantitative definitions.

The concepts of contents and Shitsukan may also apply to the visual domain. The contents of a visual stimulus typically involve object categories, while the Shitsukan includes other object properties such as materials, textures, and gloss, as well as environmental properties like lighting and haze. A visual stimulus provides information about objects because light rays reaching our eyes are reflected and modulated by those objects. It also contains information about the environment, as the light itself comes from a source in the environment and is influenced by surrounding materials. Therefore, similar to auditory perception, considering environmental factors is crucial for understanding visual Shitsukan. For example, reflections from nearby objects can affect the perceived material [37], and certain Shitsukan, such as glossiness, may only be visible under specific lighting conditions [38]. However, it is important to note a key distinction: a sound source is typically regarded as the primary focus of perceived content, while a light source is more often viewed as part of the surrounding environment, contributing to the Shitsukan of other objects [16].

5.2 Perception of Sound Source Material

Although the primary focus of this chapter is Shitsukan perception, it is worth briefly mentioning the physical mechanisms of sound production and computational approaches that simulate them. This section first outlines these mechanisms and simulations, mainly addressing impact sounds, and then turns to studies on how listeners perceive material properties from auditory cues.

5.2.1 Physical Mechanisms of Sound Production and Their Computational Simulations

The sound emitted from a source is determined by the physical properties and motion of that source [15]. The mechanism of sound emission depends on the source's state of matter (solid, liquid, or gas) and its material (e.g., wood, metal, glass for solids; water, oil for liquids). Additionally, sounds produced by interactions between different substances vary depending on how the objects move (e.g., being struck or scraped).

The sound of an object being struck with a mallet has been extensively studied (Fig. 5.2). Several mathematical models have been proposed to simulate impact sounds. For instance, Aramaki and Kronland-Martinet [3] modeled the damping of spectral components by applying a time-varying filter to a noise signal. The specific parameters of this model are determined through an analysis-synthesis framework, where the parameters are estimated by fitting the model to a recorded impact sound.

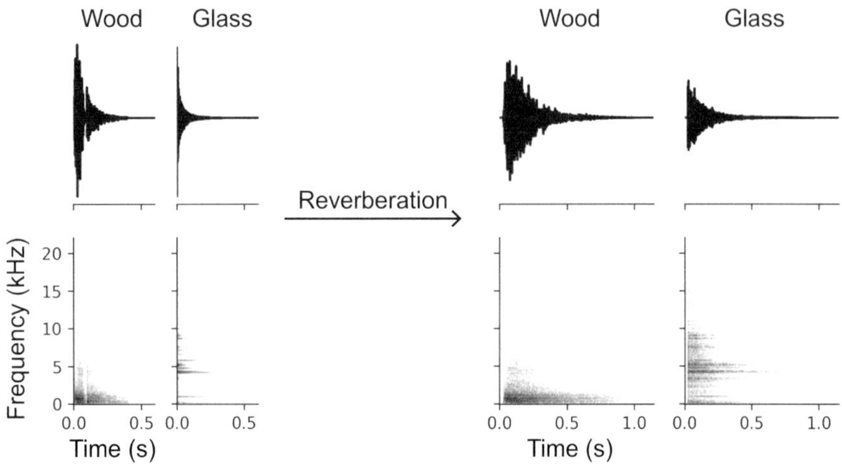

Fig. 5.2 Examples of impact sounds in waveforms and spectrograms. It can be seen that different materials produce distinct waveforms and spectrograms. When reverberation is applied (right panels), the decay rate of the waveforms slows down, and the energy in the spectrogram spreads over time. The spectrogram was calculated using a short-time Fourier transform with linear frequency scaling. The power is logarithmically scaled for better visualization. The wood and glass impact sounds are sourced from https://freesound.org/people/ldezem/sounds/386226/ and https://freesound.org/people/an2netto/sounds/379408/ respectively, both included in the FSD50K dataset [12] and available under the Creative Commons 0 license. Reverberation was simulated in a rectangular room (shoebox model) with dimensions of $10 \times 200 \times 6$ m, using the pyroomacoustics library [52]

Additionally, Owens et al. [45] demonstrated that it is possible to statistically estimate impact sounds from video footage of the moment of impact. Using a neural network (NN), they predicted sound features from visual inputs, which were then either used to synthesize sound or retrieve the closest matching sound based on the estimated features.

Other studies have focused on simulating scraping sounds based on the surface material and the scraping motion [1, 62]. Agarwal et al. [1] broke down the surface-object interaction during scraping into distinct components, such as object motion, normal force, and surface depth, each of which was mathematically modeled. These components are combined to synthesize a scraping sound from a novel combination of motion and force. The surface material is represented by recorded impulse responses from multiple positions on the surface. In addition, some models have been proposed for synthesizing or retrieving sounds generated by various liquid motion patterns [50, 67].

5.2.2 *Material Perception of an Impact Sound*

Aramaki et al. [2] applied the analysis-synthesis method to generate impact sounds. Leveraging their parametric model, they performed material morphing, synthesizing sounds with intermediate materials between wood, metal, and glass. Through subjective categorization of these intermediate sounds, they discovered that a small number of sound features could effectively capture the perceived material differences among wood, metal, and glass. Of the features tested, the amplitude decay rate was the most influential in explaining the perceived material, followed by roughness calculated from the amplitude spectrum.

Rakovec et al. [48] broadened the range of materials considered for impacted objects, including metal, wood, plastic, glass, stone, ceramic, and cardboard, as well as their shapes, such as bars, tubes, plates, blocks, and bowls. Their findings revealed that perceived materials tend to be divided into two categories: metal, glass, stone, and ceramic, in one group, and wood, plastic, and cardboard in the other. Additionally, they observed an interaction between the perceived material and the shape.

As one can expect, the perception of an object's material from impact sounds is strongly influenced by visual information [13]. When estimating the material category of an impacted object, the subjective rating is best explained by a multiplicative model, where the final perception is based on the agreement between auditory and visual stimuli. In contrast, when estimating specific material properties (e.g., surface brightness, sound loudness, hardness, and coldness), the perception follows an additive model, where the contributions of the audio and visual stimuli are independent of each other. The authors suggest that both models can be unified within a Bayesian framework.

5.3 Shitsukan Produced by Environmental Sound Modulation

As previously mentioned, once a sound is emitted by a source, it is modulated by the surrounding environment [16]. This environmental modulation is primarily shaped by reverberation and ambient noise. The sound that reaches the ear is a combination of the direct or radiant sound, which travels straight from the source without any reflections, and the reflected sounds from surrounding objects. These reflected sounds create reverberation, arriving at the ear with a delay that depends on the distances between the sound source, reflecting surfaces, and the listener. The spectrum of each reflection is altered according to the material properties of the reflecting objects. A listener's own body, including their head and outer ears, also reflects sound, contributing additional modulation. Addition of ambient noise may be considered as another type of environmental modulation. It is a mixture of sounds from numerous sources, each with different reverberation.

In auditory perception, both reverberation and ambient noise significantly influence the perceived Shitsukan. Reverberation alters the perception of Shitsukan, such as the material of objects or the emotion conveyed in speech. Additionally, sound reflections from a listener's own body can create a unique Shitsukan. Some listeners are even capable of identifying object materials based solely on reflected sound. Subtle ambient noise combined with specific reverberation can evoke a sense of presence of a particular object. Ambient noise itself can carry a Shitsukan of texture, generated by the accumulation of countless sound events.

In general, sound reflection patterns (including reverberation) can be effectively modeled using an impulse response, which is the recorded sound at a specific microphone location in a particular environment, generated from an impulse sound at a defined speaker position. Once an impulse response is recorded in a given environment with a particular microphone and speaker arrangement, it becomes possible to virtually simulate different sound sources by convolving the new source signal with the pre-recorded impulse response. Reflections within a room are characterized by the room impulse response (RIR), and those around a listener's head and body by the head-related impulse response (HRIR) or its frequency-domain counterpart, the head-related transfer function (HRTF).

5.3.1 *Effects of Reverberation on Material Perception*

One notable effect of reverberation on Shitsukan perception is that the perceived material changes when reverberation is introduced, but continuous exposure to constant reverberation leads to adaptation to reverberation [32]. Koumura and Furukawa [32] used material-morphed impact sounds synthesized by Aramaki et al. [2]. Listeners heard the sounds sequentially and classified the material as wood, glass, or metal. When reverberation was applied using RIRs (Fig. 5.2), their material classifications differed from those made with non-reverberant sounds. The shift in responses was smaller, that is, the classifications remained relatively unchanged by reverberation, when reverberation from the same room was applied consistently throughout the sequence, compared with when different reverberation sources were applied to each sound within the sequence. This finding suggests that listeners adapted to reverberation when exposed to impact sounds in the same acoustic environment. Additionally, the contribution of spectrum-related sound features to material classification was influenced by the listening context. It is also worth noting that adaptation to reverberation occurs in speech perception as well [63], which has been studied more extensively than its counterpart in material perception.

5.3.2 *Effects of Temporal Resolution on Shitsukan Perception*

The temporal envelope is one of the most important sound features in auditory perception in general [26]. Listeners can not only classify everyday sounds and recognize speech using only the envelope cue [9, 18, 54], but they also perceive sensations such as pitch and roughness from specific envelope patterns [26]. It is also possible to discriminate between the sounds of bouncing and breaking bottles based on their temporal patterns [66]. A temporal envelope is typically calculated as the amplitude envelope of each subband of a frequency-decomposed sound signal. In studies considering auditory peripheral processing, a nonlinearly compressed amplitude envelope is sometimes used instead. The temporal envelope is often characterized by its power spectrum, referred to as the modulation power spectrum.

One effect of reverberation on a sound signal is that it distorts or "smears" the temporal envelope, meaning that amplitude peaks are flattened and troughs are filled [5, 23] (Fig. 5.3), as a result of multiple delayed reflections overlapping with the direct sound. This distortion of the temporal envelope leads to a reduction in temporal resolution. Therefore, to better understand how the acoustic environment influences Shitsukan perception, it is crucial to investigate the effect of reduction in temporal resolution.

Temporal resolution influences the perception of emotion and speaker identity, which, as mentioned earlier, can be considered as forms of Shitsukan in speech. Zhu et al. [69] manipulated the temporal resolution of speech by applying a low-pass filter to set an upper limit on the modulation frequency in each subband of the sound signal. To minimize the use of spectral cues by listeners, they replaced the temporal fine structure in each subband with white noise. This type of speech is referred to as noise-vocoded speech. Emotion recognition accuracy was measured based on the intended emotion conveyed by the speaker, who was a professional actress. The accuracy of emotion recognition and speaker identification increased as the upper limit of modulation frequency approached 16 Hz. These findings suggest that the perception of emotion and speaker identity relies on features associated with relatively high modulation frequencies. This contrasts with speech content recognition, for which crucial information is found at lower modulation frequencies [17, 56]. This aligns with the modulation frequency range where the temporal envelope is distorted by reverberation, as shown by Avendano and Hermansky [5]. Zhu et al. [68] further explored the effects of additive background noise and reverberation on emotion recognition and speaker identification using noise-vocoded speech. They found that background noise and reverberation impacted listener performance only when the sound was severely distorted. This indicates robustness in the perception of emotion and speaker identity, suggesting existence of perceptual constancy across environmental changes in everyday life.

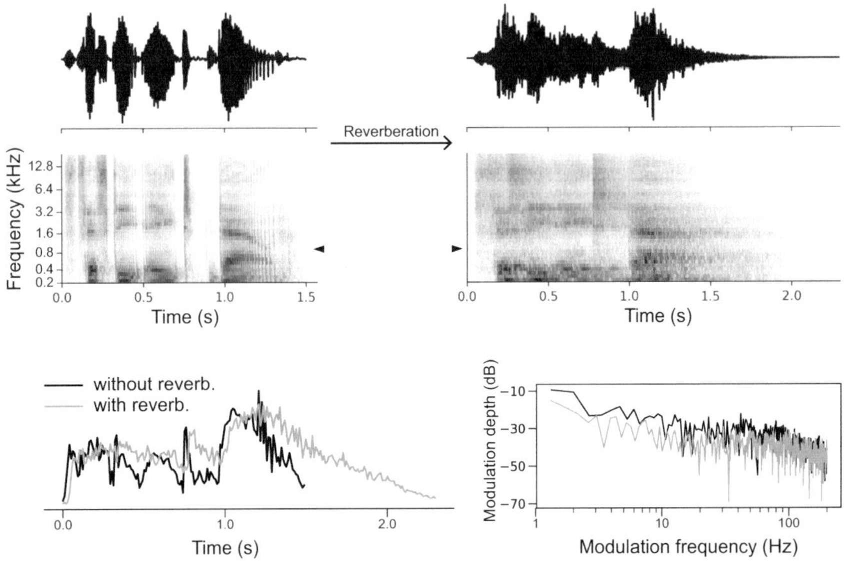

Fig. 5.3 Example of a speech sound with and without reverberation, illustrated through waveforms and auditory spectrograms. An auditory spectrogram, or cochleagram, is a type of spectrogram that simulates the output of auditory peripheral processing [42]. The waveform was decomposed into frequency bands using a gammatone filterbank that mimics auditory peripheral processing [42]. The Hilbert envelopes of the filtered waveforms were computed and then raised to the power of 0.3 to simulate nonlinear compression. The envelopes displayed in the lower-left panel correspond to the 1028.87 Hz band (closest to 1 kHz), low-pass filtered and downsampled to 50 Hz for better visualization. The effect of reverberation on the temporal envelope is clearly visible: the peaks and troughs become broader, and their magnitudes are reduced. In the lower-right panel, the modulation spectra for the same band are shown, calculated as the Fourier transforms of the envelopes. Spectra between 1 and 200 Hz are displayed for clearer visualization. The magnitude of the spectrum was normalized by the direct-current component and expressed in decibels, resulting in a scale known as modulation depth. This scale represents the strength of temporal modulation relative to the overall amplitude of the waveform. Reverberation reduced the modulation depth in the middle range of modulation frequencies, indicating a reduction in temporal resolution. Please note that the "without reverberation" sound may already contain some reverberation from the recording environment. The original speech sound is included in the FSD50K dataset [12] and sourced from https://freesound.org/people/bcimmet/sounds/236553/ under the CC BY 3.0 license. The reverberation was simulated using the same parameters as in Fig. 5.2

5.3.3 Auditory Temporal Processing and Its Emergence

Given the importance of temporal envelopes in auditory perception, their processing has become one of the most extensively studied topics in auditory science [42]. Psychophysical research has shown that sensitivity to temporal modulation depends on the modulation frequency. This dependence is referred to as the (psychophysical) temporal modulation transfer function [64]. It can be explained by the theoretical filter bank operating on temporal envelopes [7]. The theory is further supported by the presence of neurons in the auditory nervous system that are selectively tuned to specific modulation frequencies. Once sound reaches the ear, it is processed by the inner ear, which converts sound waves into neural signals and transmits them to the brain via the auditory nerve. In the brain, these signals are further processed across multiple regions, including the brainstem, thalamus, and cortex, before subjective perception occurs [46]. Notably, neuronal tuning to modulation frequencies transforms systematically across these regions [26]. Neural activities in peripheral brain regions tend to synchronize with higher modulation frequencies, although their overall activity levels remain relatively unaffected by the modulation frequency. In contrast, neural activities in central brain regions synchronize with lower modulation frequencies, and their overall activity levels are also tuned to the modulation frequency.

Computational simulation studies suggest that these psychophysical and neurophysiological characteristics emerge as a result of adaptation to the natural environment [34, 36]. Computational models designed to classify everyday sounds or speech phonemes exhibited auditory-system-like modulation-related characteristics. Crucially, they were not designed to reproduce auditory characteristics but to accurately classify sounds using machine learning techniques. Additionally, auditory-like properties did not emerge when the models were constructed with sounds without natural Shitsukan (such as temporally shuffled waveforms or sounds with flattened temporal envelopes). Natural Shitsukan might also be essential for the emergence of behavioral sensitivity and neuronal tuning to the temporal modulation.

5.3.4 Neural Processing of Musical Beat

Research consistently shows that the brain exhibits temporal synchronization with auditory stimuli. While many studies focus on simple and regular temporal patterns, such as sinusoidal modulations or pulse trains, the brain also synchronizes to more complex patterns, such as a musical beat—one of the most common temporal patterns in everyday life. Ito et al. [25] discovered that rats show head movements and neural activity in the auditory cortex synchronized with a musical beat at a tempo around 100 beats per minute. This range of tempo is similar to that in humans, suggesting that beat synchronization is governed by neural mechanisms rather than body size. If body size were the key factor, rats, being smaller than humans, would be expected to synchronize with a faster beat. Interestingly, this tempo aligns with common tempos in music, indicating that such synchronization may serve as a neural foundation for both the perception and production of music.

5.3.5 Perception of a Silent Object Through Sound Reflection

The presence of a silent object may evoke Shitsukan perception through ambient noise and reverberation. Even an object that does not emit sound alters the sound reflection simply by existing in the environment, which can lead to detectable changes in the sound signal reaching the listener's ear. Miura et al. [40] recorded impulse responses both with and without a silent object and found significant differences in the acoustic features between the two conditions. These differences were observed in the power spectrum and interaural level difference (the difference in sound intensity between the left and right ears). In a follow-up study, they applied these impulse responses to pink noise and discovered that a listener's ability to detect the presence of a silent object depended on the object's position relative to the sound source [41]. Their analysis indicated that changes in the spectrum were the primary factor contributing to the perceptual difference. In real-world situations, a listener might detect subtle changes in ambient noise caused by the altered reverberation when a silent object appears. This could be a mechanism for perceiving an object's presence, a form of Shitsukan that allows us to sense the existence of an object without seeing it, either consciously or unconsciously.

Some individuals can identify the Shitsukan of a silent object by listening to the reflection or echo of their own sound, a skill known as echolocation [31, 58]. While the term originally refers to locating objects through self-generated echoes, sometimes it also describes the ability to discern physical properties such as size, shape, and material from both self- and non-self-generated sounds. Rice and Feinstein [49] demonstrated that blind individuals could successfully use echoes to discriminate object sizes. Size discrimination can be aided by cues such as overall sound level and the sound level of the echo relative to the emission. Other factors like surface material, object shape, and distance to the object also influence echo characteristics. Both blind individuals and blindfolded sighted individuals have shown the ability to recognize simple shapes and differentiate between materials with performance well above chance [19]. Soft materials like carpet tend to absorb high frequencies, while harder materials, such as plexiglass, reflect both high and low frequencies [31]. Echo intensity can also offer clues about object shape and concavity, as concave surfaces amplify returning echoes compared to flat ones [4]. While echolocation is common in bats and dolphins, some humans also possess this ability. Visually impaired individuals tend to be more proficient, likely due to their greater reliance on auditory cues, whereas sighted people typically depend on visual input. However, sighted individuals can also develop echolocation skills through training [10, 60]. Both groups exhibit significant individual variability in their echolocation strategies and accuracy [19, 53, 59].

5.3.6 *Frisson Sensation Invoked by a Moving Sound Source at Close Distance*

Sound emitted from a source is not only reflected and attenuated by surrounding objects but also modulated by the listener's own head and body. This type of modulation can be considered an environmental influence in a broad sense and is usually modeled as an impulse response referred to as an HRIR. Differences in HRIRs across various sound source positions become more pronounced as the source moves closer to the listener. Therefore, when a sound source near the listener's head is in motion, substantial modulation occurs due to its positional changes. Depending on the sound characteristics, this kind of moving sound evokes sensations such as frisson or tingling [24, 33, 61].

Honda et al. [24] recorded binaural sounds rotating around a binaural microphone with a distance of just 6 cm, using the following sound sources: white noise, rolling beads, frictional sounds of a plastic bag, and music. These recordings were played back through headphones, and listeners rated their frisson and pleasant sensation. Faster sound rotations and binaural presentations generally resulted in higher frisson ratings compared to slower rotations and monaural presentations. Interestingly, non-musical noise-like sounds were rated as unpleasant, while music was rated as pleasant. The study found that frisson and pleasantness ratings correlated with binaural sound features (interaural time and level differences), while frisson ratings of binaural sounds also correlated with their loudness.

Koumura et al. [33] further explored frisson, finding that it correlates with sensations of tingling or tickling, but not with pleasantness. These frisson ratings were highly consistent even two weeks later. They identified correlations between frisson and sound features (amplitude, spectral centroid, and spectral bandwidth). They also found that the time lag between interaural differences in these features and frisson responses was shorter than the lag from the interaural average of these features. Moreover, frisson responses were found to be influenced by mood states, particularly tension-anxiety, rather than long-term personality traits. This suggests that frisson might be linked to temporary states rather than enduring personal characteristics.

Terashima et al. [61] mitigated the limitations of Honda et al. [24] and Koumura et al. [33] by expanding the variety of stimuli and incorporating both auditory and visual stimuli in video presentations. They tested two types of stimuli: those designed to evoke autonomous sensory meridian response (ASMR) [6] in viewers and those recorded in other natural scenes. Their findings showed that these different types of videos elicited distinct distributions of tingling and pleasantness ratings. They predicted tingling and pleasant sensations using temporal marginal statistics, originally developed to describe sound textures (mentioned below). Tingling sensations were primarily predicted by the average power of the temporal envelope around 5 kHz. Overall, tingling sensations were more accurately predicted than pleasant sensations. Their results also support that frisson and tingling sensations might form the auditory basis for the pleasant sensations associated with ASMR when accompanied with a visual stimulus.

5.3.7 Sound Texture

Generally, ambient noise reduces perceptual accuracy by lowering the signal-to-noise ratio. However, when the ambient noise itself becomes the focus of perception, it can evoke a specific Shitsukan. For example, when trying to listen to a friend speaking in a room, the sound of the air conditioner or rain outside may act as noise, distracting the listener from the conversation. But if the goal is to determine whether the air conditioner is functioning properly or to assess whether the rain is too heavy to go outside, those previously distracting sounds become the primary perceptual target. These ambient noise-like sounds, often produced by many overlapping sound events, evoke distinct Shitsukan that differ from the perception of individual sounds [16]. Such sounds are referred to as sound textures [39], a concept similar to image textures [47] (Fig. 5.4). Sound textures can be characterized by the temporal marginal statistics of their features, and when the durations are sufficiently long, different sounds sharing similar statistics become difficult to distinguish.

Sound textures can be synthesized using a method analogous to those developed for image texture synthesis [47]. Given a sound texture, a new instance can be synthesized by matching its marginal statistics to those of the original [39]. Extending this principle, a method has been proposed for converting the Shitsukan of speech and music (Fig. 5.5) [35]. This approach synthesizes sounds that preserve the marginal feature statistics of a texture while maintaining the temporal feature patterns of speech or music. For instance, it enables the creation of speech that sounds as if spoken by bubbling water and music that sounds as if sung by a flock of birds. Such Shitsukan

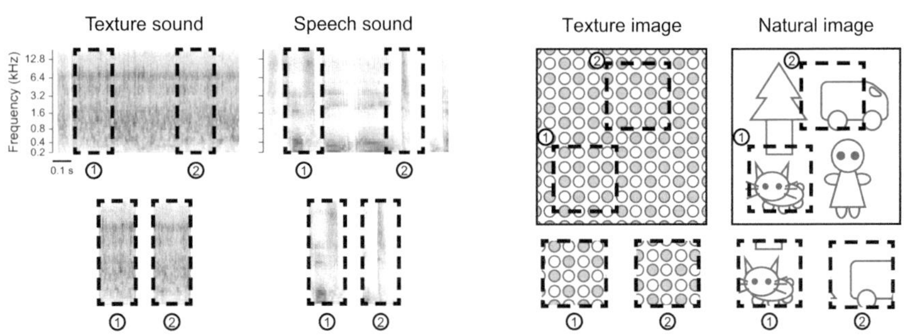

Fig. 5.4 Examples of sound and image textures. A texture sound is characterized by its relatively uniform temporal patterns, making individual excerpts (e.g., Excerpts 1 and 2) difficult to distinguish from one another. In contrast, in sounds like speech, where temporal patterns play a crucial role in perception, excerpts are easily distinguishable. This distinction mirrors the difference between texture images and other types of images. In texture images, patches (e.g., Patches 1 and 2) are not easily distinguishable due to the relatively uniform spatial pattern, unlike natural images, where unique spatial details make different patches easily identifiable. The texture sound is included in the FSD50K dataset [12] and sourced from https://freesound.org/people/VKProduktion/sounds/215709/ under the Creative Commons 0 license. The speech sound is the same as in Fig. 5.3. The illustration of the natural image is sourced and modified from [35] under the CC BY 4.0 license

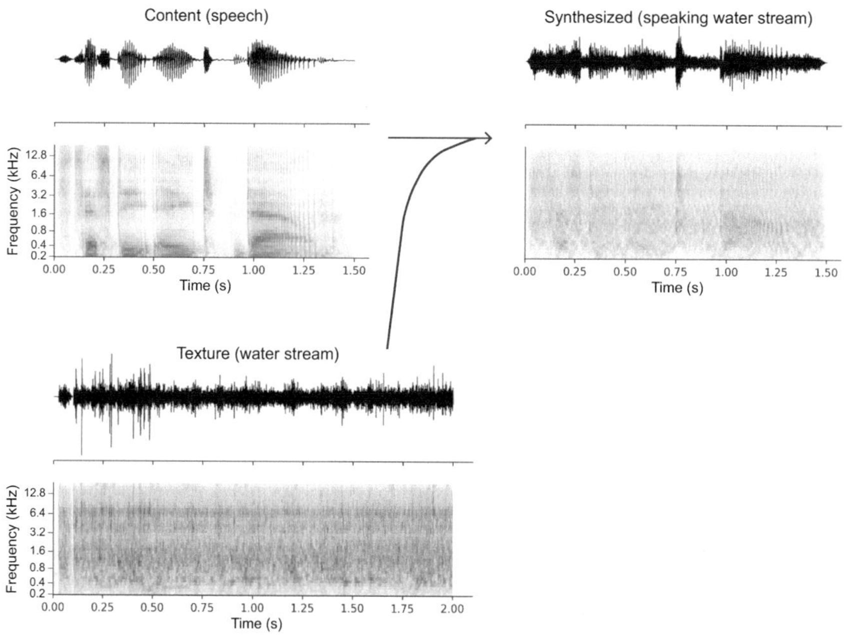

Fig. 5.5 Sound texture transfer. A texture of a water stream was transferred to a speech content, resulting in a sound heard like a speaking water stream. Sound waveforms and auditory spectrograms are shown. The original content and texture sounds are the same as in Fig. 5.4

conversion is inspired by image style transfer, where an image is synthesized to preserve the marginal statistics of a texture while retaining the spatial patterns of another image [14], a method that is in turn an extension of image texture synthesis [47].

The Shitsukan of sound textures can be influenced by stimuli from other perceptual modalities. Watanabe et al. [65] asked listeners to rate multiple aspects of Shitsukan (naturalness, luxuriousness, modernness, and comfortableness) of texture sounds while looking at different visual stimuli. When paired with an image that is presumably more natural, the same sound stimuli were rated higher in naturalness and comfortableness, but lower in luxuriousness and modernness. To further explore real-life environmental effects, they presented the sounds in different rooms with different presumed levels of naturalness. Changing the room altered not only the visual stimuli but also tactile cues and more abstract Shitsukan aspects such as the atmosphere. The effects of the room on the Shitsukan ratings were similar to those observed with visual stimuli. Additionally, they used an onomatopoeia-analysis system to quantify more implicit impressions of the sound stimuli [8, 51].

5.4 Toward Understanding More Abstract Shitsukan

Integrating the knowledge of Shitsukan perception could offer insights into previously abstract, hard-to-quantify concepts such as physical and mental states, the cuteness of acting voices, and the unique qualities of traditional songs.

5.4.1 Sound Shitsukan as an Indicator of Physical and Mental States

It is well known in clinical communities that a person's laryngeal condition affects the acoustic properties of their voice [55]. Clinicians have developed standard methods to assess physical states by analyzing vocal characteristics [22, 28]. Acoustic features also correlate with mood and could serve as biomarkers for mental disorders [11, 43]. Even without clinical training, it is easy to imagine that when someone has a sore throat from a cold, changes in their throat physiology affect their voice. These vocal changes are often recognizable and might be rooted in the Shitsukan conveyed through voice quality.

5.4.2 Shitsukan in Acting Voices

Acting voices evoke impressions that differ from those of natural voices [21]. They also provide listeners with impressions unique to the characters being portrayed, which are suggested to be governed by multiple acoustic features [20]. Among them, one of the most culturally and commercially important impressions is the cuteness of voice, which has been studied extensively [44].

A related but more abstract, elusive concept is "moe." Admittedly, its precise meaning is challenging to define, but in simple terms it refers to a kind of affectionate feeling (often experienced by men) toward a cute (typically female) character. The concept originated in Japanese pop culture roughly three decades ago. Kawahara describes moe as it is "characterized by a set of adjectives like 'pretty, cute, small, accessible, friendly, and cheerful'," but is "admittedly very difficult to define precisely" [27]. Despite its abstract nature, researchers have begun to quantify the relationship between perceived moe and the acoustic features of vocal stimuli [27, 57].

5.4.3 *Shitsukan in Traditional Songs and Performances*

Longstanding Shitsukan concepts, such as those associated with traditional songs and performances, can also be difficult to quantify. When live data are unavailable and only historical records remain, the available information is often fragmented or incomplete, which prevents a precise analysis. Another difficulty arises when performance practices have been transmitted orally without written documentation, since this leaves almost no objective records for analysis. One example of the latter is the quality of a genre of traditional Japanese songs [29, 30]. Understanding the Shitsukan of such music is not only academically valuable but also vital for preserving and passing down cultural heritage to future generations.

5.5 Conclusion

Hearing a sound provides us with various Shitsukan of both the sound source and the surrounding environment. This is partly because the sound signal carries information about these Shitsukans, and partly because our auditory system is equipped to perceive this information. This chapter explored how sound properties interact with their environment and shape human perception. We examined how people perceive Shitsukan attributes, such as the material of sound sources, and how environmental modulation influences and produces Shitsukan, including emotional responses in speech, frisson sensations, and sound textures. These insights open new possibilities for quantifying and understanding more abstract and complex auditory phenomena, both in modern and traditional contexts.

References

1. Agarwal, V., Cusimano, M., Traer, J., McDermott, J.: Object-Based synthesis of scraping and rolling sounds based on non-Linear physical constraints. In: 2021 24th International Conference on Digital Audio Effects (DAFx), pp. 136–143 (2021). ISSN: 2413-6689
2. Aramaki, M., Besson, M., Kronland-Martinet, R., Ystad, S.: Controlling the perceived material in an impact sound synthesizer. IEEE Trans. Audio, Speech Lang. Process. **19**(2):301–314 (2011). ISBN: 1558-7916
3. Aramaki, M., Kronland-Martinet, R.: Analysis-synthesis of impact sounds by real-time dynamic filtering. IEEE Trans. Audio, Speech Lang. Process. **14**(2):695–704 (2006). ISBN: 9783200001657
4. Arnott, S.R., Thaler, L., Milne, J.L., Kish, D., Goodale, M.A.: Shape-specific activation of occipital cortex in an early blind echolocation expert. Neuropsychologia **51**(5), 938–949 (2013)
5. Avendano, C., Hermansky, H.: Study on the dereverberation of speech based on temporal envelope filtering. In: Proceeding of Fourth International Conference on Spoken Language Processing. ICSLP '96, vol. 2, pp. 889–892 1(996)
6. Barratt, E.L., Davis, N.J.: Autonomous sensory meridian response (ASMR): a flow-like mental state. PeerJ **3**, e851 (2015). ISBN: 2167-8359 (Electronic)

7. Dau, T., Kollmeier, B., Kohlrausch, A.: Modeling auditory processing of amplitude modulation .1. Detection and masking with narrow-band carriers. J. Acoust. Soc. Am. **102**(5), 2892–2905, (1997). ISBN: 0001-4966 (Print) 0001-4966(Linking)
8. Doizaki, R., Watanabe, J., Sakamoto, M.: Automatic Estimation of Multidimensional Ratings from a Single Sound-Symbolic Word and Word-Based Visualization of Tactile Perceptual Space. IEEE Trans. Haptics **10**(2):173–182 (2017)
9. Dudley, H.: Remaking speech. J. Acoust. Soc. Am. **11**(2), 169–177 (1939)
10. Ekkel, M.R., van Lier, R., Steenbergen, B.: Learning to echolocate in sighted people: a correlational study on attention, working memory and spatial abilities. Exp. Brain Res. **235**(3), 809–818 (2017)
11. Ellgring, H., Scherer, K.R.: Vocal indicators of mood change in depression. J. Nonverbal Behav. **20**(2), 83–110 (1996)
12. Fonseca, E., Favory, X., Pons, J., Font, F., Serra, X.: FSD50K: an open dataset of human-labeled sound events. IEEE/ACM Trans. Audio Speech Lang. Process. **30**, 829–852 (2022). arXiv: 2010.00475. ISBN: 2010.00475v2
13. Fujisaki, W., Goda, N., Motoyoshi, I., Nishida, S., Komatsu, H.: Audiovisual integration in the human perception of materials. J. Vis. **14**(2014), 1–20 (2014)
14. Gatys, L.A., Ecker, A.S., Bethge, M.: Image Style Transfer Using Convolutional Neural Networks. In: 2016 IEEE Conference on Computer Vision and Pattern Recognition (CVPR), pp. 2414–2423 (2016)
15. Gaver, W.W.: How do we hear in the world? Explorations in ecological acoustics. Ecol. Psychol. **5**(4), 285–313 (1993). ISBN: 1040-7413
16. Gaver, W.W.: What in the world do we hear?: an ecological approach to auditory event perception. Ecol. Psychol. **5**(1):1–29 (1993). ISBN: 1040-7413
17. Greenberg, S., Arai, T.: The relation between speech intelligibility and the complex modulation spectrum. In: 7th European Conference on Speech Communication and Technology (Eurospeech 2001), pp. 473–476. ISCA (2001)
18. Gygi, B., Kidd, G.R., Watson, C.S.: Spectral-temporal factors in the identification of environmental sounds. J. Acoust. Soc. Am. **115**(3):1252–1265 (2004). ISBN: 0001-4966 (Print) 0001-4966 (Linking)
19. Hausfeld, S., Power, R.P., Gorta, A., Harris, P.: Echo perception of shape and texture by sighted subjects. Percept Mot Ski. **55**(2), 623–632 (1982)
20. Hayashi, D., Morise, M.: Acoustical features relating to the representation of age and gender in acting voices by female voice actors (2025)
21. Hayashi, D., Osugi, T.: Investigation into impressions about voice qualities in anime: comparison with daily life and drama (2021)
22. HIRANO, M.: Clinical examination of voice. Disord. Hum. Commun. **5**, 1–99 (1981)
23. Hirobayashi, S., Nomura, H., Koike, T., Tohyama, M.: Speech waveform recovery from a reverberant speech signal using inverse filtering of the power envelope transfer function. Electronics and Communications in Japan (Part III: Fundamental Electronic Science), vol. 83(6), pp. 77–85 (2000). _eprint: https://onlinelibrary.wiley.com/doi/pdf/10.1002/%28SICI%291520-6440%28200006%2983%3A6%3C77%3A%3AAID-ECJC9%3E3.0.CO%3B2-B
24. Honda, S., Ishikawa, Y., Konno, R., Imai, E., Nomiyama, N., Sakurada, K., Koumura, T., Kondo, H.M., Furukawa, S., Fujii, S., Nakatani, M.: Proximal Binaural Sound Can Induce Subjective Frisson. Front. Psychol. (2020). Publisher: Frontiers
25. Ito, Y., Shiramatsu, T.I., Ishida, N. Oshima, K. ,Magami, K., Takahashi, H.: Spontaneous beat synchronization in rats: neural dynamics and motor entrainment. Sci. Adv. **8**(45), eabo7019 (2022)
26. Joris, P.X., Schreiner, C.E., Rees, A.: Neural processing of amplitude-modulated sounds. Physiol Rev. **84**(2), 541–577 (2004). ISBN: 0031-9333 (Print)
27. Kawahara, S.: The prosodic features of the “moe” and “tsun” voices. J. Phon. Soc. Jpn. **20**(2), 102–110 (2016)
28. Kempster, G.B., Gerratt, B.R., Verdolini, A.K., Barkmeier, K.J., Hillman, R.E.: Consensus auditory-perceptual evaluation of voice: development of a standardized clinical protocol. Am. J. Speech-Lang. Pathol. **18**(2), 124–132 (2009)

29. Kidani, S.: Evaluation of the sound quality of Noh songs using timbre assessment words. In Enriched MultiMedia (EMM) **124**, 80–82 (2025)
30. Kidani, S., Isoyama, T., Unoki, M.: Study on spectro-temporal modulation information that contributes to quality Noh song. In: 2023 Autumn Meeting, Acoustical Society of Japan (2023)
31. Kolarik, A.J., Cirstea, S., Pardhan, S., Moore, B.C.J.: A summary of research investigating echolocation abilities of blind and sighted humans. Hear. Res. **310**, 60–68 (2014)
32. Koumura, T., Furukawa, S.: Context-dependent effect of reverberation on material perception from impact sound. Scientific Reports **7**(1), 16455 (2017)
33. Koumura, T., Nakatani, M., Liao, H.-I., Kondo, H.M.: Dark, loud, and compact sounds induce frisson. Q. J. Exp. Psychol. **74**(6), 1140–1152 (2021)
34. Koumura, T., Terashima, H., Furukawa, S.: Cascaded tuning to amplitude modulation for natural sound recognition. J. Neurosci. **39**(28), 5517–5533 (2019)
35. Koumura, T., Terashima, H., Furukawa, S.: Chimeric sounds with shuffled "textureâŁž and "contentâŁž synthesized by a model of the auditory system. Acoust. Sci. Tech. **41**(1), 337–340 (2020)
36. Koumura, T., Terashima, H., Furukawa, S.: Human-Like modulation sensitivity emerging through optimization to natural sound recognition. J. Neurosci. **43**(21):3876–3894 (2023)
37. Lagunas, M., Serrano, A., Gutierrez, D., Masia, B.: The joint role of geometry and illumination on material recognition. J. Vis. **21**(2), 2 (2021)
38. Leloup, F.B., Pointer, M.R., Dutré, P., Hanselaer, P.: Geometry of illumination, luminance contrast, and gloss perception. J. Opt. Soc. Am. A, JOSAA **27**(9), 2046–2054 (2010)
39. McDermott, J.H., Simoncelli, E.P.: Sound texture perception via statistics of the auditory periphery: evidence from sound synthesis. Neuron **71**(5), 926–940 (2011). ISBN: 0896-6273
40. Miura, T., Ifukube, T., Furukawa, S.: Analyses of acoustic cues for the auditory perception of silent object. J. Acoust. Soc. Jpn. **67**(7), 261–270 (2011)
41. Miura, T., Ifukube, T., Furukawa, S.: Contribution of acoustical characteristics to auditory perception of silent object. In: Conference Proceedings-IEEE International Conference on Systems, Man and Cybernetics, pp. 1074–1079 (2011). ISBN: 9781457706523
42. Moore, B.C.J.: An introduction to the psychology of hearing. Brill (2012)
43. Mundt, J.C., Vogel, A.P., Feltner, D.E., Lenderking, W.R.: Vocal acoustic biomarkers of depression severity and treatment response. Biol. Psychiat. **72**(7), 580–587 (2012)
44. Ohno, R., Morise, M., Kitahara, T.: Relationship between perception of cuteness in female voices and their durations. In: Karpov, A., Potapova, R., Mporas, I. (eds.) Speech and Computer, vol. 10458, pp. 642–650. Springer International Publishing, Cham (2017). Series Title: Lecture Notes in Computer Science
45. Owens, A., Isola, P., McDermott, J., Torralba, A., Adelson, E.H., Freeman, W.T.: Visually indicated sounds. In: The IEEE Conference on Computer Vision and Pattern Recognition (CVPR) (2016). arXiv: 1512.08512
46. Pickles, J.O.: An introduction to the physiology of hearing. Emerald Group Pub (2012)
47. Portilla, J., Simoncelli, E.P.: A parametric texture model based on joint statistics of complex wavelet coefficients. Int. J. Comput. Vision **40**(1), 49–71 (2000)
48. Rakovec, C.-E., Aramaki, M., Kronland-Martinet, R.: Perception of material and shape of impacted everyday objects. In: Proceeding of 10th CMMR, pp. 943–959 (2013)
49. Rice, C.E., Feinstein, S.H.: Sonar system of the blind: size discrimination. Science **148**(3673), 1107–1108 (1965)
50. Saito, H., Sato, S., Dobashi, Y.: A liquid sound retrieval using history of velocities in physically-based simulation. In: SIGGRAPH Asia 2021 Posters, SA '21 Posters, pp. 1–2, Association for Computing Machinery, New York, NY, USA (2021)
51. Sakamoto, M.: System to quantify the impression of sounds expressed by onomatopoeias. Acoust. Sci. Technol. **41**(1), 229–232 (2020)
52. Scheibler, R., Bezzam, E., Dokmanić, I.: Pyroomacoustics: a Python package for audio room simulations and array processing algorithms. In: 2018 IEEE International Conference on Acoustics, Speech and Signal Processing (ICASSP), pp. 351–355 (2018). arXiv:1710.04196 [cs, eess]

53. Schenkman, B.N., Nilsson, M.E.: Human echolocation: pitch versus loudness information. Perception **40**(7), 840–852 (2011)
54. Shannon, R.V., Zeng, F.-G., Kamath, V., Wygonski, J., Ekelid, M.: Speech recognition with primarily temporal Cues. Science **270**(5234), 303–304 (1995). ISBN: 0036-8075 (Print)
55. Stemple, J.C., Roy, N., Klaben, B.K.: Clinical Voice Pathology: Theory and Management, Sixth Edition. Plural Publishing (2018). Google-Books-ID: miuQDwAAQBAJ
56. Tachibana, R.O., Sasaki, Y., Riquimaroux, H.: Relative contributions of spectral and temporal resolutions to the perception of syllables, words, and sentences in noise-vocoded speech. Acoust. Sci. Technol. **34**(4), 263–270 (2013)
57. Takano, S., Yamada, M.: Perception and analysis of "Moe "voice. J. Acoust. Soc. Am. **140**(4_Supplement), 3399 (2016)
58. Teng, S.: Human Echolocation. PhD thesis, UC Berkeley (2013)
59. Teng, S., Puri, A., Whitney, D.: Ultrafine spatial acuity of blind expert human echolocators. Exp. Brain Res. **216**(4), 483–488 (2012)
60. Teng, S., Whitney, D.: The acuity of echolocation: spatial resolution in the sighted compared to expert performance. J. Vis. Impair Blind **105**(1), 20–32 (2011)
61. Terashima,H., Tada, K., Kondo, H.M.: Predicting tingling sensations induced by autonomous sensory meridian response (ASMR) videos based on sound texture statistics: a comparison to pleasant feelings. Philos. Trans. R. Soc. B: Biol. Sci. **379**(1908), 20230254 (2024)
62. Traer, J., Cusimano, M., McDermott, J.: A perceptually inspired generative model of rigid-body contact sounds (2019). ISSN: 2413-6689
63. Tsironis, A., Vlahou, E., Kontou, P., Bagos, P., Kopčo, N.: Adaptation to reverberation for speech perception: a systematic review. Trends Hear. **28**, 23312165241273399 (2024)
64. Viemeister, N.F.: Temporal modulation transfer functions based upon modulation thresholds. J. Acoust. Soc. Am. **66**(5), 1364–1380 (1979)
65. Watanabe, R., Koumura, T., Terashima, H., Furukawa, S., Sakamoto, M.: The influence of visual context on the naturalness impression of auditory stimuli. In: Yada, K., Takama, Y., Mineshima, K., Satoh, K. (eds.) New Frontiers in Artificial Intelligence. pp, pp. 317–329. Springer Nature Switzerland, Cham (2023)
66. William, J., Warren, H., Verbrugge, R.R.: Auditory perception of breaking and bouncing events: psychophysics. (1988). Publication Title: Natural Computation
67. Zheng, C., James, D.L.: Harmonic fluids. ACM Trans. Graph. **28**(3), 1–12 (2009)
68. Zhu, Z., Kawamura, M., Unoki, M.: Study on the perception of nonlinguistic information of noise-vocoded speech under noise and/or reverberation conditions. Acoust. Sci. Technol. **43**(6), 306–315 (2022)
69. Zhu, Z., Miyauchi, R., Araki, Y., Unoki, M.: Contributions of temporal cue on the perception of speaker individuality and vocal emotion for noise-vocoded speech. Acoust. Sci. Technol. **39**(3), 234–242 (2018)

Part II
Shitsukan in The Brain

Chapter 6
Decoding Shitsukan in The Brain

Yukiyasu Kamitani, Misato Tanaka, and Tomoyasu Horikawa

Abstract Understanding *Shitsukan*, or realistic qualities of the world, in visual experiences requires more than simple models or language-based descriptions. This chapter introduces a brain decoding approach centered on mid-level visual features represented in both the brain and deep neural networks (DNNs). By translating brain activity into DNN features and using generative models to reconstruct detailed visual images, we achieve high-fidelity decoding of subjective experiences, including mental imagery and visual illusions. Our approach extends beyond individual subjects, demonstrating inter-individual and inter-site generalization of these brain-derived patterns. Despite these advances, challenges persist in ensuring accurate hierarchical correspondence between brain and DNN features and mitigating spurious reconstructions. We propose a new research direction, the *Neuroverse*, which aims to externalize not only sensory representations but also the brain's internal model of the world. This framework opens new avenues for exploring how Shitsukan and other complex perceptual experiences are constructed and represented in the brain.

6.1 Introduction

The concept of *Shitsukan* refers to the perception of realistic qualities of the world. It encompasses how humans perceive and interpret the intrinsic properties of objects and the environment in relation to their physical and sensory characteristics. Unlike basic visual attributes like color or shape, Shitsukan represents a more complex sensory experience, providing a sense of "reality" to the materials we observe. This

Y. Kamitani (✉) · M. Tanaka
ATR Computational Neuroscience Laboratories, Kyoto, Japan

Kyoto University, Kyoto, Japan
e-mail: kamitani@i.kyoto-u.ac.jp

M. Tanaka
e-mail: mtanaka@i.kyoto-u.ac.jp

T. Horikawa
NTT Communication Science Laboratories, Atsugi-shi, Kanagawa, Japan

S. Nishida and K. Nishino (eds.), *Shitsukan—Understanding and Manipulating Material and Quality Perception*, https://doi.org/10.1007/978-981-95-4762-3_6

perception is crucial for understanding how we interact with our environment, guiding not only recognition but also decisions on how to handle objects. However, Shitsukan is challenging to define using simple models or linguistic descriptions. It relies on subtle visual cues that are often difficult to articulate, making it a prime target for advanced decoding approaches that aim to capture and reproduce these nuanced experiences.

In the context of cognitive neuroscience, brain decoding refers to the process of inferring perceptual or cognitive states based on patterns of brain activity, typically using neuroimaging techniques like functional Magnetic Resonance Imaging (fMRI) [11, 21]. This technique has opened up new avenues for understanding the neural underpinnings of complex mental phenomena, allowing researchers to predict or reconstruct what a person is seeing, thinking, or imagining. Brain decoding is particularly relevant to the study of Shitsukan because traditional univariate models struggle to capture the complex, distributed nature of the neural representations involved. By leveraging multivariate pattern recognition approaches and deep learning models, brain decoding provides a way to translate the brain's rich, high-dimensional signals into meaningful visual features, potentially revealing the brain's internal representations of Shitsukan.

Early work on visual material perception highlighted how surface properties like glossiness, roughness, and translucency are processed by specific neural mechanisms in the visual cortex, particularly in regions such as the fusiform gyrus and the lateral occipital cortex [24]. For instance, gloss perception has been linked to the integration of multiple image cues, including highlights and surface shading, processed by visual areas sensitive to surface properties [5]. Similarly, Chadwick et al. [4] demonstrated how neural substrates differentiate between translucent and opaque materials, capturing the unique interaction of light within a material. However, much of this research has focused on isolated features rather than the mid-level properties that define complex qualities of visual experiences. This mid-level range is crucial for the richness of visual qualities yet often remains underrepresented in existing models. High-level semantic models, in contrast, excel at capturing categorical knowledge but fail to decode the fine-grained sensory attributes that are key to Shitsukan. As a result, this gap has made it challenging to fully decode or reconstruct the richness of visual perception from brain activity, leaving a significant portion of human perceptual experience unexplored.

Our approach addresses this limitation by focusing on feature decoding from brain activity, targeting the mid-level representations in both human brains and deep neural networks (DNNs) (Fig. 6.1). Unlike low-level visual features, which are simple and easily modeled, or high-level features tied to linguistic descriptions, mid-level features are "faceless" and "nameless." They encode complex properties that are essential for realistic perception, such as surface texture, translucency, and softness, without necessarily invoking semantic labels. To achieve this, we establish a correspondence between the visual cortical areas and layers in DNNs, allowing us to decode brain activity into DNN features that align with these mid-level properties.

We further extend this approach to visual image reconstruction, where the decoded DNN features are used to generate detailed visual representations that reflect the

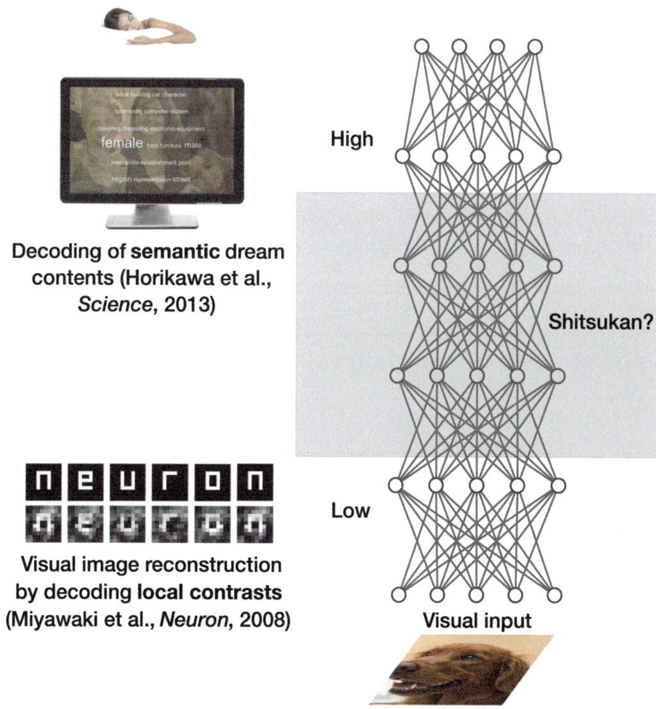

Fig. 6.1 Brain decoding approach to Shitsukan. We hypothesize that Shitsukan is represented in the mid-level features of both the human brain and deep neural networks (DNNs). In contrast to our previous studies, which focused on low-level visual features, such as local contrast and orientation, easily modeled by simple computational filters [27], or high-level visual features linked to semantic representations [16], we suggest that Shitsukan is represented in nameless, faceless features found in the middle layers of the visual system. These features capture more complex properties that are crucial for realistic perceptual experiences without necessarily invoking semantic associations. Left bottom panel adapted with permission from Miyawaki et al. [27], Neuron 60:915–29. ©2008 Elsevier Inc

perceptual contents encoded in brain activity. This process not only reveals what the brain "sees" but also sheds light on the role of mid-level features in shaping holistic visual perception. The reconstructed images allow us to probe subjective experiences, such as mental imagery and visual illusions, providing a window into the brain's internal model of reality. Through this approach, we show that subjective experiences can be captured and decoded, moving beyond the constraints of conventional brain decoding techniques.

In this chapter, we begin by providing an overview of brain decoding and the NeuroAI approach, including the use of hierarchical correspondence between brain regions and DNN layers. Next, we present the results of visual image reconstruction experiments, demonstrating the ability to reveal complex perceptual contents and subjective experiences. We then explore inter-individual and inter-site reconstructions, showing how the decoded features can be generalized across different individuals and research sites. Afterward, we address the challenges and critical evaluations of our approach, focusing on issues such as the accuracy of hierarchical alignment and the risk of spurious reconstructions. Finally, we conclude with an outlook on the future of brain decoding research, introducing the concept of the Neuroverse. This new direction aims to move beyond the reconstruction of sensory inputs, focusing instead on the externalization of the brain's internal model of reality.

6.2 Decoding Visual Experiences from Brain Activity

Brain decoding is a powerful technique that translates patterns of brain activity, captured through methods like fMRI, into perceptual or semantic outputs, such as visual images or object categories [11, 21, 36]. By leveraging machine learning models, it allows researchers to infer what a person is seeing, thinking, or imagining, providing a deeper understanding of how the brain processes sensory information.

Unlike traditional neuroimaging approaches that assign broad functions to distinct brain regions, machine learning-based brain decoding can detect fine-grained patterns imperceptible to the human eye. Early studies on visual perception decoding focused on low-level visual features [20–22], which are thought to be represented in neural structures beyond the spatial resolution of conventional fMRI. Kamitani and Tong [21] pioneered the use of machine learning to analyze fine-grained multivoxel patterns and decode stimulus orientation from distributed fMRI signals, revealing that even subtle neuroimaging signals contain rich perceptual information. Building on this, Miyawaki et al. [27] reconstructed simple visual images by predicting local contrasts, showing that low-level visual attributes could be translated into recognizable images. Their modular approach combined outputs from multiple decoders to achieve zero-shot prediction, allowing for the reconstruction of novel images that had not been previously seen. However, these models fell short in handling more complex textures and material properties, limiting their applicability for decoding the intricate perceptual qualities essential for Shitsukan.

High-level semantic decoding has significantly advanced the field by revealing complex mental representations that extend beyond basic perceptual features. Horikawa et al. [16] successfully decoded the semantic content of dreams from brain activity recorded during sleep. By training their model on brain activity data collected while subjects viewed natural images during wakefulness, they were able to predict broad object categories such as "animals" and "vehicles," demonstrating that even subjective experiences like dreaming can be decoded to reveal meaningful semantic information. Similarly, other studies have decoded high-level categories and abstract concepts, yet these approaches often overlook mid-level features that are crucial for capturing the nuanced visual qualities. Addressing this limitation requires integrating low-, mid-, and high-level features to fully decode the complexity of visual perception.

6.3 NeuroAI Approach

The advent of deep neural networks (DNNs) has revolutionized both artificial intelligence and neuroscience, providing powerful tools for modeling brain function. The breakthrough began with AlexNet [25], which set a new standard in visual recognition by leveraging deep hierarchical architectures to automatically learn complex visual features. This success spurred the development of even more sophisticated models like VGGNet [35], ResNet [13], and Inception [37], whose multi-layered designs began to mirror the hierarchical processing stages in the human visual system, giving rise to the field of NeuroAI [8, 26].

These DNNs served as functional models for understanding visual perception, inspiring researchers to explore how artificial networks could simulate the brain's extraction and synthesis of visual information. Parallel advancements in generative models, such as Generative Adversarial Networks (GANs) [10] and diffusion models [14], provided new capabilities for synthesizing high-quality images, capturing details like texture and shading. Their ability to produce photorealistic images made them promising tools for reconstructing visual experiences from brain data.

Hierarchical correspondence between the brain and deep neural networks (DNNs) has been established through multiple approaches, revealing a convergence of evidence. One key method, neural encoding models, involves using DNN features to predict neural responses to visual stimuli, thereby identifying which layers of the network correspond to specific brain regions [40]. Another approach, representational similarity analysis (RSA), constructs similarity matrices based on patterns of brain activity across different stimuli and compares them to DNN-derived representations [23]. They show that mid-level DNN layers align with mid-level visual areas like V4, while deeper layers correspond to higher-level regions such as the inferior temporal cortex. This hierarchical correspondence demonstrates that DNNs can serve as effective computational proxies for visual processing, capturing both the structure and function of the human visual system.

Our research extends this alignment through a translator–generator pipeline designed to reconstruct visual experiences from brain activity (Fig. 6.2). The pipeline begins with a translator module that maps brain activity patterns into latent representations within a pre-trained DNN. Unlike conventional brain decoding, this process is framed as a transformation from neural to machine representations, emphasizing that brain activity itself can be viewed as a latent encoding of the perceived image. The translator focuses on aligning hierarchical visual features between the brain and the DNN layers, creating a shared representational space.

In the second stage, the generator module uses these translated features to produce a visual image that corresponds to the content encoded in the original brain activity, achieving a coherent reconstruction of the perceived image. By leveraging the translated hierarchical features, the generator captures complex properties of visual experiences. This two-step process thus enables a seamless transformation from brain signals to high-fidelity visual outputs, bridging the gap between neural and computational representations.

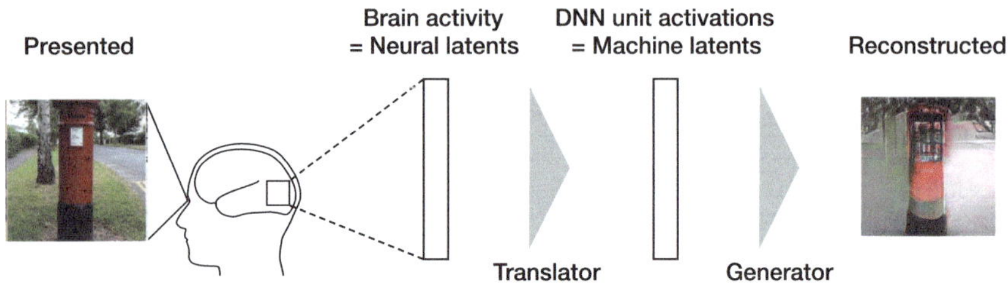

Fig. 6.2 Image reconstruction pipeline. The image reconstruction process begins by translating brain activity patterns into latent representations in a machine vision model. While this procedure is used to be commonly referred to as "feature decoding," here we prefer the term "translation" to emphasize that brain activity itself can be considered a latent representation of an image. This frames the process as a transformation from neural to machine representations. We seek to find a mapping between the brain's mid-level representations and DNN's mid-level representations. In the second step, a generator module utilizes these translated latent features to generate a visual image that corresponds to the content encoded in the original brain activity, thus achieving a reconstruction of the perceived image. Concept and graphic elements adapted from Shen et al. [33], licensed under CC BY 4.0

6.4 DNN Feature Decoding and Brain–AI Alignment

Deep neural networks (DNNs) have become essential tools for modeling visual processing in the brain due to their ability to hierarchically represent visual features, progressing from simple attributes to complex features and objects. Convolutional neural networks (CNNs), such as AlexNet and VGG, have been particularly impactful because their layered structure closely mirrors the multi-stage organization of the human visual cortex—from early stages like the primary visual cortex (V1) to higher-order areas involved in object recognition.

In our approach, the "translator" model, as outlined in the previous section, leverages DNN representations to decode brain activity. First introduced by Horikawa and Kamitani [18], this translator model lies at the core of brain–AI alignment. It maps patterns of brain activity, measured through functional MRI (fMRI), onto the latent feature space of a pre-trained CNN. This linear mapping process effectively "translates" brain signals into corresponding unit activations within the DNN. By doing so, it enables the prediction of how specific regions of the visual cortex respond to various visual features, thus creating a functional bridge between brain and machine representations.

Horikawa and Kamitani [18] established a foundational understanding of the hierarchical correspondence between visual processing in the human brain and artificial neural networks. Their experiments demonstrated that brain activity from early visual areas—those sensitive to fundamental image properties like orientation and contrast—could be accurately decoded into features represented in the early layers of a DNN. As one moves up the visual hierarchy to regions like V4, which process more complex visual information, the corresponding DNN layers reflect increasingly sophisticated patterns, such as object shapes and semantic categories. This discovery underscores both the structural and functional parallels between DNN architectures and biological visual systems, suggesting that DNNs, despite being artificial constructs, effectively replicate key mechanisms of how the brain processes visual information.

The robustness of brain–DNN mappings across different individuals was further confirmed by Horikawa et al. [17] through the use of a standardized dataset of fMRI responses and DNN features. Their findings revealed that the layer-wise correspondence between brain regions and DNN layers is highly reproducible across individuals, further solidifying the reliability of the hierarchical correspondence. This standardized dataset has since become a benchmark in the field, serving as a crucial resource for researchers testing and refining brain decoding models. The high degree of reproducibility underscores the biological validity of the decoded DNN features, making them a powerful tool for studying visual processing in the human brain.

6.5 Visual Image Reconstruction

In brain decoding research, visual image reconstruction involves generating coherent, recognizable images from patterns of neural activity. This process is integral to the "generator" component of our framework, where brain activity is translated into visual representations. While the "translator" section focuses on mapping brain activity to deep neural network (DNN) features, the generator synthesizes these features into the actual images, reconstructing the visual stimuli perceived by the subject.

Early approaches, such as the method developed by Miyawaki et al. [27], laid the groundwork for image reconstruction but did not involve a complex generator. Their method used a straightforward linear combination of image bases to approximate the visual content from brain activity. This involved a fixed set of predefined image bases, where brain activity determined the weights for combining these bases. Although this approach was effective for reconstructing simple shapes and patterns, it was limited in its ability to capture the intricate visual details found in natural images.

As the field progressed, more sophisticated methods were developed to map latent DNN representations to images, an essential task for creating high-quality reconstructions. Unlike the simple basis combination used by Miyawaki et al. [27], mapping the mid- or high-level latent space of DNNs to visual images is not trivial. This challenge led to the development of techniques like the inverse CNN (iCNN) approach, which optimized image generation by iteratively refining the generated image to match the decoded DNN features from brain activity [33]. The iCNN method, as a generator, takes brain-decoded features as input and uses optimization techniques to transform them into visual output, bridging the latent DNN space and the final image.

Figure 6.3 provides examples of the reconstructed images produced by this reconstruction model. These images closely resemble the original stimuli observed by the subjects, showcasing the generator's ability to synthesize accurate visual scenes from brain data. The quality of these reconstructions highlights the efficacy of the latent

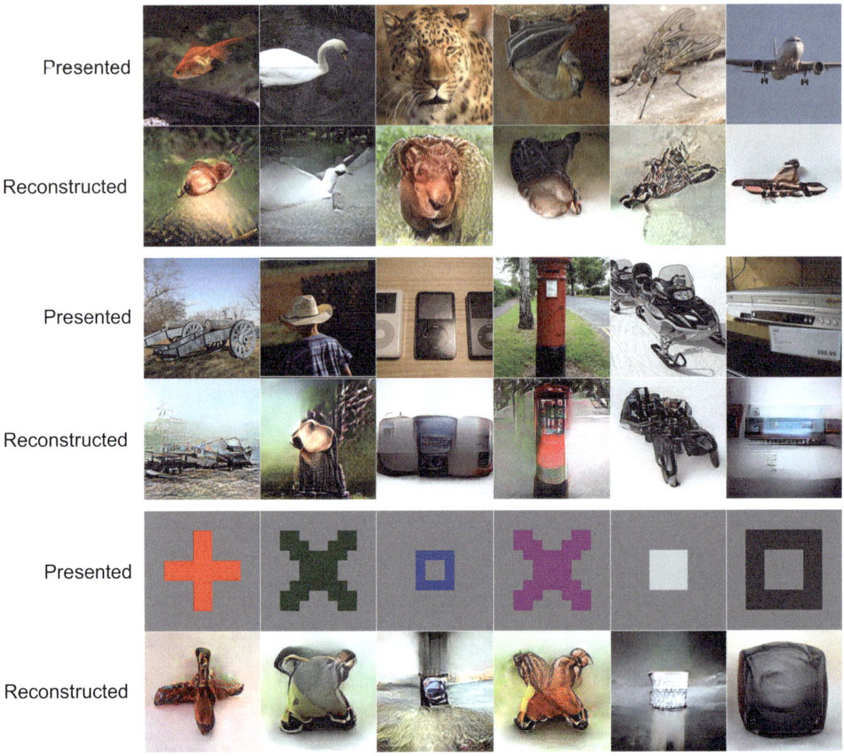

Fig. 6.3 Reconstructed images of perception. Representative examples of visual reconstructions from brain activity recorded during perception. Using trial-averaged fMRI signals from the entire visual cortex, the iCNN method [33], along with updated signal processing techniques [28], generates these visual reconstructions from decoded latent features. The stimuli are composed of (1) images reproduced with permission from the original copyright holders, (2) images licensed under CC BY 2.0, and (3) original images created by the authors

representation from DNN, translator, and generator, which is capable of capturing fine-grained visual experiences.

An alternative approach is the end-to-end deep image reconstruction model [32]. This method bypasses the need to decode brain activity into predefined DNN features, directly learning a mapping from fMRI patterns to visual outputs. In contrast to iCNN's two-step decoding and generation process, this model learns the entire generative procedure, making it a generator-only method in our framework.

The end-to-end model has excelled in material image reconstruction, particularly in capturing key material properties like texture, gloss, and translucency—crucial aspects of Shitsukan, or material perception. Figure 6.4 provides examples of how the model successfully reconstructs material surfaces, such as glossy textures, demonstrating its ability to represent fine-grained visual features essential for understanding complex perceptual experiences.

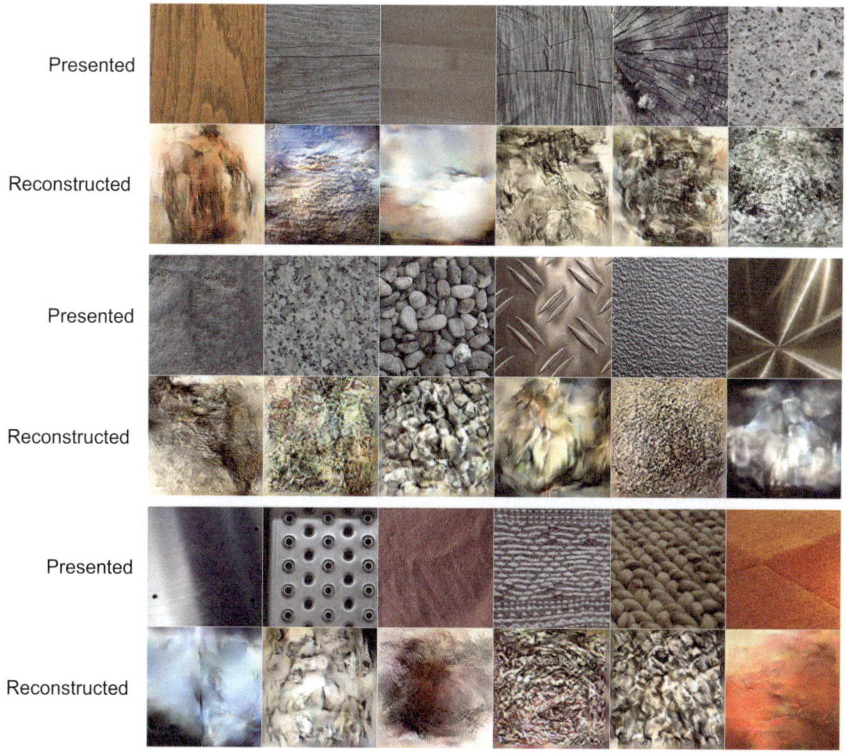

Fig. 6.4 Reconstructed images of material perception. Visual reconstructions from brain activity during material perception. Using trial-averaged fMRI signals from the entire visual cortex, the end-to-end deep image reconstruction model [32] reconstructs material-specific features, such as gloss and texture, from neural data. The stimuli were adopted from the Material Image Database (MID) [38]

6.6 Externalizing Subjective Experiences

One of the most exciting frontiers in brain decoding research is the ability to externalize subjective experiences, such as mental imagery, attention, and perceptual illusions, by reconstructing these internal states into visual representations. While traditional neural decoding methods focus on mapping externally presented stimuli to neural activity, recent advancements extend these techniques to capture experiences that originate within the mind. This approach hinges on the assumption that subjective experiences share a common representational framework with perceptual processes, making it possible to leverage models trained on stimulus-driven brain activity to decode and visualize internally generated content.

The basic strategy for reconstructing subjective experiences involves two main steps. First, a reconstruction model is trained using brain activity elicited by external visual stimuli. During this phase, subjects view a set of images while their brain responses are recorded, creating a training dataset that maps specific features of the stimuli to patterns of neural activity. Because the stimulus features are known, the resulting model can be calibrated to accurately translate neural signals into visual outputs, ensuring that the reconstructed images reflect the original stimuli. This training phase establishes a robust link between external visual features and their corresponding neural representations.

The model is then tested on brain activity collected during subjective experiences, such as mental imagery or attention-modulated perception. The assumption is that brain activity will overlap between external perception and internal experiences for similar visual content. For example, imagining a familiar object—like an apple—activates neural circuits similar to those used when seeing it. By applying a model trained on stimulus-driven brain activity to these subjective tasks, one can evaluate how closely the internal representations of subjective experiences align with those from external stimuli.

This framework allows researchers to assess not only whether the reconstructions reflect the external stimuli but also to what extent they capture the subjective visual experiences. By training on stimulus-driven brain activity, the model learns the fundamental correspondences between neural signals and visual content, enabling it to be applied to subjective experiences where exact features are not provided.

An example of this approach is the work by Shen et al. [33], where a model trained on perception-based brain activity was applied to decode mental imagery. Before brain scans, subjects were familiarized with test images, which are supposed to be remembered to imagine during fMRI scans. During the fMRI experiment, subjects were asked to imagine these same images while their brain activity was recorded. These test data were analyzed to create reconstructions using the perception-trained reconstruction model.

Figure 6.5 shows the reconstructions of mental imagery. The decoded images reveal a close match between the reconstructions derived from mental imagery and those from perception, particularly for simple shapes. However, more complex images remain challenging to reconstruct accurately. This may indicate a discrepancy between the neural representations of imagery and perception. Further research is needed to better understand these differences and improve the reconstruction of more intricate visual experiences.

Similarly, Horikawa and Kamitani [19] explored the influence of attention on visual perception using a model trained on stimulus-driven neural activity. In their study, they demonstrated that by modulating attention, subjects could alter the neural representation of the same stimulus. The stimulus consisted of two overlapping natural images, and subjects were instructed to focus their attention on one of them. The reconstruction model, which had been trained on brain activity induced by stimuli without attention modulation, was applied to decode the brain activity during selective attention. The researchers successfully reconstructed images that emphasized the features of the attended image, thereby externalizing the subjective experience of selective attention. This finding demonstrates that the same visual stimulus can be

Fig. 6.5 Reconstructed images of visual imagery. Representative examples of visual reconstructions derived from brain activity during visual imagery tasks. The same model used for perception-based reconstruction (Fig. 6.3) was applied here, where the translator was trained on brain responses to natural images. It was then used to decode trial-averaged brain activity recorded while subjects imagined these images on a blank screen, recalling the images they had been familiarized with prior to the fMRI experiment. Similar to the perception-based reconstructions, the visual outputs were generated from the decoded latent representations using the iCNN method [33], further refined by an updated signal processing pipeline [28]. The stimuli are composed of (1) original images created by the authors, (2) images reproduced with permission from the original copyright holders, and (3) images purchased under license

decoded into different reconstructions depending on the observer's internal cognitive state, highlighting the role of attention in shaping visual representation.

Another demonstration comes from Cheng et al. [6], where visual illusions were reconstructed using a similar framework. Visual illusions often create perceptual experiences that do not correspond to the actual physical properties of a stimulus, making them an ideal case for studying the brain's internal models of reality. Cheng et al. trained a decoding model on neural data from veridical perception and applied it to fMRI patterns elicited by illusory stimuli, such as illusory lines and neon-color spreading, which induce the subjective appearance of lines and colors that do not physically exist. The reconstructed images effectively captured the illusory content as perceived by the subjects, even when it deviated from the physical reality of the stimulus (Fig. 6.6). This result suggests that the brain's interpretation of visual inputs during illusions is encoded similarly to standard perception, enabling the reconstruction of altered perceptual states.

While these findings highlight the utility of assuming a shared representational space between perception and subjective experience, this assumption is not always straightforward. Subjective experiences, shaped by individual history and cognitive

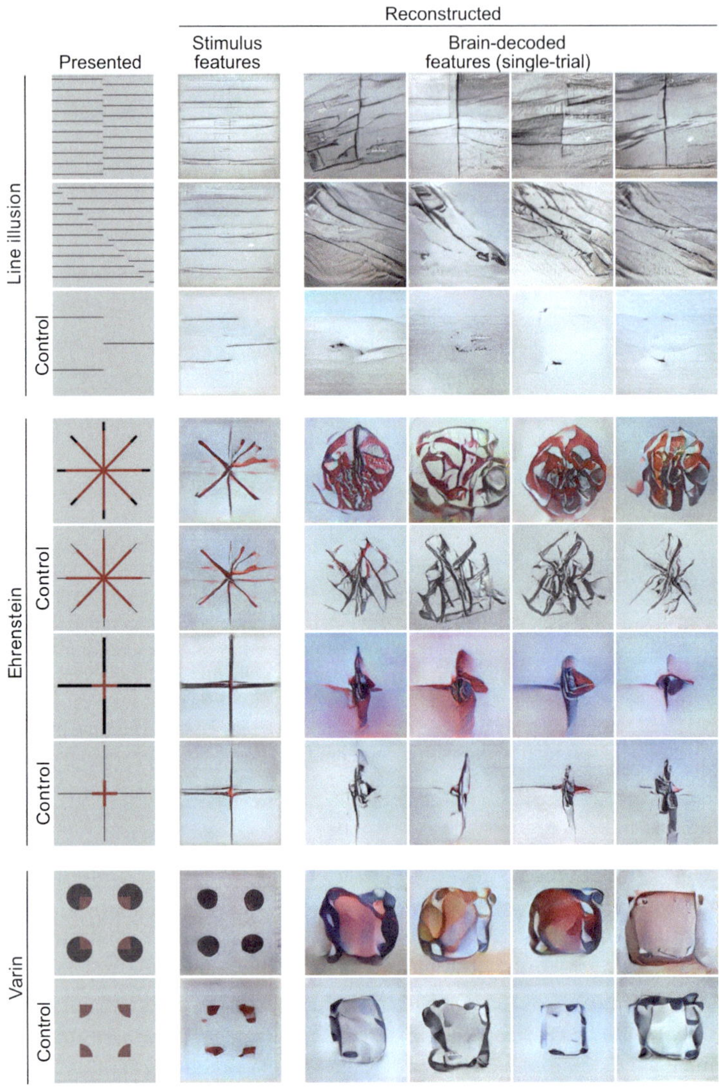

Fig. 6.6 Reconstructed images of illusory perception. Representative examples of visual reconstructions derived from brain activity recorded while subjects viewed illusory images. The reconstruction model, trained on single-trial fMRI signals from the entire visual cortex in response to natural images, was applied to decode brain activity elicited by the illusory stimuli. The resulting reconstructions successfully capture the illusory content as perceived by the subjects. As a control, we included reconstructions from non-illusory images with similar visual elements. Additionally, we confirmed that stimulus-derived latent features alone are insufficient to explain the perceptual attributes unique to illusory perception. Adapted from Cheng et al. [6], licensed under CC BY 4.0

states, can introduce neural variability not captured by models trained solely on perception data. For instance, imagining abstract or personalized concepts may activate different neural circuits, leading to less accurate reconstructions.

To address this, models could be trained on brain activity from subjective tasks, such as voluntary imagery, to better capture internal visual generation. Additionally, incorporating multimodal data, including emotional and contextual information, could enhance the decoding of subjective experiences. Refining models to handle the complexity of internal states is essential for improving the accuracy of these reconstructions and deepening our understanding of how the brain represents subjective experiences.

6.7 Neural Code Conversion

The challenges of brain decoding stem from individual variability in neural representations. Despite general anatomical consistency, fine-scale differences in cortical structure and neural response patterns complicate translating brain activity into a shared representational space. This often requires subject-specific training, limiting the scalability of brain decoding models and their application in large-scale studies or clinical settings.

Small differences in cortical folding and neural coding schemes result in divergent brain activity patterns, even with identical stimuli. This makes it difficult to develop universal decoders that work across individuals. Functional alignment techniques, such as hyperalignment, attempt to standardize neural responses by aligning brain activity across subjects [12]. While effective at harmonizing large-scale patterns, it has not been shown that fine-scale representations representing detailed perceptual contents can be preserved, which is necessary for high-fidelity image reconstruction.

Recent work addresses this challenge by mapping fine-scale neural codes between individuals using a neural code converter [39]. This method aligns brain activity across subjects by presenting the same set of stimuli and training a machine learning model to translate one subject's brain activity into another's while preserving the underlying visual content. Ho et al. [15] advanced this approach by translating the converted brain activity into DNN latent representations and generating reconstructions using a neural generator. They examined brain activity across the hierarchical visual pathway, exploring how the converter established correspondences between two brains and how these correspondences aligned with the DNN's hierarchical structure.

The results showed that the converted brain activity accurately decoded the DNN features of the stimulus. The converter automatically mapped hierarchical correspondences between subjects. This alignment extended to DNN layers, confirming a close match between neural activity and DNN representations. Using the converted brain activity and decoded DNN features, they successfully reconstructed images across individuals, achieving inter-individual decoding and reconstruction, where one subject's brain data was used to reconstruct perceived images using another subject's trained decoder.

These developments have significant implications for large-scale neuroscience and clinical applications, where brain activity can now be decoded across diverse populations. Neural code conversion opens the door to scalable, universal decoding models that generalize across contexts and individuals, much like foundation models in artificial intelligence. This approach paves the way for broader applications, including personalized brain–computer interfaces and inter-subject neural communication, revolutionizing the potential of brain decoding research.

6.8 Challenges and Critical Evaluations

The field of brain decoding has seen remarkable progress in recent years, largely driven by the application of deep neural networks (DNNs) and generative models that enable researchers to decode and reconstruct perceptual and cognitive states from brain activity. However, this rapid advancement has sparked debate, particularly regarding the use of DNNs as models of the visual system and the validity of current reconstruction methods. Critics emphasize the need for more rigorous validation, better interpretative frameworks, and caution against over-interpreting results that may reflect model artifacts rather than genuine neural correspondence.

One key area of criticism is the concept of the brain–AI hierarchical correspondence, which suggests that DNNs' hierarchical feature representations mirror the neural processing layers in the human visual cortex [18, 23, 40]. Nonaka et al. [29] argued that while models like AlexNet and VGG exhibit similarities to early and mid-level visual processing, this alignment is not universal (Fig. 6.7). Their study found that only a limited subset of DNNs showed strong correspondence to neural representations, primarily in early feedforward models. This highlights the need to develop models that more accurately mimic human visual processing, making them better proxies for translating latent representations between humans and machines.

Many initial studies relied on neural encoding accuracies of DNN features to assess brain-like properties, but recent critiques suggest that this metric does not fully capture the true similarity between DNNs and the brain [3, 7, 31]. As a result, there is growing demand for more nuanced evaluations of brain–AI methodologies, with a focus on understanding how well these models truly reflect human neural processing.

A significant issue in the field is spurious reconstruction, where generated images appear realistic but do not accurately reflect the underlying brain activity. Shirakawa et al. [34] raised this concern in their study of text-guided generative AI methods, which have gained popularity in recent image reconstruction research. These methods often rely on text features from pre-trained models like Contrastive Language–Image Pretraining (CLIP) as well as visual features as targets for decoding. The decoded

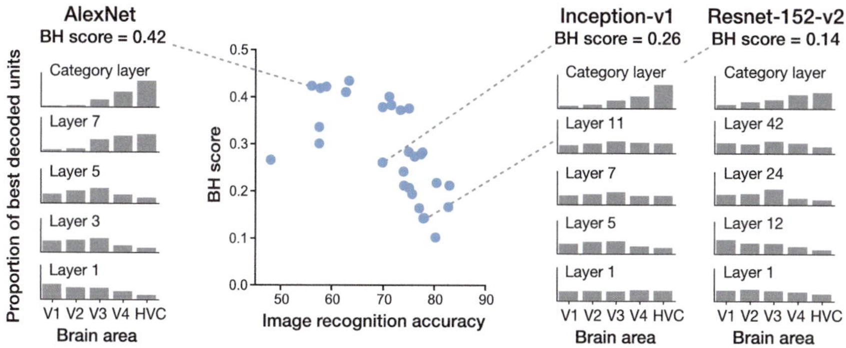

Fig. 6.7 Brain hierarchy (BH) score. The brain hierarchy (BH) score is a metric used to quantify the alignment between the hierarchical structure of deep neural network (DNN) architectures and the human visual system. It evaluates how closely the representational patterns in each DNN layer correspond to the hierarchical organization of brain activity across visual cortical regions, such as V1, V2, V4, and higher-order areas. This figure illustrates the relationship between BH scores and ImageNet top-1 accuracy, showing how brain-like hierarchical organization correlates with task performance in various DNN architectures. It also visualizes the distribution of top regions of interest (ROIs) across layers for AlexNet, Inception-v1, and ResNet-152-v2, offering insights into the layer-wise correspondence between DNN units and brain regions. Adapted from Nonaka et al. [29], licensed under CC BY 4.0

features are then used to generate images through diffusion models. However, Shirakawa et al. demonstrated that such models can produce visually convincing images that match the text prompts but not the true content of brain-derived signals. This creates a risk of inflated results, where the images appear plausible but are not grounded in genuine neural data. The problem is compounded when researchers cherry-pick results from multiple reconstruction attempts, each producing different outputs.

A related issue is the limited diversity of training data. The Natural Scenes Dataset (NSD) [1], a widely used benchmark for brain decoding, is designed to cover a broad range of visual categories, but Shirakawa et al. [34] found that its diversity is limited. The dataset consists of a small number of semantic categories with similar visual features, which are shared between the training and test sets. This lack of diversity hinders the ability of decoders trained on this dataset to generalize beyond the categories included, limiting their real-world applicability. This can lead to "output dimension collapse," where the translation from brain activity to latent features becomes confined to the subspace of DNN features driven by the narrow range of training stimuli. As a result, outputs fail to capture the true variability of visual inputs, though spuriously good results may occur if training and test stimuli are similar.

The choice of latent representation is critical for the accuracy of visual reconstructions. Shirakawa et al. [34] emphasized that the latent space must map coherently onto the image space to ensure that generated images truly reflect neural activity. While vision-based DNN features map well to images, even at higher layers, text features like CLIP embeddings do not map as accurately to the original image. To address this, they suggest using compositional representations that preserve the complexity and richness of visual experiences.

As the field moves forward, researchers need to take a more critical approach, rigorously evaluating each model's assumptions and limitations, and exploring alternative approaches beyond the current NeuroAI framework. This includes developing better metrics for assessing the similarity between brain activity and DNNs, refining latent spaces and translation methods, and ensuring that generative outputs are grounded in genuine neural data rather than superficial correlations. By addressing these challenges, the field can build a stronger foundation for decoding and understanding the brain's representation of visual and subjective experiences.

6.9 Discussion

The preceding sections have explored the core methodologies and advancements in brain decoding, particularly in the context of visual experiences and the complex phenomenon of Shitsukan. We began by reviewing the foundations of brain decoding, tracing the evolution from early feature-based models to advanced deep neural networks (DNNs) capable of capturing the nuanced details of perceptual content. Central to this approach is the translator–generator pipeline, which decodes brain activity into DNN features and reconstructs detailed visual representations, enabling the decoding of not only external stimuli but also subjective states such as mental imagery, attention, and perceptual illusions. Additionally, the development of inter-individual decoding models has addressed individual variability in neural representations, opening the door to scalable, universal approaches. However, challenges remain, such as spurious reconstructions and the need for improved alignment between brain and DNN features, underscoring the importance of ongoing refinement and validation in these brain decoding techniques.

Against this technical backdrop, a central question arises: what exactly is Shitsukan? From an evolutionary perspective, Shitsukan plays a crucial role in how we interact with our environment. While basic visual attributes like color and shape help us identify objects, Shitsukan provides essential information about how we might engage with or respond to them. The ability to perceive material qualities stems from a deeper evolutionary drive: the need to predict and model our surroundings. Early in evolution, organisms developed the motility to seek energy and survive [2]. As mobility became essential, so did the capacity to internally simulate the environment, allowing organisms to anticipate changes without direct interaction. This led to increasingly complex sensory and cognitive systems capable of representing the world not as static objects but as dynamic surfaces, textures, and affordances.

In humans, this evolutionary path took a unique turn [2]. Our intelligence evolved to simulate the environment in more sophisticated ways such that physical movement became less central to survival. Instead of engaging with every aspect of our surroundings, we developed the ability to create rich internal models, integrating visual, tactile, and even social cues. Our brains evolved to construct rich representations of

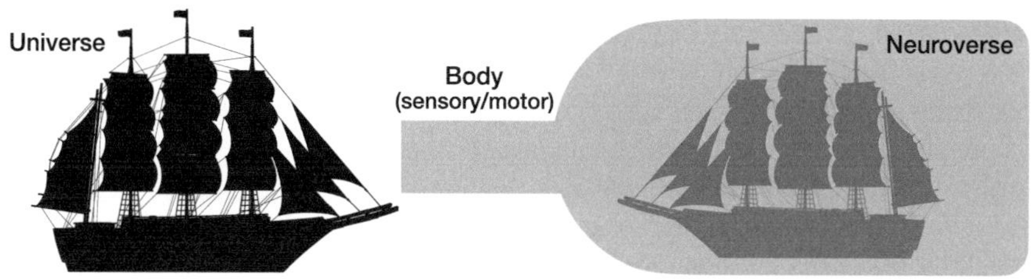

Fig. 6.8 Neuroverse refers to the brain's internal model of the experienced reality, updated by the limited sensory information it receives via the "bottleneck." Just as the physical world is termed the *universe*, the brain's internal representation of the reality is called the Neuroverse

the external world, simulating not only physical interactions but also the thoughts and intentions of others. This capacity for simulation lies at the heart of Shitsukan, enabling us to perceive subtle material properties without direct interaction.

Our work in brain decoding has shed light on the neural basis of Shitsukan. By using advanced techniques to decode and reconstruct perceptual experiences, we have demonstrated how these qualities are encoded in the visual cortex. More importantly, our approach goes beyond reconstructing basic visual stimuli to capture subjective experiences, such as mental imagery and attention-modulated perception. However, these reconstructions still largely reflect the form of immediate visual data the retina receives from the environment. This sensory-based decoding does not fully capture the deeper representational structures that shape our perception of reality.

As many lines of studies suggest, we believe that the brain's representations are not simple reflections of sensory inputs but models of the underlying causes of those inputs. This perspective aligns with predictive coding and the free energy principle, which suggest that the brain continuously generates and refines predictions about the world based on sensory inputs [9, 30]. In this view, perception is not the direct interpretation of raw sensory data but an inference about the world that best explains that data. This inferential process gives rise to the perceptual richness of Shitsukan, allowing us to experience material qualities in a way that transcends direct sensory input.

To fully capture these internal representations, we introduce the concept of the *Neuroverse*, the brain's comprehensive internal model of the external world (Fig. 6.8). Just as the universe encompasses all that exists physically, the Neuroverse represents the brain's integrated simulation of reality. This model is continuously updated through sensory and interoceptive input, interaction, and interpretation. Until now, our research has focused on externalizing small components of the Neuroverse, such as visual features and subjective imagery. The next challenge lies in reconstructing the Neuroverse as a whole, capturing the brain's broader expectations, interpretations, and predictions—beyond what is directly defined by the sensory space.

The Neuroverse offers a new framework for understanding how the brain constructs its perceptual reality. It suggests that the neural basis of Shitsukan, and perception more broadly, is not merely a mapping of sensory attributes but the active generation of an internal model of the world. This model is informed not only by visual cues but also by interoceptive signals, our perception of internal bodily states, that shape our emotional and visceral responses. Interoception plays a crucial role in our subjective experience, influencing, for instance, whether we perceive textures as pleasant or threatening and surfaces as inviting or repulsive. Thus, a full understanding of Shitsukan must integrate both external sensory data and internal bodily signals to reflect the full complexity of how we experience material qualities of the world.

By moving toward this integrative understanding, we can bridge the gap between the raw, stimulus-bound reconstructions we have achieved so far, and the rich, subjective experiences that define our perception of the material world. This approach not only deepens our understanding of Shitsukan but also sheds light on broader questions of consciousness, embodiment, and the nature of perceptual reality. The concept of the Neuroverse represents a stepping stone toward a more holistic view of brain function—one that includes not just the sensory aspects of perception but also the brain's ability to construct and navigate an intricate, evolving model of the world. Through this lens, the study of Shitsukan becomes key to unlocking deeper principles of human perception and intelligence.

References

1. Allen, E.J., St-Yves, G., Wu, Y., Breedlove, J.L., Prince, J.S., Dowdle, L.T., Nau, M., Caron, B., Pestilli, F., Charest, I., Hutchinson, J.B., Naselaris, T., Kay, K.: A massive 7T fMRI dataset to bridge cognitive neuroscience and artificial intelligence. Nat. Neurosci. **25**, 116–126 (2021)
2. Bennett, M.: A Brief History of Intelligence: Evolution, AI, and the Five Breakthroughs That Made Our Brains. Mariner Books, New York (2023)
3. Bowers, J.S., Malhotra, G., Dujmović, M., Montero, M.L., Tsvetkov, C., Biscione, V., Puebla, G., Adolfi, F., Hummel, J.E., Heaton, R.F., Evans, B.D.: Deep problems with neural network models of human vision. Behav. Brain Sci. **46**, e385 (2023)
4. Chadwick, A.C., Heywood, C.A., Smithson, H.E., Kentridge, R.W.: Translucence perception is not dependent on cortical areas critical for processing colour or texture. Neuropsychologia **128**, 209–214 (2019)
5. Chadwick, A.C., Kentridge, R.W.: The perception of gloss: a review. Vision. Res. **109**, 221–235 (2015)
6. Cheng, F.L., Horikawa, T., Majima, K., Tanaka, M., Abdelhack, M., Aoki, S.C., Hirano, J., Kamitani, Y.: Reconstructing visual illusory experiences from human brain activity. Sci. Adv. **9**(46), eadj3906 (2023)
7. Conwell, C., Prince, J.S., Kay, K.N., Alvarez, G.A., Konkle, T.: What can 1.8 billion regressions tell us about the pressures shaping high-level visual representation in brains and machines? (2023)
8. Doerig, A., Sommers, R.P., Seeliger, K., Richards, B., Ismael, J., Lindsay, G.W., Kording, K.P., Konkle, T., Van Gerven, M.A., Kriegeskorte, N., Kietzmann, T.C.: The neuroconnectionist research programme. Nat. Rev. Neurosci. **24**(7), 431–450 (2023)
9. Friston, K.: The free-energy principle: a unified brain theory? Nat. Rev. Neurosci. **11**(2), 127–138 (2010)
10. Goodfellow, I.J., Pouget-Abadie, J., Mirza, M., Xu, B., Warde-Farley, D., Ozair, S., Courville, A., Bengio, Y.: Generative adversarial nets. In: Advances in Neural Information Processing Systems 27 (NIPS2014), Montreal, December 2014 (2014)

11. Haxby, J.V., Gobbini, M.I., Furey, M.L., Ishai, A., Schouten, J.L., Pietrini, P.: Distributed and overlapping representations of faces and objects in ventral temporal cortex. Science **293**(5539), 2425–2430 (2001)
12. Haxby, J.V., Guntupalli, J.S., Nastase, S.A., Feilong, M.: Hyperalignment: modeling shared information encoded in idiosyncratic cortical topographies. eLife **9**, e56601 (2020)
13. He, K., Zhang, X., Ren, S., Sun, J.: Deep residual learning for image recognition. In: IEEE Conference on Computer Vision and Pattern Recognition (CVPR2016), Las Vegas, June 2016, pp. 770–778 (2016)
14. Ho, J., Jain, A., Abbeel, P.: Denoising diffusion probabilistic models. In: Advances in Neural Information Processing Systems 33 (NIPS2020), Virtual-only, December 2020, pp. 6840–6851 (2020)
15. Ho, J.K., Horikawa, T., Majima, K., Cheng, F., Kamitani, Y.: Inter-individual deep image reconstruction via hierarchical neural code conversion. Neuroimage **271**, 120007 (2023)
16. Horikawa, T., Tamaki, M., Miyawaki, Y., Kamitani, Y.: Neural decoding of visual imagery during sleep. Science **340**(6132), 639–642 (2013)
17. Horikawa, T., Aoki, S.C., Tsukamoto, M., Kamitani, Y.: Characterization of deep neural network features by decodability from human brain activity. Sci. Data **6**, 190012 (2019)
18. Horikawa, T., Kamitani, Y.: Generic decoding of seen and imagined objects using hierarchical visual features. Nat. Commun. **8**, 15037 (2017)
19. Horikawa, T., Kamitani, Y.: Attention modulates neural representation to render reconstructions according to subjective appearance. Commun. Biol. **5**(1), 34 (2022)
20. Kamitani, Y., Sawahata, Y.: Spatial smoothing hurts localization but not information: pitfalls for brain mappers. Neuroimage **49**(3), 1949–1952 (2010)
21. Kamitani, Y., Tong, F.: Decoding the visual and subjective contents of the human brain. Nat. Neurosci. **8**(5), 679–85 (2005)
22. Kamitani, Y., Tong, F.: Decoding seen and attended motion directions from activity in the human visual cortex. Curr. Biol. **16**(11), 1096–1102 (2006)
23. Khaligh-Razavi, S.-M., Kriegeskorte, N.: Deep supervised, but not unsupervised, models may explain IT cortical representation. PLoS Comput. Biol. **10**(11), e1003915 (2014)
24. Komatsu, H., Goda, N.: Neural mechanisms of material perception: quest on Shitsukan. Neuroscience **392**, 329–347 (2018)
25. Krizhevsky, A., Sutskever, I., Hinton, G.E.: ImageNet classification with deep convolutional neural networks. In: Advances in Neural Information Processing Systems 25 (NIPS2012), Nevada, December 2012, pp. 1097–1105 (2012)
26. Macpherson, T., Churchland, A., Sejnowski, T., DiCarlo, J., Kamitani, Y., Takahashi, H., Hikida, T.: Natural and artificial intelligence: a brief introduction to the interplay between AI and neuroscience research. Neural Netw. **144**, 603–613 (2021)
27. Miyawaki, Y., Uchida, H., Yamashita, O., Sato, M., Morito, Y., Tanabe, H.C., Sadato, N., Kamitani, Y.: Visual image reconstruction from human brain activity using a combination of multiscale local image decoders. Neuron **60**(5), 915–929 (2008)
28. Muraki, Y.: Perceptual image reconstruction from brain activity considering spatial characteristics of DNN feature maps. Master's thesis, Kyoto university (2024)
29. Nonaka, S., Majima, K., Aoki, S.C., Kamitani, Y.: Brain hierarchy score: which deep neural networks are hierarchically brain-like? iScience **24**(9), 103013 (2021)
30. Seth, A.K., Suzuki, K., Critchley, H.D.: An interoceptive predictive coding model of conscious presence. Front. Psychol. **2** (2012)
31. Sexton, N.J., Love, B.C.: Reassessing hierarchical correspondences between brain and deep networks through direct interface. Sci. Adv. **8**(28), eabm2219 (2022)
32. Shen, G., Dwivedi, K., Majima, K., Horikawa, T., Kamitani, Y.: End-to-end deep image reconstruction from human brain activity. Front. Comput. Neurosci. **13**, 21 (2019)
33. Shen, G., Horikawa, T., Majima, K., Kamitani, Y.: Deep image reconstruction from human brain activity. PLoS Comput. Biol. **15**(1), 1006633 (2019)
34. Shirakawa, K., Nagano, Y., Tanaka, M., Aoki, S.C., Muraki, Y., Majima, K., Kamitani, Y.: Spurious reconstruction from brain activity. Neural Netw. **190**, 603–613 (107515) (2024)

35. Simonyan, K., Zisserman, A.: Very deep convolutional networks for large-scale image recognition (2015)
36. Soon, C.S., Brass, M., Heinze, H.J., Haynes, J.D.: Unconscious determinants of free decisions in the human brain. Nat. Neurosci. **11**(5), 543–545 (2008)
37. Szegedy, C., Liu, W., Jia, Y., Sermanet, P., Reed, S., Anguelov, D., Erhan, D., Vanhoucke, V., Rabinovich, A.: Going deeper with convolutions. In: IEEE Conference on Computer Vision and Pattern Recognition (CVPR2015), Boston, June 2015, pp. 1–9 (2015)
38. Wiebel, C.B., Valsecchi, M., Gegenfurtner, K.R.: The speed and accuracy of material recognition in natural images. Atten. Percept. Psychophys. **75**, 954–966 (2013)
39. Yamada, K., Miyawaki, Y., Kamitani, Y.: Inter-subject neural code converter for visual image representation. Neuroimage **113**, 289–297 (2015)
40. Yamins, D.L., DiCarlo, J.J.: Using goal-driven deep learning models to understand sensory cortex. Nat. Neurosci. **19**(3), 356–365 (2016)

Chapter 7
The Neural Processing of Shitsukan Perception

Hidehiko Komatsu

Abstract Material perception likely plays a significant role in the understanding of Shitsukan in the real world. Significant advancements have been made in recent years on the understanding of neural mechanisms related to material perception especially in the domain of vision. Many studies provide converging evidence that the ventral visual pathway, one of the cortical visual pathways, processes information related to material perception. Information on the natural texture that is tightly related to the categorization of materials is hierarchically processed in the middle visual areas along the ventral visual pathway, and multimodal impression of materials is formed in the higher ventral visual areas as a result of association between visual and tactile experiences of objects. Information on the surface reflection properties of objects which is another important aspect of material perception, is also represented in the ventral higher visual area. Neurons selectively responsive to object images of specific reflection properties are recorded in the macaque monkey, and it is found that these neurons precisely represent perceptual gloss parameters defined by human psychophysics experiments on gloss perception.

Keywords Cerebral cortex · Ventral visual pathway · Gloss perception · Texture perception

7.1 Brain Structure Related to Vision

Information from the outside world is converted from physical energy into nerve signals by peripheral sensory receptor cells. The converted nerve signals are transmitted to the cerebrum through sensory nerves. In the cerebrum, which occupies most of the skull, most of the nerve cells are concentrated on the surface of the cerebral

---

H. Komatsu (✉)
National Institute for Basic Biology, Okazaki-Shi, Aichi, Japan
e-mail: komatsu@nips.ac.jp

Brain Science Institute, Tamagawa University, Machida-shi, Tokyo, Japan

National Institute for Physiological Sciences, Okazaki-shi, Aichi, Japan

S. Nishida and K. Nishino (eds.), *Shitsukan—Understanding and Manipulating Material and Quality Perception*, https://doi.org/10.1007/978-981-95-4762-3_7

cortex. The cerebral cortex is a sheet-like structure with nerve cells densely arranged 2–3 mm thick (Fig. 7.1a). Each area of the cerebral cortex receives different signals and is involved in different functions. If you look closely, you will also see that the arrangement of cells is different, and they have different names. The area related to vision (visual cortex) occupies a wide area at the back of the cerebral cortex.

Let's take a look at how visual information related to material perception, a key task for Shitsukan understanding, is sent from the sensory organs to the cerebrum. The visual sensory receptor cells (photoreceptor cells) that receive light energy and convert it into nerve signals are located in the retina of the eye, and signals from the eye are relayed by the nerve cells of the lateral geniculate body through the optic nerve and then head to the cerebral cortex. The area that first receives visual signals in the cerebral cortex is called the primary visual cortex (or V1), located at the very back of the cortex (Fig. 7.1b).

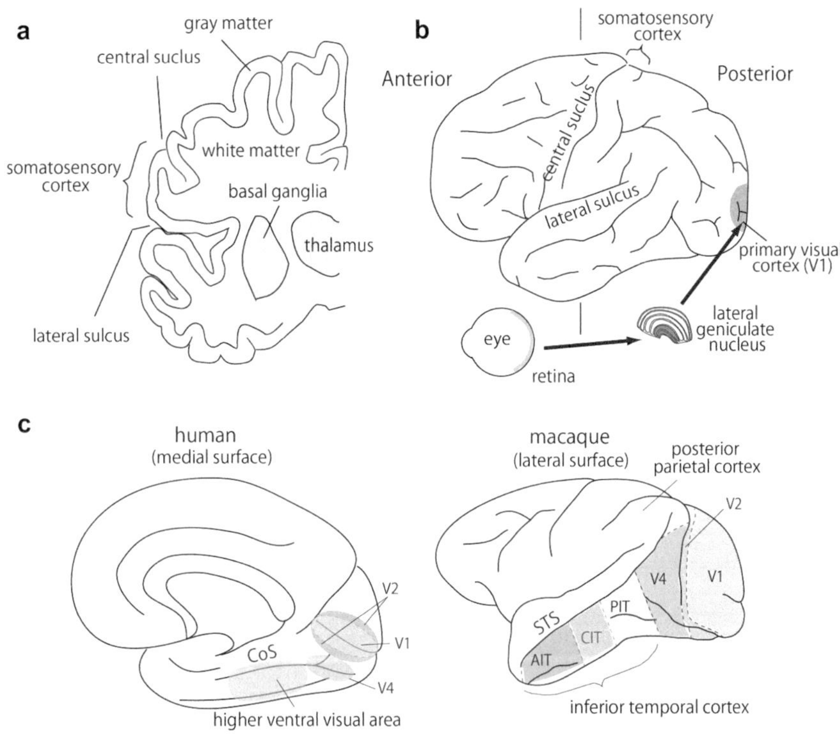

Fig. 7.1 **a** Schematic illustration of the structure of the cerebrum. **b** Lateral view of the cerebral cortex and the visual pathway from the eye to the cerebral cortex. Vertical lines indicate the position of the cross section depicted in A. **c** Schematic illustration of the visual cortical areas belonging to the ventral visual pathway in humans (left, medial view) and in the macaque monkey (right, lateral view). AIT: anterior part of the inferior temporal cortex, CIT: central part of the inferior temporal cortex, PIT: posterior part of the inferior temporal cortex, CoS: collateral sulcus, STS: superior temporal sulcus

There are two types of photoreceptor cells, which are the starting point of visual processing: rods, which are involved in visual functions in dim environments, and cones, which are involved in visual functions in bright environments. There are three types of cones with different spectral sensitivity characteristics, and color vision occurs by taking the difference between the signals from the different types of cones. Information on various attributes related to visual perception, including shape, movement, depth, and texture is contained in the signals from the same photoreceptor cells, and is extracted in subsequent information processing.

7.2 Information Processing in the Early Visual System

In the neural circuits of the retina, information on brightness and color is extracted by taking the difference between signals detected by adjacent photoreceptor cells. The area of the visual field that each cell in the visual nervous system is responsible for (receptive field) has a concentric structure for cells that send signals from the retina and cells in the lateral geniculate nucleus (LGN). The polarity of the response is different between the center and the periphery of the concentric receptive field. For example, in one type of cell, when the center responds to an increase in light intensity (on response), the periphery responds to a decrease in light intensity (off response). In another type of cell, the center shows an off response and the periphery shows an on response. In this way, because the center and the periphery have different response polarities, cells with concentric receptive fields respond more strongly when there is a change in brightness, that is, a contrast, on the receptive field than when there is no change in brightness. However, the strength of the response of cells in the retina and LGN does not depend on the direction of the light–dark contrast in the visual field. On the other hand, there are many cells in the primary visual cortex whose response strength changes depending on the direction (orientation) of the light–dark contrast in the visual field. Since the contour of an object has a light–dark contrast in a specific orientation, these cells have orientation selectivity and strongly responds to contours in a specific orientation [19].

Cells that show orientation selectivity include simple cells, in which the areas that show on-responses and the areas that show off-responses are separated in the visual field, and complex cells, in which they are not separated [16]. The response of cells with orientation selectivity also depends on how the contrast of light and dark changes in the visual field. For example, some cells respond strongly to patterns in which the light–dark contrast changes over a short distance, while other cells respond strongly to patterns that change slowly over a long distance. These cells are also selective for the spatial period of repetition of the light–dark contrast, or for the spatial frequency. In this way, a group of cells that have selectivity for both the local orientation and spatial frequency of the visual field can be considered to represent images as Gabor wavelets [7]. In addition, V1 contains a variety of cells with selectivity not seen in the stages before LGN, such as selectivity for motion direction, binocular disparity, and hue-saturation selectivity [8].

Visual information processed in V1 is sent to the anterior visual cortex. Approximately, 30 areas are distinguished in the visual cortex [9]. These areas are named, for example, V2 and V4 (Fig. 7.1c). Most of the signals from V1 are transmitted to V2, which is located immediately in front of V1, and the information processed in V2 is transmitted to the anterior areas. In this way, the visual cortex processes information hierarchically. In addition, there are two destinations of higher brain areas for signals from V2: one is in the anterior and lower direction, namely, ventral higher visual cortex and the other is in the anterior superior direction, namely, parietal association cortex. Each visual cortical area is positioned on a route to one of these destinations. These routes are functionally different, with the route to the higher ventral visual cortex (ventral visual pathway) transmitting information related to object recognition, and the route to the parietal association cortex (dorsal visual pathway) transmitting information related to spatial cognition and motion processing. Previous studies have shown that the ventral visual pathway transmits various information related to material perception [22]. The orientation selectivity of V1 cells was first revealed in a study using cats [15], but research on the functioning of the visual cortical areas has since focused on macaque monkeys which have visual functions similar to those of humans. It is known that the structure of the visual cortex in macaque monkeys and humans is also very similar [38], and the studies described in the following sections are based on findings in macaque monkeys unless noted as human studies.

7.3 Visual Information Processing in the Ventral Pathway

Image features extracted in the early and middle stages of the ventral visual pathway of the cerebral cortex are transmitted to the higher ventral visual cortex. The higher ventral visual cortex is located anterior to area V4 and is involved in the discrimination and identification of complex image information such as objects, faces, bodies, and letters [6]. In monkeys, it corresponds to a brain area called the inferior temporal cortex. The inferior temporal cortex has many cells that respond to complex image features compared to the early and middle stages, and it has been shown that the hierarchical information processing from the early stage of the visual cortex to the inferior temporal cortex corresponds well to the processing of artificial neural networks that have high ability to recognize object images [41].

The ventral visual pathway processes various information related to object recognition, such as shape, color, and depth. Regarding shape, the information on the orientation of the local contour extracted in V1 is spatially integrated as the stages progress. Area V2 represents angles formed by combining contours [17], while area V4 represents the curvature of contours, and it has been shown that complex shapes are represented by the activity of V4 neuronal populations [34]. The ventral visual pathway also processes binocular disparity information, and the gradient of binocular disparity is combined to represent three-dimensional curved object shapes [18].

Color information is extracted by taking the difference between signals from cones in the retina, but in areas prior to V1, color is represented by two types of neurons corresponding to the two axes of color space, *L-M* and $S - (L + M)$. However, in V1, the responses of these neurons are nonlinearly combined to form selectivity for various hues and saturations [21]. It has been shown that in the ventral visual pathway, sharper hue selectivity is created, and separation of color and luminance information progresses in the inferior temporal cortex [28].

As one progresses through the stages of the ventral visual pathway, the number of cells that selectively respond to complex features that combine shape, pattern, and color information increases [20]. In addition, the inferior temporal cortex contains neurons that respond strongly to face patterns (face neurons), and that such neurons are clustered in multiple small areas of a few millimeters in size within the inferior temporal cortex (face patches) [37]. Color-selective cells are also clustered in multiple small areas (color patches). Functional magnetic resonance imaging (fMRI) studies in monkeys have shown that face patches and color patches are adjacent to each other and exist in multiple locations along the anterior–posterior axis of the inferior temporal cortex [24].

7.4 Processing of Natural Textures and Materials

We can judge the material and surface condition of an object to some extent just by looking at it. This is thought to be because there are image features specific to different materials and surface conditions, which are extracted by the visual nervous system. One of the characteristics of objects that is related to material perception of objects is the unique surface pattern (texture) that various materials have for each type. For example, many cloths have textures created by their weave structure, and the surfaces of trees have unique bark textures that form as they grow. In this way, the surfaces of many materials have textures that can serve as clues for determining the category of the material. These textures have the interesting property that, although the detailed patterns differ from place to place on the surface when viewed locally, they are indistinguishable when viewed over a relatively wide area. This suggests that the visual system uses the statistical properties of images when identifying textures. In other words, various features are extracted from a certain extent of the image range in the visual system, and if the statistics of these features match, the images are perceived as having the same texture. Portilla and Simoncelli showed that image statistics (*P-S* statistics) calculated by combining the outputs of Gabor wavelet-like filters expressed in the primary visual cortex may be related to texture perception. When a set of statistics showing the relationship between the outputs of different Gabor wavelet filters are identical, two images are perceived as having the same texture [35].

The relationship between the response of neurons to texture images and *P-S* statistics has been investigated in the visual cortex of macaque monkeys. As mentioned in Sect. 7.2, V1 contains many neurons with receptive field characteristics similar to those of Gabor wavelets. These cells respond to the orientation and spatial frequency components (low-order statistics) contained in texture images. Therefore, even if texture images appear different, cells in V1 respond in the same way as long as the low-order statistics (orientation and spatial frequency) are the same as the original image. On the other hand, the response of cells in the V2 area, the next level after V1, changes when such manipulation is performed. Even if the low-order statistics are the same for images, the response is weaker if the feature components (higher-order statistics) that combine the outputs of different orientation and spatial frequency filters are different, and the response is stronger for images with matching higher-order statistics [11]. This indicates that extraction of higher-order image statistics begins at the stage of area V2.

Okazawa and colleagues [32] created texture image sets based on images of eight types of materials and examined neuronal responses in V2 and V4. They first collected 550 images for each of the eight types of materials (bark, fabric, fur, leather, stone, wood, water, sand) and extracted their P-S statistics (740 items) (Fig. 7.2c). They reduced the dimensions to seven dimensions using Fisher Linear Discrimination Analysis (FLDA) and generated 10,355 texture images that were distributed as uniformly as possible in the seven-dimensional space (Fig. 7.2a, b). In this texture image space, they mapped the neuronal responses to examine the optimal texture images and texture selectivity, but the number of images is too large to map this space uniformly. To achieve the goal, they used an evolutionary strategy [40]. That is, they first randomly selected 50 images from the stimulus image set to examine the neuronal responses, and then selected 50 images based on the responses. At this time, more images were selected from among the textures nearby the strongly active ones in the sampling space. This procedure was repeated 5–10 times, and the response to a total of 250–500 images was examined for each neuron. This method made it possible to capture the texture selectivity of the neuron well (Fig. 7.3a).

Next, they expressed the neuron's response as a linear weighting of P-S statistics, and investigated what statistics contributed to the response. Because the dimensionality of the P-S statistics is also high, this analysis was conducted after reducing its dimensionality to 29 dimensions. In Fig. 7.3b, to show what P-S statistics contributed to each neuron's response, different types of P-S statistics are represented in different colors, and the weight of the contribution is represented by the brightness of the dot. It can be seen that in both areas V2 and V4, a relatively small number of P-S statistics contributed to each neuron's response. The proportion of neurons that showed the maximum weighting on the low-order statistics (orientation and spatial frequency) expressed as spectral is higher in V2 than in V4. In contrast, the proportion of cells responding to higher-order statistics is larger in V4 than in V2. These results indicate that the calculation of higher-order image statistics proceed from V2 to V4 in the intermediate stage of the cortical visual processing, and this likely contributes to discrimination of natural textures which is important for material judgment [33].

Freeman and colleagues conducted a psychophysical experiment to investigate what P-S statistics contribute to the discrimination between noise images that have the same low-order statistics and texture images [11]. They divided the P-S statistics into seven types and examined the contribution of each type of P-S statistics based on the degree to which the discrimination sensitivity changes when each type of statistics is included or excluded. The results are shown in Fig. 7.4 right. Okazawa

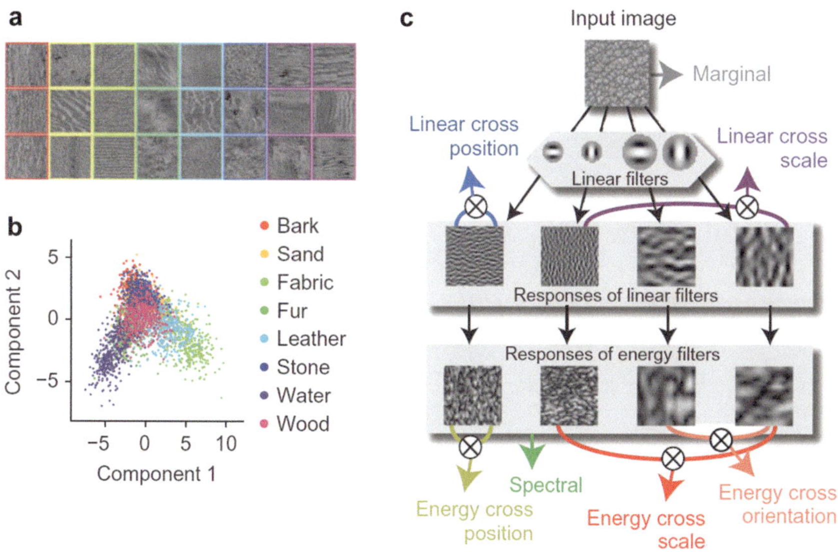

Fig. 7.2 **a** Examples of natural texture images of 8 material categories synthesized using P-S statistics. **b** Distribution of 10,355 texture images in the texture space. **c** Schematic illustration of P-S statistics [33]

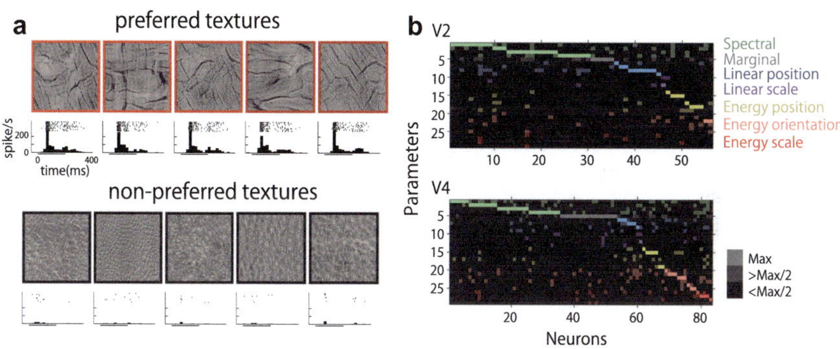

Fig. 7.3 **a** Responses of an example of texture-selective neurons recorded from area V4. Top row depicts responses to the most preferred textures, and the bottom row depicts those to the least preferred textures. **b** Weights of the contribution of 8 classes of P-S statistics on the responses of texture-selective neurons in V2 (top) and V4 (bottom) [32, 33]

and colleagues [32] applied a similar method to the responses of a population of texture-selective V4 neurons to texture and noise images to examine which types of P-S statistics contribute to their discrimination. The results are shown in Fig. 7.4 left, and are very similar to those of humans shown by Freeman and colleagues, supporting the idea that the responses of V4 neurons are involved in the discrimination of natural textures.

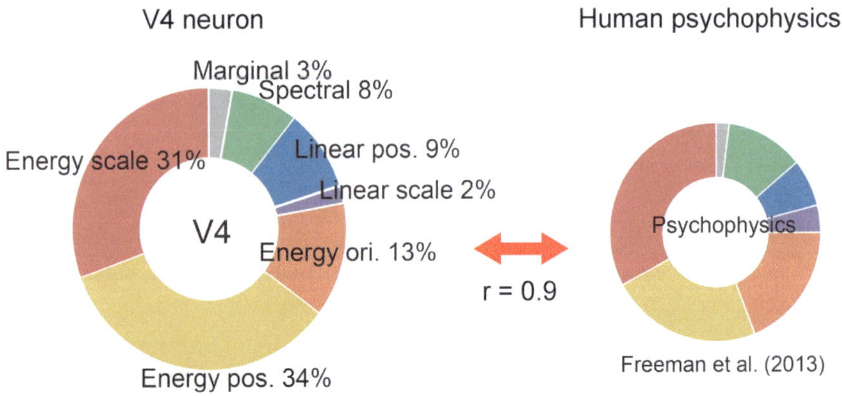

Fig. 7.4 Contribution of 7 classes of P-S statistics on the discrimination between natural textures and noise images in the responses of V4 neurons (left) and human psychophysics (right) [32]

7.5 Processing of Material Information in Human Ventral Visual Cortex

7.5.1 Processing of Natural Textures

In human fMRI studies, strong responses to texture and material images are observed along the anterior–posterior axis of the ventral visual cortex (Fig. 7.5) [22]. Many experiments have shown that natural textures are processed in the medial part of the ventral visual cortex, while object shape information is processed in the more lateral area. For example, Cant and Goodale [4] presented CG images of objects with material textures to human subjects and performed fMRI measurements. They showed that when subjects paid attention to the texture, the area around the Collateral sulcus (CoS) in the medial part of the ventral visual cortex was highly active, and when subjects paid attention to the shape of the object, the lateral occipital (LO) area located more laterally was highly active. In addition, Cavina-Pratesi and colleagues [5] showed a double dissociation between texture processing and shape processing in tests on patients with brain damage. One patient with damage near the CoS showed impaired discrimination of natural textures but normal discrimination of shapes, whereas a patient with damage near the LO showed the opposite pattern of impairment.

Responses of human V2-V4 to natural textures synthesized using P-S statistics have been shown to be stronger than responses to noisy images synthesized using only lower-order statistics [11]. In addition, when the responses of human visual cortex to many object images were measured by fMRI and analyzed for each small region (voxel) of the brain, the activities of not only the early and the intermediate visual cortex but also the ventral higher-order visual cortex can be explained to some extent by a combination of *P-S* statistics [13]. This suggests that processing based

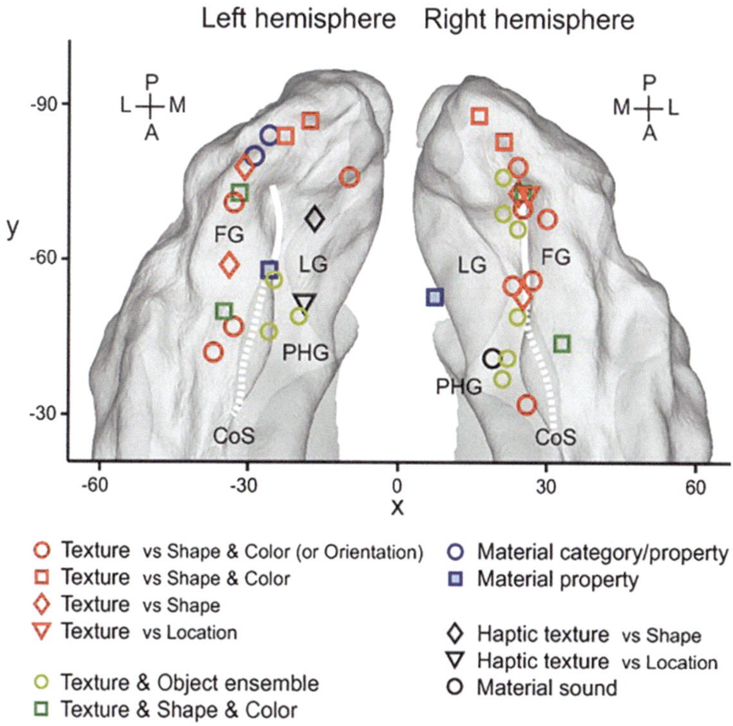

Fig. 7.5 Regions of activation in fMRI experiments related to the material perception in the human ventral visual cortex [22]. CoS: collateral sulcus, FG: fusiform gyrus, LG: lingual gyrus, PHG: parahippocampal gyrus

on image statistics is carried out throughout the ventral visual pathway, and that the extraction of higher-order image statistics may also be involved in the formation of selectivity for complex object images seen in the ventral higher visual cortex. This study used a database of high-resolution brain activity measurements [1] taken from eight subjects for a total of over 70,000 images. In the field of brain research, the sharing of measurement data has been delayed compared to genomic data, but in recent years, large-scale brain research projects have been carried out around the world, and databases and sharing of brain activity are becoming more common. Such developments will be particularly effective in brain research on material perception because it requires complex and diverse stimuli.

7.5.2 Multisensory Material Information Processing

There is important difference between the early and higher stages of the visual cortex with regard to the information related to the discrimination of materials that each stage represents. When images of various materials are shown and brain activity is examined with fMRI, it is possible to discriminate materials from the activity of both the early and higher cortical areas. Whereas the activity at higher levels reflects the differences in various impressions of materials (e.g., gloss, transparency, roughness, softness), the activity at the early stage reflects the differences in image features between materials. Hiramatsu, Goda and colleagues [14] focused on two types of information contained in CG images of nine types of materials (metal, glass, ceramics, stone, leather, bark, wood, fabric, and fur), measured brain activity using fMRI while subjects were looking at these images, and performed multi-voxel pattern analysis (MVPA) to examine the differences in information expressed by the early visual cortex (V1/V2) and the ventral higher visual cortex. One type of information they considered was low-level image features that differ depending on the material. For this, they extracted a total of 20 features, including the intensity of a total of 12 bands consisting of a combination of four orientations and three spatial frequencies, and eight statistics related to the histograms of brightness and chromaticity for each image. The other type of information was the perceptual impression caused by the image. To investigate the subjects' perceptual impressions, they asked subjects to rate each image on a 5-point scale for 12 pairs of adjectives, such as (glossy-matte), (transparent-opaque), (simple-complex), (cold-warm), and (hard-soft). Based on these quantifications, the distance between the materials in the images can be calculated for each of the image features and perceptual impressions. The top left of Fig. 7.6 shows a distance matrix that indicates the distance between nine types of materials based on image features using the brightness of the squares, and the top right shows a distance matrix created based on perceptual impressions. They created distance matrices (bottom left and right of Fig. 7.6) based on the responses of 500 voxels that responded strongly to material images in both the early visual cortex and the ventral higher visual cortex to each material, and examined whether they were similar to either the matrix based on the image features or that based on the perceptual impressions. While the brain activity of the early visual cortex resembles the pattern of a distance matrix derived from image features, that of the ventral visual cortex resembles the pattern of a distance matrix based on perceptual impressions which indicates that information about materials represented along the ventral visual pathway is converted from image features into perceptual impressions.

This study also showed that the difference in activity due to materials in the ventral visual cortex represents not only visual but also tactile impressions (rough-smooth, wet-dry, cold-warm, heavy-light, etc.), suggesting that the ventral visual cortex is also involved in multisensory material recognition. When macaque monkeys were given the experience of seeing and touching objects made of various materials, and the activity of the visual cortex was compared before and after the experience using fMRI, the correlation between the perceptual impression of the material and the activity of the ventral visual cortex was significantly increased after the visual-tactile experience of the real object [12]. This suggests that the ventral visual cortex is involved in the learning of multisensory aspects of material perception.

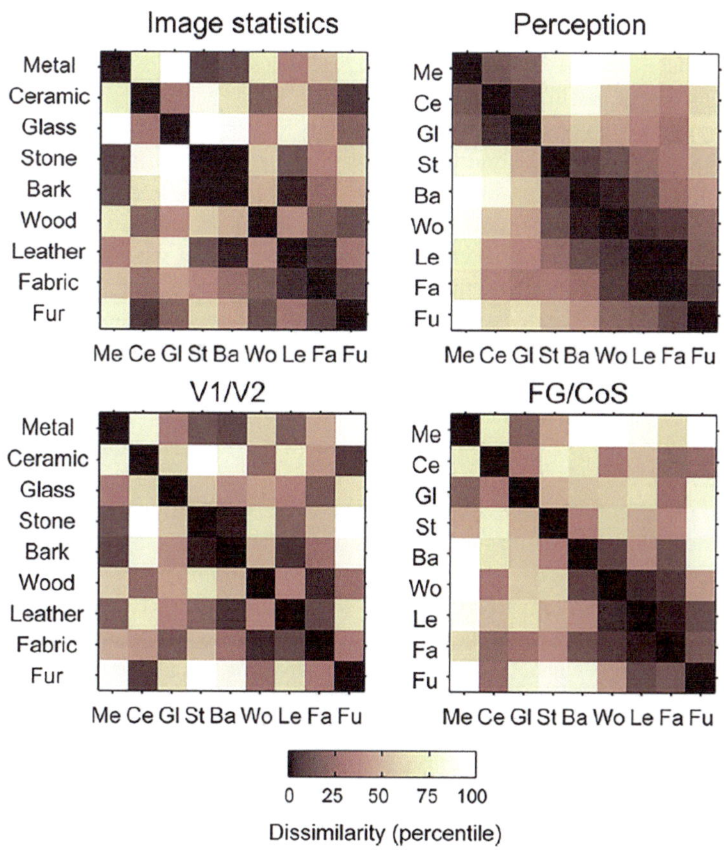

Fig. 7.6 Dissimilarity matrices depicting the distances between different types of materials with regard to the low-level image features (top left), perceptual impression (top right), activities in the early visual areas V1/V2 (bottom left), and those in the higher ventral visual areas around fusiform gyrus (FG) and collateral sulcus (CoS) (bottom right) [14]

7.6 Processing of Gloss in the Ventral Visual Cortex

7.6.1 Gloss-Selective Neurons

Another important object property involved in material perception of objects is surface reflectance (or more generally, optical properties). Surface attributes such as glossiness and transparency are generated by the properties of how the object's surface reflect and transmits light. In order to understand the features in the retinal image that these optical properties generate, psychophysical studies have been actively conducted. As a result, it has been shown that the visual features such as luminance contrast of an image, the statistics of luminance histograms, and the relationship between the luminance gradient with the orientation and curvature of the contour contribute to gloss perception [2, 27]. These visual features are relatively simple features and may be extracted at an early stage of the visual cortex, but their actual processing is still not well understood.

Our group conducted a series of experiments to clarify how the glossiness of an object is represented in the brain. Okazawa et al. [31] used fMRI to measure brain activity in monkeys performing a fixation task to the images of rotating objects, including shiny and matte objects, and images of objects shuffled while retaining their spatial frequency components (Fig. 7.7a). The area in which the response to the shiny stimuli was stronger than that to any other stimuli was distributed along the ventral visual pathway from V1 to the inferior temporal cortex (Fig. 7.8b). In the inferior temporal cortex, strong activity was observed in three small patch-like areas several millimeters in size (arrows in Fig. 7.7b). The fact that the ventral higher visual cortex shows strong responses to glossy stimuli has also been confirmed by fMRI measurements in humans [36, 39] although these human studies also showed activation in more dorsal areas.

Next, our group conducted an experiment to record neuronal activity from an area in the middle of the inferior temporal cortex (the area roughly corresponding to the red arrow in Fig. 7.7b) to investigate how information on gloss is represented. Nishio et al. [29] investigated the neuronal responses to 33 types of reflectance characteristics selected from the MERL BRDF database [25] using three parameters (specular reflectance (ρ_s), diffuse reflectance (ρ_d), and roughness (α)) of a parametric reflectance model (Ward-Duer model) (Fig. 7.8a) of 10 3D objects rendered in computer graphics. As a result, it was found that there are many gloss-selective neurons in this region whose response strengths change depending on the reflectance parameters. The reflectance parameters to which the neurons respond strongly differed from neuron to neuron. Figure 7.8b shows the responses of two examples of gloss-selective neurons to each stimulus indicated by the diameter of

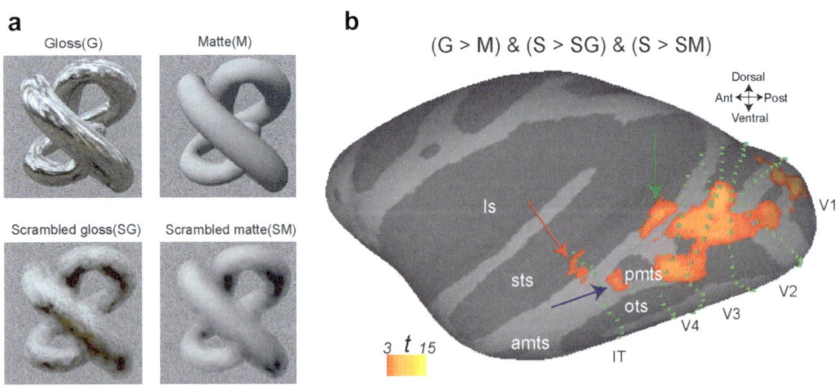

Fig. 7.7 **a** Examples of images used in the fMRI experiment to study the activation by the shiny object images in the macaque visual cortex. **b** Regions showing stronger activity to shiny objects are indicated by the orange colors in the lateral view of the cerebral cortex [31]

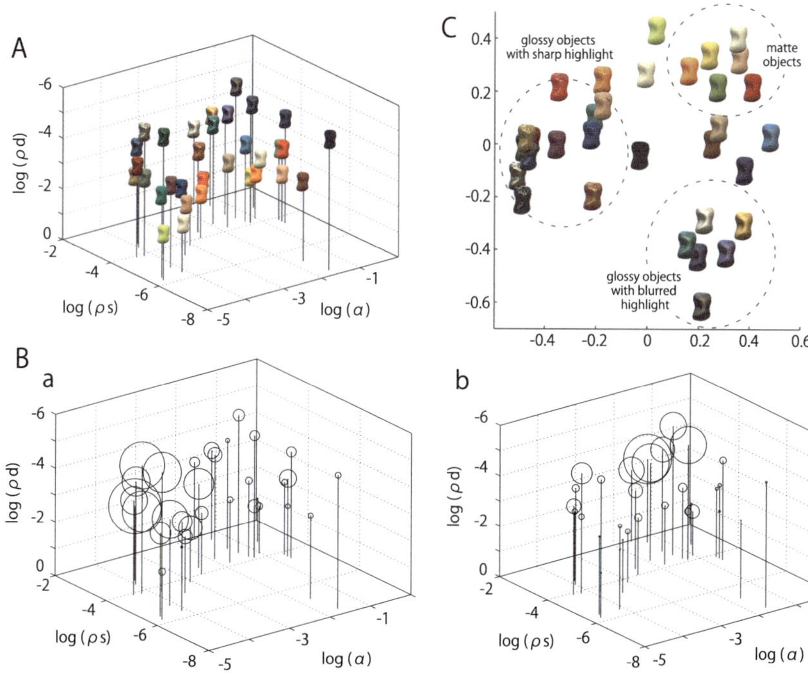

Fig. 7.8 **a** Parameters of surface reflection (ρs, ρd, α) of 33 stimuli used to test the gloss selectivity of neurons in the inferior temporal cortex of the macaque monkey. **b** Responses of two examples of gloss-selective neurons. Diameter of circle indicates the magnitude of the response to each stimulus. **c** Results of the multidimensional scaling analysis showing the distance relationships between stimuli based on the responses of gloss-selective neurons [29]

the circle. The neuron depicted in Fig. 7.8a responded strongly to stimuli with sharp highlights that have large specular reflectance and small roughness. The neuron depicted in Fig. 7.8b responded strongly to stimuli with shiny surface with blurred highlights due to large specular reflectance and large roughness. Although the shape of the highlight changes when the shape of the object changes, the stimulus selectivity of all of these neurons was maintained even when the object shape was changed. Moreover, stimuli in which pixels were randomly rearranged within the contour of the object showed no response or no significant correlation with the response to the original stimulus. This leads us to conclude that the stimulus selectivity of these neurons is due to differences in the glossiness of the stimuli, not to the local highlight pattern or the average color or brightness of the stimuli.

To investigate how the population of these gloss-selective neurons express different glosses, we calculated the correlation of the responses of the population of gloss-selective neurons for all combinations of 33 types of reflection parameters and determined the distance between the reflection parameters based on the neural responses. We then applied multidimensional scaling analysis to the resulting distance matrix, and the stimuli were arranged based on the similarity of the responses

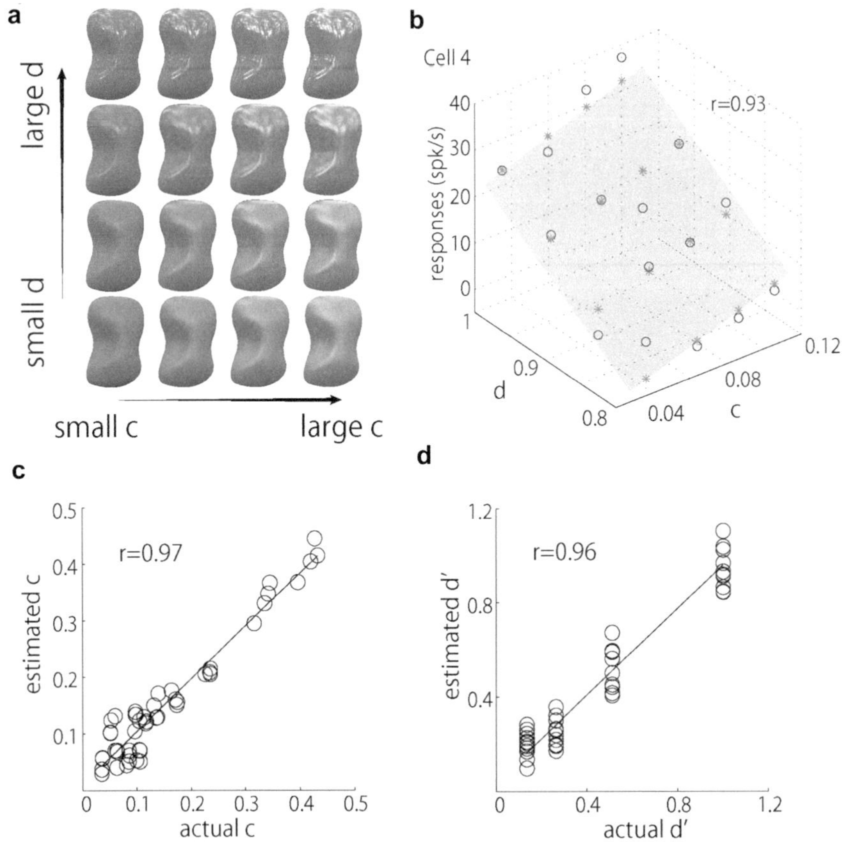

Fig. 7.9 **a** Stimuli used to test the responses of gloss-selective neurons in the perceptual gloss space (*c*-*d* space). **b** Three-dimensional plots of the responses of an example of gloss-selective neuron (black circles) to the stimuli with various *c* and *d* values and responses estimated by the multiple regression analysis (asterisks on the gray plane). **c** Relationship between the actual and estimated values of *c*. **d** Relationship between the actual and estimated values of d' [30]

of the neural populations (Fig. 7.8c). Glossy objects with sharp highlights are clustered on the left side of this figure, glossy objects with blurred highlights are clustered on the bottom right, and matte objects are clustered on the top right, showing that various glosses are systematically represented in the activities of the population of gloss-selective neurons.

7.6.2 Relationship with Gloss Perception

Ferwerda and colleagues [10] conducted a psychophysical experiment to investigate the relationship between physical gloss parameters and gloss perception, and showed that the gloss perception space is composed of the axis formed by two parameters, c and d. c represents the contrast of highlights and is expressed by the following formula:

$$c = \sqrt[3]{(\rho_s + \rho_d/2)} - \sqrt[3]{\rho_d/2)} \qquad (7.1)$$

where ρ_s is the specular reflectance and ρ_d is the diffuse reflectance. d is expressed as $1 - \alpha$ and represents the sharpness of highlights where α is roughness. In the space formed by c and d (c-d space), two pairs of stimuli that are the same distance apart are considered to have the same difference in perceived gloss intensity. Our group examined whether parameters related to gloss perception can be estimated from the responses of gloss-selective neurons [30]. For this purpose, we examined the responses of gloss-selective neurons using 16 stimuli (Fig. 7.9a) selected so that c and d were equally spaced. We found that the responses of most gloss-selective neurons can be expressed as a linear sum of c and d (Fig. 7.9b). Next, we investigated whether the perceptual gloss parameters of a stimulus could be estimated from the responses of the population of gloss-selective neurons. Since the number of neurons was 39, and the dimensionality was too high, we performed linear fitting based on the results of reducing the dimension to four using PCA. In addition, since it is known that the effect of roughness decreases nonlinearly for d, we used $d' = \exp(-\alpha/0.1)$ instead of $d = 1 - \alpha$. As a result, a high correlation of 0.97 for c and 0.96 for d' was observed (Fig. 7.9c, d), indicating that the activity of the population of gloss-selective neurons quite accurately represents perceptual gloss parameters.

If the activity of these gloss-selective neurons recorded in the middle part of the inferior temporal cortex is involved in gloss perception, it was expected that artificial manipulation of the activity of these neurons would affect the perception of gloss. Therefore, we examined the behavioral effects of micro-stimulation (35 μA, 200 Hz, 200 ms) applied from the tip of the electrode or microinjection of the GABA agonist muscimol while macaque monkeys were performing a gloss discrimination task [3]. The gloss discrimination task involved the presentation of seven types of gloss stimuli equally spaced along the diagonal of the perceptual gloss space (c-d space). Within a trial, two stimuli were sequentially presented with a short inter-stimulus interval. The first stimulus (reference stimulus) always had a medium gloss, while the second stimulus (test stimulus) presented a short time later was randomly selected from one of the seven types of gloss, and the monkeys selected which of the reference and test stimuli was more glossy. When micro-stimulation was applied during the presentation of the test stimulus at the site where the gloss-selective neurons were recorded or slightly anterior to it, the monkeys tended to answer that the test stimulus was glossier. In addition, when muscimol was injected into the site where the gloss-selective neurons were recorded, the sensitivity of gloss discrimination tended to decrease after the first injection. However, the effect was weakened with repeated injections. This suggests that compensation occurred in the neural circuitry that processes glossiness.

7.6.3 Network for Gloss Information Processing

The experiments of recording and manipulating neural activity described above were conducted in a small area of the middle part of the inferior temporal cortex. However, as shown by an fMRI experiment in monkeys [31], there are small areas in other parts of the inferior temporal cortex that respond strongly to glossy stimuli. Although analysis of the properties of the neurons in these areas and their relationship to glossiness perception remains to be done in the macaque monkey, an interesting observation is made in marmoset. Miyakawa and colleagues found that neurons that respond strongly to glossy stimuli exist in a small area in the temporal lobe [26]. They also found that this region is anatomically connected to a small area in the more posterior part of the temporal cortex where neurons which respond strongly to glossy stimuli exist. These experiments suggest that there may be a network that processes gloss information in the inferior temporal cortex.

Our group examined neural connectivity patterns in the inferior temporal cortex of a macaque monkey by microinjecting a retrograde tracer, Cholera Toxin B-Subunit (CTB), into a small area of the middle part of the inferior temporal cortex where gloss-selective neurons were recorded [23]. Retrogradely labeled neurons were widely distributed in the inferior temporal cortex, but were especially densely distributed in three small subregions (Fig. 7.10). Of these, two sites posterior to the injection site were in good agreement with areas that showed strong activity in response to gloss stimuli in the monkey's fMRI recordings. This supports the idea that there is a neural network in the inferior temporal cortex that is involved in processing gloss information. The other site was located anterior to the injection site. This site could not be detected in the fMRI experiment, which may be due to a susceptibility artifact in which the anterior inferior temporal cortex is close to the base of the brain, making it difficult to detect fMRI signals. Interestingly, in an electrical micro-stimulation experiment of the middle part of the inferior temporal cortex [3], the effect tended to be more pronounced when stimulation was applied to more anterior sites. If a small area in the anterior part of the inferior temporal cortex is strongly involved in judging glossiness, this result may be explained by interpreting that axons projecting from the middle part of the inferior temporal cortex to the anterior part were stimulated. It is expected that the neural mechanisms underlying gloss perception will be better understood by examining the functioning of these neural networks in detail.

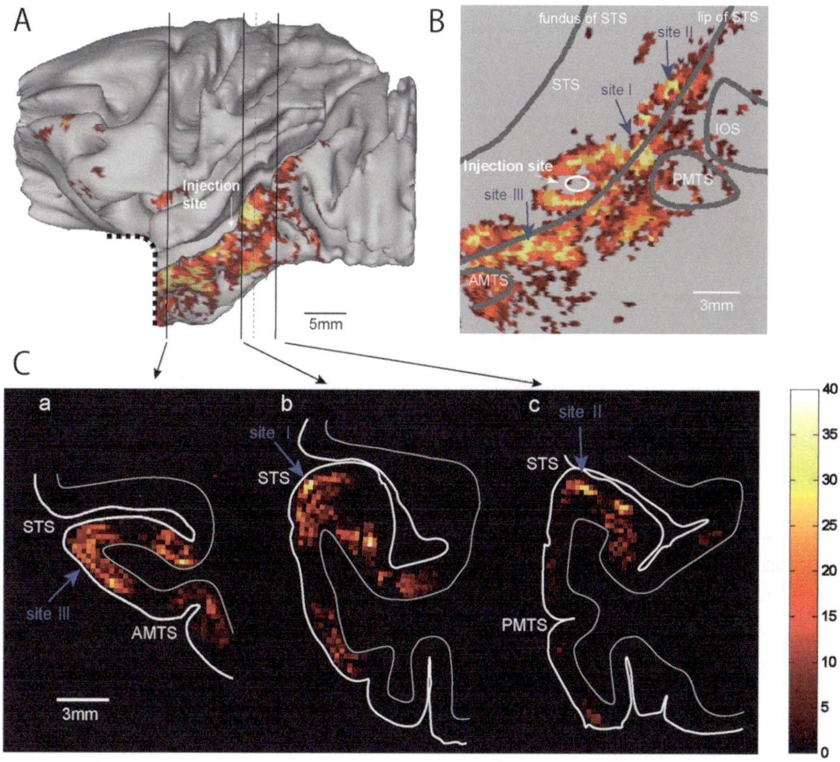

Fig. 7.10 Distribution of the neurons labeled by microinjection of a retrograde tracer cholera toxin B-subunit (CTB) into the middle part of the inferior temporal cortex where gloss-selective neurons were recorded. Location of the labeled cells are plotted on the surface of the 3D reconstructed cortical surface of the monkey (**a**), the sulcus-unfolded view of the inferior temporal cortex (**b**), and three sections whose positions are indicated by vertical lines in A (**c**). Colors represent the density of labeled cells. AMTS: anterior middle temporal sulcus, IOS: inferior occipital sulcus, PMTS: posterior middle temporal sulcus, STS: superior temporal sulcus [23]

7.7 Discussion

As we have reviewed in this chapter, neuron recordings and neuroimaging studies on humans and non-human primates provide accumulating evidence that visual information related to material perception is processed mainly along the hierarchy of the ventral visual pathway. Clinical observations on human patients with brain damage and neurological disorders also support this view (Suzuki et al. chapter in this book). However, it should be noted that these observations do not exclude the possibility that the posterior parietal cortex, the target of the dorsal visual pathway, plays important roles in material perception or related behaviors. Material perception plays important roles when we manipulate objects. By using experimental designs in which such aspects are more relevant, we should clarify the role of the posterior parietal cortex in material perception.

Another important direction that should be pursued is how the sensory information related to material perception processed in the visual cortex is linked to the evaluation or preference/avoidance of objects based on material perception. This is an essential function for both animals and humans to adapt to the natural environment, for example, by determining whether food is edible. In humans in particular, it plays an important social/economical roles by influencing the value judgment of products. In recent years, there has been great progress in understanding the mechanisms of value judgment by neural circuits including the orbitofrontal cortex, striatum, and amygdala (Minamimoto and Murata chapter in this book). However, how sensory information related to material perception processed in the higher visual cortex is transformed in the brain and linked to value judgment largely remains an unsolved problem.

Finally, I would like to add one point regarding our understanding of how information related to material perception is represented in the brain. Many studies have been conducted on what image cues are used for gloss perception (Nishida and Sawayama chapter in this book). In this article, I explained research on gloss-selective neurons in the inferior temporal cortex of monkeys, but these experiments were conducted based on stimuli created by manipulating the physical parameters of light reflection related to gloss, and it is not clarified what image cues these neurons are responding to. For natural textures, the relationship between image features and neuronal responses has been analyzed in detail. However, with regard to the neural processing related gloss perception, the question of how image features and neuronal responses are linked remains to be answered in future.

References

1. Allen, E.J., St-Yves, G., Wu, Y., Breedlove, J.L., Prince, J.S., Dowdle, L.T., Nau, M., Caron, B., Pestilli, F., Charest, I., Hutchinson, J.B., Naselaris, T., Kay, K.: A massive 7T fMRI dataset to bridge cognitive neuroscience and artificial intelligence. Nat. Neurosci. **25**(1), 116–126 (2022). https://doi.org/10.1038/s41593-021-00962-x
2. Anderson, B.L.: Mid-level vision. Curr. Biol. **30**(3), R105–R109 (2020). https://doi.org/10.1016/j.cub.2019.11.088
3. Baba, M., Nishio, A., Komatsu, H.: Relationship between the activities of gloss-selective neurons in the macaque inferior temporal cortex and the gloss discrimination behavior of the monkey. Cereb Cortex Commun. **2**(1):tgab011 (2021). https://doi.org/10.1093/texcom/tgab011
4. Cant, J.S., Goodale, M.A.: Attention to form or surface properties modulates different regions of human occipitotemporal cortex. Cereb Cortex **17**(3), 713–731. http://www.ncbi.nlm.nih.gov/entrez/query.fcgi?cmd=Retrieve&db=PubMed&dopt=Citation&list_uids=16648452
5. Cavina-Pratesi, C., Kentridge, R.W., Heywood, C.A., Milner, A.D.: Separate channels for processing form, texture, and color: evidence from FMRI adaptation and visual object agnosia. Cereb. Cortex **20**(10), 2319–2332 (2010). https://doi.org/10.1093/cercor/bhp298
6. Conway, B.R.: The organization and operation of inferior temporal cortex. Annu Rev Vis Sci **4**, 381–402 (2018). https://doi.org/10.1146/annurev-vision-091517-034202

7. Daugman, J.G.: Uncertainty relation for resolution in space, spatial frequency, and orientation optimized by two-dimensional visual cortical filters. J. Opt. Soc. Am. A **2**(7), 1160–1169 (1985). https://doi.org/10.1364/josaa.2.001160
8. DeYoe, E.A., Van Essen, D.C.: Concurrent processing streams in monkey visual cortex. Trends Neurosci. **11**(5), 219–226 (1988). https://doi.org/10.1016/0166-2236(88)90130-0
9. Felleman, D.J., Van Essen, D.C.: Distributed hierarchical processing in the primate cerebral cortex. Cereb. Cortex **1**(1), 1–47 (1991). https://doi.org/10.1093/cercor/1.1.1-a
10. Ferwerda, J.A., Pellacini, F., Greenberg, D.P.: A psychophysically-based model of surface gloss perception. Proc. SPIE Hum. Vis. Electron. Imaging **4299**, 291–301 (2001)
11. Freeman, J., Ziemba, C.M., Heeger, D.J., Simoncelli, E.P., Movshon, J.A.: A functional and perceptual signature of the second visual area in primates. Nat. Neurosci. (2013). https://doi.org/10.1038/nn.3402
12. Goda, N., Yokoi, I., Tachibana, A., Minamimoto, T., Komatsu, H.: Crossmodal association of visual and haptic material properties of objects in the monkey ventral visual cortex. Curr. Biol. **26**(7), 928–934 (2016). https://doi.org/10.1016/j.cub.2016.02.003
13. Henderson, M.M., Tarr, M.J., Wehbe, L.: A Texture statistics encoding model reveals hierarchical feature selectivity across human visual cortex. J. Neurosci. **43**(22), 4144–4161 (2023). https://doi.org/10.1523/JNEUROSCI.1822-22.2023
14. Hiramatsu, C., Goda, N., Komatsu, H.: Transformation from image-based to perceptual representation of materials along the human ventral visual pathway. Neuroimage **57**(2), 482–494 (2011). https://doi.org/10.1016/j.neuroimage.2011.04.056
15. Hubel, D.H., Wiesel, T.N.: Receptive fields of single neurones in the cat's striate cortex. J. Physiol. **148**(3), 574–591 (1959). https://doi.org/10.1113/jphysiol.1959.sp006308
16. Hubel, D.H., Wiesel, T.N.: Receptive fields and functional architecture of monkey striate cortex. J. Physiol. **195**(1), 215–243 (1968). https://doi.org/10.1113/jphysiol.1968.sp008455
17. Ito, M., Komatsu, H.: Representation of angles embedded within contour stimuli in area V2 of macaque monkeys. J. Neurosci. **24**(13), 3313–3324 (2004). https://doi.org/10.1523/JNEUROSCI.4364-03.2004
18. Janssen, P., Vogels, R., Orban, G.A.: Selectivity for 3D shape that reveals distinct areas within macaque inferior temporal cortex. Science **288**(5473), 2054–2056 (2000). https://doi.org/10.1126/science.288.5473.2054
19. Kandel, E.R., Koester, J.D., Mack, S.H.: Principles of Neural Science. McGraw-Hill Education (2021)
20. Kobatake, E., Tanaka, K.: Neuronal selectivities to complex object features in the ventral visual pathway of the macaque cerebral cortex. J Neurophysiol **71**(3), 856–867 (1994). http://www.ncbi.nlm.nih.gov/pubmed/8201425
21. Komatsu, H.: Mechanisms of central color vision. Curr. Opin. Neurobiol. **8**(4), 503–508 (1998). https://doi.org/10.1016/s0959-4388(98)80038-x
22. Komatsu, H., Goda, N.: Neural mechanisms of material perception: quest on shitsukan. Neuroscience **392**, 329–347 (2018). https://doi.org/10.1016/j.neuroscience.2018.09.001
23. Komatsu, H., Nishio, A., Ichinohe, N., Goda, N.: Structure and function of neural circuit related to gloss perception in the macaque inferior temporal cortex: a case report. Brain Struct. Funct. **226**(9), 3023–3030 (2021). https://doi.org/10.1007/s00429-021-02324-6
24. Lafer-Sousa, R., Conway, B.R.: Parallel, multi-stage processing of colors, faces and shapes in macaque inferior temporal cortex. Nat. Neurosci. **16**(12), 1870–1878 (2013). https://doi.org/10.1038/nn.3555
25. Matusik, W., Pfister, H., Brand, M., McMillan, L.: A data-driven reflectance model. ACM Trans. Graphics **22**(23) (2002)
26. Miyakawa, N., Banno, T., Abe, H., Tani, T., Suzuki, W., Ichinohe, N.: Representation of glossy material surface in ventral superior temporal sulcal area of common marmosets. Front. Neural Circuits **11**, 17 (2017). https://doi.org/10.3389/fncir.2017.00017
27. Motoyoshi, I., Nishida, S., Sharan, L., Adelson, E.H.: Image statistics and the perception of surface qualities. Nature **447**(7141), 206–209 (2007). https://doi.org/10.1038/nature05724

28. Namima, T., Yasuda, M., Banno, T., Okazawa, G., Komatsu, H.: Effects of luminance contrast on the color selectivity of neurons in the macaque area v4 and inferior temporal cortex. J. Neurosci. **34**(45), 14934–14947 (2014). https://doi.org/10.1523/JNEUROSCI.2289-14.2014
29. Nishio, A., Goda, N., Komatsu, H.: Neural selectivity and representation of gloss in the monkey inferior temporal cortex. J. Neurosci. **32**(31), 10780–10793 (2012). https://doi.org/10.1523/JNEUROSCI.1095-12.2012
30. Nishio, A., Shimokawa, T., Goda, N., Komatsu, H.: Perceptual gloss parameters are encoded by population responses in the monkey inferior temporal cortex. J. Neurosci. **34**(33), 11143–11151 (2014). https://doi.org/10.1523/JNEUROSCI.1451-14.2014
31. Okazawa, G., Goda, N., Komatsu, H.: Selective responses to specular surfaces in the macaque visual cortex revealed by fMRI. Neuroimage **63**(3), 1321–1333 (2012). https://doi.org/10.1016/j.neuroimage.2012.07.052
32. Okazawa, G., Tajima, S., Komatsu, H.: Image statistics underlying natural texture selectivity of neurons in macaque V4. Proc. Natl. Acad. Sci. USA **112**(4), E351-360 (2015). https://doi.org/10.1073/pnas.1415146112
33. Okazawa, G., Tajima, S., Komatsu, H.: Gradual development of visual texture-selective properties between macaque areas V2 and V4. Cereb Cortex **27**(10), 4867–4880 (2017). https://doi.org/10.1093/cercor/bhw282
34. Pasupathy, A., Connor, C.E.: Population coding of shape in area V4. Nat. Neurosci. **5**(12), 1332–1338 (2002). https://doi.org/10.1038/nn972
35. Portilla, J., Simoncelli, E.P.: A parametric texture model based on joint statistics of complex wavelet coefficients. Int. J. Comput. Vis. **40**, 49–71 (2000)
36. Sun, H.C., Ban, H., Di Luca, M., Welchman, A.E.: FMRI evidence for areas that process surface gloss in the human visual cortex. Vision. Res. **109**, 149–157 (2015). https://doi.org/10.1016/j.visres.2014.11.012
37. Tsao, D.Y., Freiwald, W.A., Tootell, R.B., Livingstone, M.S.: A cortical region consisting entirely of face-selective cells. Science **311**(5761), 670–674 (2006). https://doi.org/10.1126/science.1119983
38. Van Essen, D.C.: Organization of visual areas in macaque and human cerebral cortex. In: Chalupa, L.M., Werner, J.S. (eds.) The Visual Neuroscience, vol. 1, pp. 507–521. MIT Press (2003)
39. Wada, A., Sakano, Y., Ando, H.: Human cortical areas involved in perception of surface glossiness. Neuroimage **98**, 243–257 (2014). https://doi.org/10.1016/j.neuroimage.2014.05.001
40. Yamane, Y., Carlson, E.T., Bowman, K.C., Wang, Z., Connor, C.E.: A neural code for three-dimensional object shape in macaque inferotemporal cortex. Nat. Neurosci. **11**(11), 1352–1360 (2008). https://doi.org/10.1038/nn.2202
41. Yamins, D.L., Hong, H., Cadieu, C.F., Solomon, E.A., Seibert, D., DiCarlo, J.J.: Performance-optimized hierarchical models predict neural responses in higher visual cortex. Proc. Natl. Acad. Sci. USA **111**(23), 8619–8624 (2014). https://doi.org/10.1073/pnas.1403112111

Chapter 8
Shitsukan Perception When Impaired

Kyoko Suzuki, Shigeki Nakauchi, and Yuya Kinzuka

Abstract Material perception can dramatically change as people age. It can also be altered with brain damage. Studying these changes give us important insights into the perceptual mechanism of materials. Material perception in a broad sense, or Shitsukan perception, includes surface quality and object appearance as well as the texture, which are related to preference or emotional reaction toward an object. Thus, Shitsukan integrates multiple sensory modalities and is essential for object recognition and emotional processing. This chapter examines the influence of neurological disorders and aging on human Shitsukan perception. Two investigative approaches are highlighted: (1) evaluating performance in tasks related to material perception and recognition ("surface Shitsukan") and (2) analyzing neurophysiological responses to visual appearance changes ("deep Shitsukan"). Findings reveal that aging and brain damage impair Shitsukan perception across visual, tactile, and auditory modalities. In individuals with brain lesions, the extent and modality of perceptual impairment of Shitsukan are determined by lesion localization. Moreover, studies on pupil responses to glare illusions indicate that aging and brain damage diminishes physiological responses, reflecting a decline in Shitsukan perception. These results underscore that surface and deep Shitsukan perception are differently affected by aging and neurological disorders. Addressing these changes through environmental adaptations could significantly enhance the quality of life for older adults and individuals with brain dysfunctions.

Keywords Material · Texture · Shitsukan · Aging · Dementia

K. Suzuki (✉)
Department of Behavioral Neurology and Cognitive Neuroscience, Tohoku University Graduate School of Medicine, Sendai, Japan
e-mail: kyoko.suzuki.a7@tohoku.ac.jp

S. Nakauchi · Y. Kinzuka
Department of Computer Science and Engineering, Toyohashi University of Technology, Toyohashi, Japan

S. Nishida and K. Nishino (eds.), *Shitsukan—Understanding and Manipulating Material and Quality Perception*, https://doi.org/10.1007/978-981-95-4762-3_8

8.1 Introduction

Material perception in a broad sense, or Shitsukan perception, includes surface quality and object appearance including its texture. These perceptual attributes are closely linked to preference and emotional responses toward objects. Shitsukan thus integrates information from multiple sensory modalities and plays a fundamental role in both object recognition and emotional processing. Although Shitsukan is a central aspect of daily perception, its alterations with aging or brain damage have received little systematic investigation. Studying such changes offers valuable insights into the perceptual and neural mechanisms underlying Shitsukan.

Shitsukan can be perceived through various sensory modalities, including visual, auditory, tactile, olfactory, and gustatory sense. Information from each modality is integrated through learning and stored in semantic memory [1]. This integrated representation enables recognition of a material and its properties based on information from a single sensory source. For example, one may infer the hardness or texture of an object solely from its visual appearance, drawing upon previously acquired knowledge.

Shitsukan perception also plays an essential role in controlling behavior. Based on Shitsukan, we avoid eating food that appears spoiled, and instinctively adjust our grip or bite force based on its hardness. Additionally, pleasant Shitsukans can evoke positive emotions, influencing subsequent behavior.

Importantly, material properties may influence perception even in the absence of conscious awareness. Such implicit effects can be probed through neurophysiological indices, such as pupillometry. Certain visual patterns that modulate perceived brightness provide a useful paradigm for examining these latent processes; one such example, the glare illusion, will be described in detail later in this chapter.

The neural basis of human Shitsukan perception has been explored in a limited number of studies, including neuropsychological examinations of brain-damaged patients [2] and functional neuroimaging studies in healthy subjects (see Chap. 6). These studies have identified cortical regions involved in Shitsukan processing, yet the overall neural mechanisms remain only partially understood. Investigating the qualitative features of Shitsukan impairment and their relationship to specific neuronal damage will be essential for clarifying the mechanisms underlying Shitsukan perception.

This chapter addresses the impact of neurological disorders and aging on Shitsukan perception. Two complementary methodological approaches are emphasized: (1) behavioral evaluation of material perception and recognition ("surface Shitsukan") and (2) analysis of neurophysiological responses to alterations in visual appearance that may reveal implicit, or "deep Shitsukan," processing. Together, these approaches seek to bridge perceptual neuroscience with translational applications for the preservation and enhancement of Shitsukan in aged and brain-damaged subjects.

8.2 Shitsukan Perception and Aging

With aging, sensory processing deteriorates at multiple levels, from peripheral sensory nerves to central neural circuits. In the visual system, age-related changes span from the lens and retina to the primary visual cortex and visual association areas. In auditory pathways, hearing impairment becomes increasingly prevalent after age 65, affecting not only pure-tone thresholds but also speech discrimination and temporal resolution. Similarly, both passive touch [3] and active touch [4] exhibit age-related decline. Olfactory [5] and gustatory [6] systems also experience functional degradation with age. Thus, in examining texture perception in older adults, it is critical to consider the underlying decline in basic sensory functions.

While basic sensory functions are known to decline with age, this chapter demonstrates that aging also impacts material perception, an important component of Shitsukan, independent of these basic sensory declines. To investigate age-related changes in Shitsukan perception, we first assessed material recognition in older adults using neuropsychological testing. Additionally, we employed a physiological approach by measuring pupil responses to the glare illusion, a visual effect that alters perceived visual appearance through a perceptual illusion. This combined methodology enables us to examine Shitsukan perception change both behaviorally and physiologically in older adults. Although longitudinal studies are ideal for capturing age-related changes; here, we report the results of a cross-sectional study comparing younger and older adults. This approach allows us to identify age-related differences in Shitsukan perception.

8.2.1 Visual and Tactile Material Perception in Older Adults

To investigate age-related changes in Shitsukan perception, we employed material recognition and discrimination tasks that we had previously described in our earlier studies [7]. These material discrimination and identification tests used rod-shaped stimuli made from six distinct materials—glass, ceramic, metal, wood, leather, and fabric. Participants completed both visual and tactile versions of the tasks, with the tactile assessments performed using the dominant hand. For the assessment of visual material perception, we also employed computer-generated images depicting these materials to control for extraneous visual cues [8].

Regarding visual material perception, we found that older adults exhibit significantly reduced accuracy in identifying materials from both real objects and images compared to younger individuals [9]. Similarly, in tactile material perception using active touch, older adults showed a significant decline in material identification. No correlation was found with two-point discrimination, a measure of cortical somatosensory function, indicating that impairment of tactile perception was not due to cortical sensory loss [9].

Skedung et al. reported that older adults perform worse than younger individuals in surface texture discrimination tasks using the wrinkle-patterned surface [10]. This decline is associated with skin friction, moisture, and elasticity, and moisturizing the skin improved texture perception in older adults.

In contrast, it is important to acknowledge that even in advanced age, certain individuals, such as expert craftsmen, may acquire or maintain highly refined Shitsukan perception in the visual or tactile modalities [11]. This suggests that prolonged and specialized experience can modulate or compensate for age-related decline of Shitsukan perception in specific contexts.

8.2.2 Glare Illusion-Induced Pupil Responses in Younger and Older Adults

As described above, aging is associated with a decline in the ability to perceive material properties. Such Shitsukan perception, which involves the conscious appraisal of an object's surface characteristics, may be regarded as explicit "surface Shitsukan" perception. In contrast, even without conscious awareness, differences in Shitsukan can influence neurophysiological responses. In this section, we address the concept of implicit, "deep Shitsukan" perception by examining pupillary changes elicited by the glare illusion.

Pupil diameter is widely known to reflect not only the physical luminance of the incoming light but also a range of physiological internal states and the subjective brightness evoked by stimuli [12–14]. As such, several studies have demonstrated that pupil diameter can indicate the perceptual brightness caused by the glare illusion, despite the actual luminance being the same as that of the control stimuli [15–17]. Based on this, we assessed the pupil diameter as a marker of perceptual brightness for the glare illusion in younger and older adults.

We have used the stimuli shown in Fig. 8.1, glare and halo stimuli. Both stimuli consist of inducers with luminance gradient toward the center or the periphery. The central region of the stimuli in glare condition (left) typically appears brighter than the halo condition (right) even though the physical luminance is the same in both conditions.

Fig. 8.1 Glare and halo stimuli. Both consist of luminance gradient circles as inducers that either converge to the center (left) or the periphery (right)

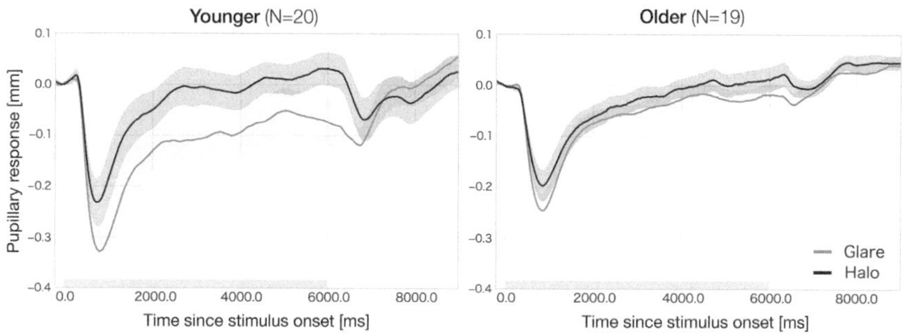

Fig. 8.2 Pupillary responses to glare (gray) and halo (black) stimulus in younger (left) and older (right) adults

We compared the magnitude of the brightness illusion effect between younger ($N = 20$; mean age = 28.8, SD = 7.08) and older ($N = 19$; mean age = 74.0, SD = 3.42) adults using pupil responses as an index. Figure 8.2 presents the pupil responses induced by stimulus presentation, categorized by each stimulus and participant group. In both cases, after the stimulus presentation, the pupil constricts with a slight delay (a response known as the light reflex), and then gradually returns to its original size. This response to light is referred to as the pupillary light reflex (PLR). Differences in the magnitude of pupil responses to the stimuli were observed between younger and older adults. Additionally, there also appear to be differences between the glare and halo conditions.

To quantitatively compare pupil responses across different stimulus conditions and participant groups, we extracted four key features based on established pupillometry methods. PLR amplitude represents the maximum constriction strength: it is calculated as the difference between baseline pupil size and the minimum diameter achieved after stimulus onset. PLR latency measures the time delay from stimulus onset until the pupil reaches that minimum diameter, providing insight into reflex speed and neural conduction efficiency. We quantified the area under the curve (AUC) from the moment of minimum diameter until stimulus offset, summarizing the depth and duration of pupil recovery. Finally, PLR velocity captures the peak speed of constriction—it is determined from the maximum rate of change in pupil size during the constriction phase, derived from the first derivative of the pupil diameter trace. By applying these four complementary metrics—amplitude, latency, AUC, and velocity—we are able to characterize not only how strongly and quickly the pupil responds, but also how prolonged the constriction effect is.

Figure 8.3 illustrates the comparisons of these feature parameters between younger and older adults for both glare and halo stimuli. Differences were evident across the extracted parameters, reflecting the influence of both stimulus condition and age group. With stimulus condition (glare or halo) as the within-subject factor and group (younger or older) as the between-subject factor, a two-way repeated measures ANOVA was conducted for each of the four feature parameters.

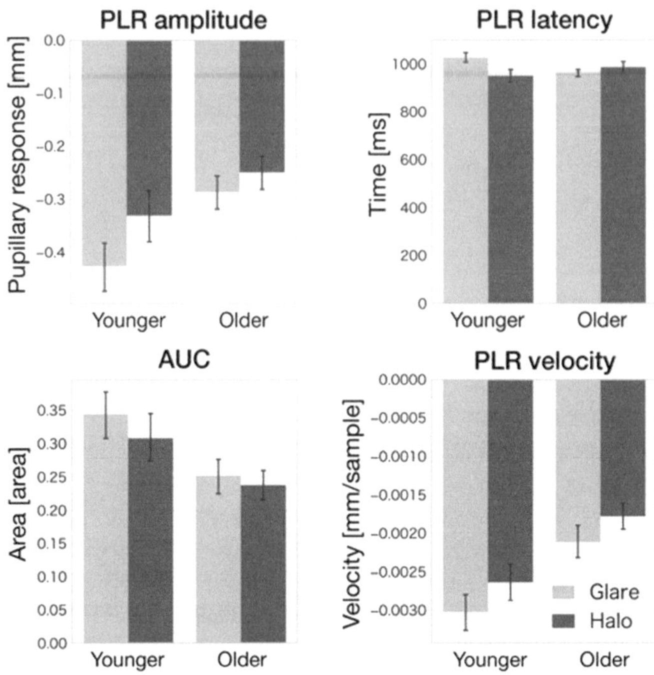

Fig. 8.3 Comparison of feature parameters extracted from pupillary responses to glare and halo stimuli in younger and older adults

The ANOVA results are summarized in Table 8.1. This table highlights differences in pupil response characteristics across stimulus conditions and age groups, with significant effects observed for PLR amplitude and PLR velocity. The interaction effects for PLR latency suggest age-related differences in response to glare and halo stimuli, potentially reflecting distinct perceptual processing in younger versus older adults.

The main effect of stimulus condition in PLR amplitude indicates that the glare stimulus elicits stronger pupil constriction than the halo across both age groups. This supports previous findings that glare illusions can intensify perceived brightness, triggering a more substantial pupillary response [18]. The significant interaction in the PLR latency suggests that the latency of the pupillary response differs based on age and type of stimulus. This may indicate that younger and older adults process the illusion differently in terms of timing, with potential age-related differences in visual or cognitive processing speeds.

For instance, the significant main effect of stimulus condition in PLR velocity, with glare stimuli producing faster pupil responses, aligns with the notion that the glare illusion accelerates perceptual brightness processing, leading to a quicker constriction response. In addition, the significant main effect of group indicates that younger adults generally exhibit faster pupillary responses than older adults,

Table 8.1 Summary of ANOVA results for main effects and interactions of stimulus condition and age group on pupil features

Feature parameter	Stimulus condition (main effect)	Group (main effect)	Stimulus × Group (interaction)
PLR amplitude	Significant ($p < 0.001$) Glare > Halo	n.s	n.s
PLR latency	n.s	n.s	Significant ($p = 0.012$) Simple effects show glare faster in younger adults
AUC	n.s	n.s	n.s
PLR velocity	Significant ($p < 0.001$) Glare > Halo	Significant ($p = 0.006$) Younger > Older	n.s

likely reflecting age-related declines in response speed. This finding suggests that although both groups perceive the brightness illusion, younger adults have a more rapid physiological response, which could be due to differences in sensory processing efficiency.

Overall, these findings contribute to the understanding of how perceptual illusions, like the glare illusion, affect physiological responses across age groups. The results indicate that while both younger and older adults perceive the brightness induced by the glare illusion, age-related changes in pupillary responses suggest that older adults may experience these perceptual effects differently.

8.3 Visual Texture Agnosia in Patients with Focal Brain Lesions and Dementia

This section addresses impairments of explicit, or surface, Shitsukan resulting from brain dysfunction. Visual texture agnosia is characterized by the inability to identify or discriminate the textures or materials of objects despite intact elementary visual functions. It is most often associated with damage to the ventral visual pathway, arising from either focal brain lesions or neurodegenerative processes. Studying texture agnosia provides a unique opportunity to investigate the mechanisms of texture perception and, more broadly, the neural basis of Shitsukan. Such investigations not only illuminate how the brain integrates visual texture information but also clarify how this integration breaks down in disease, thereby advancing our understanding of material perception in both health and pathology.

8.3.1 Visual Texture Agnosia with Focal Lesions

Reports of visual texture agnosia due to focal brain lesions are rare, with detailed accounts available for only seven cases, including information on lesion localization. Among these, three cases presented with visual texture agnosia accompanied by impairments in color recognition or prosopagnosia, associated with bilateral occipitotemporal lesions caused by stroke [19–21]. In one case, visual texture agnosia occurred without deficits in color recognition, although face perception was not evaluated [22]. Another case exhibited visual texture agnosia, but assessments of color and face recognition were not performed [23]. Both of these cases involved extensive bilateral occipitotemporal lesions, though precise lesion localization was not described. A separate case demonstrated visual texture agnosia for both real materials and images, alongside color agnosia but without prosopagnosia. This was linked to a lesion in the left medial temporal lobe, encompassing the fusiform, lingual, and parahippocampal gyri [24]. Another case displayed visual texture agnosia for images and impaired recognition of regions defined by textons, but intact color and face recognition [19]. This was attributed to a unilateral left occipital subcortical hemorrhage. These case reports suggested that the neural networks involved in texture processing are situated in proximity to, but functionally independent from, regions responsible for color and face processing.

We conducted a case series study to evaluate Shitsukan perception in both tactile and visual modalities [25]. Ten stroke patients participated, including seven with occipital lobe lesions and three with parietal lobe lesions (Table 8.2). The material discrimination and identification tasks, previously described in this chapter [7], were administered using rod-shaped stimuli representing six materials (glass, ceramic, metal, wood, leather, and fabric). Tactile testing was performed with the unaffected hand. Performance was classified as impaired when it fell below the mean minus two standard deviations of the healthy control group. General cognitive status was assessed with the Mini-Mental State Examination (MMSE), and color vision was evaluated using the City University Color Vision Test (Part 2).

In the material identification task, three patients with lesions involving the left occipital lobe exhibited significantly low scores compared to the control group (Cases 1, 2, and 3). Among them, two patients with lesions in the left fusiform and lingual gyri showed distinct impairments: case 2 demonstrated deficit in both visual and tactile texture perception, while case 1 exhibited impairment in visual texture perception alone (Fig. 8.4). Case 3, with a lesion confined to the left lingual gyrus and collateral sulcus, showed impairment in tactile texture perception. In contrast, no deficits in texture perception were observed in patients with lesions in the right occipital lobe or in the right and/or left parietal lobes. Additionally, a significant positive correlation was identified between visual and tactile texture perception scores ($R = 0.68$, $p < 0.05$), suggesting the involvement of shared processes underlying both modalities of texture perception. Among these patients with impaired texture identification, two underwent the color vision test, which revealed no abnormalities. These findings

Table 8.2 Demographic and clinical data of patients

Case	Sex	Age	Etiology	MMSE (/30)	CUCVT (/6)	Lesion	
1	m	80	CI	14	6	L, R	O-F, Li
2	m	80	CI	19	6	L	O-F, Li
3	m	78	CI	27	–	L	O-Li
4	f	68	CI	28	6	L	O-F(lateral)
5	f	55	CI	27	3	R	O-F, Li
6	f	51	BT	24	5	R	O-F, Li
7	m	54	CI	30	6	R	O-F
8	m	63	CI	29	6	L, R	P
9	m	66	CH	25	6	L	P
10	m	38	CH	29	6	R	P

MMSE Mini-Mental State Examination, *CICVT* City University Color Vision Test, *CI* cerebral infarction, *BT* brain tumor, *CH* cerebral hemorrhage, *L* left, *R* right, *O* occipital lobe, *F* fusiform gyrus, *Li* lingual gyrus, *P* parietal lobe

suggest that the left medial occipital lobe plays a crucial role in texture perception, which can be impaired independently of color vision.

Neuroimaging studies have identified distinct activations for shape, color, and texture discrimination [20]. Texture discrimination activated the posterior collateral sulcus, color discrimination the anterior collateral sulcus and lingual gyrus, and shape discrimination the lateral occipital cortex, with bilateral activation and no hemispheric dominance reported.

These clinical and neuroimaging findings suggest that texture processing is primarily localized to the left or bilateral medial occipital lobe, with separate regions dedicated to color and shape processing.

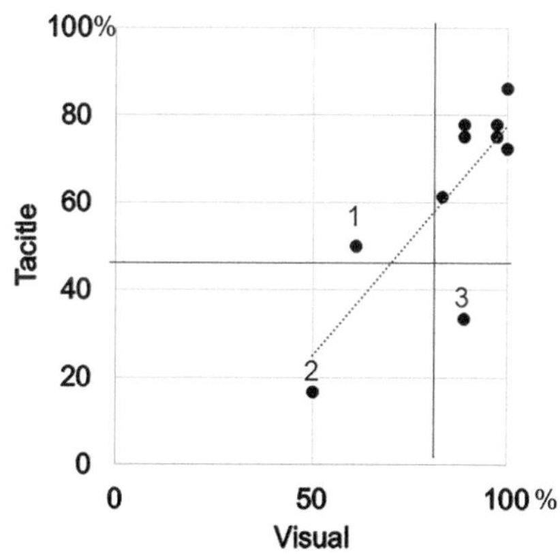

Fig. 8.4 Correlation of performance between visual and tactile material identification tasks. The lines indicate the mean—2SD of the normal control group. The number above each marker indicates the case number

8.3.2 Visual Texture Agnosia in Dementia

8.3.2.1 Visual Texture Agnosia in Dementia with Lewy Bodies

Dementia with Lewy bodies (DLB) is a neurodegenerative disorder characterized by the pathological accumulation of α-synuclein within the nervous system, predominantly affecting posterior cortical regions. Patients with DLB exhibit deficits in basic visual functions, including reduced visual acuity, diminished contrast sensitivity at mid-to-high spatial frequencies [26], impaired color vision [27, 7], and reduced stereopsis [27]. Other hallmark features involve visual misidentifications (pareidolia) and complex visual hallucinations. Pareidolia refers to the misperception of ambiguous visual stimuli as meaningful objects (e.g., faces or animals) and occurs more frequently in DLB than in Alzheimer's disease (AD) [28, 29]. Uchiyama et al. developed a scene pareidolia test using Gaussian-filtered blurred images optimized to elicit pareidolia. This test revealed a high prevalence of pareidolia in patients with DLB, making it a valuable tool for differentiating DLB from AD [29]. In DLB patients, pareidolia is more easily induced when the texture or shape of objects are blurred with filtering. These findings suggest that impaired texture and shape perception in DLB may contribute to visual misidentifications, including pareidolia.

We investigated visual texture perception in DLB and its influence on object recognition and occurrence of pareidolia [7, 30]. We found that object recognition in DLB patients was significantly impaired by both changes in visual texture and viewpoint. The texture identification was positively correlated with object recognition in DLB, but not in AD (Fig. 8.5). Pareidolic responses, where objects are misidentified as entirely different categories, were absent in the healthy controls but appeared in both the DLB and AD groups under non-canonical view conditions. These responses occurred mostly with blurred texture and were significantly more frequent in the DLB group than in the AD group. Deficits in visual texture recognition could be one of key underlying factors in the impaired visual object recognition and occurrence of pareidolic responses commonly observed in DLB.

Texture perception is crucial not only for object identification but also for determining the state of an object. For example, the freshness of fruits or the aging of furniture is often judged by texture. In DLB, deficits have been reported in both visual object recognition and the ability to visually assess object quality. We found that DLB patients demonstrate difficulty in judging the freshness of vegetables through visual inspection, which appears to be associated with impaired visual texture recognition [31].

8.3.2.2 Visual Texture Agnosia in Alzheimer's Disease

In Alzheimer's disease (AD), spatial dysfunctions, such as constructional impairments and topographical disorientation, typically emerge relatively early, while visual object recognition is less affected in the early stages. Although visual texture

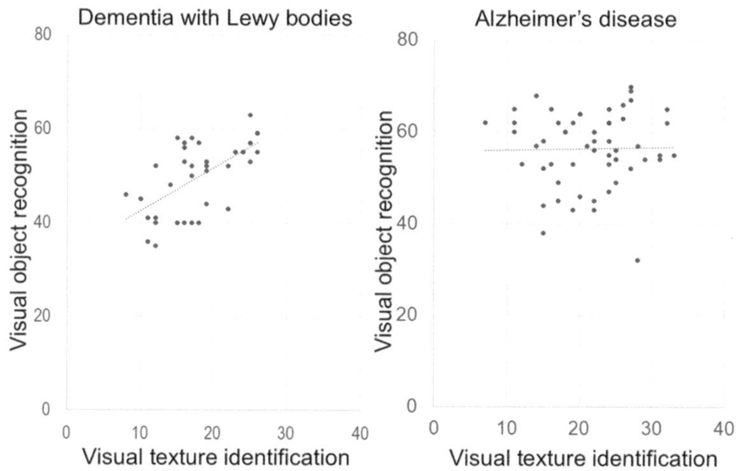

Fig. 8.5 Correlation between visual object recognition and visual texture identification in dementia with Lewy bodies and Alzheimer's disease. A positive correlation is observed only in dementia with Lewy bodies

perception declines compared to healthy older adults, the impairment is less severe than in DLB [7]. Visual object recognition remains intact when seen from canonical views based on shape, but performance declines when objects are presented from non-canonical views. This decline becomes more pronounced when texture is blurred under non-canonical view conditions, revealing significant object recognition deficits [30].

In patients with AD, no significant deficits are observed in tasks that involve judging the freshness of vegetables from photographs [31]. However, as the disease progresses, behaviors such as eating slightly spoiled food may emerge. This may be due to the combination of olfactory dysfunction, commonly reported in AD, and impairments in visual texture perception. The interaction between these sensory deficits can result in difficulties assessing food quality, potentially leading to inappropriate eating behaviors.

8.4 Auditory Texture Perception Impairment in Patients with Focal Brain Lesions and Dementia

The definition of auditory texture has not been formally established, but the concept broadly encompasses complex, often continuous acoustic patterns that convey information through their spectral and temporal structure. Examples include touch-produced sounds, musical sound textures such as consonant/dissonant chords or major/minor scales [32], and environmental natural sounds. In the perception of surface texture, roughness could be judged on the basis of touch-produced sounds alone [33]. As musical sound texture, minor tonalities, relative to major tonalities, receive higher sadness ratings and evoke increased limbic activity on fMRI; thus, changes in auditory texture are associated with mood shifts and differential network engagement [34]. Another phenomenon potentially related to auditory texture is the hypersonic effect, in which the presence of ultrasonic frequency components alters sound texture and produces measurable physiological and psychological changes [35].

8.4.1 Auditory Agnosia

Auditory agnosia refers to an impairment in the perception and identification of sounds that occurs despite normal hearing and preserved general cognitive function. It is traditionally classified into three clinical types: word deafness, involving difficulty recognizing speech sounds; environmental sound agnosia, affecting the recognition of non-speech environmental sounds; and amusia, impairing the perception of musical elements.

Auditory agnosia can also be categorized into two principal subtypes: apperceptive auditory agnosia and associative auditory agnosia. Apperceptive auditory agnosia is characterized by deficits in the basic perceptual analysis of sounds, such that individuals have difficulty discriminating their structural or acoustic features. In contrast, associative auditory agnosia reflects an inability to link accurately perceived sounds to their semantic or contextual meanings.

Considering the nature of auditory texture, apperceptive auditory agnosia may correspond to auditory texture agnosia—a form of impairment involving difficulty in perceiving the fine-grained spectral–temporal and harmonic properties that define auditory texture, affecting both verbal and nonverbal sounds. In such cases, the recognition of sound identity is compromised not because of semantic association failure, but because the perceptual representation of the sound texture is incomplete or degraded.

8.4.2 Auditory Agnosia in Patients with Focal Lesions

Auditory agnosia is usually related to bilateral temporal lesions, affecting primary and/or associate auditory cortices and their subcortical pathways. Verbal auditory agnosia (word deafness) is caused by bilateral or left temporal lobe lesions, while auditory agnosia for environmental sound or music is mainly related to the right temporal cortico-subcortical lesions.

We reported a patient with the bilateral temporal lesions, who demonstrated word deafness and impaired perception of environmental sounds [36]. MR imaging revealed a left subcortical lesion mainly affecting the auditory radiation, and a right subcortical lesion underlying the superior temporal gyrus and the primary auditory cortex. The patient identified vowels better than consonants. Additionally, he showed a differential ability to identify the five Japanese vowels. The vowel [a] was correctly identified in more than 70% of auditory presentations, while the vowel [i] was identified in only 30% of presentations. Accuracy was significantly correlated with the difference between the first and second formant frequencies, suggesting that vowel perception in this case relied heavily on the analysis of formant interactions—a core component of auditory texture in speech.

Another patient with a right auditory cortical lesion involving the planum temporale, but sparing the primary auditory cortex, demonstrated impaired auditory segregation of complex acoustic patterns in the left ear [37]. Both speech-in-noise perception and segregation of musical elements were affected, indicating a disruption of higher-order auditory scene analysis that likely degraded the perception of auditory texture.

Auditory agnosia specific to environmental sounds is rare. One reported patient who developed environmental sound agnosia following bilateral putaminal hemorrhage, initially presenting with cortical deafness and generalized auditory agnosia [38]. This patient often confused environmental sounds with acoustically similar ones, indicating impaired perception of sound texture. Another patient with lesions in the left posterior temporal and parietal regions demonstrated persistent nonverbal auditory agnosia after recovering from aphasia [39]. Sound–picture matching was more impaired for environmental sounds than for corresponding verbal phrases, yet performance improved when the environmental sounds had speech-like auditory textures, such as specific spectral weighting and harmonicity changes.

8.4.3 Auditory Agnosia in Dementia

Environmental sound agnosia has been reported to be common in Alzheimer's disease; however, patients with difficulty recognizing environmental sounds often have poorer pure-tone hearing than those without such deficits [40]. Verbal auditory agnosia was also been documented in a patient with Alzheimer's disease [41].

Primary progressive aphasia (PPA) is a neurodegenerative dementia in which aphasia is the most prominent clinical feature. Some patients with PPA also present with deficits in phonemic recognition in addition to their aphasic symptoms [42]. We found that eight out of 27 patients with primary progressive aphasia exhibited impaired phonological identification, as indicated by phonological identification scores falling below expected levels based on their pure-tone threshold results [43]. Several of these patients also had difficulty perceiving environmental sounds, suggesting that both speech and non-speech deficits may stem from a shared disruption of auditory texture processing. Furthermore, phonological identification ability was positively correlated with regional cerebral blood flow in the bilateral superior temporal gyrus and primary auditory cortex—regions implicated in extracting the fine-grained spectral–temporal features that underlie auditory textures.

8.5 Tactile Texture Impairment in Autism Spectrum Disorder

Autism spectrum disorder (ASD) is a neurodevelopmental condition marked by persistent deficits in social communication and reciprocal interaction from early childhood. Core features include restricted, repetitive behaviors and atypical sensory responses, such as hyper- or hypo-reactivity to stimuli. These may manifest as reduced sensitivity to pain or temperature, heightened sensitivity to sounds or textures, excessive touching or smelling, or intense focus on lights or movement. Atypical sensory behaviors are reported in 53–92% of individuals with ASD based on parent-reported questionnaires [44, 45].

Tactile perceptual impairments in ASD have been widely reported, primarily based on caregiver observations. The Sensory Profile, a standardized questionnaire commonly used in clinical and research settings, asks caregivers to rate behaviors suggestive of sensory abnormalities—for example, avoiding barefoot walking, particularly on grass or sand, or showing distress during grooming. However, few studies have directly investigated tactile texture perception in ASD. In passive touch applied to the forearm, texture preferences in individuals with ASD have been reported as comparable to those of typically developing (TD) individuals [46, 47]. Similarly, roughness judgments with active touch on sandpaper did not differ significantly between ASD and TD subjects [48], although one study reported superior performance in ASD [49]. Given these inconsistent findings, the nature of tactile texture perception in ASD remains poorly understood.

We investigated both objective and subjective aspects of tactile texture perception in individuals with ASD using two paradigms that we designed and implemented: a tactile–visual texture matching task and a subjective texture preference task [50]. In the matching task, we asked participants to palpate a texture concealed behind a screen and then to select, from visually presented options, the texture that matched the one they had touched. Our results showed no significant differences in texture recognition performance between the ASD and TD groups. In the preference task, we found that the ASD group did not consistently avoid prickly materials, in contrast to the sensory hypersensitivity frequently reported in caregiver-based assessments. Furthermore, when we analyzed the relationship between texture recognition scores and Sensory Profile parameters obtained from caregiver questionnaires, we found no significant correlations.

Although sensory hypersensitivity or sensory avoidance behaviors are frequently observed in caregiver reports, our findings revealed no significant differences between ASD and TD participants in tactile texture recognition or preference. Several explanations may account for this discrepancy. First, the ASD group exhibits considerable individual variability, which may reduce the likelihood of significant differences at the group level. Additionally, while active touch was used in this study, sensory avoidance in daily life may sometimes arise from passive touch where the child is touched rather than touching actively. With active touch, individuals can self-modulate the contact, possibly reducing discomfort and leading to less unpleasantness.

Neuroanatomical factors may also help explain the mismatch between sensory abnormalities reported through the Sensory Profile and the absence of texture perception impairments in our tasks. Light touch on hairy skin, such as a gentle stroke on the forearm, is conveyed via C-fibers to a network centered on the insula, a region associated with socio-emotional processing. In contrast, stimulation of the palm is processed via Aβ fibers that project to the primary sensory cortex and are involved in tactile discrimination and recognition. Functional MRI studies indicated that in ASD, insular activation in response to C-fiber-mediated stimuli (e.g., stroking the forearm) is decreased, while Aβ-mediated activation in the primary sensory cortex (e.g., from palm stimulation) is increased compared with TD individuals [51]. Given that the texture discrimination tasks in the present study involved active touch, it is plausible that they primarily recruited Aβ-mediated pathways. Accordingly, the perceptual processes engaged by these tasks may differ from the socio-emotional responses detected by the Sensory Profile, which are more closely linked to C-fiber–mediated processing.

8.6 Alteration of Shitsukan by Electrocortical Stimulation

Beyond lesion-based evidence, transient modifications of Shitsukan perception can be elicited during electrocortical stimulation, offering unique insights into its cortical substrates. Resection of epileptic focus is a therapeutic intervention for patients with drug-resistant epilepsy. During the preoperative evaluation, subdural and depth electrodes are implanted to identify the epileptic foci and to map eloquent cortex through electrical stimulation. The following case reports describe instances in which alterations in Shitsukan perception were observed as part of these clinically indicated procedures. Electrode implantation sites were determined exclusively according to clinical requirements.

8.6.1 Alteration of Face Shitsukan by Electrocortical Stimulation

Previous clinical and neuroimaging studies have identified face-selective regions in the brain, including the inferior occipital gyrus [52], fusiform gyrus [53], and superior temporal sulcus [54]. Face processing is proposed to involve two neural pathways: The ventral pathway, encompassing the inferior occipital gyrus and fusiform gyrus, which primarily processes static facial features, and the dorsal pathway, involving the anterior and posterior superior temporal sulcus which is specialized for dynamic facial features such as motion and expressions.

The inferior occipital gyrus, also referred to as the occipital face area, represents the initial stage of the ventral pathway. It is organized along gradients of spatial and face-part selectivity, serving as a foundation for higher-order facial processing. The fusiform gyrus plays a critical role in face detection, face identification, and the recognition of facial expressions.

Subtle differences in facial Shitsukan, such as complexion, glossiness, and shading, play a critical role in conveying information about a person's emotions and health status. Damage to face-processing regions has been associated with conditions such as metamorphopsia for faces, characterized by distortions in facial shape or color. Furthermore, electrical stimulation of these regions can induce transient prosopagnosia, marked by an inability to identify faces.

We observed a unique case demonstrating altered perception of facial Shitsukan elicited by electrocortical stimulation, offering novel insights into the neural mechanisms of facial Shitsukan processing (unpublished data). A patient with drug-resistant epilepsy, experiencing seizures since the age of seven, underwent presurgical evaluation for focal resection of epileptic foci in the left temporo-occipital region. Subdural electrodes were implanted in this area, and electrocorticography and electrical stimulation mapping were performed as a part of presurgical evaluation. Electrocorticography recordings revealed the face-specific high-gamma activity in a restricted region of the left inferior occipital gyrus. Electrical stimulation of this site reproducibly induced perceptual changes in the eyes of human and animal face pictures. The patient reported that "the left eye of the face (on the patient's right side) appears emphasized" only during electrical stimulation. No changes in facial shape or color were observed. Electrical stimulation of the same site did not affect the perception of non-facial objects.

These findings suggest that the restricted area of the left occipital face area may process the facial features on the right side, including the Shitsukan of face parts. Within the ventral pathway of face processing, specific subregions correspond to different stages of processing. Facial Shitsukan appears to be processed at a relatively early stage in the occipital face area.

8.6.2 *Alteration of Sound Texture by Electrocortical Stimulation*

The language-dominant hemisphere is engaged in semantic and syntactic language processing, while the language non-dominant hemisphere plays a crucial role in prosody perception. Specifically, individuals may interpret affective cues and infer emotional states through the suprasegmental modulations of sound texture in emotional prosody. The frontotemporal network responsible for decoding emotional prosody encompasses regions in the right superior temporal gyrus and the bilateral inferior frontal gyrus [55]. Significant variability in activation patterns across studies suggests distinct functional roles within each subregion. Within the inferior frontal gyrus, right Brodmann area (BA) 45 appears to be involved in cognitive evaluation of emotional stimuli, whereas right BA 47 relates to assessing the reward value and emotional quality of auditory cues [56]. Implicit processing of emotional prosody activates regions in the posterior superior temporal gyrus and bilateral inferior frontal gyrus, while explicit processing engages the middle superior temporal gyrus, left inferior frontal gyrus, amygdala, and anterior cingulate cortex [55].

We observed a drug-resistant epilepsy patient in whom electrocortical stimulation mapping revealed the right medial inferior frontal gyrus's causal role in higher-order auditory perception [57]. This right-handed patient, with a history of limbic encephalitis, displayed cognitive integrity with Wechsler Adult Intelligence Scale-III scores of 101 in verbal IQ, 129 in performance IQ, and 114 in full-scale IQ. She played the piano as a hobby. Intracranial propofol injection test demonstrated that the left hemisphere was language dominant. The epileptic focus was localized to the right temporal-frontal regions. For presurgical evaluation, subdural grid and depth electrodes were implanted in the right hemisphere to further investigate epileptic foci and eloquent areas.

Electrical stimulation of the medial inferior frontal gyrus (IFG) elicited subjective auditory perceptual changes, prompting additional assessments. Auditory stimuli included music, vocalizations (human voice and animal calls), and monotonic sounds (pure tone, white noise, single-pitch modes, and chords). The patient was instructed to press a handheld button upon noticing pitch changes and release it once the perceived pitch returned to baseline. Stimulation was applied to the right medial IFG under four conditions: (1) eyes closed with examiner-cued stimulation, (2) eyes closed with self-cued stimulation, (3) eyes open with examiner-cued stimulation, and (4) eyes open with self-cued stimulation.

The results revealed altered pitch perception depending on the context of stimulation, regardless of the type of sound. The patient perceived sounds as higher when she had greater control over the conditions (eyes open, self-cued stimulation) and as lower under examiner-controlled, eyes-closed conditions. Electrocorticography revealed low gamma band augmentation in the right medial IFG concurrent with her vocal response, indicating that this region responds to auditory stimuli. These findings suggest that the right medial IFG may modulate auditory perception in a context-dependent manner, reflecting implicit emotional change.

This study highlights the distinct role of the right medial IFG in modulating auditory perception, contrasting with previous research that emphasized the lateral IFG's involvement in processing implicit emotional stimuli [55]. These findings shed light on the involvement of a previously underrecognized region, offering a new perspective on the relationship between auditory perception and emotional processing. The human frontotemporal network involved in higher-order auditory perception consists of distinct subregions, each associated with different levels of processing. Within this network, there is likely a reciprocal relationship: sound texture can influence emotional responses, while emotional states can alter the perception of sound.

8.7 Optimal Shitsukan Environments in Super-Aged Societies

As outlined in this chapter, Shitsukan perception changes due to aging, focal brain lesions, and neurodegenerative disorders. In Japan, a super-aged society with the highest global aging rate in the world, the prevalence of dementia and mild cognitive impairment is projected to reach approximately 12 million by 2040. Although the mechanisms underlying changes in texture perception in dementia has gradually been elucidated, their impact on behavior remains poorly understood.

Recent studies have emphasized the importance of tailoring environments to individual needs, including texture preferences, in dementia care [58]. For example, PARO, a therapeutic pet-type robot, has been shown to improve mood and reduce agitation in dementia patients more effectively than standard care [59]. However, no significant difference was found between PARO and a soft toy animal in reducing agitation, suggesting that soft, fluffy texture itself may contribute to emotional stabilization.

Shitsukan perception plays a critical role in activities of daily living, encompassing food, clothing, and furniture, and its deterioration may significantly affect quality of life in dementia patients. Moreover, emotional stabilization is crucial for mitigating behavioral and neuropsychiatric symptoms of dementia, underscoring the relevance of emotionally salient Shitsukan. Advances in Shitsukan-creating technologies could enable the development of individualized sensory environments, potentially improving quality of life and alleviating behavioral and neuropsychiatric symptoms in dementia.

Technological innovations, including virtual reality, now allow for the flexible creation and modification of Shitsukan environments. Such tools offer the potential to design personalized sensory settings tailored to individual needs, providing a promising non-pharmacological approach to enhancing quality of life in individuals with brain damage and dementia.

8.8 Conclusions

The environment surrounding us is rich in Shitsukans across multiple sensory modalitie. These Shitsukans are perceived both consciously and unconsciously, contributing not only to object recognition but also to emotional and physiological responses. Our findings indicate that visual, tactile and auditory Shitsukan perception can be affected by aging, focal brain lesions, and dementia. Studying these alterations offers valuable insights into the neural mechanisms underlying Shitsukan perception. Moreover, identifying modality-specific changes in Shitsukan perception can inform the development of targeted interventions and the design of optimized Shitsukan environments to support function and well-being.

References

1. Komatsu, H., Goda, N.: Neural mechanisms of material perception: quest on shitsukan. Neuroscience **392**, 329–347 (2018)
2. Cavina-Pratesi, C., Kentridge, R.W., Heywood, C.A., Milner, A.D.: Separate processing of texture and form in the ventral stream: evidence from fMRI and visual agnosia. Cereb. Cortex **20**(2), 433–446 (2010)
3. Kalisch, T., Kattenstroth, J.C., Kowalewski, R., Tegenthoff, M., Dinse, H.R.: Cognitive and tactile factors affecting human haptic performance in later life. PLoS ONE **7**, e30420 (2012)
4. Wolpe, N., Ingram, J.N., Tsvetanov, K.A., Geerligs, L., Kievit, R.A., Henson, R.N., et al.: Ageing increases reliance on sensorimotor prediction through structural and functional differences in frontostriatal circuits. Nat. Commun. **7**, 13034 (2016)
5. Whitcroft, K.L., Altundag, A., Balungwe, P., Boscolo-Rizzo, P., Douglas, R., Enecilla, M.L.B., et al.: Position paper on olfactory dysfunction: 2023. Rhinology **61**, 1–110 (2023)
6. Mojet, J., Heidema, J., Christ-Hazelhof, E.: Taste perception with age: generic or specific losses in supra-threshold intensities of five taste qualities? Chem. Sens. **28**, 397–413 (2003)
7. Oishi, Y., Imamura, T., Shimomura, T., Suzuki, K.: Visual texture agnosia in dementia with Lewy bodies and Alzheimer's disease. Cortex **103**, 277–290 (2018)
8. Hiramatsu, C., Goda, N., Komatsu, H.: Transformation from image-based to perceptual representation of materials along the human ventral visual pathway. Neuroimage Clin. **57**, 482–494 (2011)
9. Iseki, C., Hommura, T., Sato, H., Koyama, S., Ohta, Y., Suzuki, K.: Texture perception in the elderly inhabitants of a local community. Clin. Neurol. **61**, s355 (2021)
10. Skedung, L., El Rawadi, C., Arvidsson, M., Farcet, C., Luengo, G.S., Breton, L., et al.: Mechanisms of tactile sensory deterioration amongst the elderly. Sci Rep-Uk. **8**, 5303 (2018)
11. Nakauchi, S.: Shitsukan created by experts. In: Komatsu, H. (ed.) Science of Shitsukan, pp. 142–153. Asakura Shoten, Tokyo (2016)
12. Binda, P., Pereverzeva, M., Murray, S.O.: Pupil constrictions to photographs of the sun. J. Vis. **13**, 8 (2013)
13. Laeng, B., Endestad, T.: Bright illusions reduce the eye's pupil. Proc. Natl. Acad. Sci. USA **109**, 2162–2167 (2012)
14. Naber, M., Nakayama, K.: Pupil responses to high-level image content. J. Vis. **13**, 7 (2013)
15. Laeng, B., Færevaag, F.S., Tanggaard, S., von Tetzchner, S.: Pupillary responses to illusions of brightness in autism spectrum disorder. I-Perception **9**, 2041669518771716 (2018)
16. Zavagno, D., Tommasi, L., Laeng, B.: The eye pupil's response to static and dynamic illusions of luminosity and darkness. I-Perception **8**, 2041669517717754 (2017)
17. Suzuki, Y., Minami, T., Nakauchi, S.: Pupil Constriction in the glare illusion modulates the steady-state visual evoked potentials. Neuroscience **416**, 221–228 (2019)
18. Laeng, B., Endestad, T.: Bright illusions reduce the eye's pupil. Proc. Natl. Acad. Sci. **109**, 2162–2167 (2012)
19. Suzuki, K.: Visual texture agnosia in humans. Brain Nerve **67**, 701–709 (2015)
20. Cavina-Pratesi, C., Kentridge, R., Heywood, C.A., Milner, A.D.: Separate channels for processing form, texture, and color: evidence from fMRI adaptation and visual object agnosia. Cereb. Cortex **20**, 2319–2332 (2010)
21. Sato, M., Kobayashi, Y., Hitosugi, M.: Visual texture agnosia caused by bilateral posterior cerebral artery stroke: a case study. Neurocase **27**, 190–195 (2021)
22. Battelli, L., Casco, C., Sartori, G.: Dissociation between contour-based and texture-based shape perception: a single case study. Vis. Cogn. **4**, 275–310 (1997)
23. Vaina, L.M.: Common functional pathways for texture and form vision—a single case-study. Synthese **83**, 93–131 (1990)
24. Oishi, Y., Nagasawa, H., Hirayama, K., Suzuki, K.: Neural bases of color-specific semantic loss: two cases of object-color knowledge impairment. Cortex **141**, 211–223 (2021)
25. Suzuki, K., Uno, Y.: Neuronal bases of texture discrimination and identification. J. Int. Neuropsychol. Soc. **18**, 25–26 (2012)

26. Mosimann, U.P., Mather, G., Wesnes, K.A., O'Brien, J.T., Burn, D.J., McKeith, I.G.: Visual perception in Parkinson disease dementia and dementia with Lewy bodies. Neurology **63**, 2091–2096 (2004)
27. Wood, J.S., Firbank, M.J., Mosimann, U.P., Watson, R., Barber, R., Blamire, A.M., et al.: Testing visual perception in dementia with Lewy bodies and Alzheimer disease. Am. J. Geriat. Psychiat. **21**, 501–508 (2013)
28. Mamiya, Y., Nishio, Y., Watanabe, H., Yokoi, K., Uchiyama, M., Baba, T., et al.: The pareidolia test: a simple neuropsychological test measuring visual hallucination-like illusions. PLoS ONE **11**, e0154713 (2016)
29. Uchiyama, M., Nishio, Y., Yokoi, K., Hirayama, K., Imamura, T., Shimomura, T., et al.: Pareidolias: complex visual illusions in dementia with Lewy bodies. Brain **135**, 2458–2469 (2012)
30. Oishi, Y., Imamura, T., Shimomura, T., Suzuki, K.: Visual texture agnosia influences object identification in dementia with Lewy bodies and Alzheimer's disease. Cortex **129**, 23–32 (2020)
31. Oishi, Y., Imamura, T., Shimomura, T., Suzuki, K.: Vegetable freshness perception in dementia with Lewy bodies and Alzheimer's disease. Dement Ger. Cogn. Dis. Extra. **10**, 74–85 (2020)
32. Shiramatsu Isoguchi, T., Takahashi, H.: Neural representation of sound texture in the auditory cortex. Brain Nerve **67**, 679–690 (2015)
33. Lederman, S.J.: Auditory texture perception. Perception **8**, 93–103 (1979)
34. Green, A.C., Baerentsen, K.B., Stodkilde-Jorgensen, H., Wallentin, M., Roepstorff, A., Vuust, P.: Music in minor activates limbic structures: a relationship with dissonance? NeuroReport **19**(7), 711–715 (2008)
35. Oohashi, T., Nishina, E., Honda, M., Yonekura, Y., Fuwamoto, Y., Kawai, N., et al.: Inaudible high-frequency sounds affect brain activity: hypersonic effect. J. Neurophysiol. **83**, 3548–3558 (2000)
36. Tanji, K., Suzuki, K., Okuda, J., Shimizu, H., Seki, H., Kimura, I., et al.: Formant interaction as a cue to vowel perception: a case report. Neurocase **9**, 350–355 (2003)
37. Holmes, E., Utoomprurkporn, N., Hoskote, C., Warren, J.D., Bamiou, D.E., Griffiths, T.D.: Simultaneous auditory agnosia: systematic description of a new type of auditory segregation deficit following a right hemisphere lesion. Cortex **135**, 92–107 (2021)
38. Taniwaki, T., Tagawa, K., Sato, F., Iino, K.: Auditory agnosia restricted to environmental sounds following cortical deafness and generalized auditory agnosia. Clin. Neurol. Neurosurg. **102**(3), 156–162 (2000)
39. Saygin, A.P., Leech, R., Dick, F.: Nonverbal auditory agnosia with lesion to Wernicke's area. Neuropsychologia **48**(1), 107–113 (2010)
40. Coebergh, J.A.F., McDowell, S., van Woerkom, T., Koopman, J.P., Mulder, J., Bruijn, S.: Auditory agnosia for environmental sounds in Alzheimer's disease: not hearing and not listening? J. Alzheimers Dis. **73**(4), 1407–1419 (2020)
41. Buciuc, M., Josephs, K.A., Jones, D.T., Whitwell, J.L., Graff-Radford, J.: Progressive auditory verbal agnosia secondary to Alzheimer disease. Neurology **97**, 908–909 (2021)
42. Kawakami, N., Morita, A., Kanno, S., Ogawa, N., Kakinuma, K., Saito, Y., et al.: Case report: semantic variant primary progressive aphasia with impaired verbal word discrimination. Front. Neurol. **13**, 873735 (2022)
43. Kawakami, N., Kanno, S., Ota, S., Morihara, K., Ogawa, N., Suzuki, K.: Auditory phonological identification impairment in primary progressive aphasia. Cortex **168**, 130–142 (2023)
44. Green, D., Chandler, S., Charman, T., Simonoff, E., Baird, G.: Brief report: DSM-5 sensory behaviours in children with and without an autism spectrum disorder. J. Autism Dev. Disord. **46**, 3597–3606 (2016)
45. Jussila, K., Junttila, M., Kielinen, M., Ebeling, H., Joskitt, L., Moilanen, et al.: Sensory abnormality and quantitative autism traits in children with and without autism spectrum disorder in an epidemiological population. J. Autism. Dev. Disord. **50**(1), 180–188 (2020)
46. Cascio, C., McGlone, F., Folger, S., Tannan, V., Baranek, G., Pelphrey, K.A., et al.: Tactile perception in adults with autism: a multidimensional psychophysical study. J. Autism Dev. Disord. **38**, 127–137 (2008)

47. Cascio, C.J., Moana, E.J., Guest, S., Nebel, M.B., Weisner, J., Baranek, G.T., et al.: Perceptual and neural response to affective tactile texture stimulation in adults with autism spectrum disorders. Autism Res. **5**, 231–244 (2012)
48. O'Riordan, M., Passetti, F.: Discrimination in autism within different sensory modalities. J. Autism Dev. Disord. **36**, 665–675 (2006)
49. Haigh, S.M., Minshew, N., Heeger, D.J., Dinstein, I., Behrmann, M.: Over-responsiveness and greater variability in roughness perception in autism. Autism Res. **9**, 393–402 (2016)
50. Chonan, Y.: Active touch-mediated haptic texture perception in adolescents with autism spectrum disorder. Doctral dissertation, Tohoku University Graduate Shool of Medicine (2025)
51. Kaiser, M.D., Yang, D.Y.J., Voos, A.C., Bennett, R.H., Gordon, I., Pretzsch, C., et al.: Brain mechanisms for processing affective (and Nonaffective) touch are atypical in autism. Cereb. Cortex **26**, 2705–2714 (2016)
52. de Haas, B., Sereno, M.I., Schwarzkopf, D.S.: Inferior occipital gyrus is organized along common gradients of spatial and face-part selectivity. J. Neurosci. **41**, 5511–5521 (2021)
53. Kanwisher, N.: The quest for the FFA and where it led. J. Neurosci. **37**, 1056–1061 (2017)
54. Haxby, J.V., Hoffman, E.A., Gobbini, M.I.: The distributed human neural system for face perception. Trends Cogn. Sci. **4**, 223–233 (2000)
55. Frühholz, S., Ceravolo, L., Grandjean, D.: Specific brain networks during explicit and implicit decoding of emotional prosody. Cereb. Cortex **22**, 1107–1117 (2012)
56. Schirmer, A., Kotz, S.A.: Beyond the right hemisphere: brain mechanisms mediating vocal emotional processing. Trends Cogn. Sci. **10**, 24–30 (2006)
57. Osawa, S.I., Suzuki, K., Asano, E., Ukishiro, K., Agari, D., Kakinuma, K., et al.: Causal involvement of medial inferior frontal gyrus of non-dominant hemisphere in higher order auditory perception: a single case study. Cortex **163**, 57–65 (2023)
58. Ludden, G.D.S., van Rompay, T.J.L., Niedderer, K., Tournier, I.: Environmental design for dementia care—towards more meaningful experiences through design. Maturitas **128**, 10–16 (2019)
59. Moyle, W., Jones, C.J., Murfield, J.E., Thalib, L., Beattie, E.R.A., Shum, D.K.H., et al.: Use of a robotic seal as a therapeutic tool to improve dementia symptoms: a cluster-randomized controlled trial. J. Am. Med. Dir. Assoc. **18**, 766–773 (2017)

Chapter 9
The Neural Value Transformation from Shitsukan

Takafumi Minamimoto and Koshi Murata

Abstract The sensory system enables the recognition and categorization of objects, allowing us to interpret the surrounding environment and guide our actions. Beyond this initial stage of sensory processing lies another level, where sensory representations are evaluated based on their biological significance. At this level, sensory representations give rise to value-based judgments, emotional responses, and motivational regulation, which in turn lead to decision-making and behavioral responses. Understanding sensory stimuli on the basis of their biological significance requires different computational frameworks distinct from those used for object identification—a transformation from recognizing surface attributes to evaluating deeper, context-dependent, and biologically grounded meaning. This deeper level of processing reflects the essence of "deep Shitsukan." Despite its importance for adaptive behavior, this neural transformation remains poorly understood. This chapter reviews the neural mechanisms underlying object perception in both vision and olfaction, focusing on how the brain recognizes and categorizes sensory inputs. We then move beyond this surface-level object perception to explore how the brain derives biological meaning—such as value judgments—from these sensory representations. Finally, we discuss open questions and future directions for understanding how the brain transforms perception to value-based decisions.

Keywords Vision · Olfaction · Category · Value

T. Minamimoto (✉)
Advanced Neuroimaging Center, National Institutes for Quantum Science and Technology, Chiba, Japan
e-mail: minamimoto.takafumi@qst.go.jp

K. Murata
Division of Brain Structure and Function, Faculty of Medical Sciences, University of Fukui, Fukui, Japan

S. Nishida and K. Nishino (eds.), *Shitsukan—Understanding and Manipulating Material and Quality Perception*, https://doi.org/10.1007/978-981-95-4762-3_9

9.1 Background: Sensory to Value-Based Processing as Part of "Deep Shitsukan"

In everyday life, we evaluate objects not only by recognizing what they are, but also by judging what they mean for survival, wellbeing, and action. This distinction parallels two levels of information processing. At one level, the sensory system constructs a representation of objects based on their surface attributes—shape, color, odor, and texture. At the other level, it transforms these sensory representations into value-based judgments that reflect the biological and ecological significance of those objects.

At the first level, sensory inputs are recognized and categorized, enabling the brain to construct a representation of objects and events. This stage—referred to here as "surface-level Shitsukan"—is evident across multiple sensory modalities, including vision and olfaction, and allows the brain to differentiate between objects on the basis of sensory details, thereby facilitating a structured understanding of the external world.

Beyond the first categorical stage, the second level of processing assigns value to sensory inputs, linking them to motivational and emotional meaning. This valuation stage enables the brain to assess the significance of sensory stimuli on the basis of factors such as reward, threat, or social relevance. Unlike the categorical level, which focuses on object recognition, value-based processing determines the desirability or aversiveness of an object and influences the resulting behavior. We refer to this deeper stage as "deep Shitsukan," a process that integrates internal states, prior learning, emotional context, and environmental conditions. Deep Shitsukan thus represents a core aspect of neural value computation, transforming sensory recognition into biologically meaningful signals that guide adaptive behavior.

In the following sections, overview of categorical sensory processing in vision and olfaction will be introduced, along with insights into how this information translates into behavior. Subsequently, theoretical and technical challenges will be discussed to illustrate how the second-level transformation—from perception to value-based processing—unfolds in the visual (by Minamimoto) and olfactory systems (by Murata). Using primate and rodent models, recent studies attempt to address these challenges by elucidating the neural circuitry and pathways involved in linking sensory recognition to adaptive, value-based decision-making and behavior. These findings address current gaps in our understanding of the pathway between sensory recognition and value processing and have important implications for future research.

9.2 Visual Information Processing

Vision plays a significant role in our perception of the world. Visual signals generated in the retina are processed in the lateral geniculate nucleus of the thalamus before reaching the primary visual cortex (V1). From V1, visual information ascends through a hierarchical stream known as the ventral visual pathway, which passes through areas V2 and V4 and reaches the inferior temporal (IT) cortex. This pathway is crucial for object recognition, as it transforms basic visual features into complex representations that support the identification and categorization of objects, such as faces [1, 2]. It also underlies material perception, where information about surface attributes is processed to form impressions of object materials [3].

The hierarchical structure of the ventral pathway is remarkably similar between macaques and humans [2], making macaques a valuable model for research in visual cognition with invasive methodology such as neuronal recordings. Individual neurons in the IT cortex—at the final stage of this pathway—exhibit strong selectivity for object shapes while maintaining a certain degree of invariance, meaning that their responses remain stable regardless of variations in image position, size, or orientation [4]. At the same time, IT responses are not entirely fixed, learning and experiences can modify the response properties of individual neurons [5], indicating IT representations are stable yet remain flexible and modifiable.

Consistent with these neural properties, the IT is essential for object recognition. In macaques, surgical lesions in the IT cortex lead to impairments in object recognition and categorization abilities [6–8]. In humans, lesions in specific areas of the IT cortex can cause prosopagnosia—a selective impairment in facial recognition [9]. These findings indicate that certain regions of the IT cortex are specialized for category-specific recognition.

As such, surface-level Shitsukan, involving the categorization of objects based on their visual features, is largely accomplished within the ventral visual pathway, with the IT cortex serving as its final and primary processing stage. One projection target of IT is the lateral prefrontal cortex (LPFC), which is involved in flexible categorization and decision-making [10]. Notably, visual category recognition remains possible even when LPFC function is disrupted [11], suggesting that the core process of categorization is largely implemented within IT. Nevertheless, the LPFC contains neuronal populations that represent objects as categories, supporting flexible use of these representations in behavior [12].

9.2.1 Transformation of Visual Information into Value: Beyond the IT Cortex

When we see an apple, we do more than just decide on our next action—we also experience various emotions, feelings, and thoughts, such as "That looks delicious." Additionally, even if we do not act on it immediately, we may store the information as an important memory. This shift illustrates the transition from what we have called surface-level Shitsukan—concerned with recognizing what an object category is—to deep Shitsukan, which evaluates what the object means in terms of biological value. The transformation of surface-level to deep Shitsukan is essential when experiencing feelings or making decisions on the basis of the relative importance or utility of visual objects, rather than on their physical attributes. This complex transformation involves multiple brain regions with strong anatomical connections to the IT cortex, including the amygdala, perirhinal cortex (Rh), orbitofrontal cortex (OFC), and posterior striatum, whose interactions with the IT cortex are crucial for linking visual input to emotional responses, memory storage, and adaptive behavior [13] (Fig. 9.1, top).

The amygdala is central to emotional processing and plays a key role in evaluating the value of visual stimuli [14]. Through its direct connection with the IT cortex, it regulates emotional responses to recognized objects, allowing the brain to determine the emotional significance of a visual stimulus, which in turn influences corresponding behavioral reactions [15]. The Rh, known for its role in memory and object recognition, interacts with the IT cortex to evaluate the value of objects based on past experiences, linking visual stimuli to prior rewards [16]. The OFC is

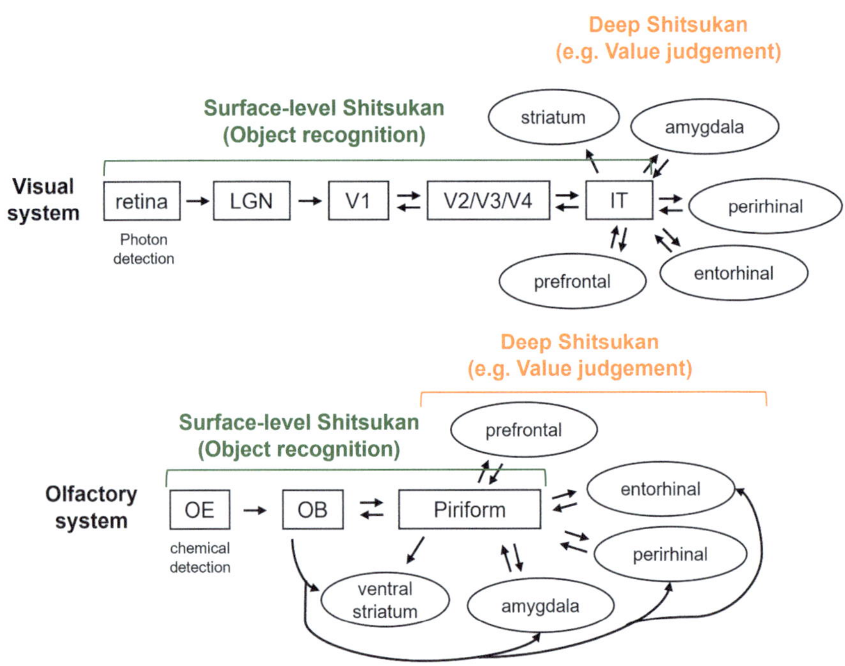

Fig. 9.1 Neural circuitries of sensory-to-value-based processing in vision and olfaction. The figure shows parallel neural systems in vision (top) and olfaction (bottom), where sensory information is processed hierarchically. Sensory information detected by peripheral receptors progresses through sensory areas from lower- to higher-order regions (inferior temporal [IT] cortex in vision and piriform cortex in olfaction) for category recognition, referred to as "surface-level Shitsukan." This process is followed by connections to limbic cortical and subcortical regions, including the striatum and amygdala, which integrate value and drive emotional and behavioral responses on the basis of sensory inputs—a process referred to as "deep Shitsukan." LGN, lateral geniculate nucleus; OB, olfactory bulb; OE, olfactory epithelium

critical for decision-making, reward processing, and emotional regulation. It integrates information from multiple sensory modalities, including the visual, gustatory, olfactory, and somatosensory inputs, through its connections with the IT cortex and other sensory areas, facilitating the evaluation of stimuli's reward value and guiding adaptive behavior [17]. The posterior striatum, particularly the caudate tail, plays a key role in reward and motivation, translating value assessments of visual stimuli into action plans. The caudate tail encodes the long-term value of visual objects and guides saccadic eye movements via projections to the substantia nigra, thereby facilitating attention and motor responses toward valued objects [18].

Together, these regions form an interconnected network that extends beyond the IT cortex, each contributing to the transformation of visual information into value-based representations. This network evaluates visual stimuli for their emotional and motivational significance, enabling the brain to guide behavior in alignment with the perceived value of what is seen.

9.2.2 Unraveling the Neural Circuits of Visual Value Transformation: Technical Challenges

The transformation of visual object representations into value-based signals relies on the interconnections between IT cortex and brain regions including OFC, amygdala, and striatum. Due to fundamental structural differences between primate and non-primate visual systems, nonhuman primates serve as essential models for studying these circuits. Because these value-related regions are also interconnected with one another, establishing causal relationships within the network requires the application of advanced neural manipulation techniques originally developed in rodents, such as optogenetics and chemogenetics.

Optogenetics involves introducing light-sensitive ion channels into specific neurons so that their activity can be turned on or off using light, offering millisecond-level temporal precision [19]. In contrast, chemogenetics uses engineered receptors (such as designer receptors exclusively activated by designer drugs; DREADDs) that can be selectively activated by administering otherwise inert designer drugs, allowing for sustained and targeted modulation of neural activity [20]. These tools make it possible to manipulate specific neuronal populations and test their causal roles in behavior.

However, applying these techniques to nonhuman primates remains challenging. The larger brain volume, limited light penetration, and difficulties in achieving specific and stable gene expression complicate reliable targeting of deep brain regions. Despite these limitations, ongoing efforts to adapt optogenetics and chemogenetics for use in primates are opening new avenues for investigating the causal roles of the neural circuits involved in visual processing and value-based decision-making. In particular, chemogenetic approaches have enabled manipulation of neural connections with deep brain regions implicated in value processing, providing novel insights into the transformation from visual recognition to value computation [21].

9.2.3 Neural Circuits of Visual Value-Based Motivation Control

The pathway from the IT cortex to the Rh, and ultimately to the OFC, where the value of reward is represented, has been considered crucial for value-based decision-making associated with visual recognition. To explore this process, a behavioral paradigm was developed using macaques, enabling subjective valuation of visual objects to be inferred from the monkeys' performance [22] (Fig. 9.2a).

In this paradigm, thirsty monkeys were required to perform a simple task: releasing a lever at the correct moment to receive a juice reward. The reward amount, presented at four levels, was signaled by specific visual stimuli before each trial. Monkeys rapidly learned to associate each visual cue with the corresponding reward amount,

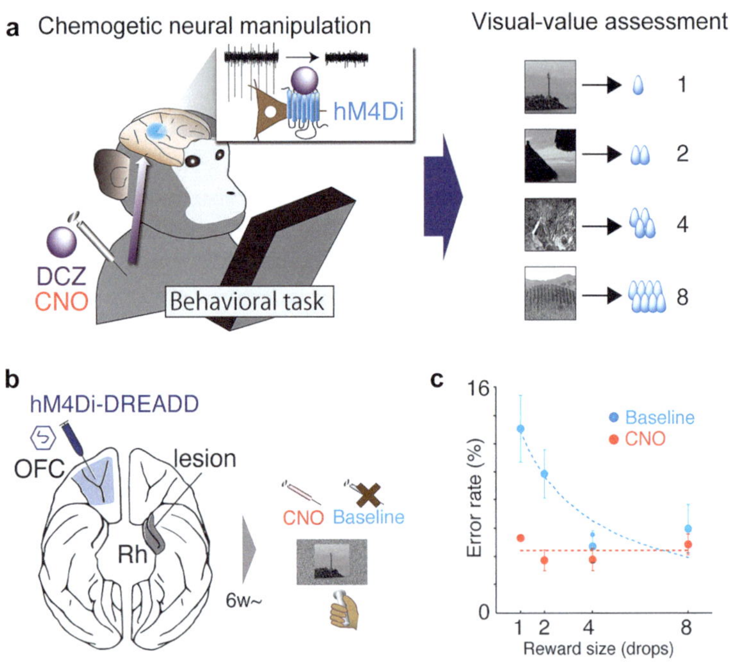

Fig. 9.2 Chemogenetic disconnection between the orbitofrontal cortex (OFC) and perirhinal cortex (Rh) disrupts visual value assessment. a Visual value assessment paradigm. **b** Combination of chemogenetic silencing of OFC and contralateral Rh lesion. **c** Behavioral results. Administration of clozapine-N-oxide (CNO) resulted in flattened error rates, indicating insensitivity to visual value. DREADD, designer receptor exclusively activated by designer drugs. DCZ, deschloroclozapine

demonstrating higher motivation to complete the task when larger rewards were expected. Conversely, when a visual stimulus indicated a smaller reward, the monkeys exhibited a higher likelihood of refusing the task. This behavior established a clear relationship between the probability of task refusal and the anticipated reward size, suggesting that any impairment in the monkeys' ability to evaluate the value of visual stimuli would likely disrupt this relationship.

To determine whether the connection between the Rh and OFC is essential for value evaluation, the neural link was temporarily disrupted using chemogenetics, and its impact on reward-refusal behavior was observed. In this setup, the Rh was surgically removed on one side of the brain, and inhibitory DREADDs were introduced into the OFC neurons on the opposite side (Fig. 9.2b). Administering a DREADD agonist, clozapine-N-oxide (CNO), suppressed the activity of these receptor-expressing neurons, enabling a temporary disruption of the Rh–OFC connection. Under disruption, monkeys' reward-refusal pattern was no longer dependent on the reward-predicting cues, indicating that the Rh–OFC pathway plays an essential role in visual value assessment (Fig. 9.2c) [23]. This study marked a significant advancement, being the first to successfully apply DREADD technology to the non-human primate brain.

A subsequent investigation focused on the role of the rostromedial caudate nucleus (rmCD), a region receiving projections from the OFC [24]. In this study, inhibitory DREADDs were virally introduced into the rmCD neurons of both hemispheres in monkeys. Systemic administration of CNO led to observable impairments in visual value-based decision-making, as evidenced by a disruption in the reward–refusal relationship.

Further insights into value representation in the rmCD were obtained through single-unit recordings conducted while the monkeys performed a value-based decision-making task [25]. Neural recordings from the rmCD and its primary output target, the ventral pallidum (VP), showed that many neurons adjusted their activity in response to visual stimuli, with the magnitude of this activity correlating with the reward value signaled by the visual cue. Pharmacological suppression of neural activity in both the rmCD and VP resulted in impairments in value judgments, underscoring the critical role of these regions in processing value information.

Taken together, these findings indicate that the IT cortex–Rh–OFC–rmCD–VP pathway is essential for assessing the value of visual stimuli and translating these evaluations into motivated behavior. The OFC serves as a hub for value-based assessments, whereas the rmCD and VP mediate motor responses on the basis of value representations. This integrated circuit ensures that visual stimuli are not only recognized but also evaluated in terms of their reward significance, shaping goal-directed behavior (Fig. 9.3).

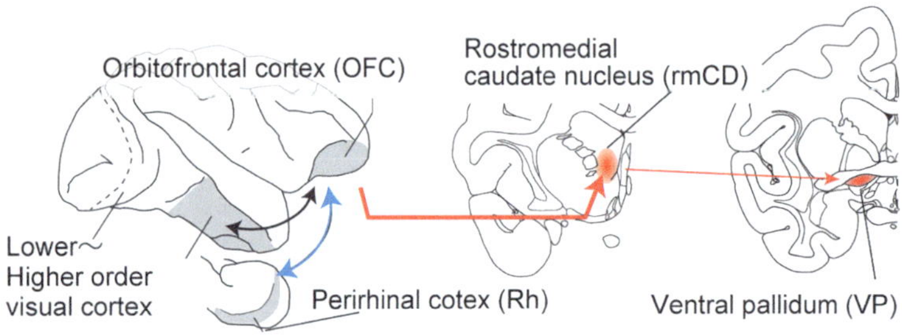

Fig. 9.3 Neural circuit for visual value transformation. By manipulating neural activity in monkeys through chemogenetics and other techniques, our studies have identified the pathway that includes the perirhinal cortex (Rh), orbitofrontal cortex (OFC), rostromedial caudate nucleus (rmCD), and ventral pallidum (VP) as an essential neural circuit for visual value transformation in motivational control

9.2.4 Visual Value is not Always the Same: Neural Circuit for Internal State-Dependent Value Transformation

The value associated with objects is inherently dynamic, adapting to changing in physiological states, prior experiences, environmental contexts, and emotional conditions. For example, even a favorite food, like an apple, can lose its appeal after overconsumption. This flexible evaluation process reflects the brain's ability to predict and update the value of objects and events in response to situational demands. However, the precise neural mechanisms that support this dynamic value computation remain largely unknown.

Research has investigated the neural mechanisms by which the perceived value of visual stimuli changes according to physiological states, such as satiety. The OFC is known to contain neurons that adjust their activity in response to food stimuli as physiological needs shift [26]. Building on this functional adaptability, a study explored the causal contribution of the neural pathway between the OFC and its projection target, the rmCD, using DREADDs to temporarily disrupt communication between these regions [27].

In this experiment, viral vectors expressing inhibitory DREADD receptors were injected into one side of monkey OFC, and receptor expression in both the OFC and the rmCD was confirmed using positron emission tomography (PET) imaging. To enable selective disruption of the OFC–rmCD pathway, additional DREADDs were introduced into the contralateral rmCD, creating a setup where the functional connection could be selectively inhibited by administering a designer drug. Monkeys were then presented with a single-option task involving visual objects associated with various reward levels. Under normal conditions, as the monkeys became satiated, their motivation to complete the task declined, while the likelihood of refusal of lesser rewards increased. However, when a DREADD agonist was administered to inhibit the OFC–rmCD connection, this adaptive behavior pattern disappeared, which indicates that the monkeys could no longer adjust their value judgments on the basis of their internal state of satiety (Fig. 9.4).

These findings suggest that the neural connection between the OFC and rmCD is essential for assessing and responding according to the value of visual stimuli in line with internal physiological states. This circuit likely plays a crucial role in maintaining flexible and adaptive value judgments, ensuring that behaviors align with the organism's current physiological needs and environmental conditions.

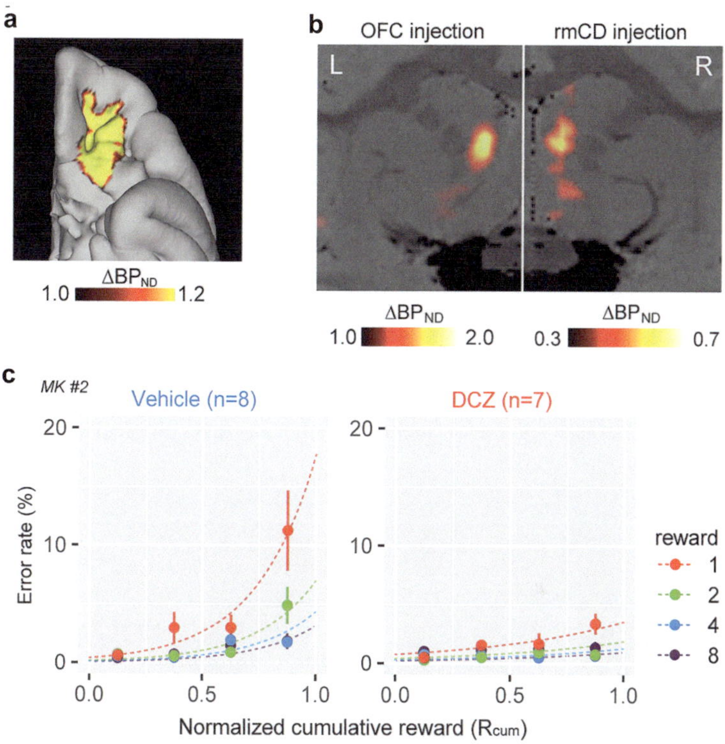

Fig. 9.4 Neural circuit essential for visual value based on internal state. **a** Positron emission tomography (PET) imaging of artificial receptor (hM4Di-DREADD) expression in monkey orbitofrontal cortex (OFC). **b** hM4Di-DREADD expression in the rostromedial caudate nucleus (rmCD), as the projection site of DREADD-positive OFC neurons (left) and via local viral injection (right). **c** Behavioral results: error rates in the single-option task depending on cumulative reward acquisition for each reward size. In control condition, monkeys showed increased error when they approaching satiation, while silencing of the OFC–rmCD pathway eliminated this adaptive change. Adapted from [27]

9.2.5 Neural Circuit for Visual Object Memory

We often retain visually significant or emotionally impactful images in our memory for a period of time. The anterior ventral temporal cortex (aVTC), a subregion of IT and the final stage of the ventral visual pathway, is a critical area for visual object memory. Neurons in aVTC encode complex visual objects; however, the source of top-down signals that determine which visual objects should be retained in memory has remained unclear. Recent chemogenetic imaging studies have provided insight into the frontal–temporal cortical network involved in object memory [28]. Using $[^{15}O]H_2O$-PET, a specific region of the OFC was identified as the site of neural activation associated with memory load during a visual memory task, named the "delayed matching to sample task." Focal chemogenetic silencing of the identified OFC region led to the downregulation of both local OFC activity and remote activation in the aVTC, which was accompanied by impaired mnemonic performance in the task. Further electrophysiological investigations revealed that top-down modulation from the OFC enhances delay period activity, that is, stimulus-selective mnemonic signals in individual anterior temporal neurons. Thus, dynamic top-down regulation of the OFC–aVTC pathway mediates short-term object memory via specific retention of the delay activity of individual aVTC neurons encoding the to-be-remembered object (Fig. 9.5). Such selective retention of biologically significant visual objects can be regarded as a component of deep Shitsukan, ensuring that perception is not only recognized but also prioritized for memory when it carries ecological or motivational relevance.

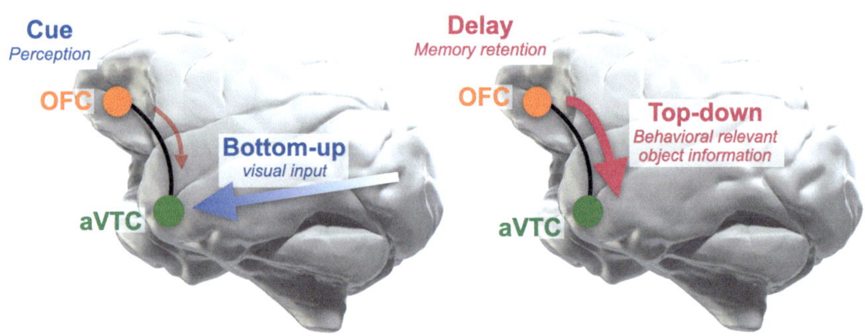

Fig. 9.5 Neural circuit for visual object memory. Schema of the ventral fronto–temporal network supporting visual object memory. During the cue period (left), anterior ventral temporal cortex (aVTC) neurons are primarily activated by bottom-up visual input for perception, during which the effect of top-down regulation is minimal. During the delay period without visual input (right), top-down signals from the orbitofrontal cortex (OFC) strongly enhance aVTC neurons carrying behaviorally relevant object information, thereby maintaining the representation of the presented cue. Reproduced from [28]

9.3 Olfactory Information Processing

The olfactory system is the sensory system responsible for detecting volatile chemicals. The evolutionary history of chemosensory systems traces back to single-celled organisms that exhibit attraction behaviors toward nutrient sources. For animals and humans alike, olfaction is a critical sensory modality for survival, offering vital cues to determine whether food is nutritious or spoiled and whether dangers such as predators are nearby. Humans and rodents are similar not only in terms of the biological significance of olfaction but also in terms of its neural mechanism, which makes mice and rats valuable models for investigating the Shitsukan mechanisms of olfaction (e.g., [29, 30]). Recent studies have revealed that olfactory neural mechanisms extend beyond merely recognizing objects—which can be referred to as sensing "surface-level Shitsukan"—to include value judgements that evoke strong emotional and behavioral responses, termed "deep Shitsukan." This part of the chapter first describes the neural mechanisms underlying the differentiation of chemical compounds and the recognition of objects emitting complex chemical mixtures, focusing on the olfactory epithelium (OE)–olfactory bulb (OB)–olfactory cortex circuit. It then explores the neural mechanisms driving both innate and learned odor value judgements, extending beyond the olfactory cortex (Fig. 9.1, bottom).

9.3.1 From Odor Detection to Object Recognition—Surface-Level Shitsukan

Scents encountered in daily life, such as those from food, typically consist of mixtures of multiple monomolecular components. It is thought that the brain recognizes objects by analyzing the individual components of these mixtures and integrating the information. The neural circuits of the OE and OB are responsible for detecting and processing individual chemical components [31]. Object recognition via chemical compounds emitted by a given target is believed to occur through comparison with a database of past experiences, particularly within the piriform cortex of the olfactory cortex [32]. The following two subsections describe how individual chemical compounds are detected and represented by the OE–OB circuit, and how this chemical information contributes to object recognition via the OB–olfactory cortex circuit.

9.3.1.1 Chemical Identification in the OE and OB

When we perceive odors, volatile chemicals in the air are detected by olfactory receptors expressed on olfactory sensory neurons located in the OE, a specialized region of the nasal mucosa. Mammals possess a large repertoire of olfactory receptors, with approximately 400 types in humans, enabling the discrimination of potentially over 1 trillion olfactory stimuli [33]. Each olfactory sensory neuron expresses only one type of olfactory receptor. This phenomenon is known as the "one neuron–one receptor rule" (Fig. 9.6a top) [34]. The axons of olfactory sensory neurons project to the OB, a brain region responsible for the initial processing of olfactory information. Neurons expressing the same type of olfactory receptor converge their axons onto a common area on the surface of the OB, forming structures known as glomeruli. This phenomenon corresponds to another important rule, the "one neuron–one glomerulus rule," which governs the formation of OE–OB neural circuits (Fig. 9.6a top) [34].

The relationship between olfactory receptors and chemical compounds is many-to-many: a single olfactory receptor can detect multiple chemical compounds with similar molecular structures, whereas a single chemical compound can activate multiple olfactory receptors with similar protein structures (Fig. 9.6a, bottom) [34, 36, 37]. The expression of olfactory receptors and the axonal projections to the OB are predominantly governed by genetic mechanisms [34]. As a result, the information detected by olfactory sensory neurons for a given chemical compound is transmitted to specific glomerular groups in the OB that correspond to that compound [31]. In short, an "odor map" exists in the OB, demonstrating spatially organized activity patterns corresponding to different odors (Fig. 9.6b) [35, 38].

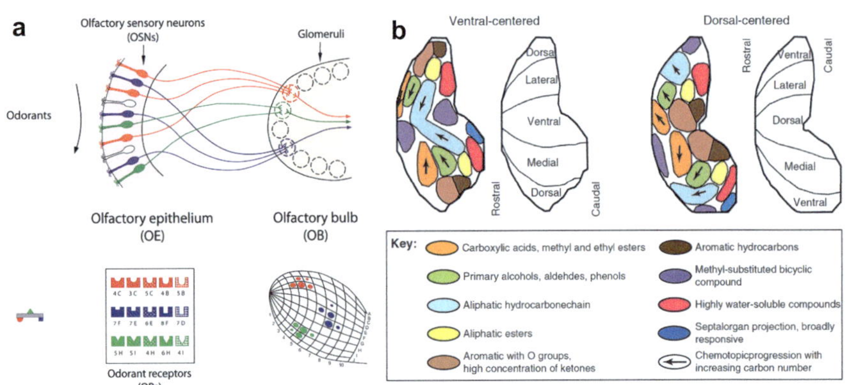

Fig. 9.6 Circuit formation between the olfactory epithelium (OE) and olfactory bulb (OB). **a**. In the OE, each olfactory sensory neuron (OSN) expresses only one functional odorant receptor (OR) gene, which is referred to as the "one neuron–one receptor rule." Furthermore, OSN axons expressing the same OR species converge to a specific glomerulus in the OB. Thus, each glomerulus represents one OR species. Because a given odorant activates multiple OR species and a given OR responds to multiple odorants, odorant signals received by OSNs in the OE are converted to a two-dimensional map of activated glomeruli with varying magnitudes of activity in the OB. **b** Odorant responses are chemotopically organized in the OB. Distinct odorant chemicals sharing certain molecular features (e.g., functional groups or aspects of hydrocarbon structure), or overall molecular properties (e.g., water solubility), stimulate overlapping but distinct sets of glomeruli that are clustered within functionally defined domains distributed across the glomerular layer. These domains are illustrated as colored areas within a ventral-centered 2D plot of the glomerular layer (left) and a dorsal-centered 2D plot (right). Reproduced with permission from [34] (A) and [35] (B)

9.3.1.2 Object Recognition by Pattern Completion and Separation in the Olfactory Cortex

The OB contains two subtypes of projection neurons: tufted cells and mitral cells. These neurons receive olfactory information from the olfactory sensory neurons in the OE and relay it to various brain regions, including the anterior olfactory nucleus, tenia tecta, ventral olfactory nucleus, piriform cortex, olfactory tubercle, cortical amygdala, and entorhinal cortex [31, 39]. Collectively, these regions, which receive axonal projections from tufted and mitral cells in the OB, are referred to as the "olfactory cortex" (Fig. 9.7a). Several studies have investigated whether the olfactory cortex, particularly the piriform cortex, the largest subregion, contains an odor map similar to that found in the OB (e.g., [40]). However, no clear correlation has been identified between chemical structure and the responding brain regions. Consequently, the olfactory cortex has since been considered to serve a function beyond merely housing an odor map [32].

Among the subregions of the olfactory cortex, the piriform cortex is thought to play an essential role in object recognition. Wilson and Sullivan [32] proposed a model in which unique combinations of odorant features, encoded in the spatiotemporal pattern of olfactory bulb glomerular output, are synthesized, stored and recalled through the activity of distributed ensembles of pyramidal cells in the piriform cortex (Fig. 9.7b, c and d). The piriform cortex thus functions as a pattern recognition system, using pattern completion and pattern separation to process the complex, dynamic combinatorial patterns of OB output [42]. The activity of individual cortical pyramidal cells reflects not only the unique combination of ongoing odorant feature inputs from tufted and mitral cells, but also the past history of synaptic input from coactive partners within the distributed pyramidal cell ensemble (auto-association). This memory-based component of the pattern recognition process facilitates the synthetic processing of odor mixtures through the experience-dependent formation of odor objects and enhances pattern completion in the presence of degraded inputs. A familiar odor—defined as a specific combination of odorant features and the corresponding spatiotemporal pattern of glomerular activation—elicits activity in a distributed, non-topographic ensemble of cortical neurons (content-addressable memory). This activation occurs because of both direct, convergent afferent input and association fiber inputs between coactive cells that were previously strengthened through experience with that odor. These processes together ensure odor discrimination (differentiation of distinct odor experiences) and perceptual stability (consistent recognition of odors under varying conditions) (Fig. 9.7). Additionally, this sparse ensemble encoding enables the storage of an extremely large number of odor patterns (odor objects) within content-addressable memory.

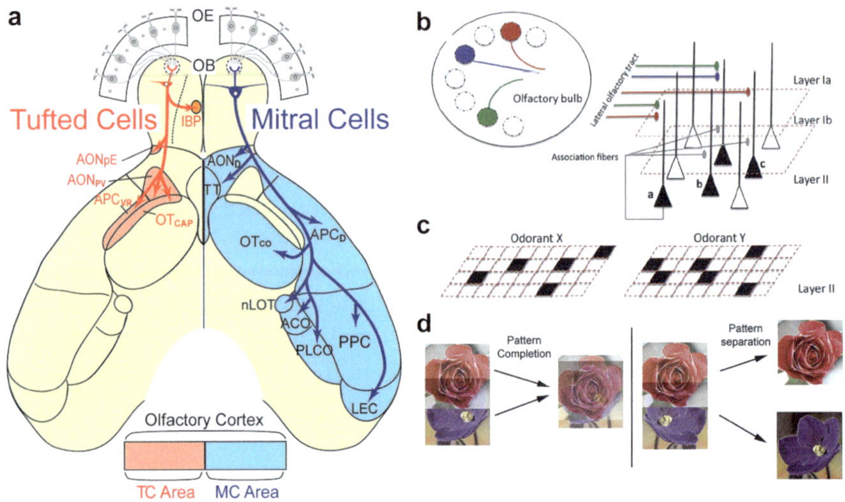

Fig. 9.7 Ensemble processing of odorants in the piriform cortex. **a** Schematic diagram of parallel pathways of mitral cells (MCs) and tufted cells (TCs) from the olfactory bulb (OB) to the olfactory cortex. The segregated projections of MCs and TCs suggest the existence of parallel MC and TC pathways in the central olfactory system. The axonal projections of the two cell types are represented on the left (TCs, red) and right (MCs, blue) sides of the ventral-view diagram of the mouse brain. In the OC, TCs route fast odor information to the anterior olfactory nucleus pars externa (AON_{pE}), posteroventral part of the anterior olfactory nucleus (AON_{pV}), anterolateral part of the olfactory tubercle that corresponds to the cap part of the olfactory tubercle (OT_{CAP}), and ventrorostral part of the anterior piriform cortex (APC_{VR}). These regions are represented as TC areas (pink). In the OB, TCs in the lateral map target the intrabulbar axons projecting to the confined, small area in the medial map (IBP). By contrast, MCs route slower odor information widely to the dorsal part of the anterior olfactory nucleus (AON_D), cortical part of the olfactory tubercle (OT_{CO}), dorsal part of the anterior piriform cortex (APC_D), tenia tecta (TT), posterior piriform cortex (PPC), lateral entorhinal cortex (LEC), nucleus of the lateral olfactory tract (nLOT), anterior cortical amygdaloid nucleus (ACO), and posterolateral cortical amygdaloid nucleus (PLCO) (MC area, cyan). The term "piriform cortex" collectively refers to the APC_{VR}, APC_D, and PPC. OE, olfactory epithelium. **b** Odorant features, encoded as spatiotemporal patterns in OB glomeruli and their outputs, converge in the piriform cortex through broadly dispersed, nontopographic projections. Information is also distributed through broad intracortical association fibers projections. Neurons activated by a given odor (black cells) are broadly distributed. Spiking in individual neurons can be driven directly by afferent input (cell a), association fiber input (cell b), or their combination (cell c). **c** Given the distributed afferent and association fiber projections, different odorants (X and Y) can activate widely distributed, overlapping ensembles of neurons. As described in the text, the plasticity of association fiber synapses allows for pattern completion in the event of degraded familiar afferent inputs. **d** Pattern completion and separation in the piriform cortex. In pattern completion, the auto-associative network of the piriform cortex enables partial or degraded odor inputs to reconstruct a complete odor representation. This process is achieved through the strengthening of synaptic connections between coactive pyramidal neurons during previous exposures to the same odor. In pattern separation, the piriform cortex uses sparse coding to distinguish similar yet distinct odor inputs. This process allows for the differentiation of closely related odor objects, preventing interference between similar scent experiences. Reproduced with permission from [41] (**a**) and [32] (**b–d**)

9.3.2 *Neural Mechanisms of Value Judgments in Olfaction—Deep Shitsukan*

The processing of olfactory information goes beyond distinguishing chemicals or recognizing the objects emitting odors (object recognition or "surface-level Shitsukan"). On the basis of whether an odor signifies food, a mate, or a danger cue, the brain makes value judgments that elicit adaptive physiological, emotional, and behavioral responses. In other words, our brain generates the sensation of "deep Shitsukan" through olfactory information. Animals and humans exhibit clear aversive emotional and behavioral responses to odors predicting life-threatening stimuli, such as spoiled food, decaying carcasses, and predators. These aversive responses are thought to be innately hard-wired into neural circuits. Furthermore, because the nutritional value, edibility, and safety of food, and environmental dangers, change over time, animals must learn to adapt to olfactory cues in their surroundings. By investigating the neural mechanisms underlying value judgments on the basis of learning and adaptive motivational control, we have identified the olfactory tubercle, a region of the ventral striatum, as a key olfactory brain area involved in learned olfactory value judgments and motivational control [43, 44]. The following sections describe the neural mechanisms underlying both innate and learned odor value judgements.

9.3.2.1 Innate Odor Value Judgements

Certain odors, such as those indicating decay or predators, trigger innate aversive responses. Recent studies have shown that these hard-wired aversive responses are mediated by specialized neural circuits. Kobayakawa et al. [45] demonstrated that genetically removing a subset of olfactory neurons from the OE projecting to the dorsal part of the OB in mice eliminates innate aversive responses to odors such as fox scent (trimethylthiazoline, TMT) and the smell of rotten food (2-methyl butyric acid). Although the mice could still detect and recognize these odors through alternative pathways involving olfactory neurons projecting to non-dorsal regions of the OB, they no longer exhibited innate avoidance behaviors. Among the subregions of the olfactory cortex, the anterior part of the cortical amygdala is necessary for mediating innate aversive behaviors toward TMT [46]. Additionally, the amygdalo–piriform transition area, a specific area of the olfactory cortex, contains neurons that are upstream of hypothalamic corticotropin-releasing hormone neurons and regulate stress hormone responses to TMT [48]. Similarly, the visual system possesses innate aversive circuits, such as those involved in snake detection, which are activated via the subcortical visual pathway, encompassing the projections from the retina to the superior colliculus, pulvinar, and amygdala [49]. These early recognition pathways underscore how sensory systems are equipped with specialized circuits to rapidly detect life-threatening stimuli and elicit immediate behavioral responses.

In contrast, certain odors, such as those found in opposite-sex urine, peanut butter, and rose flowers (which contain 2-phenylethyl alcohol), elicit innate attraction behaviors in mice [46, 49]. The innate attractive responses to 2-phenylethyl alcohol require the posterior part of the cortical amygdala [46]. When evaluating attraction behaviors toward food-associated odors, it is important to note that mammalian fetuses can experience and learn food odors. Fetal mice are exposed to odor compounds from the food consumed by their mothers through the amniotic fluid, which leads to a later attraction to those scents. This prenatal exposure enlarges the glomeruli of the OB for those odors and enhances the glomerular response to them [50]. As a result, attraction to food odors may not be entirely innate but rather influenced by early learning, making it difficult to definitively categorize attraction behaviors toward food-related odors as purely "innate."

9.3.2.2 Learned Odor Value Judgements

In addition to the aforementioned hard-wired innate responses to odors, the olfactory environment varies by region and season, requiring animals and humans to learn the smells of new food or dangerous situations and adapt to constantly changing surroundings. This adaptation necessitates a neural mechanism that learns the value of external odorants associated with rewarding or punishing objects and evaluates these odorants' significance. In the neural circuits from the OE to the piriform cortex, odorants are processed to enable object recognition—inferring what an object is. Simultaneously, the value of the odors associated with these objects is thought to be evaluated in neural circuits downstream of the piriform cortex, thereby eliciting adaptive physiological and behavioral responses; but which parts of the olfactory neural circuit are involved in the value judgment of odors learned through experience? To address this question, we took a comprehensive approach to evaluate brain activity in mice that had acquired attraction or aversion behaviors toward odors through associative learning [43]. This investigation revealed functional domains within the olfactory tubercle (OT), shedding light on the neural mechanisms underlying odor value judgments in this brain region.

Functional domains in the olfactory tubercle and their contribution to odor value judgements

To identify which subregions of the olfactory cortex are involved in odor value judgments, we performed neural activity mapping using the expression of an immediate early gene, c-fos, after mice had acquired odor cue values through associative learning. Amyl acetate and eugenol were chosen as cue odors because they induce neither clear attraction nor aversion behaviors. We established two experimental groups of mice: one trained to search for and find sugar on the basis of odor cues, and another that received an electric shock following odor cue presentation. A control group was exposed to the odor cues with neither sugar nor shock. Mice that associated the odor cue with sugar exhibited attraction behaviors, whereas those that associated the odor cue with an electric shock showed aversion. By comparing c-fos expression in brain regions downstream of the piriform cortex between these groups, we found distinct patterns of activation in the OT. In mice exhibiting attraction, c-fos responses were observed in the anteromedial domain of the OT (amOT). In those displaying aversion, c-fos responses were seen in both the amOT and the lateral domain of the OT (lOT). The OT is part of the striatum, and its projection neurons are categorized into two subtypes on the basis of the expression of dopamine receptors (D1 or D2). When evaluating dopamine receptor D1 and D2 expression in c-fos-responsive neurons, we found that D1-expressing neurons in the amOT were activated in mice displaying attraction, whereas D2-expressing neurons in the amOT, as well as D1-expressing neurons in the lOT, were activated in mice displaying aversion (Figs. 9.8). These response patterns were consistent across both amyl acetate and eugenol. These results suggest that the response patterns in the OT represent the type of behavioral reaction to odors rather than the type of odor itself. This finding provides insights into how mice judge the value of odors on the basis of OT activity [43]. Consistent with these findings, electrophysiological recordings in behaving mice revealed that the firing activity of the OT flexibly encoded the valence of conditioned odors with respect to odorant identity [51].

Involvement of olfactory tubercle functional domains in motivated behaviors

Recent advances in genetic tools for neuroscience have enabled neuronal cell-type-specific manipulation in vivo. Similar to chemogenetics with DREADDs and designer drugs described earlier, optogenetics employs light-gated ion channel

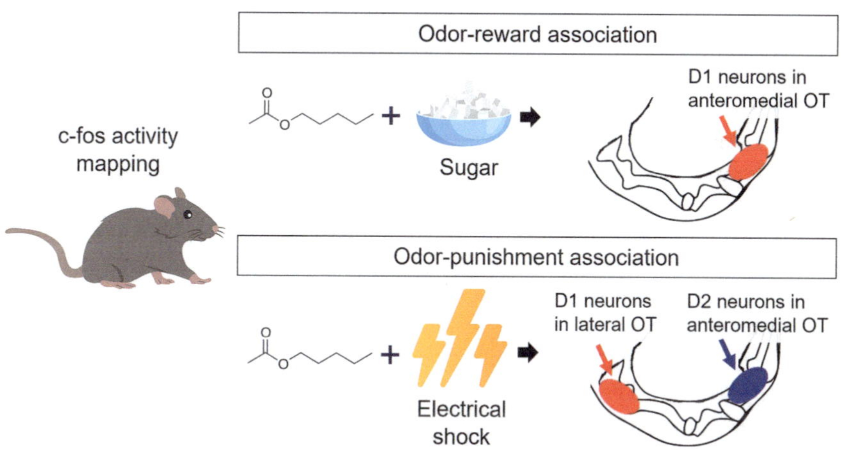

Fig. 9.8 Activation of the olfactory tubercle by odor–reward and odor–punishment associative learning. Neuronal activity mapping by an immediate early gene, c-fos, revealed functional domains of the mouse olfactory tubercle. Sugar reward-associated odor cues elicit attractive behavior and c-fos activation of dopamine receptor D1-expressing neurons in the anteromedial olfactory tubercle (OT). Electrical shock punishment-associated odor cues elicit aversive behavior and c-fos activation of dopamine receptor D1-expressing neurons in the lateral OT and D2-expressing neurons in the anteromedial OT. Adapted from [58]

proteins and light to experimentally activate or inhibit neurons. We used optogenetics to evaluate the cell-type-specific roles of dopamine receptor D1- and D2-expressing neurons in the amOT in mediating attractive and aversive behaviors [52]. Because D1- and D2-expressing neurons are intermingled in the amOT, genetic tools were essential for their selective manipulation. To achieve this, we used an adeno-associated virus encoding channelrhodopsin-2 (ChR2), a blue light-gated cation channel whose expression requires DNA recombination by Cre recombinase. Genetically modified mice that express Cre recombinase specifically in D1- or D2-expressing neurons were employed. By locally injecting the adeno-associated virus into the amOT and implanting optical fibers, we were able to selectively activate D1- or D2-expressin neurons by illuminating them with blue light. To assess attraction and aversion behaviors, we conducted real-time place preference tests. In these tests, blue light was delivered to activate the amOT neurons while the mouse stayed in one room, and the light was turned off while the mouse stayed in the other room. If neural activity manipulation increased the time spent in a specific room, it was interpreted as having an attractive effect on the mouse. Conversely, if neural activity manipulation decreased the time spent in a room, it was interpreted as having an aversive effect. Activation of D1-expressing neurons in the amOT increased the time spent in the light-stimulated area, indicating an attraction response. In contrast, activation of D2-expressing neurons decreased the time spent in the stimulated area, indicating an aversion response. These findings demonstrate that the amOT not only represents learned value judgments but also plays a role in controlling motivated behaviors such as attraction or aversion [52].

Currently, we are investigating the involvement of the amOT in hedonic "liking" reactions. As demonstrated by Berridge and colleagues at the University of Michigan, the brain contains "hedonic hotspots" where neural manipulation using optogenetics and pharmacology enhances hedonic "liking" reactions to oral infusions of sweet sucrose during taste reactivity tests [53]. These findings suggest that hedonic hotspots are critical for generating hedonic impact, or the sensation of pleasure. We hypothesized that the amOT might function as a hedonic hotspot, given that the rostromedial part of the nucleus accumbens, which forms part of the ventral striatum alongside the OT, contains its own hedonic hotspot. To test this hypothesis, we microinjected drugs such the mu-opioid receptor agonist DAMGO, the orexin-A peptide, and the $GABA_A$ receptor agonist muscimol into the amOT. These treatments significantly enhanced hedonic "liking" reactions to oral infusions of sweet sucrose (Fig. 9.9a, Murata and Berridge, unpublished observation). In contrast, when these drugs were microinjected into the lOT, no enhancement of "liking" reactions to sweet sucrose was observed. These results suggest that the amOT plays a critical role in generating positive emotions, facilitating the acquisition of positive value for odor cues and promoting motivated behavioral responses to these cues.

We also investigated the neurochemical differences between the amOT and lOT. In general, striatal D1-expressing neurons co-express *Pdyn*, an opioid precursor gene, whereas striatal D2-expressing neurons co-express *Penk*, another opioid precursor gene. In the amOT, we found that a subset of D1-expressing neurons co-express both *Pdyn* and *Penk* at a higher frequency than in the lOT (Fig. 9.9b, [54]). This

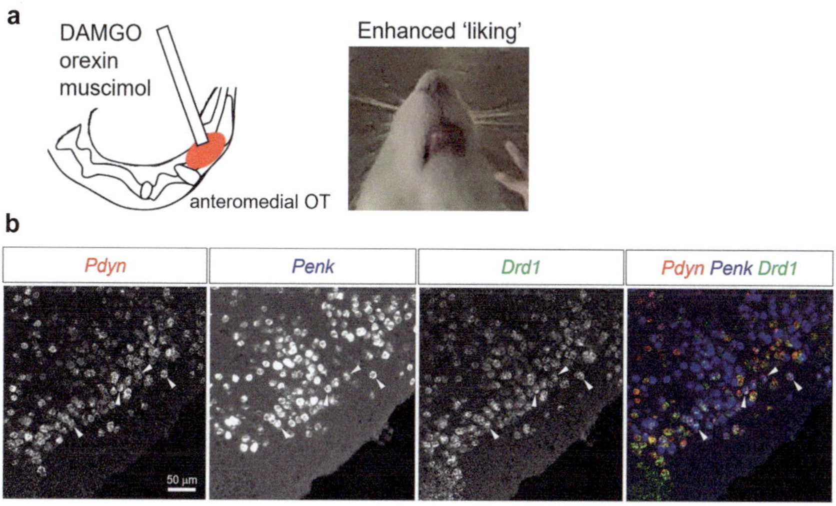

Fig. 9.9 A hedonic hotspot and opioid expression in the anteromedial olfactory tubercle. **a** Microinjection of DAMGO (a mu opioid receptor agonist), orexin-A peptide, and muscimol ($GABA_A$ receptor agonist) into the anteromedial olfactory tubercle (OT) enhances hedonic "liking" reactions to sweet sucrose infusion into the oral cavity. **b** OT projection neurons can be classified into dopamine receptor D1-expressing and D2-expressing subtypes. In general, D1-expressing neurons co-express an opioid precursor gene, Pdyn, whereas D2-expressing neurons co-express another opioid precursor gene, Penk. In the anteromedial OT, a hedonic hotspot in the olfactory system, D1-expressing neurons co-express both Pdyn and Penk at a higher frequency compared with the findings in other OT domains. Adapted from [54] and [58]

neurochemical distinction between the amOT and lOT may underlie the functional differences observed between these domains [55].

9.3.2.3 Neural Mechanisms Underlying Learned Odor Value Judgements

The functional domains of OT provide evidence for a neural mechanism that represents the odor value by altering neuronal responsiveness on the basis of past experiences, such as whether an odor was associated with rewarding or punishing outcomes. However, what neural mechanisms underlie the changes in OT response domains caused by past experiences through associative learning? Recent studies have revealed that neural plasticity in the pathways conveying olfactory information to the OT, along with dopaminergic inputs from the ventral tegmental area (VTA), play critical roles in the associative learning-driven changes in OT response domains [56, 57]. Here, we describe the involvement of neural circuit reorganization by associative learning and the dopaminergic input from the VTA to the OT in the acquisition of odor-related reward value.

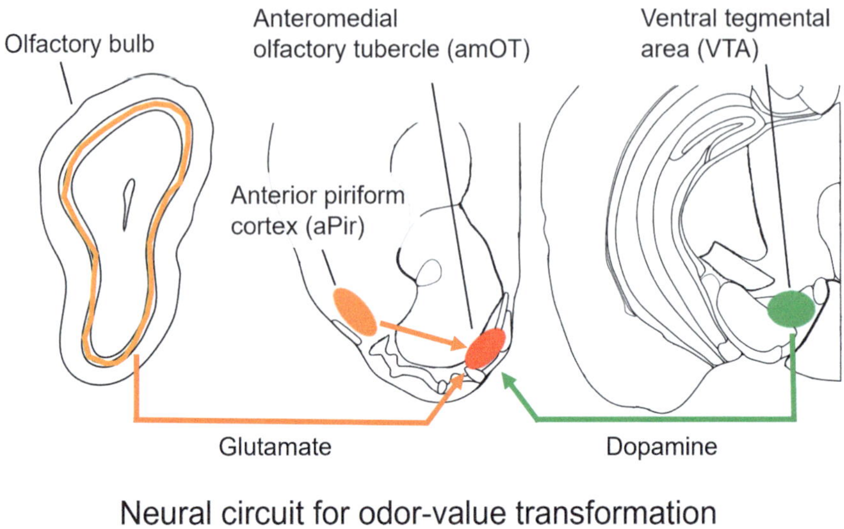

Fig. 9.10 Neural circuit for odor value transformation. Rewarding experiences such as sucrose intake drive structural changes in the amOT. This plastic reorganization of neural circuits underpins alterations in olfactory tubercle (OT) functional domain responses to odors based on past experiences. Additionally, dopaminergic input from the VTA is essential for both the acquisition and execution of attraction behaviors mediated by the medial OT (mOT) during odor–sugar reward associative learning. Together, the interplay between sensory input (olfactory bulb [OB]/aPir → OT) and reward input (VTA → mOT) leads to odor value judgments. Adapted from [58]

Neural plasticity in OB–olfactory tubercle and anterior piriform cortex–olfactory tubercle circuits through associative learning

The primary input pathways of olfactory information to the OT originate from the OB and the anterior piriform cortex (aPir). Sha et al. [56] investigated the neural plasticity of OB–OT and aPir–OT synapses during odor–reward and odor–punishment associative learning. They mimicked odor input by optogenetically stimulating ChR2-expressing projection neurons in either the OB or aPir, pairing the stimulation with either a sugar reward or an electric shock.

Similar to when real odors were used as cues, mice learned attraction or aversion behaviors toward the light stimulation. Following learning, the morphology of the axon terminals of the ChR2-expressing neurons was evaluated, revealing experience-dependent plasticity in distinct OT domains depending on the type of unconditioned stimulus. In mice that associated light stimulation with a sugar reward, axon bouton size increased in the amOT, accompanied by enhanced synaptic apposition of VGluT1 signals onto postsynaptic structures (Homer1b/c), whereas no changes were observed in the lOT. Conversely, in mice that associated light stimulation with an electric shock, similar changes occurred in the lOT but not in the amOT. These results indicate that strengthening the glutamatergic synapses of the OB and aPir onto the OT occurs in a domain-specific manner during associative learning. This reorganization of the OT functional domains is thought to underlie changes in odor responsiveness driven by associative learning through odor–reward or odor–punishment experiences [56].

Dopamine inputs from the VTA to the medial olfactory tubercle are required for odor–reward associative learning

Another factor contributing to the reorganization of OT neural circuits during the acquisition of odor value is the experience of unconditioned stimuli, such as sugar consumption and electrical shocks. Zhang et al. [57] investigated the neural pathways through which sugar consumption drives the reorganization of the amOT. Their findings revealed that dopaminergic input from the VTA plays a key role in learning positive value judgments associated with sugar rewards.

Using optogenetics and chemogenetics, they examined and manipulated the neural activity of dopaminergic inputs from the VTA to the medial OT (mOT). Sugar consumption increased the activity of dopaminergic axons projecting from the VTA to the mOT. When this pathway was inhibited during odor–sugar associative learning, mice exhibited impaired acquisition of attraction behaviors. Furthermore, inhibition of the VTA–mOT dopamine pathway after learning also disrupted attraction behaviors toward odor cues. These findings suggest that this pathway is essential for both the acquisition and execution of learned responses to odors [57].

In summary, the OT, a component of the ventral striatum, plays a crucial role in odor value judgments and motivated behaviors elicited by olfactory cues. Rewarding or punishing experiences induce domain-specific plastic changes in the axon terminals of projection neurons from the OB and aPir within the OT. Rewarding experiences specifically drive structural changes in the amOT, whereas punishing experiences lead to changes in the lOT. This plastic reorganization of neural circuits underpins alterations in OT functional domain responses to odors on the basis of past experiences. Additionally, dopaminergic input from the VTA is essential for both the acquisition and execution of attraction behaviors mediated by the mOT during odor–sugar reward associative learning. Together, these findings emphasize the interplay between sensory input (OB/aPir → OT) and reward input (VTA → mOT) in forming odor value judgments (Fig. 9.10).

9.4 Summary and Future Directions

This chapter has explored how the brain transforms sensory input into value-based representations, focusing on vision and olfaction. Sensory processing begins with categorical recognition, where objects are identified on the basis of their features, before advancing to valuation, where biological significance is assigned on the basis of internal states and past experiences. In vision, the IT cortex represents object categorizations, whereas regions such as the OFC, amygdala, and striatum integrate recognition with motivational and emotional significance. Similarly, in olfaction, the OB and piriform cortex identify odors, whereas the OT and VTA modulate odor–value associations through learning and dopaminergic signaling.

Despite significant progress in understanding these neural processes, many questions remain. The precise mechanisms by which categorical and value representations interact are still unclear, particularly how valuation arises from categorical representation at the neural level. Additionally, experience-dependent plasticity plays a key role in modifying sensory to value-based circuits, but the cellular and molecular mechanisms remain to be fully elucidated. Future research should focus on high-resolution neuroimaging, circuit-specific manipulations, and computational modeling to unravel the complex interplay between sensory processing and value-based decision-making. Comparative studies across species will also be essential for identifying conserved principles of sensory valuation. A deeper understanding of these neural mechanisms will enhance knowledge of perception and motivation. In this sense, the framework of Shitsukan—spanning from surface recognition to deep, evaluation grounded in biological significance—serves as an integrative principle that unites vision and olfaction, highlighting how diverse sensory modalities converge on common mechanisms of biological meaning and adaptive behavior.

Acknowledgements The authors thank Dr. Kenji Koyano and the editors for their helpful comments on an earlier version of this chapter. This chapter, along with some relevant studies discussed herein, was partly supported by MEXT/JSPS KAKENHI Grant Numbers JP20H05955 and JP21H05817.

References

1. Mishkin, M., Ungerleider, L.G., Macko, K.A.: Object vision and spatial vision: two cortical pathways. Trends Neurosci. **6**, 414–417 (1983). https://doi.org/10.1016/0166-2236(83)90190-X
2. DiCarlo, J.J., Zoccolan, D., Rust, N.C.: How does the brain solve visual object recognition? Neuron **73**(3), 415–434 (2012). https://doi.org/10.1016/j.neuron.2012.01.010
3. Komatsu, H.: Neural processing for material perception. In: Shitsukan: The Science Of Material and Quality Perception and Their Synthesis. Springer, Tokyo (2025)
4. Rust, N.C., DiCarlo, J.J.: Selectivity and tolerance ("invariance") both increase as visual information propagates from cortical area V4 to IT. J. Neurosci. **30**(39), 12978–12995 (2010). https://doi.org/10.1523/JNEUROSCI.0179-10.2010
5. Op de Beeck, H.P., Baker, C.I.: The neural basis of visual object learning. Trends Cogn. Sci. **14**(1), 22–30 (2010). https://doi.org/10.1016/j.tics.2009.11.002
6. Matsumoto, N., Eldridge, M.A., Saunders, R.C., Reoli, R., Richmond, B.J.: Mild perceptual categorization deficits follow bilateral removal of anterior inferior temporal cortex in Rhesus monkeys. J. Neurosci. **36**, 43–53 (2016). https://doi.org/10.1523/JNEUROSCI.2058-15.2016
7. Eldridge, M.A., Matsumoto, N., Wittig, J.H.J., Masseau, E.C., Saunders, R.C., Richmond, B.J.: Perceptual processing in the ventral visual stream requires area TE but not rhinal cortex. Elife **7**, e36310 (2018). https://doi.org/10.7554/eLife.36310
8. Setogawa, T., Eldridge, M.A.G., Fomani, G.P., Saunders, R.C., Richmond, B.J.: Contributions of the monkey inferior temporal areas TE and TEO to visual categorization. Cereb. Cortex **31**, 4891–4900 (2021). https://doi.org/10.1093/cercor/bhab129
9. Farah, M.J., Levinson, K.L., Klein, K.L.: Face perception and within-category discrimination in prosopagnosia. Neuropsychologia **33**(6), 661–674 (1995). https://doi.org/10.1016/0028-3932(95)00002-k

10. Freedman, D.J., Riesenhuber, M., Poggio, T., Miller, E.K.: A comparison of primate prefrontal and inferior temporal cortices during visual categorization. J. Neurosci. **23**(12), 5235–5246 (2003). https://www.jneurosci.org/content/23/12/5235
11. Minamimoto, T., Saunders, R.C., Richmond, B.J.: Monkeys quickly learn and generalize visual categories without lateral prefrontal cortex. Neuron **66**(4), 501–507 (2010). https://doi.org/10.1016/j.neuron.2010.04.023
12. McKee, J.L., Riesenhuber, M., Miller, E.K., Freedman, D.J.: Task dependence of visual and category representations in prefrontal and inferior temporal cortices. J. Neurosci. **34**(48), 16065–16075 (2014). https://www.jneurosci.org/content/34/48/16065
13. Kravitz, D.J., Saleem, K.S., Baker, C.I., Ungerleider, L.G., Mishkin, M.: The ventral visual pathway: an expanded neural framework for the processing of object quality. Trends Cogn. Sci. **17**(1), 26–49 (2013). https://doi.org/10.1016/j.tics.2012.10.011
14. LeDoux, J.E.: Emotion circuits in the brain. Annu. Rev. Neurosci. **23**, 155–184 (2000). https://doi.org/10.1146/annurev.neuro.23.1.155
15. Pessoa, L., Adolphs, R.: Emotion processing and the amygdala: from a "low road" to "many roads" of evaluating biological significance. Nat. Rev. Neurosci. **11**(11), 773–782 (2010). https://doi.org/10.1038/nrn2920
16. Liu, Z., Murray, E.A., Richmond, B.J.: Learning motivational significance of visual cues for reward schedules requires rhinal cortex. Nat. Neurosci. **3**(12), 1307–1315 (2000). https://doi.org/10.1038/81841
17. Rolls, E.T.: The functions of the orbitofrontal cortex. Brain Cogn. **55**(1), 11–29 (2004). https://doi.org/10.1016/S0278-2626(03)00277-X
18. Yasuda, M., Yamamoto, S., Hikosaka, O.: Robust representation of stable object values in the oculomotor basal ganglia. J. Neurosci. **32**(47), 16917–16932 (2012). https://doi.org/10.1523/JNEUROSCI.3271-12.2012
19. Deisseroth, K.: Optogenetics. Nat. Methods **8**(1), 26–29 (2011). https://doi.org/10.1038/nmeth.f.324
20. Roth, B.L.: DREADDs for neuroscientists. Neuron **89**(4), 683–694 (2016). https://doi.org/10.1016/j.neuron.2016.01.040
21. Minamimoto, T., Nagai, Y., Oyama, K.: Imaging-based chemogenetics for dissecting neural circuits in nonhuman primates. Proc. Jpn. Acad., Ser. B **100**(8), 476–489 (2024). https://doi.org/10.2183/pjab.100.030
22. Minamimoto, T., La Camera, G., Richmond, B.J.: Measuring and modeling the interaction among reward size, delay to reward, and satiation level on motivation in monkeys. J. Neurophysiol. **101**(1), 437–447 (2009). https://doi.org/10.1152/jn.90959.2008
23. Eldridge, M.A.G., Lerchner, W., Saunders, R.C., Kaneko, H., Krausz, K.W., Gonzalez, F.J., Ji, B., Higuchi, M., Minamimoto, T., Richmond, B.J.: Chemogenetic disconnection of monkey orbitofrontal and rhinal cortex reversibly disrupts reward value. Nat. Neurosci. **19**(1), 37–39 (2016). https://doi.org/10.1038/nn.4192
24. Nagai, Y., Kikuchi, E., Lerchner, W., Inoue, K., Ji, B., Eldridge, M.A.G., Kaneko, H., Kimura, Y., Oh-Nishi, A., Hori, Y., Kato, Y., Hirabayashi, T., Fujimoto, A., Kumata, K., Zhang, M.R., Aoki, I., Suhara, T., Higuchi, M., Takada, M., Richmond, B.J., Minamimoto, T.: PET imaging-guided chemogenetic silencing reveals a critical role of primate rostromedial caudate in reward evaluation. Nat. Commun. **7**, 13605 (2016). https://doi.org/10.1038/ncomms13605
25. Fujimoto, A., Hori, Y., Nagai, Y., Kikuchi, E., Oyama, K., Suhara, T., Minamimoto, T.: Signaling incentive and drive in the primate ventral pallidum for motivational control of goal-directed action. J. Neurosci. **39**(10), 1793–1804 (2019). https://doi.org/10.1523/JNEUROSCI.2399-18.2018
26. Rolls, E.T., Sienkiewicz, Z.J., Yaxley, S.: Hunger modulates the responses to gustatory stimuli of single neurons in the caudolateral orbitofrontal cortex of the macaque monkey. Eur. J. Neurosci. **1**(1), 53–60 (1989). https://doi.org/10.1111/j.1460-9568.1989.tb00774.x
27. Oyama, K., Hori, Y., Mimura, K., Nagai, Y., Eldridge, M.A.G., Saunders, R.C., Miyakawa, N., Hirabayashi, T., Hori, Y., Inoue, K.I., Suhara, T., Takada, M., Higuchi, M., Richmond, B.J., Minamimoto, T.: Chemogenetic disconnection between the orbitofrontal cortex and the

rostromedial caudate nucleus disrupts motivational control of goal-directed action. J. Neurosci. **42**(32), 6267–6275 (2022). https://doi.org/10.1523/JNEUROSCI.0229-22.2022
28. Hirabayashi, T., Nagai, Y., Hori, Y., Hori, Y., Oyama, K., Mimura, K., Miyakawa, M., Iwaoki, H., Inoue, K.I., Suhara, T., Takada, M., Higuchi, M., Minamimoto, T.: Multiscale chemogenetic dissection of fronto-temporal top-down regulation for object memory in primates. Nat. Commun. **15**(1), 5369 (2024). https://doi.org/10.1038/s41467-024-49570-w
29. Iravani, B., Arshamian, A., Lundqvist, M., Kay, L.M., Wilson, D.A., Lundström, J.N.: Odor identity can be extracted from the reciprocal connectivity between olfactory bulb and piriform cortex in humans. Neuroimage **237**(118130), 118130 (2021)
30. Kehl, M.S., Mackay, S., Ohla, K., Schneider, M., Borger, V., Surges, R., Spehr, M., Mormann, F.: Single-neuron representations of odours in the human brain. Nature **634**(8034):626–634 (2024). https://doi.org/10.1038/s41586-024-08016-5. Epub 2024 Oct 9. PMID: 39385026; PMCID: PMC11485236
31. Mori, K., Sakano, H.: How is the olfactory map formed and interpreted in the mammalian brain? Annu. Rev. Neurosci. **34**, 467–499 (2011)
32. Wilson, D.A., Sullivan, R.M.: Cortical processing of odor objects. Neuron **72**(4), 506–519 (2011)
33. Bushdid, C., Magnasco, M.O., Vosshall, L.B., Keller, A.: Humans can discriminate more than 1 trillion olfactory stimuli. Science (New York, N.Y.), **343**(6177), 1370–1372 (2014)
34. Sakano, H.: Neural map formation in the mouse olfactory system. Neuron **67**(4), 530–542 (2010)
35. Arzi, A., Sobel, N.: Olfactory perception as a compass for olfactory neural maps. Trends Cogn. Sci. **15**(11), 537–545 (2011)
36. Malnic, B., Godfrey, P.A., Buck, L.B.: The human olfactory receptor gene family. Proc. Natl. Acad. Sci. U S A. **101**(8), 2584–2589 (2004). https://doi.org/10.1073/pnas.0307882100
37. Olender, T., Lancet, D., Nebert, D.W.: Update on the olfactory receptor (OR) gene superfamily. Hum. Genomics **3**(1), 87–97 (2008). https://doi.org/10.1186/1479-7364-3-1-87.PMID: 19129093;PMCID:PMC2752031
38. Mori, K., Takahashi, Y.K., Igarashi, K.M., Yamaguchi, M.: Maps of odorant molecular features in the Mammalian olfactory bulb. Physiol. Rev. **86**(2), 409–433 (2006)
39. Murata, K., Kinoshita, T., Fukazawa, Y., Kobayashi, K., Kobayashi, K., Miyamichi, K., Okuno, H., Bito, H., Sakurai, Y., Yamaguchi, M., Mori, K., Manabe, H.: GABAergic neurons in the olfactory cortex projecting to the lateral hypothalamus in mice. Sci. Rep. **9**(1), 7132 (2019)
40. Illig, K.R., Haberly, L.B.: Odor-evoked activity is spatially distributed in piriform cortex. J. Comp. Neurol. **457**(4), 361–373 (2003). https://doi.org/10.1002/cne.10557. PMID: 12561076
41. Igarashi, K.M., Ieki, N., An, M., Yamaguchi, Y., Nagayama, S., Kobayakawa, K., Kobayakawa, R., Tanifuji, M., Sakano, H., Chen, W.R, Mori, K.: Parallel mitral and tufted cell pathways route distinct odor information to different targets in the olfactory cortex. J. Neurosci. **32**(23), 7970–7985 (2012). https://doi.org/10.1523/JNEUROSCI.0154-12.2012
42. Haberly, L.B.: Parallel-distributed processing in olfactory cortex: new insights from morphological and physiological analysis of neuronal circuitry. Chem. Senses **26**(5), 551–576 (2001)
43. Murata, K., Kanno, M., Ieki, N., Mori, K., Yamaguchi, M.: Mapping of learned odor-induced motivated behaviors in the mouse olfactory tubercle. J. Neurosci. **35**(29), 10581–10599 (2015)
44. Murata, K.: Hypothetical roles of the olfactory tubercle in odor-guided eating behavior. Front. Neural Circuits **14**, 577880 (2020)
45. Kobayakawa, K., Kobayakawa, R., Matsumoto, H., Oka, Y., Imai, T., Ikawa, M., Okabe, M., Ikeda, T., Itohara, S., Kikusui, T., Mori, K., Sakano, H.: Innate versus learned odour processing in the mouse olfactory bulb. Nature **450**(7169), 503–508 (2007)
46. Root, C.M., Denny, C.A., Hen, R., Axel, R.: The participation of cortical amygdala in innate, odour-driven behaviour. Nature **515**(7526), 269–273 (2014)
47. Kondoh, K., Lu, Z., Ye, X., Olson, D.P., Lowell, B.B., Buck, L.B.: A specific area of olfactory cortex involved in stress hormone responses to predator odours. Nature **532**(7597), 103–106 (2016)

48. Setogawa, T., Matsumoto, J., Nishijo, H., Nishimaru, H.: Neuronal mechanism of innate rapid processing of threating animacy cue in primates: insights from the neuronal responses to snake images. Front. Psychol. **29**(15), 1462961 (2024). https://doi.org/10.3389/fpsyg.2024.1462961. PMID:39268378;PMCID:PMC11391488
49. Horio, N., Liberles, S.D.: Hunger enhances food-odour attraction through a neuropeptide Y spotlight. Nature **592**(7853), 262–266 (2021)
50. Todrank, J., Heth, G., Restrepo, D.: Effects of in utero odorant exposure on neuroanatomical development of the olfactory bulb and odour preferences. Proc. R. Soc. B: Biol. Sci. **278**(1714), 1949–1955 (2011)
51. Gadziola, M.A., Tylicki, K.A., Christian, D.L., Wesson, D.W.: The olfactory tubercle encodes odor valence in behaving mice. J. Neurosci. **35**(11), 4515–4527 (2015)
52. Murata, K., Kinoshita, T., Fukazawa, Y., Kobayashi, K., Yamanaka, A., Hikida, T., Manabe, H., Yamaguchi, M.: Opposing roles of dopamine receptor D1- and D2-expressing neurons in the anteromedial olfactory tubercle in acquisition of place preference in mice. Front. Behav. Neurosci. **13**, 50 (2019)
53. Morales, I., Berridge, K.C.: "Liking" and "wanting" in eating and food reward: brain mechanisms and clinical implications. Physiol. Behav. **227**, 113152 (2020)
54. Maegawa, A., Murata, K., Kuroda, K., Fujieda, S., Fukazawa, Y.: Cellular profiles of prodynorphin and preproenkephalin mRNA-expressing neurons in the anterior olfactory tubercle of mice. Front. Neural Circuits **16**, 908964 (2022)
55. Murata, K., Maegawa, A., Imoto, Y., Fujieda, S., Fukazawa, Y.: Endogenous opioids in the olfactory tubercle and their roles in olfaction and quality of life. Front. Neural Circuits **18**, 1408189 (2024)
56. Sha, M.F.R., Koga, Y., Murata, Y., Taniguchi, M., Yamaguchi, M. Learning-dependent structural plasticity of intracortical and sensory connections to functional domains of the olfactory tubercle. Front. Neurosci. **17**(2023). https://doi.org/10.3389/fnins.2023.1247375
57. Zhang, Z., Liu, Q., Wen, P., Zhang, J., Rao, X., Zhou, Z., Zhang, H., He, X., Li, J., Zhou, Z., Xu, X., Zhang, X., Luo, R., Lv, G., Li, H., Cao, P., Wang, L., Xu, F.: Activation of the dopaminergic pathway from VTA to the medial olfactory tubercle generates odor-preference and reward. ELife **6** (2017). https://doi.org/10.7554/eLife.25423
58. Allen Reference Atlas—Mouse Brain [brain atlas]. Available from atlas.brain-map.org

Part III
Creating and Modulating Shitsukan

Chapter 10
The Haptics of Shitsukan

Hiroyuki Kajimoto, Masashi Konyo, and Shogo Okamoto

Abstract This chapter explores the role of touch in the perception of Shitsukan, referring to material qualities like texture, hardness, and temperature. Haptics plays a critical role in understanding Shitsukan through five key sensations: hardness–softness, friction, micro-level roughness, macro-level roughness, and thermal. In addition, vibrotactile perception is involved in all of these factors except heat. The chapter presents examples on how these haptic sensations can be measured and reproduced. The first example is the presentation of softness using both force and cutaneous feedback. Previous research showed that force feedback alone is insufficient to replicate soft objects, and combining it with cutaneous feedback significantly improves the realism of the sensation. Based on this finding, a method employing an electro-tactile display has been proposed to simulate variations in contact area associated with the deformation of soft objects under pressure. The second example addresses the perception of high-frequency vibrations and introduces a method for reproducing them with high fidelity based on perceptual characteristics. It also introduces a spatial vibration representation that uses multiple oscillators to express the direction and distance of external vibration sources to improve the sense of realism. The third example shows texture rendering through vibrations and friction on touch panels. Vibratory stimuli and friction control create sensations of roughness and texture, offering new possibilities for tactile interfaces. By accurately controlling skin deformation, these methods can simulate a wide range of textures, making haptic feedback increasingly useful in touch-based devices.

H. Kajimoto (✉)
The University of Electro-Communications, Chofu, Tokyo, Japan
e-mail: kajimoto@uec.ac.jp

M. Konyo
Tohoku University, Sendai, Japan
e-mail: konyo@tohoku.ac.jp

S. Okamoto
Tokyo Metropolitan Univeristy, Hino, Tokyo, Japan
e-mail: okamotos@tmu.ac.jp

S. Nishida and K. Nishino (eds.), *Shitsukan—Understanding and Manipulating Material and Quality Perception*, https://doi.org/10.1007/978-981-95-4762-3_10

10.1 Measurement and Display of Touch Experience

Haptics plays a crucial role in the perception of Shitsukan. When observing a stone, for example, we naturally form various expectations about its Shitsukan—such as its heaviness, hardness, roughness, or coldness. Many of these perceptions are intrinsically linked to haptics. It is well-established that haptic-related Shitsukan can be categorized into five distinct types: hardness–softness, friction, micro-level roughness, macro-level roughness, and thermal sensation (coldness-warmness) [29].

To effectively reproduce these haptic sensations, it is imperative to observe the physical interactions occurring at the skin's surface, distill the essential elements of these sensations, and then accurately recreate them. In considering this process of measurement and reproduction, it is beneficial to differentiate between temporal and spatial phenomena. For instance, research has shown that material perception based on temperature is largely determined by changes in skin temperature within the first few seconds of contact, making temporal change the critical factor in this aspect of Shitsukan [15]. Conversely, the roughness experienced when touching a sandpaper cannot be adequately conveyed through finger vibration alone; rather, it is generated by stimuli that are spatially distributed across the skin [8].

The following sections will explore three examples that demonstrate the reproduction of haptic Shitsukan. The first example, reported by Kajimoto, focuses on replicating the sensation of softness by combining presentations of force and cutaneous senses. The second example, reported by Konyo, addresses high-fidelity vibrotactile rendering, including high-frequency vibration over several hundred Hz, and introduces spatial haptic expression through distributed vibrations for VR applications. The third example, reported by Okamoto, highlights the presentation of textures on touch panels, a feature that is becoming increasingly sought after with the advancement of ICT devices.

As mentioned above, the five elements are considered to be associated with haptic-related Shitsukan. The three case studies presented in this chapter correspond to these elements as follows. The first case, the presentation of softness using electrical stimulation, relates to the expression of softness–hardness. The second case, involving vibrational stimuli, covers a broad range of tactile sensations other than temperature perception. The third case, texture presentation on a touch panel, corresponds to the expression of friction as well as macro-roughness and micro-roughness. In other words, these methods aim to encompass a broad area of tactile Shitsukan.

10.2 Softness Presentation by Electro-Tactile Display

This section presents a novel approach to softness presentation by simultaneously providing both force and cutaneous feedback [40]. A compact electro-tactile display was employed for cutaneous feedback, enabling spatial and temporal high-fidelity reproduction of contact area changes.

10.2.1 How to Present Softness?

Softness is a crucial aspect of haptic Shitsukan. Key haptic cues for perceiving softness include the reaction force experienced by the finger in response to displacement when pressing into an object, as well as changes in the contact area between the finger and the object [4]. The relative importance of these sensory cues in the perception of softness varies depending on the object's hardness [3, 11]. Particularly when perceiving soft objects, force sensation alone is inadequate; both force and skin sensory information are essential.

Various attempts have been made to create a rich perception of softness by simultaneously delivering both force and cutaneous feedback. Scilingo et al. [37] integrated a haptic interface with a softness display consisting of cylinders that expanded and contracted using pneumatic actuators, allowing independent control of both reaction forces and contact area changes. Ikeda et al. [18] developed a haptic display by combining a glove-type force feedback device with a tactile display that controlled fingertip contact area, enabling the representation of softness during grasping actions. Park et al. [33] introduced a method for simultaneously presenting force and cutaneous sensations by interacting with a hard surface through a force feedback device, showing that combining a cutaneous interface with force feedback significantly enhanced the perception of hardness compared to force feedback alone. However, these systems often relied on complex mechanisms for controlling contact area changes, limiting their practical application in multi-finger scenarios.

10.2.2 Contact Area Measurement

First, the changes in contact area when participants touched soft objects were measured. This served as a preparatory step for the subsequent presentation of simulated softness using an electrical stimulation pattern. The contact area measurements were conducted with six participants (four right-handed, two left-handed, all males aged 21–26).

In this experiment, two types of gels with varying softness levels were used. These gels had Asker C hardness values of 0 and 15, corresponding to the softness of a baby's skin and an adult's skin, respectively. These will be referred to as Gel 0 and Gel 15. The participants applied ink to the entire pad of their dominant index finger and pressed directly downward onto each gel, allowing the measurement of the contact area (Fig. 10.1). Measurements were recorded after pressing the gel samples to depths of 0 mm, 1 mm, 2 mm, and 3 mm. The 0 mm measurement was defined as the point at which the participant first perceived tactile feedback from the sample.

Indentation depth was measured using a laser displacement sensor (Keyence, LK-H050). An indentation error margin of ± 0.3 mm was allowed; if the peak indentation value fell outside this range, the participant was instructed to press again.

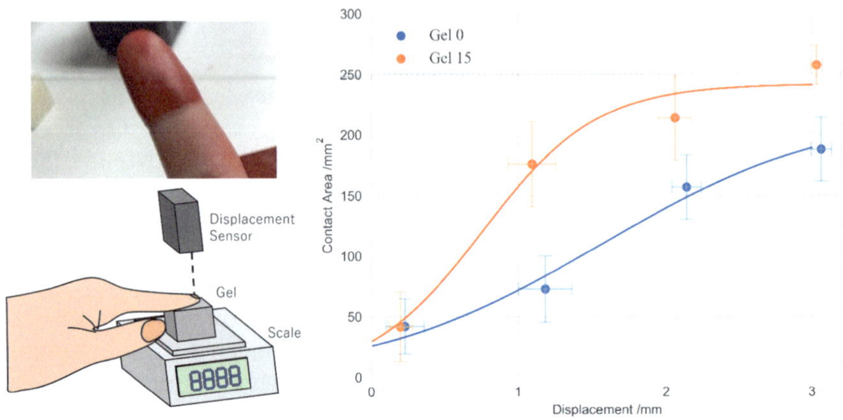

Fig. 10.1 Contact area measurement. (Top) Ink was applied to the fingertip to capture the contact area. (Bottom) Indentation depths ranging from 0 to 3 mm were applied, and the resulting data were fitted with a logistic curve. The error bars represent the standard deviations of finger displacement and contact area, respectively

Following each trial at the specified indentation depths, the inked contact area was analyzed through pixel analysis. A logistic regression model was applied to the measurement results. This process enabled us to accurately measure the changes in the fingertip's contact area when touching two objects with different levels of softness.

10.2.3 Softness Presentation Combining Force and Cutaneous Cues

Building on the data from the previous section, an experiment was conducted to assess the effectiveness of combining force and cutaneous cue feedback for softness presentation.

The experimental setup involved the Touch X USB force feedback device, a finger mount, and an electro-tactile display (Fig. 10.2) [21]. The electro-tactile display features a flexible film substrate with 64 electrodes arranged in a 2.54 mm grid. A flexible sponge beneath the electrode sheet ensured it conformed closely to the finger during use. This setup allowed us to accurately replicate contact area changes in real time while avoiding any unwanted force feedback from the cutaneous system.

The experiment compared the experience of touching real gel objects with bare hands to interacting with virtual cubes of the same size using the haptic device. Ten participants (9 males, 1 female; 7 right-handed, 3 left-handed; average age: 23.4) were recruited.

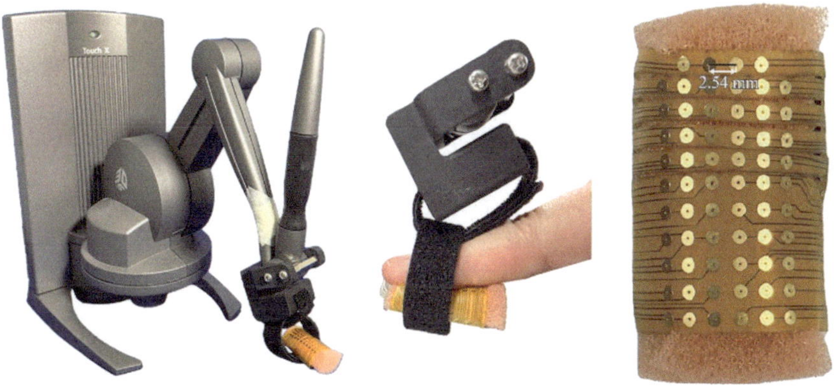

Fig. 10.2 Presentation devices. From left to right: Touch X USB force feedback device, fingertip mount, and electro-tactile display

The experiment consisted of two stages. In the first stage, participants were asked to determine the subjective point of equality for hardness–softness perception using the method of adjustment. The two real gels (Gel 0 and Gel 15) served as reference stimuli, and participants familiarized themselves with their softness by touching them with bare hands before each trial. They then adjusted the Young's modulus parameter of the force feedback control to match the perceived hardness of the two gels. Two conditions were tested: one with only force feedback and the other with both force and cutaneous feedback via the electro-tactile display to replicate the contact area changes in real time. The results showed no significant differences between the conditions, as Young's modulus was consistently adjusted by the participants to values close to those of the real objects. This suggests that for hardness perception, as represented by Young's modulus, the addition of cutaneous feedback had no notable impact.

The second stage aimed to assess changes in subjective realism. The two real gels (Gel 0 and Gel 15) were used as reference stimuli, as in the previous stage, and participants memorized their softness by touching them with bare hands before each trial. The comparison stimuli comprised nine conditions: one with only force feedback, four with simultaneous force and electro-tactile feedback, and four with only electro-tactile feedback. When force feedback was provided, it always simulated the reaction force corresponding to Young's modulus of the reference gels (i.e., the force feedback was always "accurate"). The four electro-tactile conditions consisted of two that replicated the contact area changes measured for Gel 0 and Gel 15, and two reverse playback patterns. In the reverse playback pattern, the contact area was maximized at the moment of initial contact and then reduced as the finger pressed further in, in order to prevent responses that could be based merely on average stimulation intensity.

Each combination of the two gels and nine comparison stimuli was presented once to each participant in a randomized, counterbalanced order to avoid bias. Participants answered two questions: (1) "How similar is the force sensation compared to the real sample?" and (2) "How similar is the cutaneous sensation compared to the real sample?" Responses were recorded on a 7-point Likert scale (1: not similar at all, 7: perfectly similar).

The results from the participants are presented as box plots for force and cutaneous sensations for Gel 0 and Gel 15 in Figs. 10.3 and 10.4, respectively.

In the similarity evaluation of force sensation, high ratings were observed for both Gel 0 and Gel 15 when using the force feedback device. This is unsurprising, as the device consistently simulated the reaction forces based on the Young's modulus of each gel in every trial. Furthermore, no significant effects were noted from the addition of electro-tactile stimulation.

For the cutaneous sensation evaluation, the highest ratings for Gel 0 were achieved when the contact area changes of Gel 0 were accurately reproduced, combined with force feedback. Similarly, for Gel 15, the highest ratings occurred when the contact area changes of Gel 15 were replicated along with force feedback. Notably, when force feedback was absent, the ratings for cutaneous sensation alone were lower. These findings suggest that accurately presenting the changes in skin contact area

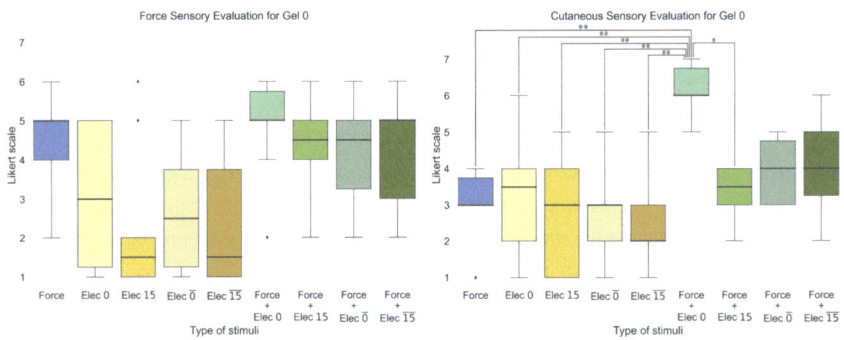

Fig. 10.3 Perceived similarity of the presented stimuli compared with Gel 0: (Left) similarity in force sensation, (Right) similarity in cutaneous sensation

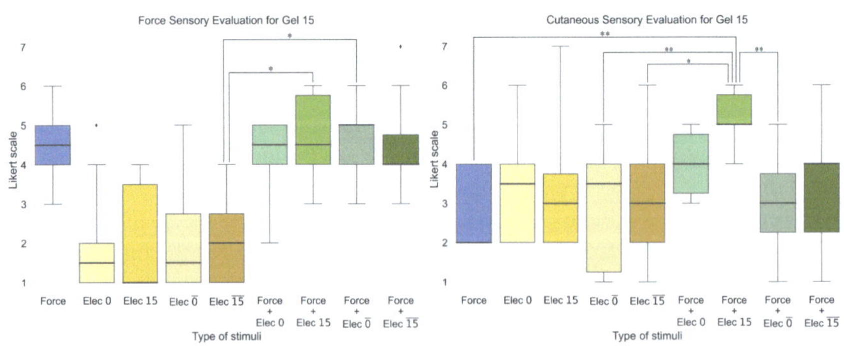

Fig. 10.4 Perceived similarity of the presented stimuli compared with Gel 0: (Left) similarity in force sensation, (Right) similarity in cutaneous sensation

in accordance with the softness of the gel is crucial for enhancing the realism of cutaneous sensations. In other words, reproducing these changes with high fidelity, based on the target object's softness, is essential.

It has been well-established that cutaneous cues dominate perception of soft object [39]; however, in this experiment, the realism of cutaneous sensations was lower when only electro-tactile stimulation was used. This result suggests that, as a standalone method for cutaneous feedback, electro-tactile stimulation is not yet a fully developed form of tactile presentation, leading to a decrease in the realism of softness.

Thus far, this experiment has examined how cutaneous feedback from electro-tactile stimulation and force feedback from the haptic device each contribute to the subjective realism of cutaneous and force sensations. However, the independence of these feedback methods requires further consideration. While the electro-tactile display does not provide force feedback—one of the reasons for its use in this experiment—the force feedback device inherently delivers reaction forces to the fingertip, making it inevitable that additional cutaneous cues are conveyed by the force feedback.

One key takeaway from this section is that the contribution of cutaneous sensations was reflected in subjective realism but did not manifest in Young's modulus adjustment task. In other words, the nature of the task dictates whether force feedback alone is sufficient or whether cutaneous feedback should also be included.

10.3 High-Fidelity Vibrotactile Feedback

Vibration is one of the most fundamental information captured by human tactile receptors. Recent studies have shown that even with a single vibrator, it is possible to replicate a realistic tactile sensation of collision or friction by reproducing vibrations over a wide range of frequencies, including high frequencies up to several hundred Hz. The experience gained through such high-frequency vibration not only distinguishes the object's properties but also makes us perceive our own movement interacting with the environment. For this reason, vibration feedback is expected to improve the intuitiveness and interactivity of content and play a crucial role in improving haptic Shitsukan.

10.3.1 Broadband Vibration Presentation Including High-Frequency Vibrations

Presenting vibrations over a broad frequency range up to several hundred Hz is an effective approach for reproducing realistic tactile sensations. It has been reported that realistic tactile sensations can be presented by measuring contact vibrations with a sensor and by reproducing the vibrations directly with a vibrator. For example, it has been shown that it is possible to present the material feel of an object by presenting the vibrations of tool contact [30]. A similar approach has also been applied to haptic feedback for a surgical robot [22], and it has been well-received by surgeons. It has also been applied to the remote control of a construction robot [27]. The TECHTILE Toolkit [26] is a system that allows users to experience the reproduction of realistic tactile sensations, such as the movement of a ball in a paper cup or the vibration of a racket. A simple setup that connects a microphone and a vibrator to an audio amplifier is sufficient to transmit tactile sensations.

These approaches are effective when the frequency of the vibration generated by the contact is within the range of human perception and the operating range of the vibrator. Consequently, it is difficult to convey sensations of vibration below a few tens of Hz or above a few hundred Hz, which is difficult to generate using the small linear resonance actuators (LRAs) commonly used in mobile devices.

Meanwhile, high-performance transducers are also becoming more widespread in commercial devices. For example, Apple smartphones and laptop touchscreens use vibration to create the sensation of pressing a physical button without actually using one. Furthermore, controllers for home video game consoles such as the Nintendo Switch and Sony PlayStation 5 use wide-band LRA types instead of conventional eccentric motors to provide vibration feedback linked to interactive content. However, in commercial applications, vibration patterns are generally designed through trial and error. This limits interactivity, as realistic sensations or stimuli linked to movement cannot be automatically generated.

The main issues with vibration feedback, including high-frequency vibration, are as follows.

- Limitations on the frequency range of small vibrators.
- Noise from the casing due to high-frequency vibration.
- Understanding the perceptual characteristics reproduced by high-frequency vibration.
- Understanding and reproducing the perception of spatial vibration distribution on the body.

Regarding the limitations of the frequency range of the vibrator, the LRA-type vibrator shows significant attenuation in the low- and high-frequency ranges. Piezoelectric vibrators improve response, but the problem of noise generated by the casing, which becomes audible from around 300 Hz, still remains. The key to solving these problems is to understand the perceptual characteristics of high-frequency vibration and to replace high-frequency vibration with different, lower-frequency vibration.

Vibrotactile perception based on the spatial distribution of vibrations on the body is a promising research field. The Pacinian corpuscle, sensitive to high-frequency vibration, has a large receptive field and can perceive vibration propagating through the body, not just vibration directly below the contact area [35]. Shao et al. [38] attached many acceleration sensors to the hand to visualize vibration and showed how vibration from contact spreads. The author's group has reported that the feeling of impact from a tennis shot can be improved by reproducing the sensation of the vibration being transmitted to the palm, wrist, and elbow [36].

The following sections introduce a method for converting vibration waveforms into perceptual equivalents based on research into the perceptual characteristics of high-frequency vibration. In addition, a method for expressing realistic high-frequency tactile sensations that spatially localizes the source of vibration outside the body will also be introduced in Sect. 10.3.4.

10.3.2 Perceptual Properties of High-Frequency Vibrations

One of the typical characteristics of human vibration perception is the frequency dependence of the vibration detection threshold [12]. The activity of the Pacinian corpuscle is dominant at vibrations of 100 Hz or higher, and the threshold is lowest around 230 Hz; i.e., the sensitivity is highest. This is why LRA-type vibrators are generally designed to resonate around 200 Hz. Recently, different approaches have been used to achieve a broader frequency representation, such as incorporating multiple resonance points for broadband performance (as in the Nintendo Switch controllers) or adding resonance below 100 Hz, where sensitivity drops, to enhance low-frequency sensation (as in the Sony PlayStation 5 controllers).

Generally, the upper limit of human vibration perception is considered to be around 1 kHz, but it is difficult to produce such a frequency with a small vibrator. Furthermore, even if the carrier wave frequency exceeds 1 kHz, if the waveform has an amplitude-modulated envelope, there is a possibility that the envelope component will be perceived [24]. This phenomenon has also been reported for ultrasonic vibrations [25]. In addition, it has been confirmed that the envelope component also affects perception in single decaying oscillation waves, such as impact waves, not just periodic vibrations [6]. As such, to understand actual perceptual characteristics, it is necessary to consider characteristics beyond single-frequency sinusoidal waves. Importantly, if we can understand how the Pacinian corpuscle, which detects high-frequency vibration, extracts the characteristics of the waveform, then we can convert or compress the signal without reproducing the original high-frequency waveform.

The perceptual characteristics of the mixed frequency of multiple high-frequency vibrations have been reported by Bensmaïa et al. [2]. By comparing with psychophysical experiments, they showed that the intensity I_s perceived by the Pacinian corpuscle could be explained by the following equation:

$$I_s = \sum_f \left(\frac{A_f^2}{T_f^2} \right)^{\alpha_f}, \tag{10.1}$$

where A_f, T_f, and α_f represent the amplitude, vibration threshold, and experimentally determined exponent coefficient for each frequency component f, respectively. The differences in perceived intensity expressed by this equation were shown to have a high correlation with the discriminability of the tactile sensation of a composite wave with three frequencies in the range of 100–400 Hz.

However, the above equation is only valid for synthesizing vibrations above 100 Hz, and in cases where there are envelope components below that, the intensity model cannot explain the differences in tactile sensation in some cases. Cao et al. [7] investigated human discrimination characteristics when the frequency of the envelope component of the amplitude-modulated wave was changed between 12 Hz and 125 Hz while maintaining the perceptual intensity of Eq. (10.1). The results showed that the correct response rate for the 1/3 discrimination task was below 60% for frequencies between 80 and 125 Hz, indicating that humans cannot discriminate the envelope component at frequencies above this range. In other words, even when the perceptual intensity is kept constant, humans can discriminate the shape of the waveform at envelope frequencies below 80 Hz.

The next section introduces a signal conversion method for high-frequency vibrations that consider the perceptual intensity and envelope perception.

10.3.3 Sensory Equivalence Conversion of High-Frequency Vibrations Considering Human Perceptual Properties

As mentioned in the previous section, reproducing the perception of high-frequency vibrations does not require maintaining the original waveform frequency as long as the perceived intensity remains the same. However, envelope components below 80 Hz also contribute to the perception of high-frequency vibrations and should be preserved. Yamaguchi et al. [43] have proposed a method that converts arbitrary vibration waveforms, including those in the high-frequency acoustic range, into a low-frequency signal while preserving the perceived intensity. The signal conversion is called intensity segment modulation (ISM), and the perceptual intensity is calculated and converted for each segment, which is determined so as to retain the fluctuations of the perceptible envelope.

As shown in Fig. 10.5, ISM first divides the high-frequency signal into short time segments, typically 10 ms long, to match the temporal resolution of the human being to detect intensity fluctuations. For each segment, the perceived intensity is calculated to reflect the frequency-dependent characteristics of the original signal according to Eq. (10.1). Finally, the ISM outputs an amplitude-modulated waveform with a single carrier frequency of typically 150–300 Hz that has the same perceptual intensity. By maintaining the original intensity for each segment, the ISM can convert any high-frequency vibrations into a different signal that retains the perceptual properties.

The ISM signal processing pipeline includes multiple steps. First, the signal is divided using overlap to ensure a smooth transition. Next, using the Empirical Mode Decomposition (EMD) [17], each segment is decomposed into its frequency components, known as Intrinsic Mode Functions (IMFs), which allow ISM to calculate the frequency-dependent intensity of each segment. In this method, high-pass and low-pass filters with a cutoff frequency of 100–200 Hz are applied to separate the high-frequency components for modulation. The modulated segments are then combined

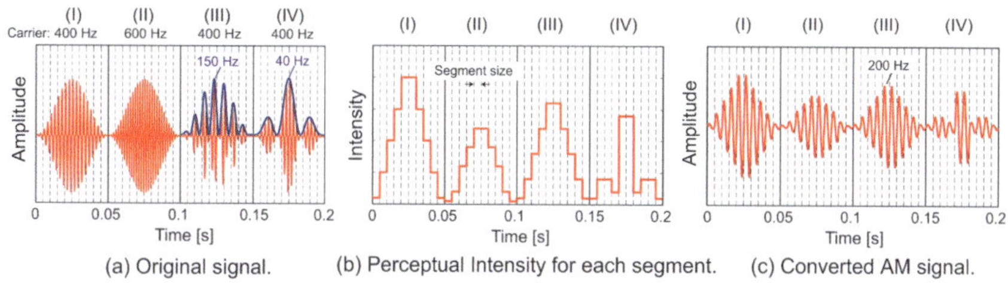

Fig. 10.5 Process of intensity segment modulation (ISM). **a** difference in carrier wave frequency (I, II) and difference in envelope frequency (III, V). **b** calculate the perceived intensity for each segment. **c** convert to a 200 Hz amplitude-modulated wave while maintaining the perceived intensity

with the low-frequency components to produce the final waveform, which captures the essence of the temporal and intensity changes of the original high-frequency signal.

A double-blind triple-stimulus (DBTS) method was used to evaluate the degradation of tactile signals and confirm the sensory equivalence of ISMs. Two artificial waveforms, harmonic vibration (amplitude-modulated wave) and impact vibration (attenuated sine wave), were tested at different envelope modulation and carrier frequencies. Tactile stimuli were provided through transducers with flat responses. In this procedure, participants were asked to identify the difference between the ISM-modulated signal and the original signal and to evaluate the level of degradation on a scale of 1 (very unpleasant) to 5 (not perceivable) to calculate a subjective difference grade (SDG) degradation scale. As a result, the average SDG value was below −1.0 for all conditions, confirming that the level of degradation was not annoying or almost imperceptible.

Compared to conventional methods like low-pass filtering (LPF), ISM offers significant improvements by preserving the perception of high-frequency components and delivering a more immersive haptic experience. This approach is particularly valuable for applications requiring high-fidelity synchronization with audio-visual media. It provides a practical haptic solution for multimedia on mobile devices and paves the way for more advanced haptic feedback possibilities.

10.3.4 Stereohaptics: Spatial Representation of Vibration Sources Localized Outside the Body

Distributed vibrations transmitted to the body surface have the potential to make us aware of the movement and direction of vibration sources outside the body. For example, we naturally recognize directional vibrations in everyday life, such as air vibrations caused by loud sounds and vibrations propagated from the floor. If these external sensations can be reproduced through vibration perception, it is expected to contribute to improving the Shitsukan of presence. By spatially representing the existence of vibration sources in the environment, it becomes possible to create a more immersive and realistic experience and improve the sense of presence and reality in virtual environments.

This section introduces "stereohaptic vibration" [28]—a new method that uses distributed vibration stimulation to project virtual vibration sources (VVS) outside the body. Figure 10.6 shows the concept image of the stereohaptic vibration.

Phantom sensation (PhS) is a phenomenon that creates the illusion of VVS by changing the strength between vibrators. Conventional studies have reported that PhS can control the position and movement of stimuli on the body surface using multiple vibrators [19, 42]. However, conventional PhS often sets vibration intensity ratios to relatively simple vibration waveforms prepared in advance and localizes them; it is generally difficult to apply it to arbitrary complex vibration waveforms, such as vibration sensations produced by sound sources.

Ohara et al. [28] addressed the limitations of conventional methods by developing a sensory-equivalent conversion method for tactile signals using ISM, as described in the previous section. This approach enables the presentation of PhS for arbitrary waveforms. Additionally, by positioning multiple vibrators in a three-dimensional arrangement on the body, it becomes possible to simulate vibration sources originating outside the body, not merely on its surface. This section briefly reports the concept of stereohaptic vibration and an example of spatial expression using multi-point stimulation on the forearm.

To represent stereohaptic vibration, this method distributes perceived intensities across multiple oscillators according to the angle between the VVS and each vibrator, as shown in Fig.10.7a. The perceived intensity at the origin is distributed such that oscillators in the same direction as the VVS emit stronger vibrations than those in the opposite direction. The approach includes a distance decay function, which adjusts perceived intensity based on distance, and an orientation distribution model, which divides intensity among oscillators according to their spatial relation to the VVS.

Figure 10.7b shows a stereohaptic display of multiple vibrators placed on the palm and forearm. Four small vibrators (audio exciters, TEAX13C02-8/RH) attached to the forearm with a wristband and one vibrator (voice coil type transducer, Acouve

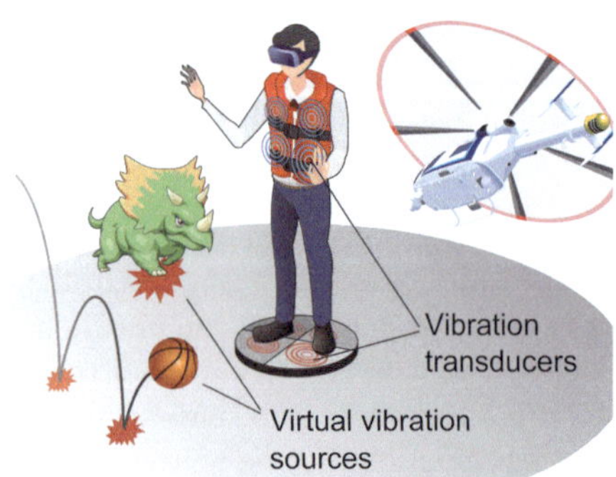

Fig. 10.6 Concept image of stereohaptic vibration. By adjusting the intensity of multiple vibration transducers attached to the body, the sensation of a virtual vibration source, such as a character or ball that exists at a specific direction and distance outside the body, is expressed

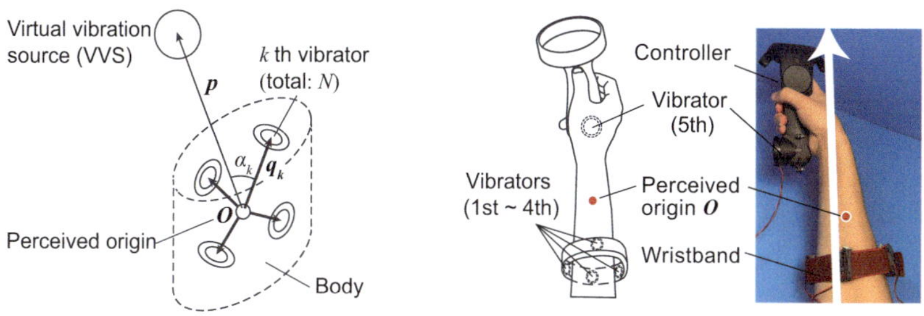

(a) Principle of stereohaptic vibrtion. (b) Overview of vibration system on the forearm.

Fig. 10.7 Schematic images of stereohaptic vibration. **a** Principle of stereohaptic vibration distribution using multiple vibrators. **b** Actual example of stereohaptic display applied to the forearm

Laboratory, Inc., Vp2) attached on the controller held in the hand were used to create a three-dimensional representation.

The experiment examined whether users could accurately localize the position of a 3D vibration source rotating around the forearm. Participants were asked to identify the trajectory of the motion around their forearm and determine if they could perceive the 3D position of VVS. As shown in Fig. 10.8a, to prevent participants from relying solely on intensity differences to identify the source, the experiment included a trajectory in which the vibration source appeared to move forward while rotating around a specific axis. Participants were then asked to indicate the direction of motion from nine possible directions. Figure 10.8b presents the response rate for each direction. The results showed that participants could identify the complex rotational trajectory with an accuracy rate significantly above chance (11.1%), achieving an average correct response rate of 30.5%. Furthermore, this study confirms that by attaching the same system to the other forearm and using the midpoint between the

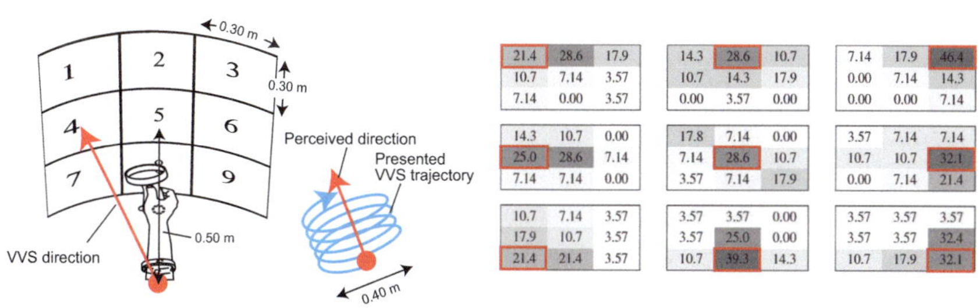

(a) Discrimination task to perceive moving direction of the rotating VVS in 3D. (b) Percentage of responses for each direction. Table positions correspond to dirctions #1~9.

Fig. 10.8 Experiments on the spatial perception of rotating VVS across nine directions. **a** Experimental conditions. **b** Response distribution for each direction. The positions of the nine tables represent the presented trajectories, and the values within the tables indicate participants' responses. Columns highlighted with red squares correspond to the correct answers

two outstretched arms as the perceptual origin, spatial information can be effectively represented.

Realistic spatial tactile vibrations significantly enhance the sense of presence for virtual objects. This method effectively represents both internal and external vibration sources, providing a natural and immersive experience, especially when combined with visual and auditory cues.

10.4 Tactile Texture Displays for Touch Panels

Until relatively recently, touch panels were primarily limited to specific applications, such as bank ATMs. Today, however, it is common for individuals to own multiple devices equipped with touch panels. Over this period of widespread adoption, the absence of haptic feedback has been repeatedly identified as a significant factor limiting usability [5, 23]. Nevertheless, touch panels that incorporate haptic feedback have yet to become the industry standard.

Interestingly, the inconvenience associated with the lack of haptic feedback appears to have become less of an issue for users in recent years. One explanation for this shift is that, whereas early touch panel interfaces simply reproduced mechanical push buttons in a visual form, the advent of gesture-based controls and multitouch functionality has substantially enhanced usability.

Originally, tactile displays for touch panels were developed to address the inconvenience caused by the lack of haptic feedback. However, today, few users consider the absence of haptic feedback to be a significant inconvenience. Instead, tactile displays are now regarded as tools for conveying the material qualities—*Shitsukan*—of objects presented on the screen more effectively.

10.4.1 Surface Tactile Display

The term "surface display" refers to touch panels equipped with haptic feedback capabilities. Conventional touch panels found in smartphones and tablet devices are typically hard and flat, offering a uniform tactile sensation regardless of the area touched. By contrast, surface displays are technologies that superimpose additional tactile sensations—such as button presses, bumps, or textures—onto the visual content presented on the screen.

In this section, we introduce the underlying principles of representative methods for achieving surface tactile displays and explore the possibilities they offer for generating diverse tactile experiences. Special emphasis is placed on the presentation of virtual tactile textures on touch panels.

At present, there are no commercially successful surface texture displays; however, the methods with the greatest potential are those that generate mechanical vibratory stimuli on the panel and those that control the panel's friction. Each approach can be further divided into several distinct techniques. In addition, high-quality tactile displays that combine both vibration and friction control are under active research and development [20, 31].

Both categories share the fundamental principle of eliciting tactile sensations by rapidly modulating the deformation of the skin on the fingertip in contact with the panel. Although it is often assumed that the tactile texture of an object is solely determined by its physical surface properties, in practice, texture perception arises from the dynamic deformation of the skin on the fingers during exploration. A tactile display is, in essence, a device that evokes tactile sensations by precisely controlling this skin deformation.

10.4.2 Vibrotactile Surface Texture Display

In this approach, tactile stimuli are produced by mechanically actuating the touch panel using dedicated actuators. The sensation is generated through deformation of the skin at the point of contact (Fig. 10.9). In devices where directly driving the touch panel is impractical—such as compact smartphones—the entire chassis can be vibrated using an internal eccentric mechanism. This method creates tactile feedback by causing subtle back-and-forth movements of the panel or device. Only minute displacements, often just a few micrometers at high frequencies, are required to evoke a distinct sensation. The critical factor is not the amplitude of movement, but the ability to modulate vibrations rapidly and precisely. For this reason, highly responsive actuators such as voice coil motors and piezoelectric actuators are commonly employed.

One of the most common and commercially successful haptic effects created by vibrotactile surface displays is the sensation of pressing a button, perceived as a "click" or "pop" (Fig. 10.10a). When tactile feedback accompanies a software button on a touch panel, users can confirm button presses by touch, thereby reducing operational errors [5, 16, 23].

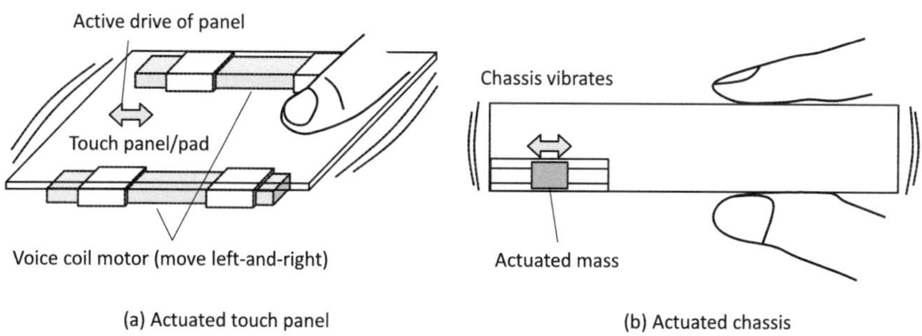

Fig. 10.9 Vibrotactile surface display. **a** Actuated touch panel: the panel itself is driven by actuators. **b** actuated chassis: the entire chassis vibrates, stimulating the fingers that hold the device

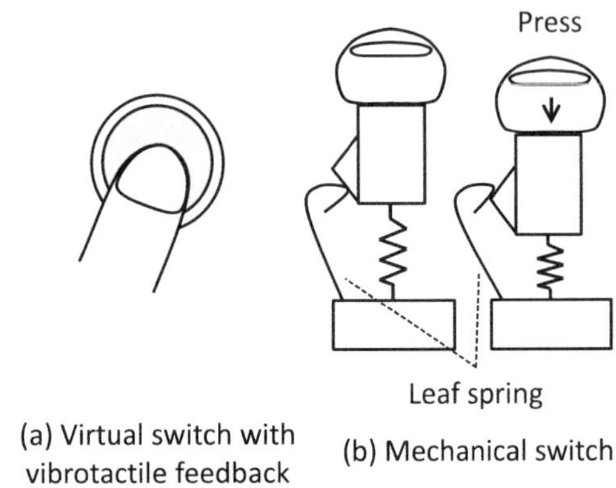

Fig. 10.10 Virtual switch with vibrotactile feedback. **a** A virtual switch drawn on a touch panel. **b** Schematic of a mechanical switch. The reaction force from the leaf spring is abruptly released when the switch is pressed to a certain depth, resulting in rapid, vibratory skin deformation

Mechanical push buttons typically incorporate springs; when pressed beyond a certain point, the spring's resistance suddenly drops and the button moves downward (Fig. 10.10b). This abrupt change in force produces a rapid deformation of the fingertip skin, yielding the familiar sensation of a button click. To replicate this effect on a tactile display, the device measures the force applied by the user's finger, and when this force exceeds a specified threshold, it delivers a mechanical displacement to the finger skin [9, 23]. Importantly, the touch panel itself does not physically move or deform under finger pressure; rather, the actuators generate the illusion of displacement. Despite this, well-designed vibrotactile feedback can closely approximate the experience of pressing a real mechanical button for many users.

10.4.3 Friction-Variable Surface Tactile Display

A friction-variable surface display creates diverse tactile sensations by actively modulating the frictional force experienced as a finger slides across the touch panel. One of the most widely used principles for controlling surface friction is electrostatic adhesion.

As illustrated in Fig. 10.11a, when both the surface of the touch panel and the user's finger are electrically charged, electrostatic attraction arises between the fingertip and the panel surface. This attraction increases the adhesive force, thereby enhancing friction. Importantly, because an insulating layer exists between the panel and the user, no electrical current actually passes through the body. By modulating the electrostatic force in response to the finger's position on the panel, the local distribution of friction can be precisely controlled. Since the attractive force depends only on the potential difference between the panel and the user, explicit grounding is unnecessary. The use of electrostatics for haptic displays offers practical advantages: the lack of moving mechanical parts simplifies device design and implementation.

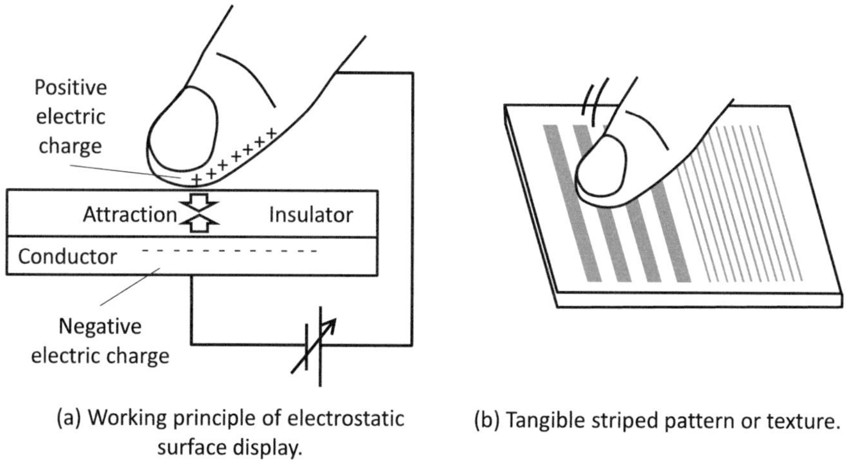

Fig. 10.11 Friction-variable surface displays. **a** Working principles. **b** Texture rendering by surface friction control

A representative application of friction-variable displays is the presentation of virtual textures. As shown in Fig. 10.11b, consider a striped pattern rendered visually on the touch panel. As a finger traverses the surface, the applied voltage is dynamically controlled according to the finger's position. For example, friction is increased when the finger passes over black stripes and decreased elsewhere. This spatial variation in friction allows the user to perceive the visual pattern as a tangible tactile sensation. By finely adjusting the frictional modulation, a wide variety of virtual textures can be simulated.

A key distinction between the two surface tactile display types discussed above is whether they actively or passively deliver tactile stimuli. In the vibrotactile approach, the panel is mechanically actuated to apply energy directly to the fingertip, classifying it as an active-type display. In contrast, the friction-variable approach modifies the friction at the surface, thereby dissipating or modulating the kinetic energy of the sliding finger, making it a passive-type display. This distinction—active versus passive—influences the applications best suited for each technology. For instance, the sensation of a button click is best rendered by an active-type display, while the presentation of tactile textures can be achieved using either approach.

10.4.4 Data-Driven Approach for Texture Rendering

One of the most widely adopted strategies for rendering tactile textures is the data-driven approach, in which frequency response models are constructed from physical interaction data recorded as a finger slides across textured surfaces [10, 14, 32]. As illustrated in Fig. 10.12, miniature accelerometers and force sensors are commonly used to capture the vibrations and forces generated during finger exploration.

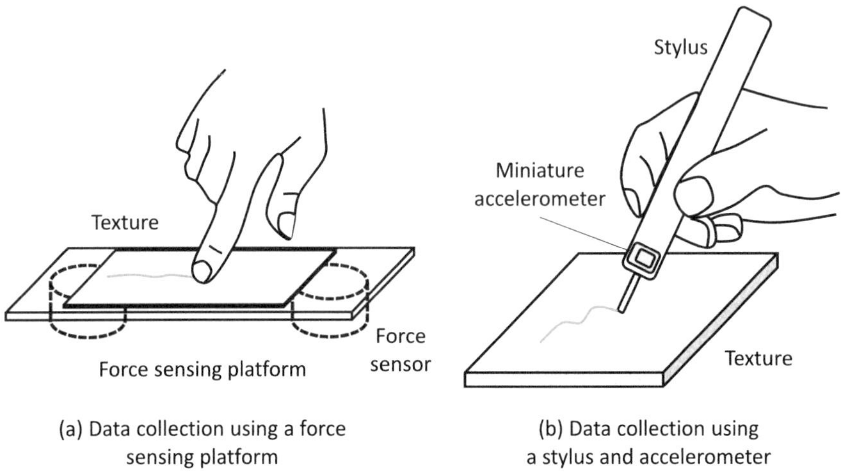

Fig. 10.12 Data collection of physical interactions during texture exploration. **a** Measurement of contact forces between the fingertip and the texture. **b** Measurement of vibrations at the tool tip

Accelerometers are rigidly affixed to the fingertip or a stylus, while force sensors are positioned beneath the platform holding the sample textures.

The accelerometer provides three-axis acceleration signals, which are typically combined to yield the resultant acceleration [34]. Force sensors measure either the normal and/or tangential forces, which can be used to compute target forces for subsequent presentation by a tactile display [41]. In addition to capturing force and vibration, it is also necessary to record the motion parameters of the finger or tool—particularly velocity.

The collected sensor data forms a set of time-series signals, from which frequency response models are computed to preserve the amplitude distribution of frequency components found in real-world tactile interactions. The spectral characteristics captured in these models play a crucial role in texture perception [1, 13]. Frequency spectra or autoregressive models are typically derived from the time-series data for this purpose.

It is important to recognize that the frequency characteristics of vibratory information are strongly dependent on the finger's exploratory motions, including sliding speed and applied normal force. As such, separate frequency models must be generated for different exploration conditions and target textures. This adaptation is essential because the manner of hand movement fundamentally shapes the experience of texture.

Once frequency models are established, they are employed in the following manner. First, the finger's motion on the touch panel is continuously monitored. Based on the real-time motion parameters, the system selects the most appropriate frequency model. Next, a white noise time-series signal is passed through a frequency-shaping filter based on the chosen model. This convolution process imparts the characteristic

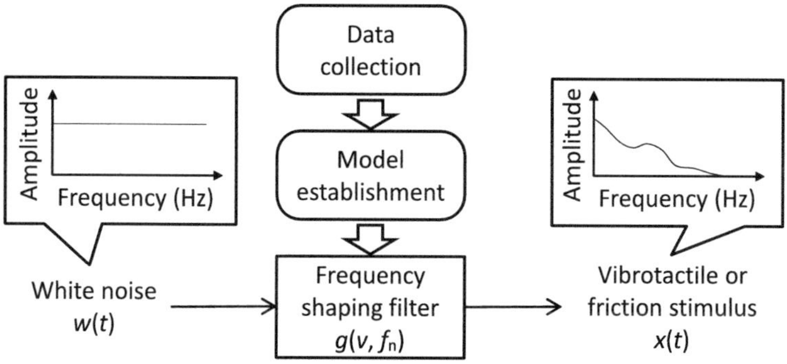

Fig. 10.13 Data-driven texture rendering. White noise signals are input to a frequency-shaping filter, designed using experimentally collected data. The filter is selected or updated in real time according to finger velocity and normal force on the touch panel. The resulting output signals retain the frequency characteristics unique to the target textures

frequency profile of the sampled material onto the output signal, thereby reproducing the original tactile experience (Fig. 10.13).

Although this data-driven approach is not yet standardized, it has been shown to render several types of textures and materials with moderate realism. For instance, when four materials—leather, cork, denim, and wood—were modeled and rendered using this method, participants were able to correctly identify the presented material 70–80% of the time [32].

10.5 Conclusion

In this chapter, we introduced three case studies from research on haptic Shitsukan: (1) softness presentation, (2) high-fidelity vibration and spatial presentation, and (3) texture presentation on touch panels. Together, these studies cover four of the five principal components of haptic Shitsukan described in Sect. 10.1.

In the work on softness presentation, coordinating kinesthetic force feedback with controlled skin presentation area with electro-tactile display was shown to markedly enhance subjective realism. Faithfully reproducing the contact area proved to be a decisive cue for perception along the "hard–soft" dimension.

The high-fidelity vibration and spatial presentation study handled frequencies above 100 Hz and developed a descriptive model that accounts for propagation characteristics within the body. Techniques such as perceptual impulse-response equivalence (ISM) and stereohaptics for locating vibration sources were identified as key to extending the perception of "roughness," "impact," and "motion" in both temporal and spatial domains.

Finally, the texture-on-touch-panel study demonstrated that combining subtle mechanical vibration with friction control can reproduce virtual materials consistent with visual cues. A data-driven rendering framework opened a path for porting "friction" and "macro-/micro-roughness" dimensions to mobile environments.

All three studies share the common principle of precisely controlling and presenting skin physical and perceptual phenomena to manipulate haptic Shitsukan. They also follow the strategic approach of identifying which physical phenomena are critical for perception and presenting those cues in the most efficient manner. While this is an obvious strategy for any sensory display, we emphasize that it remains fundamental even when recreating highly subjective experiences such as Shitsukan.

Haptic Shitsukan presentation is still in an early stage of development. Although active research is underway on individual components of Shitsukan, their fidelity is not yet comparable to that of vision or audition, where stimuli can be rendered indistinguishable from reality; the softness presentation by electro-tactile display is one such example. Developing new devices that offer high temporal and spatial resolution based on novel principles is therefore essential. On the other hand, when the application context is clearly defined, practical deployment is already feasible; the texture-on-touch-panel case exemplifies such an application-driven scenario.

Future research on haptic Shitsukan must advance both the precision of individual cues and methods for combining them naturally. Because cue integration must follow user movements in real time, engineering solutions that merge all sensations at high temporal resolution will be indispensable. Finally, concrete application scenarios that provide clear user benefits must be cultivated to drive adoption of haptic Shitsukan technologies.

References

1. Bensmaïa, S.J., Hollins, M.: Pacinian representations of fine surface texture. Percept. Psychophys. **67**(5), 842–854 (2005)
2. Bensmaia, S., Hollis, M., Yau, J.: Vibrotactile intensity and frequency information in the Pacinian system: a psychophysical model. Percept. Psychophys. **67**(5), 828–841 (2005). https://doi.org/10.3758/bf03193536
3. Bergmann Tiest, W.M., Kappers, A.M.L.: Cues for haptic perception of compliance. IEEE Trans. Haptics **2**(4), 189–199 (2009). https://doi.org/10.1109/TOH.2009.16
4. Bergmann Tiest, W.M., Kappers, A.M.: Physical aspects of softness perception, pp. 3–15. Springer London, London (2014). https://doi.org/10.1007/978-1-4471-6533-0_1
5. Brewster, S., Chohan, F., Brown, L.: Tactile feedback for mobile interactions. In: Proceedings of the SIGCHI Conference on Human Factors in Computing Systems, pp. 159–162 (2007)
6. Cao, N., Nagano, H., Konyo, M., Okamoto, S., Tadokoro, S.: Envelope effect study on collision vibration perception through investigating just noticeable difference of time constant. In: 2017 IEEE World Haptics Conference (WHC), pp. 528–533 (2017). https://doi.org/10.1109/WHC.2017.7989957
7. Cao, N., Konyo, M., Nagano, H., Tadokoro, S.: Dependence of the perceptual discrimination of high-frequency vibrations on the envelope and intensity of waveforms. IEEE Access **7**, 20840–20849 (2019). https://doi.org/10.1109/ACCESS.2019.2898029
8. Chatterjee, S., Tan, S., Choi, C., Kuchibhotla, A., Wan, G., Peshkin, M.A., Colgate, J.E., Hipwell, M.C.: Decoding roughness perception in distributed haptic devices. PNAS Nexus **3**(10), 468 (2024). https://doi.org/10.1093/pnasnexus/pgae468
9. Chen, H., Park, J., Dai, S., Tan, H.Z.: Design and evaluation of identifiable key-click signals for mobile devices. IEEE Trans. Haptics **4**(4), 229–241 (2011)

10. Culbertson, H., Kuchenbecker, K.J.: Importance of matching physical friction, hardness, and texture in creating realistic haptic virtual surfaces. IEEE Trans. Haptics **10**(1), 63–74 (2017)
11. Friedman, R.M.: Magnitude estimation of softness. Exp. Brain Res. **191**(2), 133–142 (2008). https://doi.org/10.1007/s00221-008-1507-5
12. Gescheider, G.A., Bolanowski, S.J., Hardick, K.R.: The frequency selectivity of information-processing channels in the tactile sensory system. Somatosens. Motor Res. **18**(3), 191–201 (2001). https://doi.org/10.1080/01421590120072187
13. Hasegawa, H., Okamoto, S., Yamada, Y.: Phase difference between normal and shear forces during tactile exploration represents textural features. IEEE Trans. Haptics **13**(1), 11–17 (2020). https://doi.org/10.1109/TOH.2019.2960021
14. Hassen, R., Gülecyüz, B., Steinbach, E.: PVC-SLP: perceptual vibrotactile-signal compression based-on sparse linear prediction. IEEE Trans. Multimed. **23**, 4455–4468 (2021). https://doi.org/10.1109/TMM.2020.3042674
15. Ho, H.N., Jones, L.: Modeling the thermal responses of the skin surface during hand-object interactions. J. Biomech. Eng. **130**, 021005 (2008). https://doi.org/10.1115/1.2899574
16. Hoggan, E., Brewster, S.A., Johnston, J.: Investigating the effectiveness of tactile feedback for mobile touchscreens. In: Proceedings of the SIGCHI Conference on Human Factors in Computing Systems, CHI '08. ACM, pp. 1573–1582 (2008). https://doi.org/10.1145/1357054.1357300
17. Huang, N.E., Shen, Z., Long, S.R., Wu, M.C., Shih, H.H., Zheng, Q., Yen, N.C., Tung, C.C., Liu, H.H.: The empirical mode decomposition and the Hilbert spectrum for nonlinear and non-stationary time series analysis. Proceed. Math. Phys. Eng. Sci. **454**(1971), 903–995 (1998). https://doi.org/10.1098/rspa.1998.0193
18. Ikeda, Y., Fujita, K.: Display of soft elastic object by simultaneous control of fingertip contact area and reaction force. Trans. Virtual Reality Soc. Jpn. **9**(2), 187–194 (2004). https://doi.org/10.18974/tvrsj.9.2_187
19. Israr, A., Poupyrev, I.: Tactile brush: drawing on skin with a tactile grid display. In: Proceedings of the SIGCHI Conference on Human Factors in Computing Systems, CHI '11. Association for Computing Machinery. New York, NY, USA, p. 2019–2028 (2011). URLhttps://doi.org/10.1145/1978942.1979235
20. Ito, K., Okamoto, S., Yamada, Y., Kajimoto, H.: Tactile texture display with vibrotactile and electrostatic friction stimuli mixed at appropriate ratio presents better roughness textures. ACM Trans. Appl. Percept. **16**(4), 20 (2019)
21. Kajimoto, H.: Electro-tactile display kit for fingertip. In: 2021 IEEE World Haptics Conference (WHC), pp. 587–587 (2021). https://doi.org/10.1109/WHC49131.2021.9517192
22. Koehn, J.K., Kuchenbecker, K.J.: Surgeons and non-surgeons prefer haptic feedback of instrument vibrations during robotic surgery. Surg. Endosc. **29**(10), 2970–2983 (2015). https://doi.org/10.1007/s00464-014-4030-8
23. Koskinen, E., Kaaresoja, T., Laitinen, P.: Feel-good touch: finding the most pleasant tactile feedback for a mobile touch screen button. In: Proceedings of the 10th International Conference on Multimodal Interfaces, ICMI '08. ACM, pp. 297–304 (2008). https://doi.org/10.1145/1452392.1452453
24. Lamoré, P.J.J., Muijser, H., Keemink, C.: Envelope detection of amplitude-modulated high-frequency sinusoidal signals by skin mechanoreceptors. J. Acoust. Soc. Am. **79**(4), 1082–1085 (1986). https://doi.org/10.1121/1.393380
25. Makino, Y., Maeno, T., Shinoda, H.: Perceptual characteristic of multi-spectral vibrations beyond the human perceivable frequency range. In: 2011 IEEE World Haptics Conference, pp. 439–443 (2011). https://doi.org/10.1109/WHC.2011.5945526
26. Minamizawa, K., Kakehi, Y., Nakatani, M., Mihara, S., Tachi, S.: Techtile toolkit: a prototyping tool for designing haptic media. In: ACM SIGGRAPH 2012 Emerging Technologies, SIGGRAPH'12, pp. 387–392 (2012). https://doi.org/10.1145/2343456.2343478
27. Nagano, H., Takenouchi, H., Cao, N., Konyo, M., Tadokoro, S.: Tactile feedback system of high-frequency vibration signals for supporting delicate teleoperation of construction robots. Adv. Robo.: Int. J. Robot. Soc. Jpn. **34**(11), 730–743 (2020). https://doi.org/10.1080/01691864.2020.1769725

28. Ohara, G., Kikuchi, D., Konyo, M., Tadokoro, S.: Stereohaptic vibration: Out-of-body localization of virtual vibration source through multiple vibrotactile stimuli on the forearms. IEEE Trans. Haptics **17**(1), 86–91 (2024). https://doi.org/10.1109/TOH.2024.3357574
29. Okamoto, S., Nagano, H., Ho, H.N.: Psychophysical dimensions of material perception and methods to specify textural space, pp. 3–20. Springer Japan, Tokyo (2016). https://doi.org/10.1007/978-4-431-55772-2_1
30. Okamura, A., Cutkosky, M., Dennerlein, J.: Reality-based models for vibration feedback in virtual environments. IEEE/ASME Trans. Mechatron. **6**(3), 245–252 (2001). https://doi.org/10.1109/3516.951362
31. Otake, K., Okamoto, S., Akiyama, Y., Yamada, Y.: Tactile texture display combining vibrotactile and electrostatic-friction stimuli: substantial effects on realism and moderate effects on behavioral responses. ACM Trans. Appl. Percept. **19**(4), 18 (2022). https://doi.org/10.1145/3539733
32. Otake, K., Okamoto, S., Akiyama, Y., Yamada, Y.: Tactile texture rendering for electrostatic friction displays: incorporation of low-frequency friction model and high-frequency textural model. IEEE Trans. Haptics **15**(1), 68–73 (2022). https://doi.org/10.1109/TOH.2021.3138647
33. Park, J., Oh, Y., Tan, H.Z.: Effect of cutaneous feedback on the perceived hardness of a virtual object. IEEE Trans. Haptics **11**(4), 518–530 (2018). https://doi.org/10.1109/TOH.2018.2854721
34. Romano, J.M., Kuchenbecker, K.J.: Creating realistic virtual textures from contact acceleration data. IEEE Trans. Haptics **5**(2), 109–119 (2012)
35. Saal, H.P., Delhaye, B.P., Rayhaun, B.C., Bensmaia, S.J.: Simulating tactile signals from the whole hand with millisecond precision. Proc. Natl. Acad. Sci. U.S.A. **114**(28), E5693–E5702 (2017). https://doi.org/10.1073/PNAS.1704856114
36. Sakata, S., Nagano, H., Konyo, M., Tadokoro, S.: Multipoint vibrotactile stimuli based on vibration propagation enhance collision sensation. In: Haptics: Perception, Devices, Control, and Applications, *Lecture notes in computer science*. Springer International Publishing, Cham, vol. 9775, pp. 65–74 (2016). https://doi.org/10.1007/978-3-319-42324-1_7. URLhttp://link.springer.com/10.1007/978-3-319-42324-1_7
37. Scilingo, E.P., Bianchi, M., Grioli, G., Bicchi, A.: Rendering softness: integration of kinesthetic and cutaneous information in a haptic device. IEEE Trans. Haptics **3**(2), 109–118 (2010). https://doi.org/10.1109/TOH.2010.2
38. Shao, Y., Hayward, V., Visell, Y.: Spatial patterns of cutaneous vibration during whole-hand haptic interactions. Proc. Natl. Acad. Sci. U.S.A. **113**(15), 4188–4193 (2016). https://doi.org/10.1073/pnas.1520866113
39. Srinivasan, M.A., LaMotte, R.H.: Tactual discrimination of softness: abilities and mechanisms, pp. 123–135. Birkhäuser Basel, Basel (1996). https://doi.org/10.1007/978-3-0348-9016-8_11
40. Suga, Y., Takeuchi, M., Tanaka, S., Kajimoto, H.: Softness presentation by combining electrotactile stimulation and force feedback. Front. Virtual Reality **4**, 1133146 (2023). https://doi.org/10.3389/frvir.2023.1133146
41. Tamura, A., Okamoto, S.: Richer textural information in the horizontal component of the contact force compared with the normal component. In: IEEE Haptics Symposium, pp. 13–18 (2024). https://doi.org/10.1109/HAPTICS59260.2024.10520867
42. von Békésy, G.: Neural funneling along the skin and between the inner and outer hair cells of the cochlea. J. Acoust. Soc. Am. **31**(9), 1236–1249 (1959). https://doi.org/10.1121/1.1907851
43. Yamaguchi, K., Konyo, M., Tadokoro, S.: Sensory equivalence conversion of high-frequency vibrotactile signals using intensity segment modulation method for enhancing audiovisual experience. In: 2021 IEEE World Haptics Conference (WHC). IEEE, pp. 674–679 (2021). https://doi.org/10.1109/WHC49131.2021.9517147

Chapter 11
Augmenting Reality with Shitsukan

Daisuke Iwai and Yuta Itoh

Abstract This chapter explores the capabilities and challenges of in situ Shitsukan (material appearance) manipulation through augmented reality (AR) technologies, focusing on two main approaches: projection mapping (PM) and optical see-through AR (OST-AR) systems. Digital Shitsukan manipulation allows for modifying the perceived material properties of physical surfaces, and AR enables these modifications to be experienced in real-world scenarios. We discuss various applications, including makeup simulation, product design, and tactile feedback, as well as the technical challenges of geometric alignment, radiometric compensation, and visual consistency in AR-based Shitsukan manipulation. Additionally, we address emerging hybrid systems, such as beaming displays, that combine PM and OST-AR technologies for enhanced experiences. Finally, we outline future research directions, highlighting the potential of AR-based Shitsukan manipulation in various fields.

11.1 Digital Shitsukan Manipulation

Digital image processing is a powerful tool for modifying the visual Shitsukan, i.e., the perceived material properties, of physical surfaces. Once various material components are decomposed from the captured appearance through inverse rendering or computational photography pipelines, they can be digitally adjusted independently of other properties, such as the shapes of the surfaces and the scene lighting. For example, using intrinsic image decomposition [12, 14, 20, 21] which separates an image into two layers, namely reflectance and shading, we can 'recolor' a captured surface. Integrating spatio-temporally and spectrally controllable illumination allows us to separate the appearance into more complex lighting components, such as direct and global components [48] (Fig. 11.1a), and reflective and fluorescent components [19].

D. Iwai (✉)
The University of Osaka, Toyonaka, Osaka, Japan
e-mail: daisuke.iwai.es@osaka-u.ac.jp

Y. Itoh
Institute of Science Tokyo, Yokohama, Kanagawa, Japan
e-mail: itoh@comp.isct.ac.jp

S. Nishida and K. Nishino (eds.), *Shitsukan—Understanding and Manipulating Material and Quality Perception*, https://doi.org/10.1007/978-981-95-4762-3_11

Fig. 11.1 Digital Shitsukan manipulation. **a** Separation of direct and global components [48] ©ACM. **b** Motion magnification [42] ©ACM

The Shitsukan modification can also be achieved without explicitly separating material components from the captured appearance of a physical surface. For instance, a series of 2D image operations based on multiscale image analysis can consistently change the Shitsukan [13]. By building a subband decomposition of an image and selectively modifying the coefficients within the subbands, we can alter the appearance of material properties like gloss, smoothness, or weathering. Another method involves adjusting the perceptual stiffness of an object in a captured movie sequence by selectively amplifying its small motion [42] (Fig. 11.1b).

As described so far, modifying the Shitsukan of physical surfaces using digital image processing techniques has been actively explored at the intersection of computer vision and computer graphics. However, the results of these manipulations can only be viewed on two-dimensional media, such as computer monitors or printed paper, which are not spatially and temporally aligned with the physical surfaces. This limitation restricts the potential applications of these technologies. In the next section, we will discuss the possibilities of in situ Shitsukan manipulation beyond 2D media and explore augmented reality (AR) as a promising implementation approach.

11.2 In Situ Shitsukan Manipulation in Augmented Reality

AR is a technology that overlays digital information on the user's view of the physical world. Typical AR systems place 3D virtual objects, such as text, arrows, or avatars, on top of or floating over the physical surfaces. On the other hand, in the context of Shitsukan manipulation, AR is used to alter the appearance of physical surfaces in situ, realizing non-traditional applications. Compared to the Shitsukan manipulation on 2D media, AR provides a more intuitive and immersive experience by naturally delivering the presence of the modified surfaces in the real world. Moreover, AR enables the interaction with the modified surfaces, such as touching, moving, or changing the viewpoint, which is essential for evaluating the modified Shitsukan in real-world scenarios.

The manipulation of Shitsukan in AR can be achieved through two main approaches: projection mapping (PM) and optical see-through (OST) AR. In this section, we will introduce application examples of Shitsukan manipulation using both approaches that have been explored so far and discuss the technical issues and the solutions involved in achieving them.

11.2.1 Projection Mapping

PM is a technique that optically projects digital images onto physical surfaces to create the illusion of modifying their appearance. The Shitsukan of physical surfaces can be manipulated by aligning projected imagery, which simulates desired material properties such as color or texture, with these surfaces. Since the augmentations can be viewed by multiple users from various viewpoints without requiring them to wear or hold any display devices, PM is suited for applications where Shitsukan manipulation results are shared by a group of people.

11.2.1.1 Applications

Makeup is an application domain where PM has been actively explored. PM systems have been proposed that can apply makeup in real time, adjusting to facial expressions and movements [8] (Fig. 11.2a). These systems offer a novel way to experiment with makeup styles and colors without the need to remove and reapply makeup, which is both time-consuming and costly. A cosmetics company has already adopted a PM system in their stores, allowing customers to experience virtual makeup applications [1].

Another promising application is in product design support, where PM is used to switch between different visual materials of a product prototype, allowing the evaluation of different material designs before its actual production. Cascini et al. [15] validated a PM system for creating design representations to support co-creative design sessions and confirmed that PM enables quick, real-time modifications to the surface of a physical prototype to try out new ideas. The presented PM system allowed the participants to evaluate the visual appearance of the packaging of food

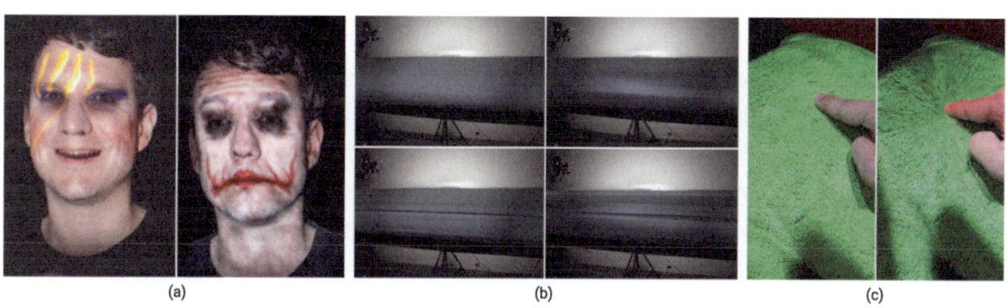

Fig. 11.2 Applications of PM-based Shitsukan manipulation. **a** Makeup [8]. **b** Car interior design [57] ©IEEE. **c** Softness manipulation based on a cross-modal effect for cushion material design [51] ©IEEE

by projecting different patterns and colors on the prototype. Similar technologies have been developed to support the design process of car interiors [57] (Fig. 11.2b) and exteriors [43].

Shitsukan of non-rigid products such as textiles and clothing can also be modified using PM. Although aligning the projected imagery with the deforming surfaces of these products is technically challenging, a system has been developed that can alter the perceived material properties of a flexible surface [44]. This system circumvents the alignment issue by determining the color of each pixel based on the normal direction of the corresponding point on the surface. PM can also adjust the mechanical Shitsukan properties of non-rigid surfaces. Researchers have found that projecting dynamic luminance patterns representing motion cues onto a static physical surface can evoke the perception of deformation in that surface [35]. By applying this illusionary effect, the perceived stiffness of a flexible surface can be adjusted, which is useful for evaluating the design of clothing and textiles [52].

It has been demonstrated that PM can also modify the Shitsukan of modalities beyond vision through cross-modal effects, expanding the potential application fields of PM-based Shitsukan manipulation. For example, it was experimentally confirmed that altering the color of the food surface with projected imagery changes the taste of the food [49]. Another study found that superimposing dynamic boiling textures on food (such as curry soup) influences perceived saltiness, spiciness, and appetite when eating [55]. The manipulation of Shitsukan using projection mapping can improve the dining experience and nutritional intake in contexts such as caregiving meals or hospital meals, potentially enhancing the well-being and satisfaction of individuals receiving these meals. Beyond the sense of taste, the sense of touch can also be manipulated using PM. A system has been developed that can adjust the perceived softness of non-rigid physical objects by projecting dynamic luminance patterns onto them [51] (Fig. 11.2c). Such haptic Shitsukan modulation can support the design of soft products like cushions and mattresses, allowing designers to adjust and evaluate the tactile properties of these products in real time.

11.2.1.2 Technical Issues and Solutions

Assuming a simple scenario where each projected pixel modifies the appearance of a single point on the physical surface, two major technical challenges need to be addressed to accurately reproduce the desired appearance: geometric alignment and radiometric compensation. Geometric alignment involves accurately registering the 2D projected imagery with the 3D physical surface. Radiometric compensation, on the other hand, deals with adjusting the colors of the projected imagery to accurately reproduce the target appearance, even on textured surfaces. A typical setup for accomplishing these tasks in PM is a projector-camera system (ProCams), where the camera is used to analyze the calibration patterns projected onto the physical surface.

Geometric alignment is technically achieved by determining pixel correspondences between the projector and the camera. For static surfaces, correspondence can be established by projecting structured light patterns, such as gray code patterns, onto the surface and capturing the reflected light with the camera. However, this method is not applicable to dynamic surfaces, as the surface must remain static during the projection and capture of multiple pattern images. For dynamic cases, it is necessary to know the position and orientation of the physical surface relative to the projector. Motion capture systems using multiple cameras, often with retroreflective markers attached to the surface, are commonly employed for tracking [47]. However, these markers are visible and can disrupt the projected appearances. One solution is to use invisible markers to human observers, such as active markers that emit infrared light [58] (Fig. 11.3a), or to minimize the visibility of markers through radiometric compensation techniques which will be discussed in the next paragraph [5] (Fig. 11.3b). Another solution involves developing markerless tracking methods that can track the position and orientation of the physical surface using feature points or landmarks, such as faces [8].

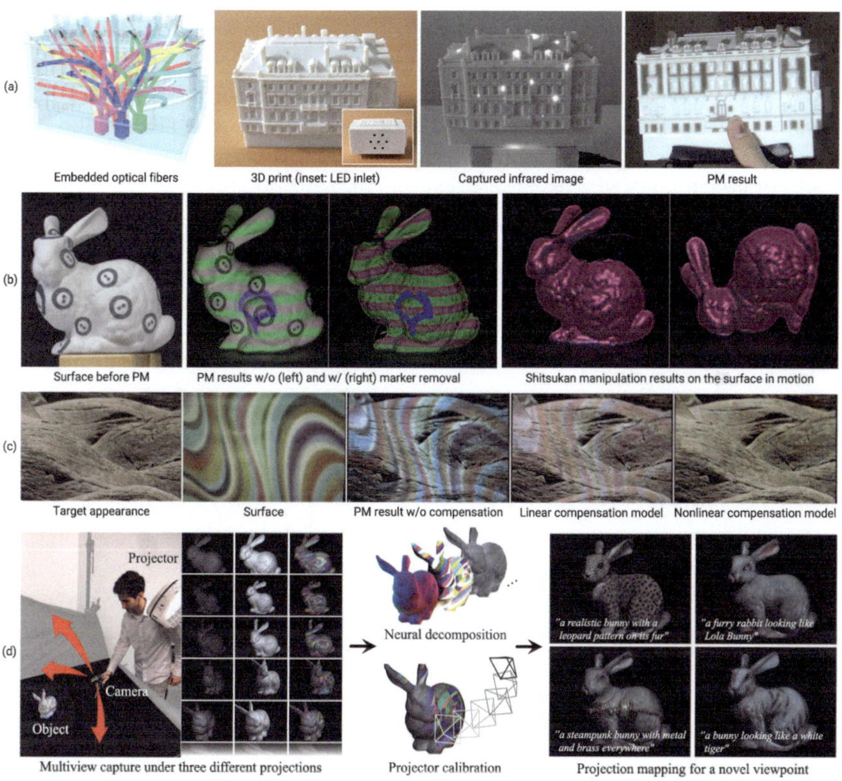

Fig. 11.3 PM technologies. **a** Geometric alignment using active IR markers embedded into the projection surface with a multimaterial 3D printer [58] ©IEEE. **b** Geometric alignment using diminishable visual markers [5] ©IEEE. **c** Radiometric compensation [23] ©IEEE. **d** DNN-based geometric alignment and radiometric compensation [17] ©IEEE

Radiometric compensation is achieved by solving the inverse problem of color transformation between the input and captured RGB values for each pixel, addressing the spatially varying reflectance properties of physical surfaces. While pioneering works explored simple linear models, more sophisticated models, including deep neural networks (DNNs), have demonstrated superior accuracy. These advanced models effectively handle the complex dependencies between color channels and the nonlinear characteristics of the projector's color processing [23, 27] (Fig. 11.3c). A recent DNN-based method has achieved both geometric alignment and radiometric compensation, even for novel viewpoints where the camera was not placed during the calibration phase [17] (Fig. 11.3d). This research also proposes integrating generative AI into PM, enabling users to create PM content using text prompts.

The techniques introduced above function well as long as each projected pixel precisely hits a single point on the physical surface. However, this condition is not always met, and the projected light may scatter within the surface, reflect multiple times between surfaces, or become defocused due to the shallow depth of field of the projector. Conventionally, these global illumination effects were compensated for by estimating the full light transport, which describes how light travels from the projector to the camera, and by solving the inverse problem of the light transport equation. However, this process involves large-scale matrix inversion which is computationally intensive [7]. Recently, researchers have applied DNNs to compensate for these global illumination effects more efficiently. For example, Kageyama et al. [32–34] demonstrated that DNNs can compensate for defocus blur almost in real time, with image quality comparable to that of conventional methods.

The above-mentioned technologies are more thoroughly summarized in a book [10] and survey articles [9, 22, 31]. Interested readers are encouraged to refer to these resources for further details.

11.2.2 Optical See-Through AR

Optical see-through AR (OST-AR) is another approach to in situ Shitsukan manipulation. It uses a transparent display, such as a head-mounted display (HMD) or a transparent screen, to overlay digital imagery on the user's view of the physical world. Unlike PM, OST-AR allows users to view the physical surfaces directly, without the need for a projector, and to interact with the surfaces while observing the digital augmentations. This feature is handy for applications that require the user to touch or manipulate the physical surfaces, such as in the fields of industry [6], medical [11], and education [53].

11.2.2.1 Applications

As an application of OST-AR, vision augmentation assists the user's vision via see-through visualization. Langlotz et al. [40] proposed ChromaGlasses, computational glasses for compensating color blindness. Their system assists people with dichromatic vision by augmenting the scene with virtual information. The system considers the user's type of dichromatic vision via user calibration. The display augments the color of textures that are hard for the user to distinguish from the surrounding colors (Fig. 11.4).

11.2.2.2 Technical Issues and Solutions

Achieving visual consistency is crucial for practical uses in OST-AR Displays [30, 60]. It ensures that virtual images seamlessly integrate with the real world, which is essential for making the visuals indistinguishable from reality. Several technical challenges must be addressed to achieve this level of visual fidelity.

- **Wide FOV:** A wide FOV is essential for immersive AR experiences, allowing virtual content to occupy a substantial portion of the user's visual field [16]. Limited FOV can break the immersion and make virtual objects appear cut off or out of place.
- **Transparency (Occlusion) and Contrast Optimization:** Balancing the display's transparency with high contrast ratios ensures that virtual images are vivid without obscuring the real-world view [37]. Poor transparency or contrast can result in virtual images that are either too faint to see clearly or too opaque, hindering the view of the real environment.
- **Vergence-Accommodation Conflict Mitigation:** When viewing virtual objects, the convergence of the eyes (vergence) and the mismatch between the focal distance (accommodation) can lead to visual discomfort and reduce the realism of virtual content. Various OST-AR displays aim to resolve these issues [54].
- **Alignment and Calibration:** Precise alignment between the virtual and real-world coordinate systems is necessary to prevent the misplacement of virtual

Fig. 11.4 As an OST-AR application, ChromaGlasses augment the dichromatic-vision users' view to assist them in distinguishing similar colors [40] (Image reconstructed from our materials)

objects. This requirement essentially means calibrating the display and the user's eye coordinates [29].

- **Color Accuracy and Gamut:** Accurate color reproduction is critical for matching virtual objects with the real-world environment [39]. Limited color gamuts or inaccurate color rendering can make virtual content appear unnatural or out of place.
- **High Dynamic Range (HDR):** Supporting HDR allows displays to show both very bright and very dark elements simultaneously, closely mimicking real-world lighting conditions [60]. Without HDR, virtual content may not blend well with varying lighting in the real environment.
- **Latency Reduction:** Low display latency is essential to ensure that virtual images update in real time with head and eye movements [41]. High latency can cause a noticeable lag, making virtual objects appear to 'swim' or lag behind, which disrupts visual consistency.
- **Precise Tracking Systems:** Accurate head and eye tracking are necessary to render virtual images in the correct location and perspective [38]. Inaccurate tracking can lead to misalignment between virtual and real objects, breaking the illusion of reality.
- **Environmental Lighting Adaptation:** An OST-AR system needs to adapt to varying ambient light conditions to maintain the visibility and realism of virtual content [3]. Failure to adjust can result in virtual images that are too bright or too dim compared to the surroundings.

Addressing the challenges related to visual consistency in OST-AR is essential for delivering an immersive and convincing AR experience. This involves a combination of high-quality optical design, advanced display technologies, precise tracking systems, and sophisticated rendering algorithms. OST-AR research focuses on these areas to enhance the seamless integration of virtual content with the real world, making visuals indistinguishable from reality.

11.3 Current Challenges for AR-Based Shitsukan Manipulation

As described in Sect. 11.2, the technical advancements in both PM and OST-AR have enabled the in situ manipulation of physical surfaces' appearances with high levels of accuracy. However, there are still challenges that need to be addressed to realize Shitsukan manipulation in AR that is both visually convincing and practically applicable. In this section, we will discuss the current challenges in AR-based Shitsukan manipulation and introduce the recent technical solutions that have been proposed to overcome them.

11.3.1 Perceptual Reflectance Control in PM

PM technologies have matured to accurately reproduce target appearances on physical surfaces, as described in Sect. 11.2.1.2. However, they still face limitations in manipulating Shitsukan, or perceived surface reflectance. This section discusses the challenges beyond conventional technical issues, focusing on how we can induce the perception of altered surface reflectance in human observers. Specifically, we will address two issues: the necessity for a dark environment and the removal of cast shadows.

Firstly, PM works effectively only in a dark room, as the contrast and saturation of the projected imagery can be significantly reduced by environmental lighting. However, in the physical world, objects are visible only when illuminated, unless they are self-luminous. Therefore, environmental lighting is necessary for physically correct Shitsukan manipulation in PM. It is also crucial for altering an object's material properties to appear specular or transparent, because the surrounding environment is reflected and refracted by these objects, respectively [18]. Additionally, without environmental lighting, projected surfaces are likely to be perceived as self-luminous rather than illuminated as shown in psychophysical studies [45].

Takeuchi et al. [56] successfully overcame this limitation by replacing the typical room lighting with projectors (Fig. 11.5a). They configured the projectors to selectively illuminate the scene, excluding the projection target, effectively replicating

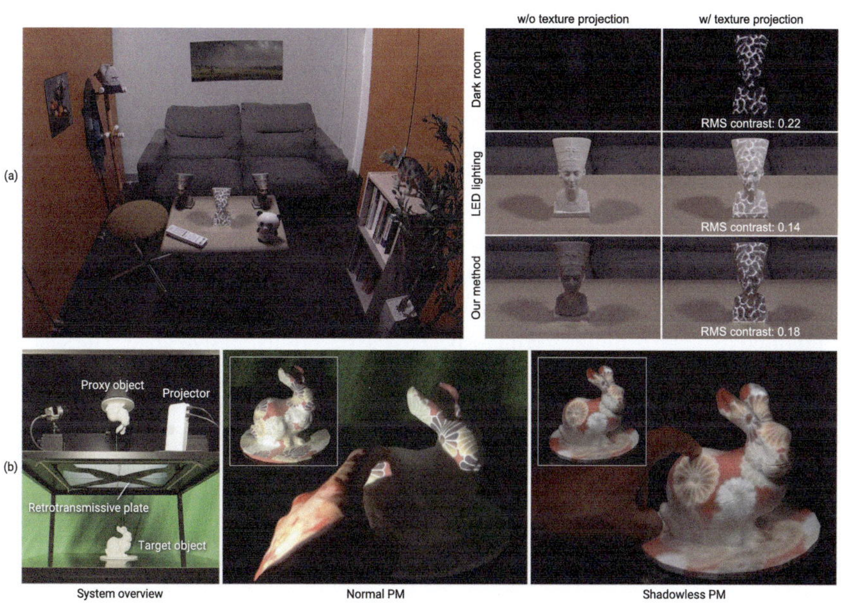

Fig. 11.5 Current challenges in PM. **a** PM in a bright environment without sacrificing the contrast [56] ©IEEE. **b** Shadowless PM using a large optical element [25]

environmental lighting while avoiding the undesirable increase in the target's luminance. Through experiments, they demonstrated that this projector-based lighting system significantly enhances the contrast and realism of PM results, even under environmental lighting conditions. They also showed that the surface material of the target object could be convincingly altered to a mirror-like specular material in a physically correct manner.

Secondly, cast shadow is an inherent limitation of PM and can disrupt the realism of Shitsukan manipulation, especially in interactive applications where a user's body may approach the target surface. In our daily scenarios, room lighting illuminates each point in the scene from a wide range of directions, ensuring that a physical surface is not completely shadowed and its texture remains visible even when an observer's body approaches it. In contrast, in PM, a projector emits light from a single direction, casting shadows on the surface which causes the projected texture to diminish.

The primary conventional solution to the cast shadow problem is a synthetic aperture technique, in which a multi-projection system is used to virtually realize a large aperture projector [46, 50]. Multiple projectors are spatially distributed such that they project images from a wide range of viewing angles onto a target projection surface. When an area of a projection surface is occluded from a projector by a user's interaction, these methods select another projector that is visible from the occluded area and project a compensation image from the selected projector. The compensation image needs to be carefully computed to avoid geometric and photometric artifacts such as overlaps or seams between images from different projectors, and color inconsistencies across them. However, because there is an inevitable delay in the compensation process from the shadow occurrence to the compensating projection, artifacts occur on the surface when the occluder moves by the user's interaction.

Hiratani et al. [25] realized shadowless PM by adopting an optical approach that eliminates the need for complex computations for shadow removal (Fig. 11.5b). They used a large format retrotransmissive plate to project images onto a surface from wide viewing angles. The retrotransmissive plate collects light rays emitted from a point in space and redirects them to a plane-symmetrical position with respect to it. Thus, they placed a white diffuse object, referred to as a proxy object, whose shape is plane-symmetrical to a projection target such that the target and proxy objects are configured in plane symmetry with respect to the retrotransmissive plate. The system projects an image onto the proxy object using standard projectors. Projected light incident on a surface point is diffusely reflected, and the reflected light rays fall on the retrotransmissive plate. After traveling through the plate, the rays converge to a point on the target object that corresponds with the projected point on the proxy object. This arrangement allows projection from a wide range of directions, thus achieving shadowless PM, without requiring the shadow removal computations used in conventional synthetic aperture approaches.

11.3.2 Beaming Displays

While there are various challenges in see-through AR displays [30], one of the most critical issues is the trade-offs among the various performance factors of the display, such as resolution, field of view, brightness, power consumption, weight, and form factor. These properties are typically interdependent, and improving one may degrade others. For example, increasing the display resolution may reduce the field of view, and increasing the display brightness may increase power consumption. Therefore, designing an OST display often faces a trade-off based on the application requirements.

To resolve this trade-off, researchers have proposed a new type of display called a beaming display [28] which is a hybrid of PM and OST displays. A beaming display is a see-through display that consists of two separate pieces of hardware: transparent light-receiving glasses without computing units and a steering projector that projects images onto the passive glasses. This approach breaks the trade-off chains and allows the display to improve and have a larger design space. For example, theoretically, a beaming display can achieve a small form factor and high brightness simultaneously thanks to the separation of the optics and the light engine. However, there are still many technical challenges to be addressed, such as the alignment between the steering projection and the glasses screen, the latency of the tracking and projection, further miniaturization of the glasses, and the installation of a set of steering projectors.

Hiroi et al. [26] proposed a low-latency beaming display to achieve fast tracking and projection of the image onto the light-receiving glasses (Fig. 11.6a). Aksit et al. [2] proposed thin and lightweight beaming display glasses using a holographic optical element (HOE) (Fig. 11.6b). Their glasses were about 2 mm thick with an HOE film. They demonstrated that an image can be projected using a DLP projector to form a virtual image in the user's field of view through the custom lens HOE. They also demonstrated image formation via computational holography, yet with an eyepiece lens instead of the HOE glass plate. Aoki et al. [4] proposed a dual steering projector system for a beaming display to expand the projection area (Fig. 11.6c). They built a geometric calibration model for dual steering projector systems and demonstrated the effectiveness of the proposed method in a prototype system.

11.4 Conclusion and Future Directions

In this chapter, we have explored the capabilities and challenges of in situ Shitsukan manipulation through AR technologies, focusing on PM and OST-AR systems. Both approaches offer more intuitive and immersive experiences than traditional 2D media, enabling users to interact with and evaluate modified material properties in real-world scenarios. We introduced applications of Shitsukan manipulation using PM and OST-AR technologies and discussed the technical issues and solutions involved in achieving these applications. Subsequently, we examined the current challenges in AR-based Shitsukan manipulation and presented recent technical solutions proposed to address them.

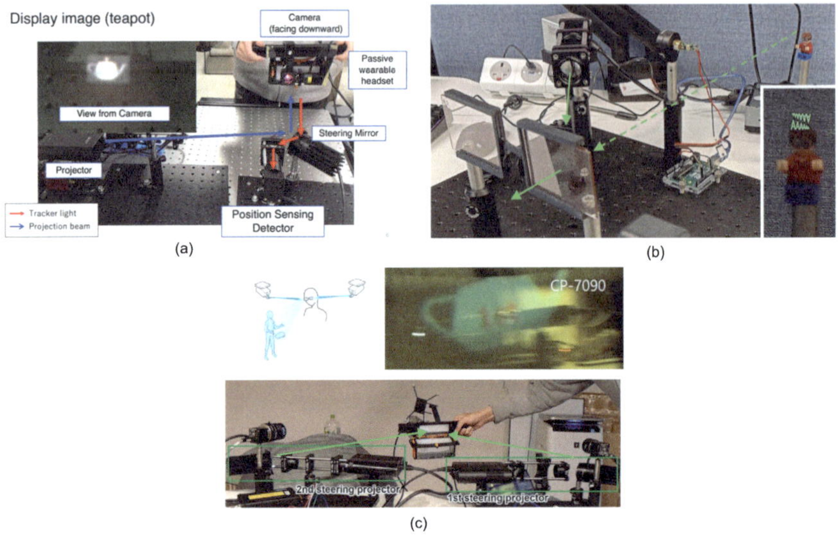

Fig. 11.6 Existing beaming display systems (images compiled from our own materials). **a** A low-latency version [26], **b** a system with thin light-receiving glasses using an HOE lens [2], and **c** a system with dual steering projectors [4]

An interesting future direction is the development of hybrid systems that combine PM and OST-AR technologies, such as beaming displays, as shown in Sect. 11.3.2, to achieve novel Shitsukan manipulation experiences. For instance, Hamasaki et al. [24] proposed integrating OST-AR technologies into PM-based Shitsukan manipulation systems, allowing view-dependent Shitsukan representation (e.g., specular reflection) and enhancing the displayable dynamic range (Fig. 11.7). Additionally, combining near-eye optics, a component of OST-AR display systems, with

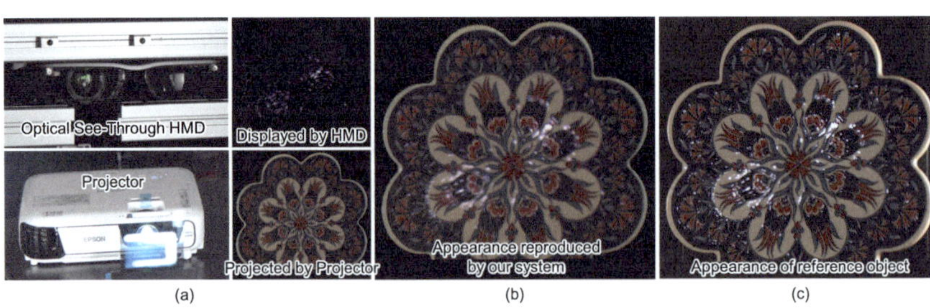

Fig. 11.7 A hybrid Shitsukan manipulation system combining PM and OST-AR technologies. **a** A static projector displays the viewpoint-independent component of the material, and the OST-AR display adds the viewpoint-dependent component of the material. **b** Hybrid spatial augmented reality (HySAR) reproduces a reference object with the viewpoint-dependent component and the viewpoint-independent component over multiple viewers. **c** The reference object has a viewpoint-independent component and a viewpoint-dependent component [24] ©IEEE

PM technologies can provide a novel immersive experience by enabling users to view three-dimensional Shitsukan manipulations without experiencing vergence-accommodation conflicts [36]. This technology can also be used to present spatial blurring effects, such as bokeh, which are difficult to achieve with conventional PM systems [59]. We believe that many unexplored possibilities remain in the hybrid approach, and we look forward to further advancements in this field.

Acknowledgements This work was supported by JSPS KAKENHI Grant Numbers JP20H05958 and JP23H03430 (JP23K28120), JST ASPIRE Grant Number JPMJAP2404, and JST FOREST Grant Number JPMJFR206E.

References

1. Maison KOSÉ, Color Machine. https://maison.kose.co.jp/freepage/store/en/concept_store.html. [Online; Accessed 2024-07-29]
2. Akşit, K., Itoh, Y.: Holobeam: paper-thin near-eye displays. In: 2023 IEEE Conference Virtual Reality and 3D User Interfaces (VR). IEEE, pp. 581–591 (2023)
3. Alhakamy, A., Tuceryan, M.: Real-time illumination and visual coherence for photorealistic augmented/mixed reality. ACM Comput. Surv. (CSUR) **53**(3), 1–34 (2020)
4. Aoki, H., Tochimoto, T., Hiroi, Y., Itoh, Y.: Towards co-operative beaming displays: dual steering projectors for extended projection volume and head orientation range. IEEE Trans. Vis. Comput. Graph. **30**(5), 2309–18 (2024)
5. Asayama, H., Iwai, D., Sato, K.: Fabricating diminishable visual markers for geometric registration in projection mapping. IEEE Trans. Vis. Comput. Graph. **24**(2), 1091–1102 (2018)
6. Bellalouna, F.: Use case of the application of the optical-see-through augmented reality technology in the engineering context. Proced. CIRP **106**, 3–8 (2022)
7. Bermano, A., Brüschweiler, P., Grundhöfer, A., Iwai, D., Bickel, B., Gross, M.: Augmenting physical avatars using projector-based illumination. ACM Trans. Graph. **32**(6), 1 (2013)
8. Bermano, A.H., Billeter, M., Iwai, D., Grundhöfer, A.: Makeup lamps: live augmentation of human faces via projection. Comput. Graph. Forum **36**(2), 311–323 (2017)
9. Bimber, O., Iwai, D., Wetzstein, G., Grundhöfer, A.: The visual computing of projector-camera systems. Comput. Graph. Forum **27**, 2219–2245 (2008)
10. Bimber, O., Raskar, R.: Spatial Augmented Reality: Merging Real and Virtual Worlds. CRC Press (2005)
11. Birlo, M., Edwards, P.E., Clarkson, M., Stoyanov, D.: Utility of optical see-through head mounted displays in augmented reality-assisted surgery: a systematic review. Med. Image Anal. **77**, 102361 (2022)
12. Bonneel, N., Kovacs, B., Paris, S., Bala, K.: Intrinsic decompositions for image editing. Comput. Graph. Forum **36**(2), 593–609 (2017)
13. Boyadzhiev, I., Bala, K., Paris, S., Adelson, E.: Band-sifting decomposition for image-based material editing. ACM Trans. Graph. **34**(5), 1–6 (2015)
14. Careaga, C., Aksoy, Y.: Intrinsic image decomposition via ordinal shading. ACM Trans. Graph. **43**(1), 1–24 (2023)
15. Cascini, G., O'Hare, J., Dekoninck, E., Becattini, N., Boujut, J.-F., Ben Guefrache, F., Carli, I., Caruso, G., Giunta, L., Morosi, F.: Exploring the use of AR technology for co-creative product and packaging design. Comput. Ind. **123**, 103308 (2020)
16. Dunn, D., Tippets, C., Torell, K., Kellnhofer, P., Aksit, K., Didyk, P., Myszkowski, K., Luebke, D., Fuchs, H.: Wide field of view varifocal near-eye display using see-through deformable membrane mirrors. IEEE TVCG (2017)

17. Erel, Y., Iwai, D., Bermano, A.H.: Neural projection mapping using reflectance fields. IEEE Trans. Vis. Comput. Graph. **29**(11), 4339–4349 (2023)
18. Fleming, R.W.: Visual perception of materials and their properties. Vis. Res. **94**, 62–75 (2014)
19. Fu, Y., Lam, A., Sato, I., Okabe, T., Sato, Y.: Separating reflective and fluorescent components using high frequency illumination in the spectral domain. In: 2013 IEEE International Conference on Computer Vision, pp. 457–464 (2013)
20. Garces, E., Rodriguez-Pardo, C., Casas, D., Lopez-Moreno, J.: A survey on intrinsic images: delving deep into lambert and beyond. Int. J. Comput. Vis. **130**(3), 836–868 (2022)
21. Grosse, R., Johnson, M.K., Adelson, E.H., Freeman, W.T.: Ground truth dataset and baseline evaluations for intrinsic image algorithms. In: 2009 IEEE 12th International Conference on Computer Vision, pp. 2335–2342 (2009)
22. Grundhöfer, A., Iwai, D.: Recent advances in projection mapping algorithms, hardware and applications. Comput. Graph. Forum. **37**(2), 653–675 (2018)
23. Grundhöfer, A., Iwai, D.: Robust, error-tolerant photometric projector compensation. IEEE Trans. Image Process. **24**(12), 5086–5099 (2015)
24. Hamasaki, T., Itoh, Y., Hiroi, Y., Iwai, D., Sugimoto, M.: Hysar: hybrid material rendering by an optical see-through head-mounted display with spatial augmented reality projection. IEEE Trans. Vis. Comput. Graph. **24**(4), 1457–1466 (2018)
25. Hiratani, K., Iwai, D., Kageyama, Y., Punpongsanon, P., Hiraki, T., Sato, K.: Shadowless projection mapping using retrotransmissive optics. IEEE Trans. Vis. Comput. Graph. **29**(5), 2280–2290 (2023)
26. Hiroi, Y., Watanabe, A., Mikawa, Y., Itoh, Y.: Low-latency beaming display: implementation of wearable, 133us motion-to-photon latency near-eye display. IEEE Trans. Vis. Comput. Graph. (2023)
27. Huang, B., Ling, H.: End-to-end projector photometric compensation. In: 2019 IEEE/CVF Conference on Computer Vision and Pattern Recognition (CVPR), pp. 6803–6812 (2019)
28. Itoh, Y., Kaminokado, T., Akşit, K.: Beaming displays. IEEE TVCG **27**(5), 2659–2668 (2021)
29. Itoh, Y., Klinker, G.: Interaction-free calibration for optical see-through head-mounted displays based on 3d eye localization. In: 2014 IEEE Symposium on 3d User Interfaces (3dui) (2014)
30. Itoh, Y., Langlotz, T., Sutton, J., Plopski, A.: Towards indistinguishable augmented reality: a survey on optical see-through head-mounted displays. ACM Comput. Surv. (CSUR) **54**(6), 1–36 (2021)
31. Iwai, D.: Projection mapping technologies: a review of current trends and future directions. Proceed. Jpn. Acad. Series B **100**(3), 234–251 (2024)
32. Kageyama, Y., Isogawa, M., Iwai, D., Sato, K.: Prodebnet: projector deblurring using a convolutional neural network. Opt. Express **28**(14), 20391–20403 (2020)
33. Kageyama, Y., Iwai, D., Sato, K.: Online projector deblurring using a convolutional neural network. IEEE Trans. Vis. Comput. Graph. **28**(5), 2223–2233 (2022)
34. Kageyama, Y., Iwai, D., Sato, K.: Efficient distortion-free neural projector deblurring in dynamic projection mapping. In: IEEE Transactions on Visualization and Computer Graphics, pp. 1–14 (2024)
35. Kawabe, T., Fukiage, T., Sawayama, M., Nishida, S.: Deformation lamps: a projection technique to make static objects perceptually dynamic. ACM Trans. Appl. Percept. **13**(2), 1–7 (2016)
36. Kimura, S., Iwai, D., Punpongsanon, P., Sato, K.: Multifocal stereoscopic projection mapping. IEEE Trans. Vis. Comput. Graph. **27**(11), 4256–4266 (2021)
37. Kiyokawa, K., Kurata, Y., Ohno, H.: An optical see-through display for mutual occlusion of real and virtual environments. In: IEEE and ACM ISAR (2000)
38. Koulieris, G.A., Akşit, K., Stengel, M., Mantiuk, R.K., Mania, K., Richardt, C.: Near-eye display and tracking technologies for virtual and augmented reality. Comput. Graph. Forum **38**, 493–519 (2019)
39. Langlotz, T., Cook, M., Regenbrecht, H.: Real-time radiometric compensation for optical see-through head-mounted displays. IEEE TVCG **22**(11), 2385–2394 (2016)
40. Langlotz, T., Sutton, J., Zollmann, S., Itoh, Y., Regenbrecht, H.: Chromaglasses: computational glasses for compensating colour blindness. In: Proceedings of the 2018 CHI Conference on Human Factors in Computing Systems, pp 1–12 (2018)

41. Lincoln, P., Blate, A., Singh, M., Whitted, T., State, A., Lastra, A., Fuchs, H.: From motion to photons in 80 microseconds: towards minimal latency for virtual and augmented reality. IEEE TVCG **22**(4), 1367–1376 (2016)
42. Liu, C., Torralba, A., Freeman, W.T., Durand, F., Adelson, E.H.: Motion magnification. ACM Trans. Graph. **24**(3), 519–526 (2005)
43. Menk, C., Jundt, E., Koch, R.: Visualisation techniques for using spatial augmented reality in the design process of a car. Comput. Graph. Forum **30**(8), 2354–2366 (2011)
44. Miyashita, L., Watanabe, Y., Ishikawa, M.: Midas projection: markerless and modelless dynamic projection mapping for material representation. ACM Trans. Graph. **37**(6), 1–2 (2018)
45. Morimoto, T., Numata, A., Fukuda, K., Uchikawa, K.: Luminosity thresholds of colored surfaces are determined by their upper-limit luminances empirically internalized in the visual system. J. Vis. **21**(13), 3 (2021)
46. Nagase, M., Iwai, D., Sato, K.: Dynamic defocus and occlusion compensation of projected imagery by model-based optimal projector selection in multi-projection environment. Virtual Reality **15**(2), 119–132 (2011)
47. Narita, G., Watanabe, Y., Ishikawa, M.: Dynamic projection mapping onto deforming non-rigid surface using deformable dot cluster marker. IEEE Trans. Vis. Comput. Graph. **23**(3), 1235–1248 (2017)
48. Nayar, S.K., Krishnan, G., Grossberg, M.D., Raskar, R.: Fast separation of direct and global components of a scene using high frequency illumination. ACM Trans. Graph. **25**(3), 935–944 (2006)
49. Nishizawa, M., Jiang, W., Okajima, K.: Projective-AR system for customizing the appearance and taste of food. In: Proceedings of the 2016 Workshop on Multimodal Virtual and Augmented Reality, MVAR '16. New York, NY, USA. Association for Computing Machinery (2016)
50. Nomoto, T., Li, W., Peng, H.-L., Watanabe, Y.: Dynamic multi-projection mapping based on parallel intensity control. IEEE Trans. Vis. Comput. Graph. **28**(5), 2125–2134 (2022)
51. Punpongsanon, P., Iwai, D., Sato, K.: Softar: visually manipulating haptic softness perception in spatial augmented reality. IEEE Trans. Vis. Comput. Graph. **21**(11), 1279–1288 (2015)
52. Punpongsanon, P., Iwai, D., Sato, K.: Flexeen: visually manipulating perceived fabric bending stiffness in spatial augmented reality. IEEE Trans. Vis. Comput. Graph. **26**(2), 1433–1439 (2020)
53. Radu, I.: Augmented reality in education: a meta-review and cross-media analysis. Pers. Ubiquit. Comput. **18**, 1533–1543 (2014)
54. Rathinavel, K., Wetzstein, G., Fuchs, H.: Varifocal occlusion-capable optical see-through augmented reality display based on focus-tunable optics. IEEE TVCG **25**(11), 3125–3134 (2019)
55. Suzuki, Y., Narumi, T., Tanikawa, T., Hirose, M.: Taste in motion: the effect of projection mapping of a boiling effect on food expectation, food perception, and purchasing behavior. Front. Comput. Sci. **3**, 662824 (2021)
56. Takeuchi, M., Kusuyama, H., Iwai, D., Sato, K.: Projection mapping under environmental lighting by replacing room lights with heterogeneous projectors. IEEE Trans. Vis. Comput. Graph. **30**(5), 2151–2161 (2024)
57. Takezawa, T., Iwai, D., Sato, K., Hara, T., Takeda, Y., Murase, K.: Material surface reproduction and perceptual deformation with projection mapping for car interior design. In: 2019 IEEE Conference on Virtual Reality and 3D User Interfaces (VR), pp. 251–258 (2019)
58. Tone, D., Iwai, D., Hiura, S., Sato, K.: Fibar: embedding optical fibers in 3d printed objects for active markers in dynamic projection mapping. IEEE Trans. Vis. Comput. Graph. **26**(5), 2030–2040 (2020)
59. Ueda, T., Iwai, D., Hiraki, T., Sato, K.: Illuminated focus: vision augmentation using spatial defocusing via focal sweep eyeglasses and high-speed projector. IEEE Trans. Vis. Comput. Graph. **26**(5), 2051–2061 (2020)
60. Zhong, F., Jindal, A., Yöntem, Ö., Hanji, P., Watt, S., Mantiuk, R.: Reproducing reality with a high-dynamic-range multi-focal stereo display. ACM Trans. Graph. **40**(6), 241 (2021)

Chapter 12
Dynamic Projection of Shitsukan

Yoshihiro Watanabe

Abstract Dynamic projection mapping (DPM) is a technology that overlays virtual imagery onto moving physical objects in real time. By creating dynamic virtual appearances that adapt to the ever-changing surroundings, DPM enables the direct manipulation of Shitsukan, namely the perceived material properties of objects. This chapter reviews the current state, capabilities, and potential of this dynamic projection of Shitsukan; examines the technological advances in sensing, tracking, and projection systems that underlie it; and explores its wide range of applications across diverse industries. Finally, the chapter discusses future trends and challenges, offering insights to guide ongoing research and development in this rapidly evolving field.

Keywords Augmented reality · Projection mapping · Projector · Image sensing · Computer graphics

12.1 Introduction

Imagine that a red object lies before us. Is it truly a red object illuminated by white light or is it a white object illuminated by red light?

Because our eyes perceive the world through reflected light, distinguishing between these two possibilities can be difficult. Determining object properties and ambient lighting conditions solely from reflected light is a complex task. The reality we perceive is subjective and can be easily manipulated.

Projection mapping exploits these gaps in perception by overlaying images onto physical objects, creating visual experiences that can be altered at will, transforming the appearance of real-world environments. Also known as spatial augmented reality (SAR) [6], projection mapping offers device-free interaction, allowing multiple users to experience the same projection simultaneously, while physical objects remain tangible and interactive. Such merging of the virtual and real worlds, powered by

---

Y. Watanabe (✉)
Institute of Science Tokyo, Yokohama, Kanagawa, Japan
e-mail: watanabe@ict.eng.isct.ac.jp

S. Nishida and K. Nishino (eds.), *Shitsukan—Understanding and Manipulating Material and Quality Perception*, https://doi.org/10.1007/978-981-95-4762-3_12

technology embedded within the environment, enables users to engage in augmented experiences without losing their natural sensory and motor functions. Projection mapping has therefore been applied in stage performances, amusement parks, digital signage, fashion, design, and work assistance [7, 17].

However, unlike conventional display technologies that emit light directly into the eyes, projection mapping relies on reflected light from real objects. This makes controlling light and maintaining a sense of realism in the virtual content particularly challenging. As discussed in the *Augmenting Reality with Shitsukan* chapter, addressing these technical hurdles is the focus of ongoing research aimed at enhancing the realism and immersion of projection-mapping experiences, which ultimately enables the manipulation of Shitsukan—the perceived material properties that shape our sense of reality.

Building on that discussion, this chapter turns to the unique case of dynamic projection mapping (DPM), which extends projection mapping to dynamically changing environments. Ideally, DPM synchronizes the movement of real objects with that of their dynamically changing virtual projections to create a sense of absolute reality. In practice, the complexity of real-time motion tracking and projection makes achieving such perfect alignment technically unfeasible. Rather than striving for flawless synchronization, DPM researchers concentrate on perceptual consistency, ensuring that visual discrepancies are undetectable. In dynamic settings, this directly translates into enhanced capabilities for Shitsukan manipulation. Such Shitsukan manipulation through DPM is expected to serve as a key to further broadening the wide range of projection-mapping applications mentioned earlier.

This chapter reviews the latest developments, explains how the challenges posed by DPM's high operational speed—particularly those related to preventing misalignment of projected images on moving targets—are being overcome, and surveys the surprisingly broad range of potential applications opened up by the dynamic projection of Shitsukan.

12.2 Foundations of Dynamic Projection Mapping

To realize immersive Shitsukan manipulation in dynamic projection mapping (DPM), it is essential to understand how projected imagery is perceived. In addition, conventional projectors were originally developed for static surfaces, but DPM requires new projection capabilities—in particular, ultra-high-speed performance—to cope with dynamically changing objects. Moreover, sensing technologies that can instantly capture the state of moving targets are indispensable. This section provides an overview of the key technological foundations of DPM that addresses these challenges.

12.2.1 Perception in Dynamic Projection Mapping

In DPM, it is essential to ensure that the real object and the projected image remain visually synchronized and consistent, with no perceived latency. The total time required for processes such as camera capture, image processing, object recognition, appropriate imagery generation, and final output projection must therefore be minimized.

Latency is a key concern not only for DPM but for all interactive technologies. As Allison et al. have pointed out, even minor latency can undermine the stability of augmented reality systems [1]. For example, researchers have examined the relationship between latency thresholds and head movements in mitigating the generation of visual artifacts by head-mounted displays (HMDs) [27, 28].

In one study of latency perception, the participants dragged their finger across a surface while a high-speed projector displayed a white square beneath it [45]. The study found that participants did not perceive any delay when the average latency between the finger's movement and the projected square was less than 6.04 ms.

However, this study does not directly address the latency requirements of DPM, because the projection was performed without aligning to the 3D geometry of the target surface, unlike in projection-mapping scenarios. Additionally, while this study focused on latency perception in relation to the user's own body movement, DPM scenarios can involve projections onto both the user's body and externally moving objects. Therefore, although the 6.04-ms latency threshold has often been used as a guideline in DPM research, it may not always be applicable.

Fukuda et al. investigated the perceptual threshold of latency in DPM using a moving flat board as the projection target [14]. The movement was controlled using a positioning stage, and the DPM system experienced a minimum latency of 2 ms due to processing limitations. However, the study did not establish the precise latency threshold at which misalignment became noticeable, since there was no perfect temporally aligned reference for comparison.

We further explored latency perception in dynamic facial projection mapping (DFPM) [51]. DFPM aims to alter the perceived appearance of facial features by overlaying images based on facial position and shape. Even slight delays between motion and projection can result in visible misalignment, as humans are highly sensitive to facial distortions; this significantly reduces the immersiveness of DFPM. The study measured the latency threshold at which a just-noticeable difference (JND) was detected in DFPM under various facial motion conditions. In this work, we designed a simulated DFPM system to precisely control latency, with a temporal resolution of 0.1 ms. We also used a high-speed projector capable of 1,000 fps, which reduced motion blur and improved temporal accuracy in displaying misalignments. The technical details of this specialized projector are discussed in the next section.

Our experiments provided several key insights. As facial motion speed increased, the minimum perceptible misalignment also increased, suggesting that faster movements may make smaller misalignments less noticeable. Additionally, we found that the relationship between facial motion speed and latency perception was non-linear, with the required latency decreasing and then increasing as motion speed rose. We also demonstrated that latency requirements varied depending on the type of facial motion, underscoring the importance of considering specific motion characteristics when designing DFPM systems. Most notably, an average latency of 3.87 ms or lower was found necessary to avoid perceptible misalignment in DFPM, offering a clear target for system designers.

12.2.2 High-Speed Projectors

Recent digital projectors can be categorized based on their liquid-crystal, laser-scanning, and digital-light-processing (DLP) configurations. DLP-type projectors, which use arrays of small mirrors known as digital micromirror devices (DMD) to modulate pixel brightness, excel in achieving high frame rates. In these projectors, each mirror tilts to either emit or block light, modulating pixel brightness through high-speed mirror flipping. The frame rate is governed by the speed of the DMD control system, which determines how fast each mirror can flip.

If the minimum time for DMD control is denoted by $\widetilde{T}$, the maximum frame rate for 8-bit projection is $\frac{1}{255\widetilde{T}}$. This is because an 8-bit grayscale value is generated by combining the display times of all eight binary bit planes. The most significant bit (MSB) must be displayed for $128\widetilde{T}$, the next bit for $64\widetilde{T}$, and so forth, down to the least significant bit (LSB) for $\widetilde{T}$. The total time required to display a full 8-bit frame is therefore $(2^8 - 1)\widetilde{T} = 255\widetilde{T}$, which sets the upper bound on the achievable frame rate. For example, when $\widetilde{T} = 44\,\mu s$, the upper bound of the frame rate for 8-bit projection is approximately 90 fps. In the case of a single-chip DMD projector producing full-color images, this frame rate is effectively reduced to one-third, since the red, green, and blue (RGB) channels must be projected sequentially. Such frame rates are acceptable for conventional DLP projectors, which are primarily designed for projection onto static screens. However, they are insufficient for DPM, as described in the previous section.

Three-chip DLP configurations, using three DMDs for RGB color channels, are commonly employed in projection systems. Although this setup is not specifically designed for DPM, it has the potential to improve the frame rate for color projection, rendering it a viable option for achieving the higher speeds. However, a significant drawback is that using three DMDs increases the size and complexity of the projector, potentially limiting its practicality in applications where compactness is essential. Furthermore, the frame rate improvement is limited to a factor of three, as each DMD handles only one color channel; consequently, further speed enhancements cannot be achieved solely through this configuration.

Conversely, specialized high-frame-rate projectors have been developed to correct misalignment in DPM [29–31] and for use in optical-see-through HMD, which enable users to view digital content overlaid directly on the real world through transparent lenses [37]. These projectors warp each bit-level image in DLP projection to ensure correct overlap on the target surface, adjusting for misalignment. Although this technique offers notable advantages, it is limited to simple warping methods such as homography, which adjusts the image to align with flat surfaces.

The most promising candidate for general-purpose DPM addresses the limitations of DMD control time in single-chip configurations by introducing synchronized high-speed light-source blinking control. By using a high-speed modulated light source, such as an LED, the minimum time for the LSB in the image can be significantly reduced compared to the time taken by the DMD itself. The principle is that even while the DMD remains fixed at its minimum switching interval $\widetilde{T}$, the illumination can be subdivided into shorter pulses by blinking the light source. For example, if the display time of the MSB is set to $\widetilde{T}$, the display time of the MSB–1 must be half of that, $\frac{\widetilde{T}}{2}$. This means that by keeping the DMD fixed for $\widetilde{T}$ and turning on the light source for only half of that duration, the MSB–1 can be represented. Subsequent lower-order bits can be controlled in the same manner, by subdividing the illumination within the DMD's minimum control time. With this method, the total time required to display all eight bit planes is reduced to $8\widetilde{T}$. Consequently, the maximum frame rate for 8-bit projection is increased to $\frac{1}{8\widetilde{T}}$, approximately 32 times higher than that of conventional DLP projection.

Although this foundational concept of high-frame-rate projection was introduced in a 2008 paper [7], we first successfully developed a high-frame-rate projector in 2015 [70]. Our technology enabled 1,000-fps 8-bit projection at a resolution of 1024 × 768, with a delay of only 3 ms from image generation to projection. In 2016, similar technology was applied to develop a high-bit-depth projector [9].

In 2019, building on this light-source blinking approach, we further developed a 947-fps 24-bit projector with a resolution of 1024 × 768 and a 2 ms delay [68]. This corresponds to an achievable frame rate of 2,841 fps for 8-bit image projection, where $\widetilde{T}$ in the utilized DMD was 44 μs. Our projector also addressed the demand for high brightness, compensating for brightness loss from high-speed light-source blinking by utilizing light sources based on luminescent concentration from LEDs and an optimized optical system. Because of these advancements, our projector maintained a compact design with a single-chip configuration. The developed projector is shown in Fig. 12.1.

Fig. 12.1 A 947-fps 24-bit projector with a resolution of 1024 × 768 and a 2 ms delay, utilizing a single-chip configuration [68]

In 2023, we proposed a novel method for higher-frame-rate projection [43]. This method divides the bit depth of an image among multiple projectors which then simultaneously project in precise synchronization. The bit images are superimposed to generate a high-bit-depth image within a reduced single-frame duration. We also introduced an optimization method to determine the division scheme, DMD control time, and light modulation tailored to the specific number of projectors and target frame rates, all aimed at maximizing brightness. Using two projectors, our system achieved a frame rate of 5,600 fps with 8-bit image projection (Fig. 12.2).

High-speed projectors are not limited to visible color images alone. For applications utilizing sensing technologies, we developed a high-speed projector capable of projecting both visible RGB and infrared (IR) images [38]. Our projector was designed to enhance DPM, including markerless techniques, by performing image sensing using IR pattern projection in parallel with visible image projection. In this system, two mounted DMDs controlled 24-bit RGB and 8-bit IR images simultaneously. The optical engine precisely aligned the images coaxially while maintaining a compact configuration and high-power projection. This projector achieved frame rates of up to approximately 1,000 fps, with image transfer from the computer occurring with a latency of only a few milliseconds.

12.2.3 Expanding the Depth of Field

In DPM, the distance between the projector and the projection target changes as the target moves. This can cause the projected image to lose focus when the target moves outside the projector's depth of field. To address this issue, it is necessary to expand the depth of field beyond that of conventional projectors.

Various methods have been proposed that combine high-speed focus-controllable lenses with projectors to solve this problem. For example, one method achieves distance-independent blur characteristics by installing a high-speed variable focus

Fig. 12.2 High-frame-rate projection with thousands of frames per second based on the multi-bit superimposition method [43]. The developed two-projector configuration is shown on the left. The four images on the right show the 5,600-fps 8-bit projection with a balloon bursting, using the developed system

liquid lens in front of a conventional projector and rapidly sweeping the focus over a specific range during the projection time of a single image [26]. Another method leverages neural networks to generate blur-compensated images without special lenses [32, 33]. However, because these techniques require pre-processing the images with blur compensation, achieving the high speed necessary for DPM is difficult.

As an alternative approach, we integrated a high-speed variable focus lens and a high-speed projector. For instance, we developed a system that detects the distance to the target using a high-speed camera and instantly adjusts the focal length of a variable focus liquid lens to focus there with a latency of 5 ms [67]. Our system maintains focus even when the target moves, effectively expanding the depth of field. We also proposed another method in which the focal length of the variable focus lens oscillates between maximum and minimum values [72]. In this approach, images are projected precisely by a synchronized high-speed projector when the lens reaches specific focal lengths during its rapid oscillation. As the oscillation frequency is too high to be perceived by the human eye, multiple images projected within one oscillation cycle are seen as a single, sharp image. In this way, focused projection is achieved over a wide depth range.

Despite these advancements, the small aperture of high-speed variable focus lenses still poses challenges, including a reduction in the projected image's light intensity and degradation of image quality caused by optical aberrations.

12.2.4 Expanding the Projection Range

Projecting images from a fixed direction with a single projector limits the area over which DPM can be effectively performed. One method of overcoming this limitation expands the projection range by adjusting the projector's direction to follow the moving object. High-speed performance can be achieved by rapidly controlling the projection direction using a lightweight mirror placed in front of the projector [25, 40, 60]. Furthermore, the high-speed projector introduced in the previous section has been integrated into this mirror-based projection direction control method [39]. This approach compensates for an object's translational and rotational motion by controlling the projection direction and projected image, respectively.

However, this method is limited to a single object. Under some circumstances, projections from all directions must be made onto the entire surface of multiple objects. Moreover, addressing the issue of shadows in areas that cannot be projected because of obstructions between the projector and the object can be problematic when expanding the projection range.

A simple and effective solution to this problem is to arrange multiple projectors around the scene and control them simultaneously. However, applying this approach to dynamic scenes is challenging. Conventional methods determine the pixel intensities for all projectors simultaneously using global optimization techniques, which are time-consuming and computationally demanding [4, 57, 58]. Consequently, reducing the latency from motion to projection is difficult.

Fig. 12.3 DPM using multiple projectors based on parallel intensity control [49]. The left image shows the developed system configuration with four networked high-speed projectors. The center image shows that a single projector (the second from the left) cannot remove shadows caused by the occlusion of the bunny. The right image shows that our multi-projector system adaptively coordinates the projections to remove such occlusion shadows, even in dynamic scenes. (Reprinted with permission from [49]. ©IEEE)

To mitigate this, we propose a pixel-parallel intensity control method that leverages the high-resolution assumption to bypass global optimization, allowing each projector's pixel values to be computed independently in real time with low latency [49]. This assumption is based on the insight that projected pixels from different projectors can be treated independently in overlapping areas if each pixel is sufficiently small relative to the surface structure. Additionally, the pixel-parallel calculation serves as a sound basis for a distributed system configuration in which the number of projectors can be increased to form a highly scalable network. The developed system uses four networked high-speed projectors and demonstrates the removal of shadows caused by occlusion, as shown in Fig. 12.3.

12.2.5 High-Speed Image Sensing

High-speed sensing of the projection scene is a crucial component of DPM technology. Methods using markers printed on the projection target to rapidly detect the object's position and deformation have proven to be effective. We developed one such method employing deformable dot cluster markers, which are designed to capture the deformation of non-rigid curved surfaces with a single camera [44]. These dot-based markers are optimized to prevent misidentification of local positions within the marker pattern, even under complex deformations or movements. Moreover, as the markers consist of simple black-and-white elements, they can easily be printed on objects. As demonstrated in Fig. 12.4, robust and high-speed tracking of non-rigid deformations is possible through the parallel execution of marker detection and continuous tracking based on high-frame-rate imaging. The system has been shown to achieve up to 1,000 fps using CPU-based processing. Even when multiple types of markers are present in the image, each can be recognized individually. We also extended this marker system to enable 3D position and orientation acquisition for 3D objects [69].

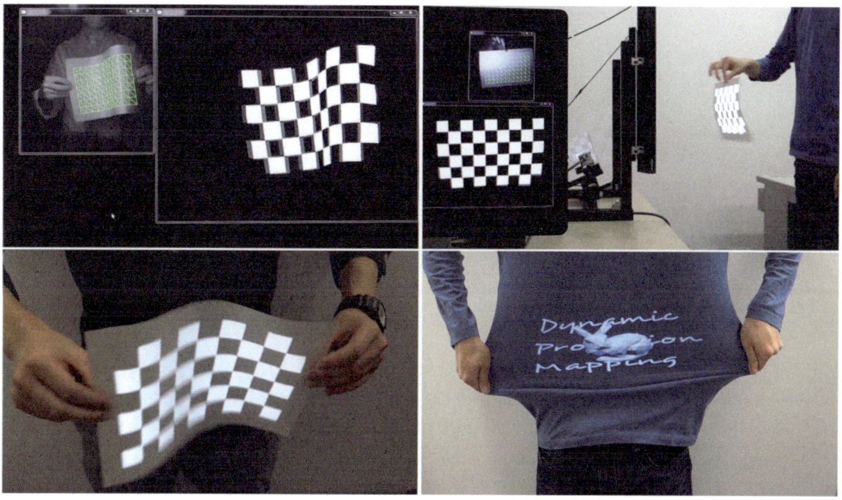

Fig. 12.4 High-speed non-rigid surface tracking using a deformable dot cluster marker [44]. The marker is printed on paper or fabric (e.g., a T-shirt) using infrared ink. Non-rigid surface deformation can be tracked at 1,000 fps

In some methods, the markers are rendered invisible by using ink that absorbs only infrared light [55], or their visibility is reduced through color correction via projection [3]. Additionally, a method has been proposed to enable recognition from a distance by embedding within the object light-emitting markers, identifiable through blinking patterns [64]. Another approach proposes acquiring the object's position and orientation by embedding light sensors within the object as an alternative to markers [36]. This method determines the positional relationship by using light sensors to detect the projected image position from a scanning laser projector.

Markerless methods, which do not require printing markers on the object or embedding any specialized devices within it, have also been proposed. For example, Hashimoto et al. developed a method to rapidly capture the 3D pose of an object by analyzing its contour edges [20]. We also proposed a technique that acquires surface normal images at 500 fps using three wavelengths of near-infrared light for mapping purposes [42]. Moreover, to achieve more flexible mapping, we developed a method to capture depth images of the entire scene and the pose of objects at 500 fps without the use of markers [21]. An example result of this method is shown in Fig. 12.5.

12.3 Realization of Dynamic Projection Mapping

This section presents the realization of dynamic projection mapping (DPM) through representative applications that demonstrate its capability to manipulate Shitsukan in diverse contexts. Specifically, we first explore Shitsukan manipulation on human

Fig. 12.5 High-speed depth image capture and 3D pose tracking using the captured depth images. The left image shows the captured image with the projection of the infrared structured-light pattern. The right image shows the acquired depth image and the estimated 3D pose results at 500 fps [21]

bodies, where projection dynamically alters the perceived appearance of living surfaces. We then turn to Shitsukan manipulation in material reproduction, highlighting how DPM can dynamically reproduce and transform material impressions. Finally, we examine Shitsukan manipulation by altering perceived real object motion, where the movement of physical targets adds an additional dimension of perceptual change.

12.3.1 Shitsukan Manipulation on Human Bodies

Human bodies are considered effective targets for DPM. The face, in particular, is a crucial area that considerably influences how a person is perceived, offering extensive possibilities for transforming Shitsukan through projection mapping. For instance, the 2017 art piece "INORI (prayer)," created in collaboration between artists and our research group, successfully projected dynamic, movement-synchronized images onto the faces of two dancers [24]. These images seamlessly integrated with the dancers' skin, effectively altering their bodily Shitsukan. Although markers were attached to the face in this project, there have been reports of markerless recognition and projection of facial expressions. For example, a system using a 480 fps, 3-chip DLP high-speed projector has achieved markerless facial projection mapping [5]. DPM on faces has also been realized using two projectors to expand the projection area [58]. Moreover, as shown in Fig. 12.6, we achieved dynamic facial projection mapping with markerless tracking using a 1,000-fps high-speed projector [11]. Building on this work, we also developed a system that improved alignment accuracy through high-speed facial tracking and a novel coaxial projector-camera optical design [52].

Applications of facial projection mapping to makeup simulators have also been reported [8, 65, 66]. In our latest development, conducted in collaboration with a cosmetics company, we successfully provided a natural makeup experience by

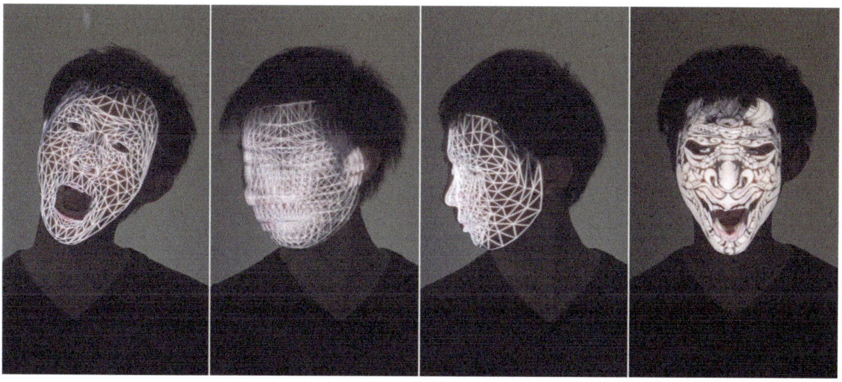

Fig. 12.6 Dynamic facial projection mapping using a 1,000-fps high-speed projector [11]. Facial movements are tracked without markers, and motion-consistent images are projected in real-time

achieving higher speeds than the conventional work, thanks to maintaining motion-to-projection latency within 6 ms [66]. Being able to try many makeup styles quickly can greatly enhance a customer's pre-purchase experience; systems facilitating this have already begun to appear in stores.

The arm is another promising target for DPM, as it is one of the few surfaces on the human body that is commonly displayed bare. Projection-mapping targeting the arm has been applied in diverse fields such as fashion [23], user interfaces [18, 19, 59, 71], prototyping [15, 16], education [22], and medical assistance [46]. However, conventional systems for projecting onto the human arm often overlook skin deformation and suffer from high latency between motion and projection, leading to noticeable misalignments between the arm surface and projected images. These issues degrade user experience and limit the potential for faithful Shitsukan reproduction.

To address these challenges, we developed a high-speed human arm projection-mapping system [53, 54]. Our system combines a state-of-the-art parametric deformable surface model with an efficient regression-based accuracy compensation

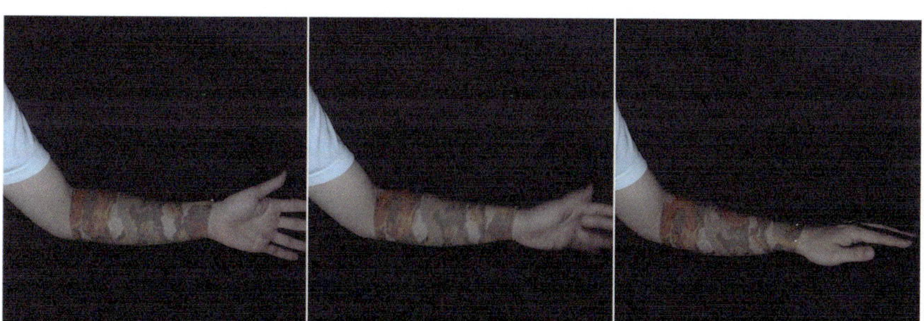

Fig. 12.7 High-speed human arm projection mapping with skin deformation [53, 54]. Skin deformation in response to arm movement is accurately reproduced through projection

method for skin deformation. The high-speed system reduces motion-to-projection latency to within 10 ms, achieving highly realistic mapping that accurately reproduces skin deformation in response to arm movement, as shown in Fig. 12.7.

Moreover, DPM has been applied to surgical assistance [47]. In this application, near-infrared images, invisible to the naked eye, are projected onto the surgical field, tracking the movement of organs in real-time. This enables safer and more accurate surgical guidance.

12.3.2 Shitsukan Manipulation in Material Reproduction

DPM can reproduce the appearance of various materials, and in particular it can dynamically simulate visual effects dependent on an object's movement, including specular reflections, thereby manipulating their Shitsukan. For example, by combining the non-rigid deformation tracking introduced in Sect. 12.2.5 with a high-speed projector, we applied DPM to freely deformable T-shirts [44]. Multiple tracking cameras can also be used to capture 3D deformations of non-rigid objects. We successfully reproduced the perceived material properties for deforming non-rigid objects based on this 3D deformation [10]. As shown in Fig. 12.8, both the reflectance properties and surface unevenness can be manipulated, creating the illusion of physical change through shading techniques that mimic 3D deformation.

While markers were used in these conventional demonstrations [10, 69], markerless material reproduction has also been reported using the sensing methods described in Sect. 12.2.5 [21, 42]. For example, we reported manipulating an object's material appearance based on 3D normal information obtained at high speed without markers [42]. Additionally, as shown in Fig. 12.9, we developed a method for manipulating the material of an entire scene using both depth and normal information obtained at high speed [21].

To further enhance the realism of material reproduction, it is necessary to simulate inter-reflections, transmission, and refraction more accurately. Path tracing [34], a rendering method that simulates the physical behavior of light, fulfills this requirement. However, due to the limited rendering time available at the 500–1000 fps required for DPM, this method generates noisy images.

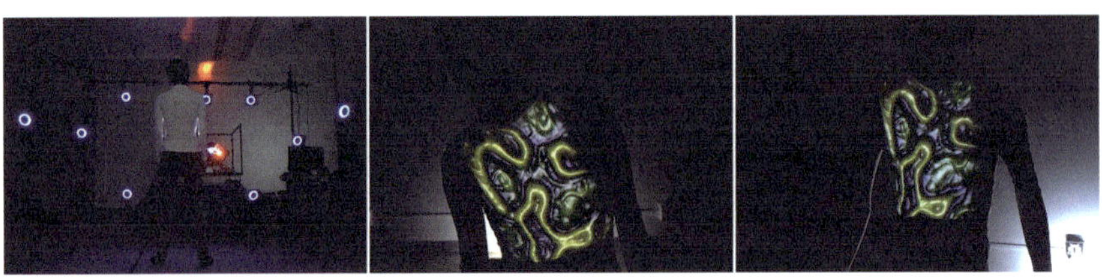

Fig. 12.8 Reproduction of material appearance on a dynamically deforming shirt through DPM. Both the material and surface unevenness can be manipulated [10]

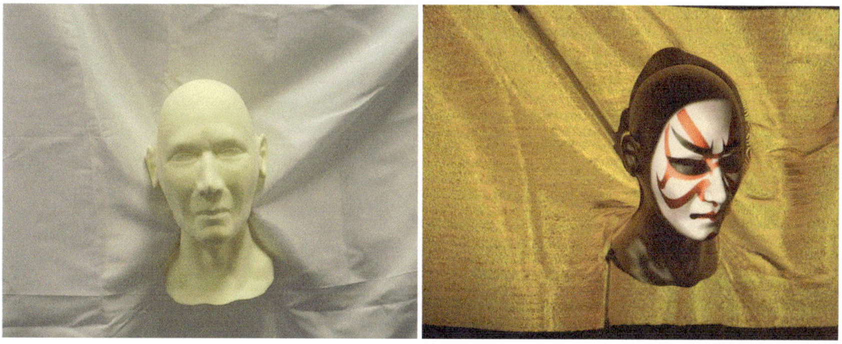

Fig. 12.9 Depth-aware DPM using high-speed RGB and IR projectors [21]. The left image shows the scene before projection. As shown on the right, the captured depth image enables the center object's appearance to be augmented through high-speed 3D markerless tracking. The material appearance of the background is augmented to align with the 3D surface structure

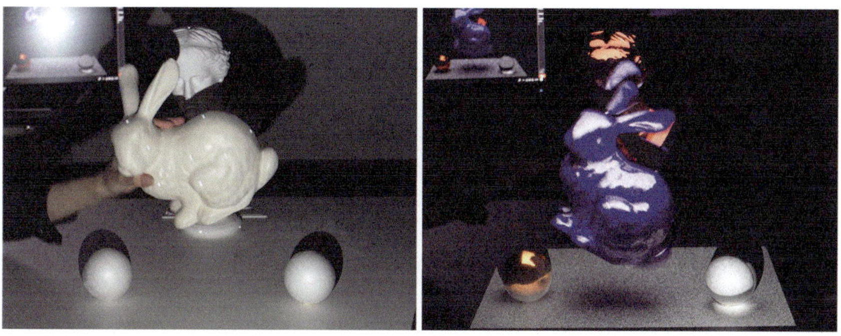

Fig. 12.10 Realistic DPM using real-time ray tracing [48]. The left image shows the scene before projection. The right image demonstrates the reproduction of several elements: the mirror-like reflection of the central rabbit object on the sphere in the lower left, the soft shadow cast by the central rabbit object on the floor, and the caustics created by the transparent glass-like sphere in the lower right

To address this limitation, we proposed a method to project intermediate images that are aligned with the projection target but contain noise as a result of the short rendering times inherent to path tracing [48]. The images are displayed at frame rates exceeding the limits of human visual perception. This approach reduces noise, which is perceived as aligned with the target due to the integrating effect of human visual persistence. Figure 12.10 shows the results. In addition, we achieved material reproduction through DPM using multiple high-speed projectors based on the method described in Sect. 12.2.4 [49]. Figure 12.11 shows the results.

Moreover, in pursuit of more realistic material reproduction, approaches have been proposed that realize material displays by directly employing physical materials, rather than simulating their appearance through projection. In this approach, the ability of DPM to project onto moving objects in real-time is exploited to create a

Fig. 12.11 Material reproduction using two high-speed projectors [49]. The appearances of the two objects are transformed into a colorful diffuse material and a glass material, respectively. (Reprinted with permission from [49]. ©IEEE)

lighting control system for objects moving periodically at high speeds. For example, we developed the material display *Phyxel*, which can flexibly change materials' locations [74], and *ZoeMatrope*, which can dynamically change their reflectance properties in the displayed content [41]. Both of these display systems manipulate material appearance using physical objects, leveraging the persistence of vision.

This concept is well-suited for applications such as a 3D swept-volume display, which achieved naked-eye stereoscopic vision without vergence-accommodation conflict over a wide viewing angle [12, 63]. However, the use of a high-speed projector led to low brightness gradation, resulting in poor texture reproduction quality for the 3D image. To address this, we proposed a method to construct the scanning screen of the 3D swept-volume display using the actual material being reproduced [2]. Our method incorporated principles for adjusting the resolution of 3D images based on the properties of the actual material and used hidden-surface removal techniques that accounted for the observer's viewpoint. As a result, both 3D display performance and texture reproduction were improved simultaneously. Figure 12.12 shows the result of displaying 3D images, e.g., of a panda, using materials such as yarn.

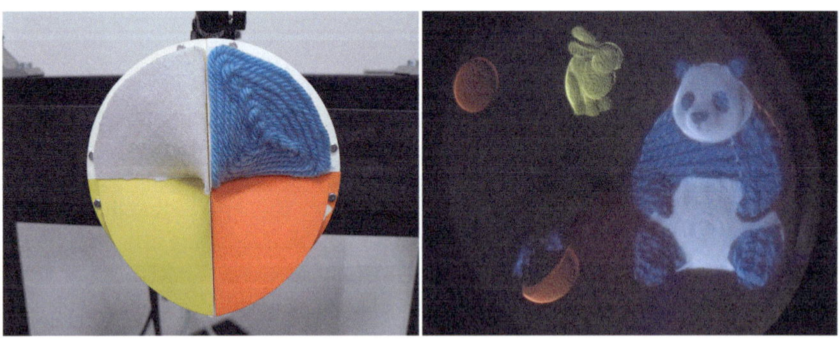

Fig. 12.12 Realistic 3D swept-volume display with hidden-surface removal using physical materials [2]. The left image shows the screen comprising white felt, blue yarn, orange rubber, and yellow nylon. The right image shows the results of the displayed 3D image

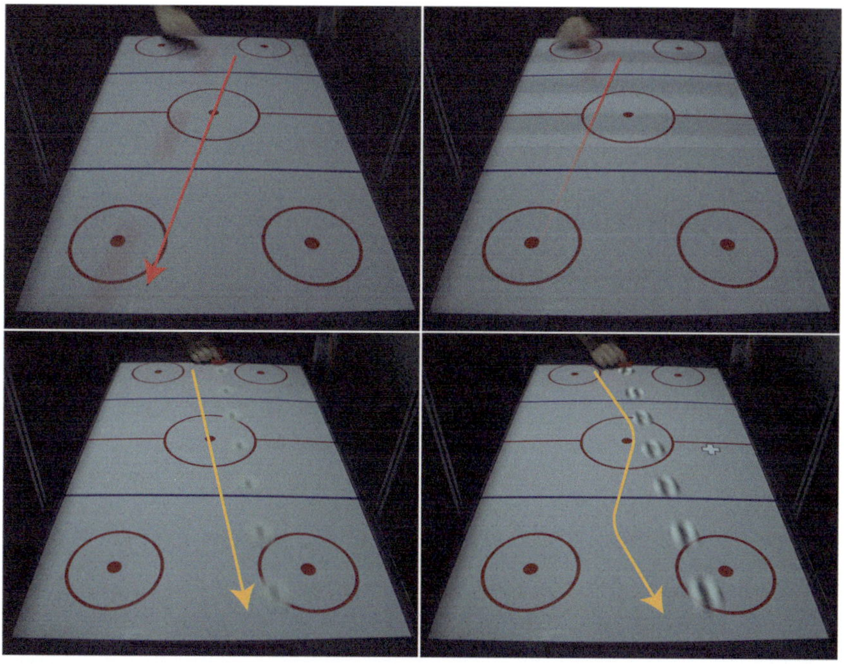

Fig. 12.13 E.S.P.: Extra-sensory puck in air hockey using projection-based illusion [56]. Through a projection-based illusion, the moving puck (top left) appears invisible (top right). In another demonstration, while the puck travels in a straight line (bottom left), its trajectory is perceived as bending into an S-shaped curve (bottom right)

12.3.3 Shitsukan Manipulation by Altering Perceived Object Motion

The movement of objects is a crucial factor in shaping our perception of reality, as dynamic motion strongly modulates Shitsukan—the material impressions we associate with objects. Several techniques have been developed to manipulate object movement through image projection using visual illusions. For instance, there are methods that make stationary objects appear to move [35], and others that create the illusion of boiling in static food samples [61].

Although these methods primarily target stationary objects, they have also been applied to moving ones. For example, the same illusion used to make stationary objects appear to move can be leveraged to make a rigid body appear elastic (giving the impression that it is soft) by projecting a secondary illusory movement synchronized with its actual motion [13].

As another example, in gaming applications, we demonstrated a method for manipulating the movement of an air hockey puck [56]. When illusion-inducing stimulus patterns are projected onto it with no delay, a moving puck can appear to vanish the moment it is hit or to follow a zigzag trajectory that seems to contradict the normal laws of motion, as shown in Fig. 12.13.

12.4 Conclusion

In this chapter, we explored the technical aspects of DPM and its applications to enhancing the sense of natural realism, with a particular focus on Shitsukan. Although DPM demonstrates significant potential, improvements are still required in projection techniques, sensing accuracy, optical systems, graphics rendering, and visual psychology.

For example, many of the cases introduced here operate primarily in unnaturally dark environments where only the projection-mapped target is prominently illuminated. This is because ambient light reduces the contrast of the projected images. However, research is beginning to address these limitations by enabling high-contrast projection mapping in bright environments [62, 73]. As shown in Fig. 12.14, we developed an approach that combines traditional projection mapping with ray-controlled ambient lighting [73]. The ray-controlled ambient light avoids direct illumination of the projection-mapping target while sufficiently illuminating the surrounding areas, thereby preserving contrast on the target. Although currently limited to stationary objects, these innovations are expected to be integrated into DPM systems in the near future. As a result, projection-mapped targets and ordinary objects could seamlessly coexist in well-lit environments, considerably enhancing the overall visual experience.

Additionally, as demonstrated in the surgical assistance work introduced in Sect. 12.3.1, projecting images captured by specialized cameras that detect wavelengths beyond human vision can effectively enhance visual perception. We have

Fig. 12.14 Projection mapping in a bright environment using a mixed light field [73]. The left image shows ray-controlled ambient light avoiding the PM target while adequately illuminating the surrounding areas. The right image illustrates optimal contrast between the mapping target and brightly lit surroundings

also explored this approach in non-destructive inspection by projecting images captured with ultra-broadband sensors operating from infrared to millimeter and shorter (terahertz) wavelengths [50]. However, projection onto dynamic targets has not yet been realized.

Although DPM is still an evolving technology, it shows considerable potential for offering precise and flexible manipulation of reality, particularly in terms of Shitsukan—the perceived material properties of objects—across a wide range of applications.

References

1. Allison, R., Harris, L., Jenkin, M., Jasiobedzka, U., Zacher, J.: Tolerance of temporal delay in virtual environments. In: Proceedings IEEE Virtual Reality 2001, pp. 247–254 (2001). doi:https://doi.org/10.1109/VR.2001.913793
2. Asahina, R., Nomoto, T., Yoshida, T., Watanabe, Y.: Realistic 3d swept-volume display with hidden-surface removal using physical materials. In: 2021 IEEE Virtual Reality and 3D User Interfaces (VR), pp. 113–121 (2021). doi:https://doi.org/10.1109/VR50410.2021.00032
3. Asayama, H., Iwai, D., Sato, K.: Fabricating diminishable visual markers for geometric registration in projection mapping. IEEE Trans. Vis. Comput. Graph. **24**(2), 1091–1102 (2018). https://doi.org/10.1109/TVCG.2017.2657634
4. Bermano, A., Brüschweiler, P., Grundhöfer, A., Iwai, D., Bickel, B., Gross, M.: Augmenting physical avatars using projector-based illumination. ACM Trans. Graph. **32**(6), 1 (2013). https://doi.org/10.1145/2508363.2508416
5. Bermano, A.H., Billeter, M., Iwai, D., Grundhöfer, A.: Makeup lamps: live augmentation of human faces via projection. Comput. Graph. Forum **36**(2), 311–323 (2017)
6. Bimber, O., Raskar, R.: Spatial augmented reality: merging real and virtual worlds. CRC press (2005)
7. Bimber, O., Iwai, D., Wetzstein, G., Grundhöfer, A.: The visual computing of projector-camera systems. Comput. Graph. Forum **27**(8), 2219–2245 (2008). https://doi.org/10.1111/j.1467-8659.2008.01175.x
8. Bokaris, P.A., Askenazi, B., Haddad, M.: Light me up: an augmented-reality projection system. In: SIGGRAPH Asia 2019 XR, SA '19, pp. 21–22 (2019). https://doi.org/10.1145/3355355.3361885
9. Chang, J.H.R., Kumar, B.V.K.V., Sankaranarayanan, A.C.: 216 shades of gray: high bit-depth projection using light intensity control. Opt. Express **24**(24), 27937–27950 (2016). https://doi.org/10.1364/OE.24.027937
10. DynaFlash v2 and post reality. http://www.vision.ict.e.titech.ac.jp/projects/dynaflashv2/
11. Dynamic Facial Projection Mapping—Basic Test. https://www.vision.ict.e.titech.ac.jp/projects/faceDPM/
12. Favalora, G.E., Napoli, J., Hall, D.M., Dorval, R.K., Giovinco, M., Richmond, M.J., Chun, W.S.: 100-million-voxel volumetric display. In: Cockpit Displays IX: Displays for Defense Applications, vol. 4712, pp. 300–312 (2002). https://doi.org/10.1117/12.480930. https://doi.org/10.1117/12.480930
13. Fukamizu, K., Miyashita, L., Ishikawa, M.: Elamorph projection: deformation of 3D shape by dynamic projection mapping. In: 2020 IEEE International Symposium on Mixed and Augmented Reality (ISMAR), pp. 164–173 (2020). https://doi.org/10.1109/ISMAR50242.2020.00038
14. Fukuda, S., Kagami, S., Hashimoto, K.: Evaluation of perceptual difference in dynamic projection mapping with and without movement of the target surface. J. Robot. Mechatron. **34**(5), 1141–1151 (2022)

15. Gannon, M., Grossman, T., Fitzmaurice, G.: Exoskin: on-body fabrication. In: Proceedings of the 2016 CHI Conference on Human Factors in Computing Systems, CHI '16, pp. 5996–6007 (2016). https://doi.org/10.1145/2858036.2858576
16. Gannon, M., Grossman, T., Fitzmaurice, G.: Tactum: a skin-centric approach to digital design and fabrication. In: Proceedings of the 33rd Annual ACM Conference on Human Factors in Computing Systems, CHI '15, pp. 1779–1788 (2015). https://doi.org/10.1145/2702123.2702581
17. Grundhöfer, A., Iwai, D.: Recent advances in projection mapping algorithms, hardware and applications. Comput. Graph. Forum **37**(2), 653–675 (2018). https://doi.org/10.1111/cgf.13387
18. Harrison, C., Benko, H., Wilson, A.D.: Omnitouch: wearable multitouch interaction everywhere. In: Proceedings of the 24th Annual ACM Symposium on User Interface Software and Technology, UIST '11, pp. 441–450 (2011). https://doi.org/10.1145/2047196.2047255
19. Harrison, C., Tan, D., Morris, D.: Skinput: appropriating the body as an input surface. In: Proceedings of the SIGCHI Conference on Human Factors in Computing Systems, CHI '10, pp. 453–462 (2010). https://doi.org/10.1145/1753326.1753394
20. Hashimoto, N., Koizumi, R., Kobayashi, D.: Dynamic projection mapping with a single IR camera. Int. J. Comput. Games Technol. **2017**, 2 (2017). https://doi.org/10.1155/2017/4936285
21. Hisaichi, S., Sumino, K., Ueda, K., Kasebe, H., Yamashita, T., Yuasa, T., Lippmann, U., Aswendt, P., Höfling, R., Watanabe, Y.: Depth-aware dynamic projection mapping using high-speed RGB and IR projectors. In: SIGGRAPH Asia 2021 Emerging Technologies, SA '21 (2021). doi:https://doi.org/10.1145/3476122.3484843
22. Hoang, T., Reinoso, M., Joukhadar, Z., Vetere, F., Kelly, D.: Augmented studio: projection mapping on moving body for physiotherapy education. In: Proceedings of the 2017 CHI Conference on Human Factors in Computing Systems, CHI '17, pp. 1419–1430 (2017). https://doi.org/10.1145/3025453.3025860
23. Ink Mapping: Video Mapping Projection on Tattoos, by Oskar & Gaspar. https://vimeo.com/143296099
24. INORI (Prayer). https://vimeo.com/210599507
25. Iuchi, M., Hirohashi, Y., Oku, H.: Proposal for an aerial display using dynamic projection mapping on a distant flying screen. In: 2023 IEEE Conference Virtual Reality and 3D User Interfaces (VR), pp. 603–608 (2023). https://doi.org/10.1109/VR55154.2023.00075
26. Iwai, D., Mihara, S., Sato, K.: Extended depth-of-field projector by fast focal sweep projection. IEEE Trans. Vis. Comput. Graph. **21**(4), 462–470 (2015). https://doi.org/10.1109/TVCG.2015.2391861
27. Jerald, J., Whitton, M.: Relating scene-motion thresholds to latency thresholds for head-mounted displays. In: IEEE Virtual Reality Conference, pp. 211–218 (2009)
28. Jerald, J.J.: Scene-motion-and latency-perception thresholds for head-mounted displays. Ph.D. thesis, The University of North Carolina at Chapel Hill (2009)
29. Kagami, S., Hashimoto, K.: A full-color single-chip-DLP projector with an embedded 2400-fps homography warping engine. In: ACM SIGGRAPH 2018 Emerging Technologies (2018). https://doi.org/10.1145/3214907.3214927
30. Kagami, S., Hashimoto, K.: Sticky projection mapping: 450-fps tracking projection onto a moving planar surface. In: SIGGRAPH Asia 2015 Emerging Technologies (2015). https://doi.org/10.1145/2818466.2818485
31. Kagami, S., Hashimoto, K.: Animated stickies: fast video projection mapping onto a markerless plane through a direct closed-loop alignment. IEEE Trans. Vis. Comput. Graph. **25**(11), 3094–3104 (2019). https://doi.org/10.1109/TVCG.2019.2932248
32. Kageyama, Y., Iwai, D., Sato, K.: Efficient distortion-free neural projector deblurring in dynamic projection mapping. In: IEEE Transactions on Visualization and Computer Graphics, pp. 1–14 (2024). https://doi.org/10.1109/TVCG.2024.3354957
33. Kageyama, Y., Iwai, D., Sato, K.: Online projector deblurring using a convolutional neural network. IEEE Trans. Vis. Comput. Graph. **28**(5), 2223–2233 (2022). https://doi.org/10.1109/TVCG.2022.3150465

34. Kajiya, J.T.: The rendering equation. SIGGRAPH. Comput. Graph. **20**(4), 143–150 (1986). https://doi.org/10.1145/15886.15902
35. Kawabe, T., Fukiage, T., Sawayama, M., Nishida, S.: Deformation lamps: a projection technique to make static objects perceptually dynamic. ACM Trans. Appl. Percept. **13**(2), 1 (2016). https://doi.org/10.1145/2874358
36. Kitajima, Y., Iwai, D., Sato, K.: Simultaneous projection and positioning of laser projector pixels. IEEE Trans. Vis. Comput. Graph. **23**(11), 2419–2429 (2017). https://doi.org/10.1109/TVCG.2017.2734478
37. Lincoln, P., Blate, A., Singh, M., Whitted, T., State, A., Lastra, A., Fuchs, H.: From motion to photons in 80 microseconds: towards minimal latency for virtual and augmented reality. IEEE Trans. Vis. Comput. Graph. **22**(4), 1367–1376 (2016). https://doi.org/10.1109/TVCG.2016.2518038
38. Lippmann, U., Aswendt, P., Höfling, R., Sumino, K., Ueda, K., Ono, Y., Kasebe, H., Yamashita, T., Yuasa, T., Watanabe, Y.: High-speed RGB+IR projector based on coaxial optical design with two digital mirror devices. In: 28th International Display Workshops, pp. 636–639 (2021)
39. Mikawa, Y., Sueishi, T., Watanabe, Y., Ishikawa, M.: Variolight: hybrid dynamic projection mapping using high-speed projector and optical axis controller. In: SIGGRAPH Asia 2018 Emerging Technologies, SA '18 (2018). https://doi.org/10.1145/3275476.3275481
40. Mikawa, Y., Sueishi, T., Watanabe, Y., Ishikawa, M.: Dynamic projection mapping for robust sphere posture tracking using uniform/biased circumferential markers. IEEE Trans. Vis. Comput. Graph. **28**(12), 4016–4031 (2022). https://doi.org/10.1109/TVCG.2021.3111085
41. Miyashita, L., Ishihara, K., Watanabe, Y., Ishikawa, M.: Zoematrope: a system for physical material design. ACM Trans. Graph. **35**(4), 1 (2016). https://doi.org/10.1145/2897824.2925925
42. Miyashita, L., Watanabe, Y., Ishikawa, M.: Midas projection: markerless and modelless dynamic projection mapping for material representation. ACM Trans. Graph. **37**(6), 1 (2018). https://doi.org/10.1145/3272127.3275045
43. Nakagawa, S., Watanabe, Y.: High-frame-rate projection with thousands of frames per second based on the multi-bit superimposition method. In: IEEE International Symposium on Mixed and Augmented Reality (2023)
44. Narita, G., Watanabe, Y., Ishikawa, M.: Dynamic projection mapping onto deforming non-rigid surface using deformable dot cluster marker. IEEE Trans. Vis. Comput. Graph. **23**(3), 1235–1248 (2017). https://doi.org/10.1109/TVCG.2016.2592910
45. Ng, A., Lepinski, J., Wigdor, D., Sanders, S., Dietz, P.: Designing for low-latency direct-touch input. In: Proceedings of the 25th Annual ACM Symposium on User Interface Software and Technology, pp. 453–464 (2012)
46. Ni, T., Karlson, A.K., Wigdor, D.: Anatonme: facilitating doctor-patient communication using a projection-based handheld device. In: Proceedings of the SIGCHI Conference on Human Factors in Computing Systems, CHI '11, pp. 3333–3342 (2011). https://doi.org/10.1145/1978942.1979437
47. Nishino, H., Hatano, E., Seo, S., Nitta, T., Saito, T., Nakamura, M., Hattori, K., Takatani, M., Fuji, H., Taura, K., Uemoto, S.: Real-time navigation for liver surgery using projection mapping with indocyanine green fluorescence: development of the novel medical imaging projection system. Ann. Surg. **267**(6), 1134–1140 (2018). https://doi.org/10.1097/sla.0000000000002172
48. Nomoto, T., Koishihara, R., Watanabe, Y.: Realistic dynamic projection mapping using real-time ray tracing. In: ACM SIGGRAPH 2020 Emerging Technologies, SIGGRAPH '20 (2020). https://doi.org/10.1145/3388534.3407297
49. Nomoto, T., Li, W., Peng, H.L., Watanabe, Y.: Dynamic multi-projection mapping based on parallel intensity control. IEEE Trans. Vis. Comput. Graph. **28**(5), 2125–2134 (2022). https://doi.org/10.1109/TVCG.2022.3150488
50. Odawara, R., Yamamoto, M., Kawano, Y., Watanabe, Y., Li, K.: Physical and chemical composition optimization of CNT imagers for augmented reality non-destructive inspections. In: 9th Workshop on Nanocarbon Photonics and Optoelectronics (2024)

51. Peng, H.L., Nishida, S., Watanabe, Y.: Studying user perceptible misalignment in simulated dynamic facial projection mapping. In: 2023 IEEE International Symposium on Mixed and Augmented Reality (ISMAR) (2023)
52. Peng, H.L., Sato, K., Nakagawa, S., Watanabe, Y.: Perceptually-aligned dynamic facial projection mapping by high-speed face-tracking method and lens-shift co-axial setup. IEEE Transactions on Visualization and Computer Graphics pp. 1–15 (2025). https://doi.org/10.1109/TVCG.2025.3527203
53. Peng, H.L., Watanabe, Y.: High-speed human arm projection mapping with skin deformation. In: SIGGRAPH Asia 2020 Emerging Technologies, SA '20 (2020). https://doi.org/10.1145/3415255.3422887
54. Peng, H.L., Watanabe, Y.: High-speed dynamic projection mapping onto human arm with realistic skin deformation. Appl. Sci. **11**(9), 3753 (2021). https://doi.org/10.3390/app11093753
55. Punpongsanon, P., Iwai, D., Sato, K.: Projection-based visualization of tangential deformation of nonrigid surface by deformation estimation using infrared texture. Virtual Reality **19**(1), 45–56 (2015)
56. Sato, K., Terashima, H., Nishida, S., Watanabe, Y.: E.S.P.: extra-sensory puck in air hockey using the projection-based illusion. In: SIGGRAPH Asia 2022 Emerging Technologies, SA '22 (2022). https://doi.org/10.1145/3550471.3558397
57. Siegl, C., Colaianni, M., Thies, L., Thies, J., Zollhöfer, M., Izadi, S., Stamminger, M., Bauer, F.: Real-time pixel luminance optimization for dynamic multi-projection mapping. ACM Trans. Graph. **34**(6), 1–1 (2015). https://doi.org/10.1145/2816795.2818111
58. Siegl, C., Lange, V., Stamminger, M., Bauer, F., Thies, J.: Faceforge: markerless non-rigid face multi-projection mapping. IEEE Trans. Vis. Comput. Graph. **23**(11), 2440–2446 (2017). https://doi.org/10.1109/TVCG.2017.2734428
59. Sodhi, R., Benko, H., Wilson, A.: Lightguide: projected visualizations for hand movement guidance. In: Proceedings of the SIGCHI Conference on Human Factors in Computing Systems, CHI '12, pp. 179–188 (2012). https://doi.org/10.1145/2207676.2207702
60. Sueishi, T., Oku, H., Ishikawa, M.: Lumipen 2: dynamic projection mapping with mirror-based robust high-speed tracking against illumination changes. Presence **25**(4), 299–321 (2016). https://doi.org/10.1162/PRES_a_00275
61. Suzuki, Y., Narumi, T., Tanikawa, T., Hirose, M.: Taste in motion: the effect of projection mapping of a boiling effect on food expectation, food perception, and purchasing behavior. Front. Comput. Sci. **3**, 662824 (2021)
62. Takeuchi, M., Kusuyama, H., Iwai, D., Sato, K.: Projection mapping under environmental lighting by replacing room lights with heterogeneous projectors. IEEE Trans. Vis. Comput. Graph. **30**(5), 2151–2161 (2024). https://doi.org/10.1109/TVCG.2024.3372031
63. Tian, F., Wang, H., Fang, Y., Pan, H., Xia, X.: A swept volume display system using a planetary gear structure based on parallel moving. J. Disp. Technol. **8**(8), 457–463 (2012). https://doi.org/10.1109/JDT.2012.2196790
64. Tone, D., Iwai, D., Hiura, S., Sato, K.: FibAR: embedding optical fibers in 3D printed objects for active markers in dynamic projection mapping. IEEE Trans. Vis. Comput. Graph. **26**(5), 2030–2040 (2020). https://doi.org/10.1109/TVCG.2020.2973444
65. Treepong, B., Mitake, H., Hasegawa, S.: Makeup creativity enhancement with an augmented reality face makeup system. Comput. Entertain. **16**(4), 1–7 (2018). https://doi.org/10.1145/3277452
66. Tsurumi, N., Ohishi, K., Kakimoto, R., Tsukiyama, F., Peng, H.L., Watanabe, Y., Masubuchi, Y.: Rediscovering your own beauty through a highly realistic 3D digital makeup system based on projection mapping technology. In: International Federation of Societies of Cosmetic Chemists (2023)
67. Wang, L., Tabata, S., Xu, H., Hu, Y., Watanabe, Y., Ishikawa, M.: Dynamic depth-of-field projection mapping method based on a variable focus lens and visual feedback. Opt. Express **31**(3), 3945–3953 (2023). https://doi.org/10.1364/OE.478416
68. Watanabe, Y., Ishikawa, M.: High-speed and high-brightness color single-chip DLP projector using high-power LED-based light sources. In: 26th International Display Workshops, IDW 2019, pp. 1350–1352 (2019). https://doi.org/10.36463/IDW.2019.1350

69. Watanabe, Y., Kato, T., Ishikawa, M.: Extended dot cluster marker for high-speed 3d tracking in dynamic projection mapping. In: 2017 IEEE International Symposium on Mixed and Augmented Reality (ISMAR), pp. 52–61 (2017). https://doi.org/10.1109/ISMAR.2017.22
70. Watanabe, Y., Narita, G., Tatsuno, S., Yuasa, T., Sumino, K., Ishikawa, M.: High-speed 8-bit image projector at 1,000 fps with 3 MS delay. In: 22nd International Display Workshops, IDW 2015, pp. 1064–1065 (2015)
71. Xiao, R., Cao, T., Guo, N., Zhuo, J., Zhang, Y., Harrison, C.: Lumiwatch: On-arm projected graphics and touch input. In: Proceedings of the 2018 CHI Conference on Human Factors in Computing Systems, CHI '18, pp. 1–11 (2018). https://doi.org/10.1145/3173574.3173669
72. Xu, H., Wang, L., Tabata, S., Watanabe, Y., Ishikawa, M.: Extended depth-of-field projection method using a high-speed projector with a synchronized oscillating variable-focus lens. Appl. Opt. **60**(13), 3917–3924 (2021). https://doi.org/10.1364/AO.419470
73. Yasui, M., Iwataki, R., Ishikawa, M., Watanabe, Y.: Projection mapping with a brightly lit surrounding using a mixed light field approach. IEEE Trans. Vis. Comput. Graph. **30**(5), 2217–2227 (2024). https://doi.org/10.1109/TVCG.2024.3372132
74. Yoshida, T., Watanabe, Y., Ishikawa, M.: Phyxel: realistic display of shape and appearance using physical objects with high-speed pixelated lighting. In: Proceedings of the 29th Annual Symposium on User Interface Software and Technology. UIST '16, pp. 453–460 (2016). https://doi.org/10.1145/2984511.2984548

Chapter 13
Digital Fabrication of Shitsukan

Masashi Nakatani, Yasuaki Kakehi, and Shinsaku Hiura

Abstract Recent advancements in digital fabrication technologies have enabled not only the shaping of physical forms but also the design of material qualities, including tactile sensations and interactive functions. This chapter explores novel approaches to designing Shitsukan through digital fabrication from three perspectives: (1) controlling haptic feedback via internal structural design, (2) developing fully flexible deformation sensors using porous and conductive materials, and (3) realizing dynamic visual and tactile transformations through methods such as 4D printing and refractive index modulation. By treating material texture as a programmable and dynamic design element of real-world Shitsukan, this work points toward new directions for embodied interaction and material-centered interface design.

13.1 Introduction

Advancements and the growing accessibility of digital fabrication technologies have made it possible not only to design the shape of physical objects but also to shape their material properties which play an important role in defining the Shitsukan of real-world objects. With the expanding range of materials available for 3D printing–such as wood-based or metallic filaments–it has become increasingly feasible to create objects with diverse tactile and visual qualities.

The potential of digital fabrication of Shitsukan goes beyond surface-level expressions of an object. Today, we can design the internal structure of an object to control

M. Nakatani
Keio University, Endo, Fujisawa, Kanagawa, Japan
e-mail: nakatani.z3@keio.jp

Y. Kakehi (✉)
The University of Tokyo, Hongo, Bunkyo-ku, Tokyo, Japan
e-mail: kakehi@iii.u-tokyo.ac.jp

S. Hiura
University of Hyogo, Shosha, Himeji, Hyogo, Japan
e-mail: hiura@eng.u-hyogo.ac.jp

S. Nishida and K. Nishino (eds.), *Shitsukan—Understanding and Manipulating Material and Quality Perception*, https://doi.org/10.1007/978-981-95-4762-3_13

its softness and tactile feel. By modifing the structural parameters allows designers to tailor a wide range of haptic responses.

Moreover, by incorporating conductive materials into the fabrication process, it becomes possible to add interactive functionality to material textures. Without embedding rigid sensors or electronic components, we can create soft objects that function as sensors in themselves–greatly expanding the possibilities for haptic interfaces.

In this chapter, we explore three key topics that exemplify this expanded notion of material Shitsukan. The first author (Nakatani) discusses the design of tactile material c through 3D printing. The second author (Kakehi) introduces technologies for embedding deformation-sensing capabilities into flexible, printed structures. The third author (Hiura) focuses on fabrication techniques for achieving dynamic changes in visual Shitsukan.

Texture is not merely a surface attribute–it is a design element that shapes rich Shitsukan experiences through our bodily interactions with objects. Exploring this potential through digital fabrication opens up new horizons for creative expression.

13.2 The Use of Digital Fabrication in Haptic Science

The rise of digital fabrication has made it possible to computationally design and build physical objects that can present not only audiovisual but also haptic domains. An advantage of digital fabrication technology is that it can continuously vary the design parameters of the object to be generated. These design parameters can alter the shape, size, material density, or internal structure of an object. By leveraging this technical merit, we can study the design parameters that can dominantly manipulate the haptic Shitsukan of objects. In other words, digital fabrication technology enables us not only to produce the shape of an object but also to investigate haptic Shitsukan of the object, such as surface texture and softness.

For texture roughness perception, Tymms et al. [31] investigated the contributions of microgeometric features—such as shape, size, spatial period, and spatial arrangement of raised elements—using specimens fabricated with a high-resolution 3D printer. According to their study, Tymms et al. [31] found that perceived roughness increases with the spatial period of the surface texture. They also reported that, when the spatial period is held constant, surfaces with smaller raised elements are perceived as rougher than those with larger ones. Moreover, even when the spatial period remains the same, differences in the spatial arrangement of raised elements lead to perceptual differences in roughness. This study demonstrates how digital fabrication makes it possible to systematically study haptic Shitsukan in roughness perception, as surface asperities are difficult to manipulate in natural materials.

Kuroki et al. [15] used a high-precision 3D printer to produce textured plates by converting grayscale images of natural scenes into height maps [15]. They ensured consistency in lower-order surface statistics (mean and variance of height), while retaining variations in both lower-order (e.g., spatial frequency and amplitude spectrum) and higher-order (e.g., joint correlations, phase patterns) image statistics. Participants easily distinguished textures varying in lower-order statistics; however; participants struggled to distinguish surface textures of similar amplitude spectra even if textures' higher-order statistics differed. Kuroki et al. [15] also created texture pairs matched in lower-order statistics but differing in higher-order properties so as to isolate the role of higher-order features in surface texture discrimination. Participants could not distinguish these texture pairs by touch, unless the textures contained salient local features. Motivated by image statistics in visual Shitsukan studies, the result implies that controlling lower-order tactile features through high-resolution digital fabrication technology is crucial for haptic texture perception.

For softness perception, it has become possible to easily produce real three-dimensional objects with complex mechanical properties by forming objects with internal geometric structures called "architected materials" [10, 19, 21]. Architected materials can evoke a nuanced perception of softness through the interplay of compliance, resistance and deformation behavior.

In the following, we briefly evaluate the emerging literature on the design of medical insoles manufactured using a 3D printer.

13.2.1 Compressibility Control by Digital Fabrication

Research has explored changing the infill inside of a 3D object by altering the internal structure [18, 28]. It is important to recognize that the tactile qualities of softness and smoothness are interconnected rather than determined by separate physical quantities; For example, softness involves both the compressibility of an object and the fluffiness of a surface texture [2].

Recent advancements in high-resolution 3D printing technology allow for the production of architected materials featuring (micro)lattice structures. These materials have a special internal structure that absorbs energy when the impact occurs, making them suitable for applications like body supports or impact-reducing packaging [26]. Architected materials exhibit a nonlinear force-stroke relationship, and their physical properties are complex. Architected materials may have high resilience or high damping characteristics. Some of the architected materials are resistant to deformation in the vertical direction but deform easily in the horizontal direction [14]. In certain architected materials, their surface deforms softly, but when pressed further, the density increases and the architected material resists deformation, resulting in a hard sensation. Architected materials may also exhibit velocity dependence, feeling soft when pressed slowly but hard when pressed quickly [11]. There has been little research on whether the unique physical properties of architected materials contribute to human softness perception or to the softness Shitsukan.

13.2.2 *Softness Perception in Humans: Evidence from 3D-Printed Lattice Structures with Heterogeneous Compliance*

This section briefly overviews an experiment investigating how humans perceive softness in heterogeneous six-layer lattice structures created exclusively by manipulating lattice beam thickness (Higuchi, Iwashita, Nagashima, Nakatani, & Ohgi, in preparation). As mentioned above, softness perception is one of the central dimensions of haptic experience, influencing how humans evaluate foods, textiles, and daily objects. In previous studies, only a few have mainly employed inhomogeneous materials, where compliance is not uniform across the object. Many real-world materials are heterogeneous. Fruits with a firm skin and soft pulp, or layered confections with distinct textures (e.g., Xu et al. [35]). How humans perceive softness in such layered heterogeneous structures remains elusive.

To address softness perception in heterogeneous material, we used 3D-printed lattice structures with controllable beam sizes to construct stimuli in which the mechanical properties of each layer could be manipulated. This methodological approach allowed us to test two specific hypotheses:

- Hypothesis 1 (Surface dominance): Stimuli with a soft contact surface layer will be perceived as softer than stimuli with a hard contact surface, regardless of deeper layers.
- Hypothesis 2 (Cumulative subsurface contribution): For stimuli with a hard contact surface, perceived softness will increase as the number of soft subsurface layers increases.

13.2.2.1 Materials and Methods

Participants
Twenty-two participants (9 male, 13 female; mean age = 21.8 years, range 21–24) took part in the experiment. All were right-handed, reported no neurological disorders, and gave informed consent prior to participation. The experimental protocol was approved by the Ethical Committee on Human Experimentation of Keio University, Shonan Fujisawa Campus (approval No. 586).

Stimuli
Stimuli were lattice blocks (3.6 × 3.6 × 3.6 cm) fabricated with a fused deposition modeling (FDM) 3D printer. Each block consisted of six lattice layers (6.0 mm thick each) stacked vertically. The bottom two layers were always hard lattices for structural stability, while the upper four lattice layers were systematically varied in compliance by adjusting beam thickness. Hard layers were printed with thicker beams (higher effective modulus), and soft layers with thinner beams (lower effective modulus).

A total of sixteen stimuli (T1–T16) were prepared, each representing a unique combination of hard (H) and soft (S) lattice layers. Among these, T1–T8 were designed specifically to test our hypotheses (H1: surface dominance; H2: cumulative subsurface contribution) by systematically manipulating the hardness/softness of the upper four layers:

T1: HHHH (All hard in the upper lattice layers)
T2: HSHH
T3: HSSH
T4: HSSS
T5: SHHH
T6: SSHH
T7: SSSH
T8: SSSS (All soft in the upper lattice layers)

Here, H = hard (thick beams) and S = soft (thin beams). Thus, each stimulus comprised six lattice layers in total, with the upper four experimentally manipulated in terms of beam size.

In addition, T9–T16 were created as additional stimuli, representing further combinations of hard and soft lattice layers. T9–T16 were included to broaden the range of heterogeneous configurations and to evaluate whether the patterns observed in T1–T8 generalized to other structural arrangements.

Each stimulus was placed on a flat base so that the first layer (contact surface) was directly accessible to finger indentation (Fig. 13.1).

Procedure
Participants sat at a desk and explored each stimulus with the right index fingertip. They were instructed to press perpendicularly into the contact surface once and rate its perceived softness using magnitude estimation. A reference stimulus (T11) was first presented and its softness magnitude was defined as '50'. Participants were told to assign numbers larger than 50 if the test stimulus felt softer, and smaller than 50 if harder, but must be more than '1'. Stimulus order was randomized across participants. Participants were allowed to apply force up to 3000 g. Participants were able to see each experimental stimulus through a half-mirror, but were unable to observe the details of how much it was being deformed under test conditions.

Data Analysis
Softness magnitude ratings were log-transformed and standardized within participants. Linear mixed-effects models (LMMs) were fitted with participant as a random intercept $(1|S)$.

To test H1, we compared models with and without L1 (contact surface softness). To test H2, we included the number of soft subsurface layers (L2–L4) as an additional predictor, restricted to trials with a hard surface layer. Model comparisons used likelihood ratio tests (LRTs), AIC, and marginal R^2. Data analysis was performed using R version 4.4.1.

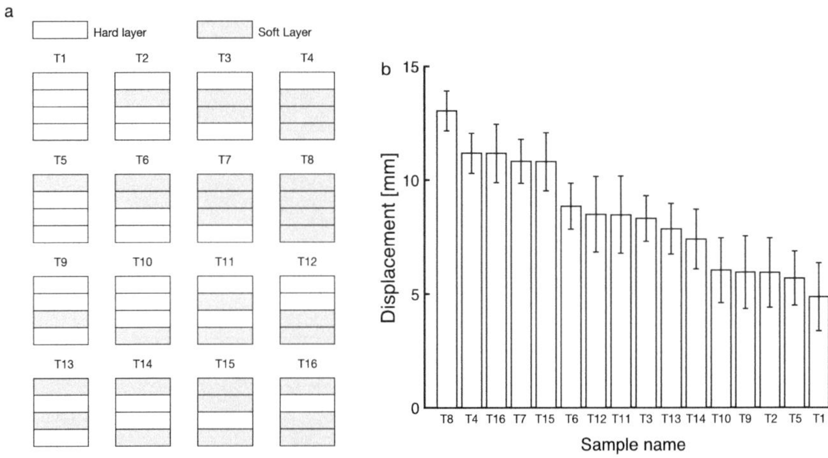

Fig. 13.1 Stimulus set of 3D-printed lattice structures (3.6 × 3.6 × 3.6 cm), each consisting of six lattice layers. The bottom two layers were always hard, while the upper four lattice layers were varied in compliance by manipulating beam thickness (hard, thick beams, 1.0 mm; soft, thin beams, 0.75 mm). **a** Sixteen stimuli (T1–T16) were prepared. T1–T8 were systematically designed to test our hypotheses regarding surface dominance (H1) and cumulative subsurface contributions (H2), whereas T9–T16 represented additional combinations of hard and soft layers to extend the stimulus set. **b** The deformation response of the specimens when subjected to a load of 3000 g

13.2.2.2 Results

A linear regression analysis was conducted with the logarithm of displacement as the predictor and the logarithm of softness magnitude as the outcome variable. The regression model was significant, $F(1, 14) = 19.1$, $P < 0.001$, with an adjusted R^2 of 0.55, indicating that the model explained about half of the variance. The slope of $\mathrm{Log}_{10}(\mathrm{displacement})$ was significant, $\beta = 1.25$, SE $= 0.29$, $t(14) = 4.37$, $P < 0.001$, and the intercept was 0.58 (SE $= 0.26$, $t(14) = 2.22$, $P < 0.05$. The regression model results showed that an explanatory model incorporating the softness of the contact surface is marginally appropriate (Fig. 13.2).

Consistent with H1, adding the contact surface factor (L1) significantly improved model fit ($\chi^2(1) = 132.56$, $P < 0.001$). Marginal R^2 was 0.51. This result indicated that stimuli with a soft surface layer were reliably judged as softer regardless of subsurface configuration.

Moreover, consistent with H2, adding the number of subsurface soft layers further improved the model ($\Delta AIC = -86.9$, $P < 0.001$), with marginal R^2 increasing to 0.68. A layer-specific model indicated that the first layer (contact surface, L1) mainly contributed the softness perception ($\beta = 38.23$, SE $= 1.95$, $P < 0.001$) Also, the second layer (L2) contributed significantly ($\beta = 15.23$, SE $= 2.76$, $P < 0.001$), the third layer (L3) showed a similar trend ($\beta = 9.82$, SE $= 2.76$, $P < 0.001$), and the fourth layer (L4) had negligible impact ($\beta = 4.05$, SE $= 2.76$, $P = 0.15$).

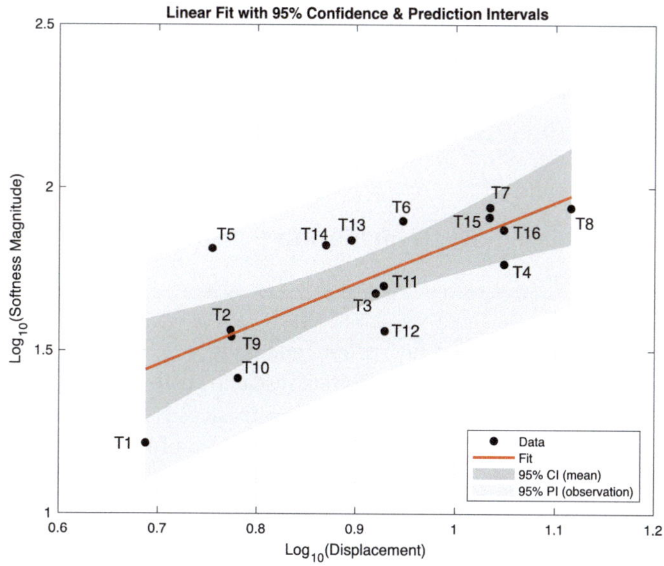

Fig. 13.2 Scatterplot of log-transformed displacement versus log-transformed softness magnitude, with fitted regression line. The regression was significant, $F(1, 14) = 19.1$, $P < 0.001$, adjusted $R^2 = 0.55$, indicating that displacement accounted for about the half of the variance in perceived softness. CI: Confidence interval, PI: Prediction Interval

13.2.2.3 Discussion

This study provided direct evidence that human softness perception depends on both surface and subsurface compliance, but with markedly different weights.

H1 is supported by the clear improvement in model fit when surface softness (L1) was included as a predictor. A soft contact surface consistently increased perceived softness regardless of subsurface configuration, indicating strong surface dominance.

H2 is partially supported by the additional variance explained when the number of subsurface soft layers was incorporated into the model. Although deeper layers contributed positively, their influence decayed with depth: the second layer exerted a significant effect, the third layer a weaker trend, and the fourth layer negligible impact.

These findings suggest that the perceptual system integrates haptic softness information across depth through a weighted integration process, in which surface input is prioritized while subsurface information is incorporated to a lesser degree. Mechanically, this pattern may reflect skin deformation gradients and receptor depth sensitivity; perceptually, it highlights a strategy that favors immediate surface cues while modulating judgments with additional subsurface softness when available.

Methodologically, the use of 3D-printed lattice structures demonstrates a novel approach for systematically manipulating layered mechanical properties to investigate haptic softness. This framework also opens avenues for investigating haptic Shitsukan in heterogeneous materials and offers applications in haptic product design.

13.3 3D-Printable Soft Deformation Sensors with Lattice Structures

In the field of Human-Computer Interaction, integrating "softness" and "flexibility" into interface design has become an important research challenge. These are referred to as Organic User Interfaces [8] or Deformable Interfaces [1], and research has been conducted on leveraging the flexibility and deformation of materials as interaction mechanisms.

One approach to utilizing the deformation of objects as computer input is to wrap existing rigid sensors with soft materials. For instance, Fuwafuwa [27] covered an optical sensor with cotton, and by analyzing changes in the reflected light when the user pressed the cotton, the system detected the deformation. Another approach involves combining optical sensors with soft materials. For example, ForceTile [12] placed a soft tile made of elastic silicone on a tabletop and computed its deformation using an optical method.

While these methods enable various input techniques, the presence of rigid components can locally restrict soft input capabilities. Additionally, when using external sensors such as cameras, constraints may arise in terms of placement flexibility and required orientation, potentially limiting the design freedom of the interface. However, these approaches still rely on external sensors or embedded rigid components, which limit the integration of sensing into soft, continuous surfaces. To address these limitations, the researchers led by the second author (Kakehi) have been exploring deformation-sensing techniques using entirely soft objects that contain no rigid components and function independently without external sensing equipment.

As one example of such efforts, FoamSense [20], proposed by Nakamaru et al., involves impregnating porous materials like sponges with conductive ink and measuring the resistance between both ends to capture the degree of deformation when compressed. As shown in Fig. 13.3, when the porous material constructed with conductive ink deforms, the resistance between the electrodes at both ends changes. In principle, these sensors are fabricated from readily available materials, which makes them highly cost-effective to produce.

Similarly, Foamin [34], proposed by Watanabe et al. is a soft sensor that uses conductive sponges but focuses on changes in capacitance due to finger contact instead of resistance. The proposed sensor is composed of a soft conductive foam, a shield covering the surface, and a cable connected to a microcontroller. The sensor is entirely made of soft materials, allowing it to capture and identify user actions such as touching or deforming the sensor with fingers or other parts of the body. In this

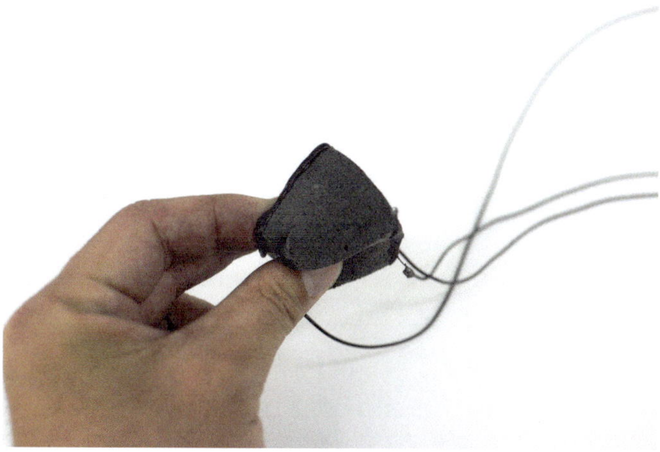

Fig. 13.3 FoamSense [20] embeds conductive ink into porous materials such as sponges and detects compression-induced deformation by measuring the resistance across the material

system, a sensor board based on the SFCS (Swept Frequency Capacitive Sensing) method [24] was used to measure the system's impedance at multiple frequencies. Similar to touch sensors, foamin can recognize contact input from fingers or hands on the surface. Additionally, when the user deforms the sensor body to provide input, the impedance changes significantly not only due to changes in the contact area, but also due to structural changes caused by compression of the body and changes in the distance between the wire contact area and the contact point. By capturing these changes in impedance, it is possible to identify different input modes and positions (see Fig. 13.4).

These examples demonstrate the potential of directly utilizing commercially available conductive sponges for soft sensing. However, such technologies also present several limitations.

First, the porous materials used in prior studies typically exhibit uniform mechanical properties, making it difficult to locally customize softness or sensitivity. Second, the fabrication of complex three-dimensional (3D) geometries often requires manual labor or specialized equipment, posing challenges to scalability and reproducibility. Third, most of these sensors are designed to support only a single deformation mode–usually compression–meaning that additional modes such as shearing or twisting require the integration of multiple sensing mechanisms, thereby increasing design complexity.

To address these challenges, Sakura et al. [22] from Kakehi's group explored the use of 3D printing technologies to develop soft sensors that can be designed not only by their external geometry but also by their internal material structure [22].

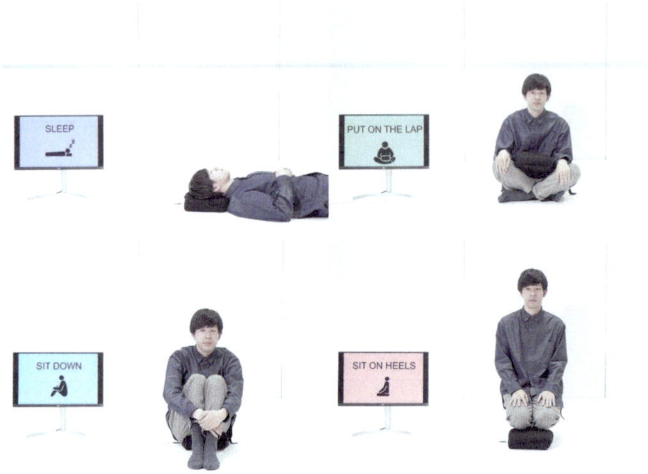

Fig. 13.4 Foamin [34] captures inputs from touch and deformation as impedance changes, enabling the identification of multiple input modes and positions. This figure illustrates posture estimation on a cushion using Foamin

13.3.1 Overview of LattiSense

LattiSense [22] is a soft deformation sensor that employs 3D-printed lattice structures composed of flexible, conductive materials, thereby increasing the degrees of freedom in both three-dimensional form and deformation (see Fig. 13.5).

While related work has explored similar approaches [5, 6], these designs are generally limited to planar configurations and provide only restricted control over material softness. In addition, practical challenges such as cable routing and connector placement remain obstacles to broader applicability.

To address these limitations, LattiSense introduces a parametric lattice design that allows tuning of unit size and structural model, enabling the detection of multiple deformation modes–including twisting, shearing, and compression–within a single body. Furthermore, varying levels of localized softness can be embedded in one print. Internal conductive pathways are also integrated, allowing flexible cable attachment and simplifying sensor integration, while enhancing both functional and aesthetic qualities of the final form.

13.3.2 Design of LattiSense

To facilitate mechanical responsiveness, LattiSense is internally structured using a three-dimensional lattice configuration (Fig. 13.6). This framework consists of spatially periodic unit cells, forming a lightweight architecture that is well-suited to

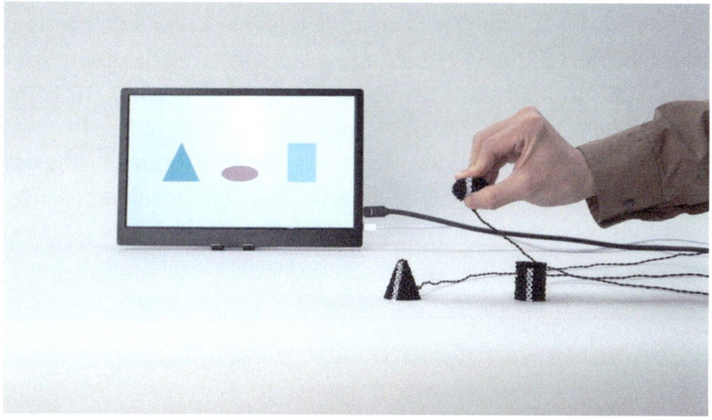

Fig. 13.5 LattiSense [22] is a soft deformation sensor built from 3D-printed lattice structures made of flexible, conductive materials

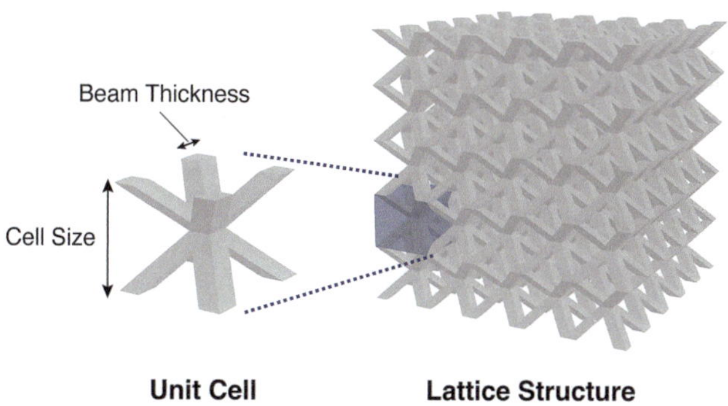

Fig. 13.6 Three-dimensional lattice structure and its parameters

additive manufacturing processes. While lattice geometries have traditionally been valued for their structural efficiency, the integration of flexible materials expands their applicability to soft systems. By parametrically tuning unit cell dimensions and types, it becomes possible to modulate both the mechanical compliance and directional deformability of the printed object.

What distinguishes LattiSense is the functionalization of the 3D lattice structure itself as a sensing medium. Constructed with electrically conductive and elastic filaments, the structure exhibits resistance changes in response to physical deformation. These changes can be monitored in real-time to capture dynamic mechanical interactions, enabling the lattice to operate as an embedded soft sensor.

To extract resistance values, electrical leads are connected to the printed structure. Proper placement requires that the conductive region lie between at least two terminals. In conventional sensing systems, such as porous-material-based approaches including FoamSense [20], electrodes are commonly affixed to opposite faces of the object, aligned with the primary deformation axis. However, this configuration can interfere with user interaction, especially in handheld or tactile use cases.

To mitigate such limitations, LattiSense introduces a design strategy in which non-conductive materials are selectively integrated into the lattice to control current flow paths (see Fig. 13.7). This allows electrodes to be positioned on the same surface or at more compact intervals, thereby avoiding obstruction and increasing flexibility in mechanical interface design.

13.3.3 Fabrication and Results

To assess the feasibility and sensing performance of the LattiSense design, multiple prototypes were fabricated using a commercially available dual-extrusion FDM 3D printer. A detailed description of the overall fabrication pipeline, including baseline design parameters and printing setup, can be found in [22]. The following discusses the design strategy, parameterization techniques, and outcomes of updated experimental evaluations.

Lattice geometries were modeled using Grasshopper, a visual programming environment for Rhino 3D, which enabled the procedural generation of complex unit cell arrangements and beam structures. The parametric nature of the design allowed for flexible control over key structural features such as unit cell size, beam thickness, cell orientation, and deformation axes. Additionally, routing channels and conductive

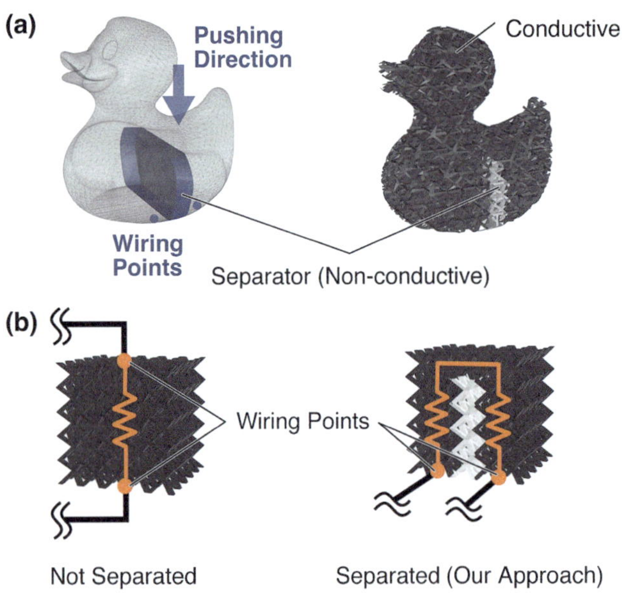

Fig. 13.7 **a** Separation structure. **b** Comparison of wiring with/without separator

segmentation were incorporated into the digital models to optimize sensor performance and improve wiring accessibility. After finalizing the geometry, the mesh was exported as STL files for fabrication.

NinjaTek Eel, a highly flexible conductive TPU, was selected for the sensing elements, while 3DXFLEX TPU was employed for the insulating structural regions. Both filaments share a similar Shore hardness (90A), ensuring uniform mechanical compliance across conductive and non-conductive regions. Printing was performed at a nozzle temperature of 225°C, with a layer height of 0.2 mm and a print speed of 15 mm/s.

A variety of lattice configurations were fabricated and tested, with systematic variations in unit cell size (e.g., 4.0, 5.0, 6.0 mm), beam thickness (e.g., 0.8, 1.0, 1.2 mm), and overall object dimensions. The resulting sensors were subjected to controlled compression, shear, and torsion using a custom mechanical testbed equipped with a load cell and linear actuator.

The results demonstrated a strong correlation between structural parameters and sensing behavior (Fig. 13.8). As expected, larger cell sizes and thinner beams yielded greater deformability and higher sensitivity. Each deformation mode produced distinct resistance profiles, confirming that the lattice geometry could be tuned to support mode-specific interactions. In most cases, linear or monotonic changes in resistance were observed with high coefficients of determination ($R^2 > 0.9$), suggesting that the sensor output can be reliably mapped to physical deformation.

13.3.4 Application Scenarios

Based on the design principles and functionalities discussed above, LattiSense is applicable to a variety of domains, including interactive systems, wearable computing, and robotics.

Tangible Interfaces By leveraging its ability to detect multiple deformation modes including compression, shear, and twist, LattiSense enables tangible interactions that extend beyond flat surfaces. For example, users can issue commands or manipulate parameters by directly pressing, pinching, or twisting volumetric objects in spatial user interfaces. Owing to its customizability, the sensor can be shaped into ergonomic input devices or sculptural forms. As demonstration examples, a one-piece game controller and a CPR training model embedded with sensing capabilities were fabricated (Fig. 13.9, top left and right).

Shape-Adaptive Interactive Surfaces Thanks to its design flexibility and softness, LattiSense can be embedded into irregularly shaped environments such as curved walls, furniture, or textile surfaces. These surfaces can detect localized deformations caused by user interaction, making them suitable for ambient intelligence applications and architectural installations. As a proof of concept, an application

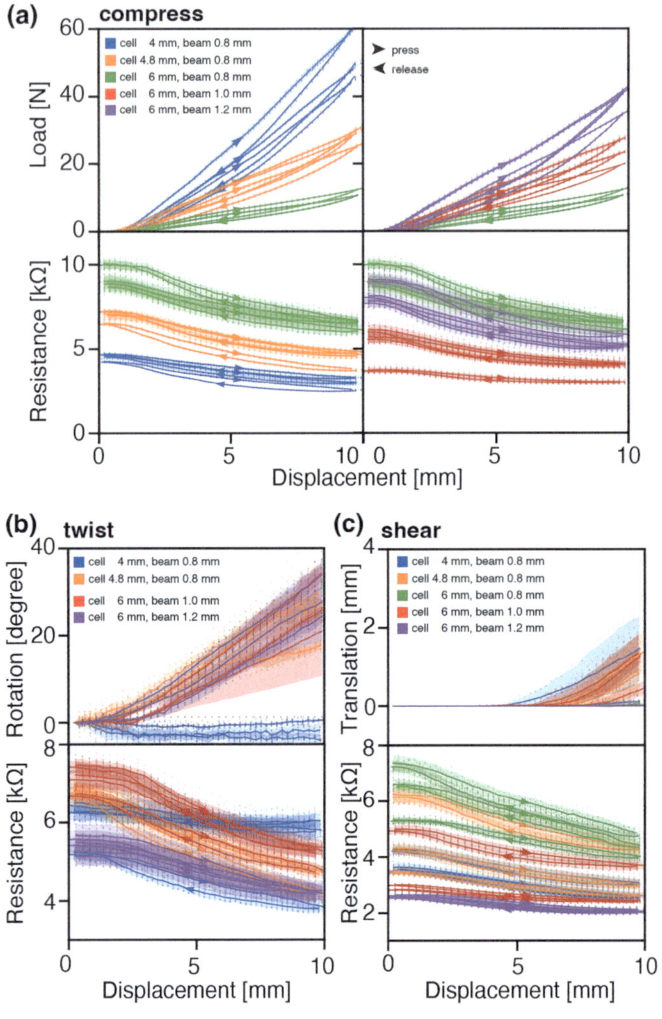

Fig. 13.8 Mechanical properties of the printed deformation structures. **a** Force-displacement and resistance characteristics of the compress model with different unit cell size and beam thickness, **b** rotation characteristic of the twist model, and **c** lateral translation of the shear model

was developed in which a grip customized to fit an existing pen alters the stroke appearance on a screen according to the pressure applied to it (Fig. 13.9, bottom left).

Wearable and Body-Attached Devices The sensor's flexibility and customizable geometry support wearable scenarios such as skin patches, joint monitors, and posture sensors. As an example, the sensor was embedded into the sole of a sandal to capture changes in pressure distribution during walking (Fig. 13.9, bottom right).

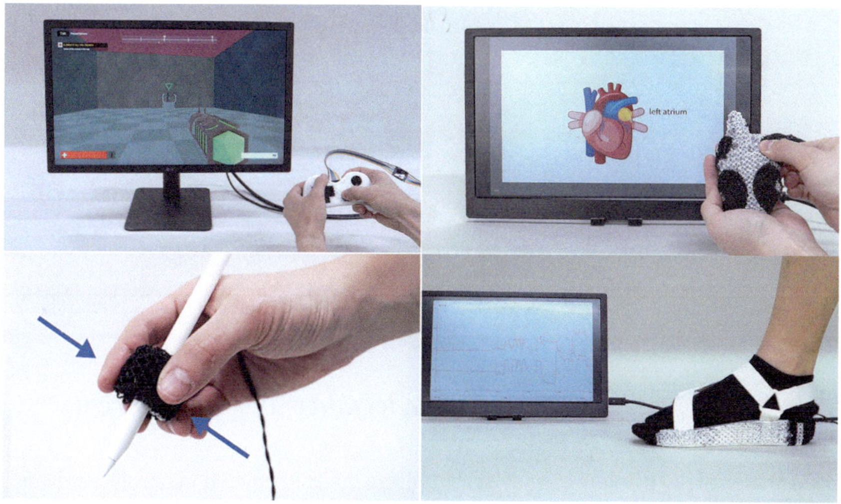

Fig. 13.9 Application examples of LattiSense. Top left: A 3D-printed game controller with compressible, twistable, and shearable buttons for intuitive input with tactile feedback. Top right: an interactive heart model for education, where pressing different parts triggers corresponding visual feedback. Bottom left: a pen grip embedded with LattiSense that alters digital stroke appearance based on grip pressure, enabling pressure-sensitive interaction. Bottom right: a wearable sandal with integrated sensors that detect pressure distribution during walking

Other Potential Applications In the field of robotics, LattiSense can serve as a skin-like layer for soft robotic systems, enabling proprioception by detecting shape changes or pressure on actuator surfaces. Furthermore, since the sensor can be fabricated as a single body with integrated wiring channels, it is well-suited for modular configurations and distributed deployment.

13.4 Digital Fabrication of Objects with Dynamically Changing Appearance

In several applications, not only the including advertisement and entertainment but also evaluation of designs related to Shitsukan, methods to change the appearance of a fixed object are widely demanded. In this section, we propose two methods to design and fabricate objects whose appearances can be changed by the direction of illumination. The first method makes it possible to represent different pictures for frontal and back illuminations by adjusting the thickness of black and white layers. The second method can render different pictures by changing the position of light sources placed at the back of the object. In both methods, we considered actual limitations and characteristics of existing multi-material 3D printers, such as the limited opacity of black materials.

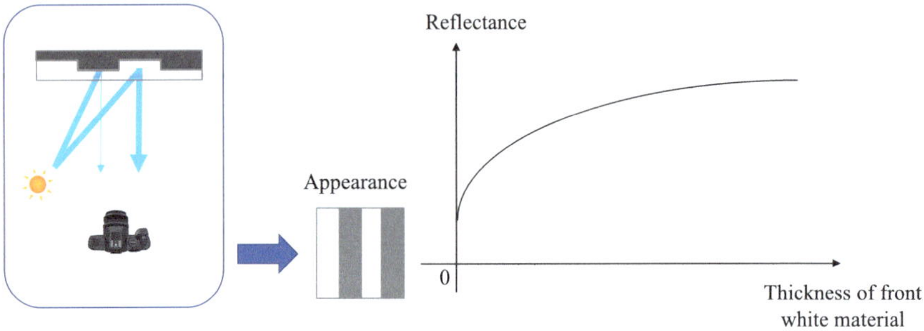

Fig. 13.10 Control of reflectance by the thickness of front white layer

13.4.1 Independent Control of Reflectance and Transparency

Multi-material 3D printers can fabricate objects made of several materials connected together. Generally, most plastics and resins are slightly translucent because their colors are controlled by pigments mixed into transparent substrates. Therefore, we can manipulate reflectance and transparency by changing the thickness of the materials. As shown in Fig. 13.10, we apply a white material on the front surface and adjust its thickness to control the reflectance under frontal illumination. Additionally, we use a black material for the back layer and control its transparency by varying its thickness.

The relationship between reflectance and the thickness of the material is nonlinear. Therefore, we made a wedge-shaped test piece in which the thickness of the white layer gradually changes, as shown in Fig. 13.11. Similarly, we varied the thickness of

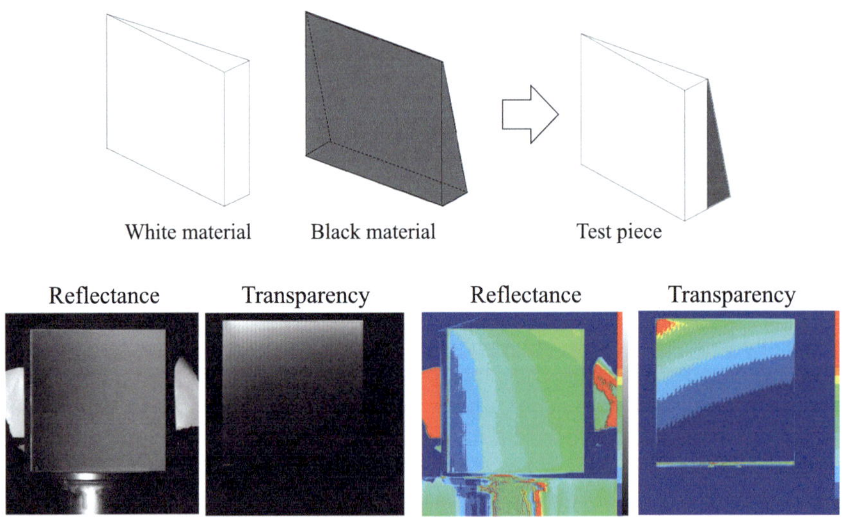

Fig. 13.11 Measurement of reflectance and transparency using wedge-shaped test piece

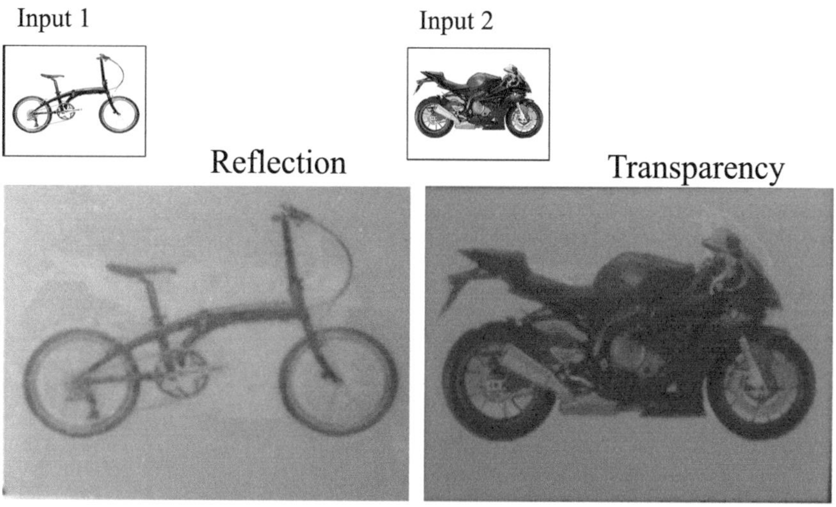

Fig. 13.12 A single object with two layers to show different images under frontal and back illuminations

the black layer vertically to measure transparency at the same time. The images shown in Fig. 13.11 are examples of photos captured under frontal and back illumination separately. The pseudo-color image clearly shows that the thicknesses of the two layers mutually affect reflectance and transparency. Therefore, we use these images to select thicknesses that provide the intended reflectance and transparency.

Figure 13.12 shows an example of an object that displays two images under frontal and back illumination independently. We used the Stratasys Objet260 Connex3 multi-material 3D printer to fabricate the actual object. The crosstalk between the two images is effectively suppressed.

13.4.2 Control of Transparency for Differently Tilted Back Illuminations

For most applications such as advertisements, it is unrealistic to control the environmental lighting in our living spaces. Therefore, we developed another method to change the appearance of objects by changing the direction of illumination placed at the back of the object. Instead of controlling the thickness of the layers, we adjust the width of pigments arranged in the transparent substrate to control the ratio of light passing through, as shown in Fig. 13.13. More specifically, the width and height of small cuboids are adjusted according to the brightness of the corresponding pixels of the input images, and then they are rotated by 45 degrees.

To improve the performance and practicality, we modified the design of the object as follows. First, we stretched the object perpendicular to the display surface to

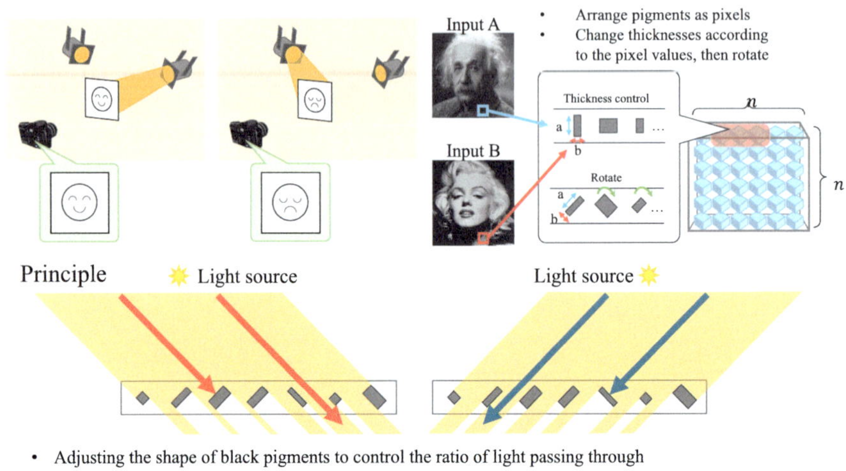

Fig. 13.13 The principle of appearance-changing object for differently tilted illuminations

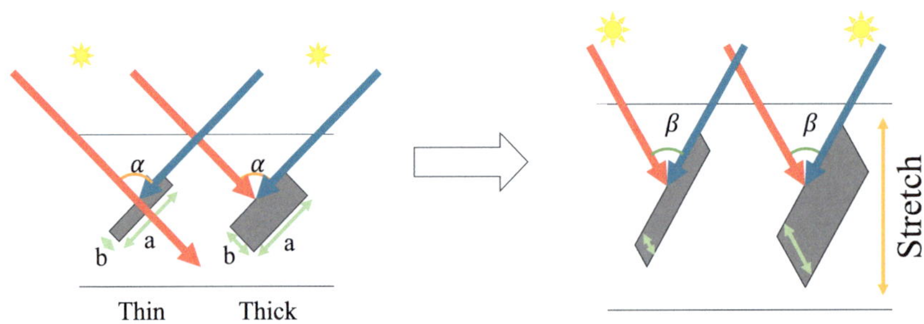

Fig. 13.14 Stretch of the thickness of the object

improve the contrast of the displayed images. If the thickness of the pigment is too thin, the light that should be blocked passes through the pigment, as shown in Fig. 13.14. The angle between the two light sources is also too large. By increasing the thickness of the object, we can solve both problems at once.

Theoretically, our design requires light sources placed at infinity, which is not practical. Therefore, we warped the object using a projective transformation (2D homographic transformation), as shown in Fig. 13.15.

Figure 13.16 shows the comparison between the input images and the corresponding displayed images. We see that the two images are clearly displayed without crosstalk between them.

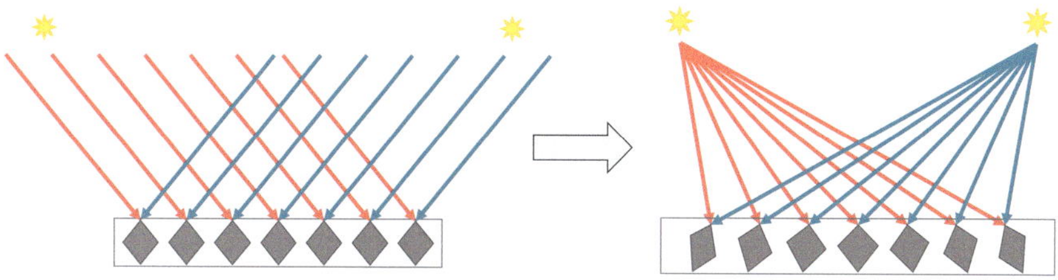

Fig. 13.15 Projective transformations to use light sources at finite distances

Fig. 13.16 Comparison between input and displayed images

13.4.3 Design of Texture Changing Objects

We proposed a method for creating three-dimensional real objects whose glossiness can change. By matching the refractive indices of two materials, we eliminate refraction and reflection that occur when light passes through a textured surface, thereby altering the glossiness. Additionally, we demonstrated that glossiness can be switched by creating an object with a curved display surface and examining changes in reflections.

As shown in Fig. 13.17, a transparent object with a textured surface scatters light. This is because the refractive indices of the transparent object and air are different, and at the interface between them, Fresnel reflections occur. The light splits into reflected and refracted rays, causing changes in their directions. Therefore, we fill the textured side of the transparent object with a liquid that has the same refractive index as the object. As a result, Fresnel reflections no longer occur between the transparent object and the liquid, and all light passes straight through the interface. This is called index matching.

As shown in Fig. 13.18, we controlled the presence or absence of texture using this principle. The 3D printer used was the Stratasys Objet260 Connex 3, and the

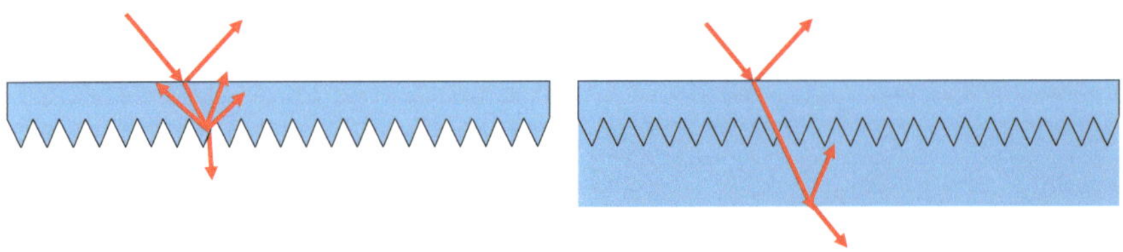

(a) Resin object only (b) Filled with index-matched liquid

Fig. 13.17 Index matching technique to suppress the light scattering of textured surface of transparent object

(a) Resin object only (air gap) (b) Filled with 2,2'-Thiodiethanol

Fig. 13.18 An example of texture changing object by index matching

refractive index of the transparent material VeroClear is 1.523. Therefore, we used thiodiethanol, which has a refractive index almost equal to that of this material. It can be observed that when this liquid is filled, the texture completely disappears.

Figure 13.19 shows an example of the measured intensity distribution under these conditions. When the liquid is not filled, the average intensity is high, and many peaks of specular reflection are observed. In contrast, when the liquid is filled, the average intensity is low, and little change in intensity is observed.

Next, we designed a three-dimensional object whose texture can change. To facilitate the insertion and removal of the liquid, we incorporated a syringe inside the object, as shown in Fig. 13.20, allowing the liquid to be injected and withdrawn by moving the piston up and down. Figure 13.21 shows an example of manipulating this object. It can be seen that when the liquid is inserted, the texture disappears. High-refractive-index liquids for index matching include immersion oils used in microscopes, but due to their high viscosity, there was a problem that the liquid was difficult to remove. Thiodiethanol has low viscosity and was more suitable for quickly controlling the presence or absence of the texture.

One drawback of this method is that the reflection from the outer surface of the object cannot be controlled and always remains. To solve this problem, applying a multi-layer anti-reflection coating to the outer surface can be considered. Additionally, even after removing the liquid, it may remain attached to the fine texture, so it is necessary to consider measures such as oleophobic coatings.

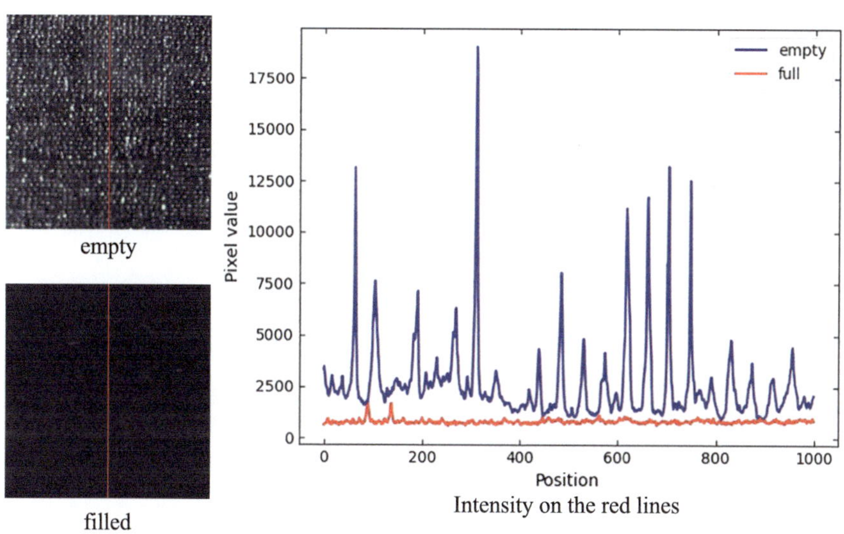

Fig. 13.19 Quantitative evaluation of appearance change by index matching technique

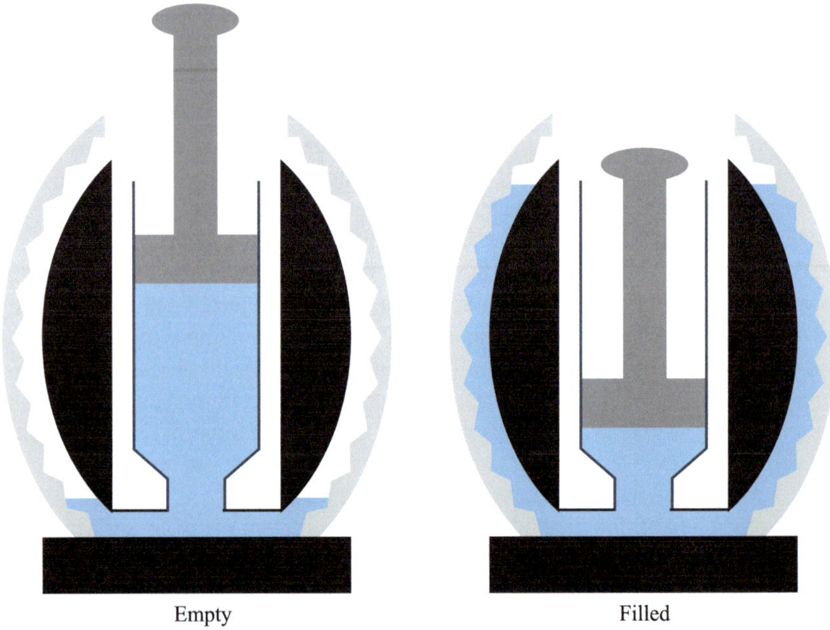

Fig. 13.20 The principle of appearance-changing object for differently tilted illuminations

Fig. 13.21 The principle of appearance-changing object for differently tilted illuminations

13.5 Conclusion

In this chapter, we examined emerging approaches to designing material texture through digital fabrication as a means to alter the Shitsukan of real-world objects, which focused on three perspectives. First, we looked at how selecting and combining materials can yield a variety of visual and tactile textures. Second, we explored how internal structural design can be used to control softness and deformation characteristics. Finally, we discussed the potential of dynamic texture expression, including methods for altering visual appearance over time or in response to external stimuli.

These practices invite us to rethink texture not as a superficial property but as an experiential quality, deeply linked to perception and interaction. Through the axes of material, structure, and change, we are now able to design not only how an object feels, but how it responds, transforms, and engages with the human body, which provides a comprehensive means to manipulate the Shitsukan in our daily lives.

Acknowledgements We thank the Kakehi Planned Research Group and the Sato Planned Research Group of the KAKENHI Grant-in-Aid for Transformative Research Areas (A), "Analysis and Synthesis of Deep SHITSUKAN Information in the Real World," for their contributions to the research presented in this chapter. We are also grateful to Ms. Rei Sakura, who led the studies on 3D-printable soft sensors. We further acknowledge Mr. Kazuo Ono for his invaluable support in advancing collaboration between the Kakehi Lab and the Nakatani Lab and for his assistance in organizing the SHITSUKAN research meetings.

References

1. Boem, A., Troiano, G.M.: Non-rigid HCI: a review of deformable interfaces and input. In: Proceedings of DIS '19, ACM, pp. 885–906 (2019)
2. Cavdan, M., Doerschner, K., Drewing, K.: Task and material properties interactively affect softness explorations along different dimensions. IEEE Trans. Haptics (2021). https://doi.org/10.1109/TOH.2021.3069626
3. Cleland, L.D., Rupani, M., Blaise, C.R., Ellmers, T.J., Saal, H.P.: Texture perception at the foot sole: comparison between walking, sitting, and to the hand. J. Neurophysiol. (2024). https://doi.org/10.1152/jn.00170.2024
4. Friedman, R.M., Hester, K.D., Green, B.G., LaMotte, R.H.: Magnitude estimation of softness. Exp. Brain Res. (2008). https://doi.org/10.1007/s00221-008-1507-5
5. Georgopoulou, A., Vanderborght, B., Clemens, F.: Multi-material 3D printing of thermoplastic elastomers for development of soft robotic structures with integrated sensor elements. AMPA 2020. Springer (2021)
6. Gong, J., Seow, O., Honnet, C., Forman, J., Mueller, S.: MetaSense: integrating sensing capabilities into mechanical metamaterial. In: Proceedings of UIST '21. ACM, pp. 1063–1073 (2021)
7. Hašan, M., Fuchs, M., Matusik, W., Pfister, H., Rusinkiewicz, S.: Physical reproduction of materials with specified subsurface scattering, ACM Trans. Graph. (2010)
8. Holman, D., Vertegaal, R.: Organic user interfaces: designing computers in any way, shape, or form. Commun. ACM **51**(6), 48–55 (2008)

9. Ion, A., Frohnhofen, J., Wall, L., Kovacs, R., Alistar, M., Lindsay, J., Lopes, P., Chen, H.-T., Baudisch, P.: Metamaterial mechanisms. In: Proceedings of UIST '16. ACM, pp. 529–539 (2016)
10. Ion, A., Kovacs, R., Schneider, O.S., Lopes, P. Baudisch, P.: Metamaterial textures. In: Proceedings of the 2018 CHI Conference on Human Factors in Computing Systems. Association for Computing Machinery. Montreal QC, Canada, pp. 1–12 (2018)
11. Janbaz, S., Narooei, K., van Manen, T., Zadpoor, A.A.: Strain rate-dependent mechanical metamaterials. Sci. Adv. **6**(25), eaba0616 (2020). https://doi.org/10.1126/sciadv.aba0616
12. Kakehi, Y., Jo, K., Sato, K., Minamizawa, K., Nii, H., Kawakami, N., Naemura, T., Tachi, S.: ForceTile: tabletop tangible interface with vision-based force distribution sensing. In: ACM SIGGRAPH,: New Tech Demos, vol. 17, pp. 1–1 (2008)
13. Kennedy, P.M., Inglis, J.T.: Distribution and behaviour of glabrous cutaneous receptors in the human foot sole. J. Physiol. (2002). https://doi.org/10.1113/jphysiol.2001.013087
14. Kladovasilakis, N., Tsongas, K., Karalekas, D., Tzetzis, D.: Architected materials for additive manufacturing: a comprehensive review. Materials **15**(17), 5919 (2022). https://doi.org/10.3390/ma15175919
15. Kuroki, S., Sawayama, M., Nishida, S.: The roles of lower—and higher-order surface statistics in tactile texture perception. J. Neurophysiol. **126**(1), 95–111 (2021). https://doi.org/10.1152/jn.00577.2020
16. Lan, Y., Dong, Y., Pellacini, F., Tong, X.: Bi-scale appearance fabrication, ACM Trans. Graph. (2013)
17. Matusik, W., Ajdin, B., Gu, J., Lawrence, J., Lensch, H., Pellacini, F., Rusinkiewicz, S.: Printing spatially-varying reflectance. ACM Trans. Graph. (2009)
18. Miyoshi, M., Punpongsanon, P., Iwai, D., Sato, K.: SoftPrint: investigating haptic softness perception of 3D printed soft object in FDM 3D printers. J. Imaging Sci. Technol. (2021). https://doi.org/10.2352/J.ImagingSci.Technol.2021.65.4.040406
19. Morita, J., Ando, Y., Komatsu, S., Matsumura, K., Okazaki, T., Asano, Y., Nakatani, M., Tanaka, H.: Mechanical properties and reliability of parametrically designed architected materials using urethane elastomers. Polymers (2021). https://doi.org/10.3390/polym13050842
20. Nakamaru, S., Nakayama, R., Niiyama, R., Kakehi, Y.: FoamSense: design of three dimensional soft sensors with porous materials. In: Proceedings of UIST '17. ACM, pp. 437–447 (2017)
21. Pelanconi, M., Ortona, A.: Nature-inspired, ultra-lightweight structures with gyroid cores produced by additive manufacturing and reinforced by unidirectional carbon fiber ribs. Materials (2019). https://doi.org/10.3390/ma12244134
22. Sakura, R., Han, C., Lyu, Y., Watanabe, K., Yamamura, R., Kakehi, Y.: LattiSense: A 3D-printable resistive deformation sensor with lattice structures. In: Proceedings of SCF '23, ACM, vol. 2, pp. 1–14 (2023)
23. Sakurai, K., Dobashi, Y., Iwasaki, K., Nishita T.: Fabricating reflectors for displaying multiple images, ACM Trans. Graph. (2018)
24. Sato, M., Poupyrev, I., Harrison, C.: Touché: enhancing touch interaction on humans, screens, liquids, and everyday objects. In: Proceedings of CHI '12. ACM, pp. 483–492 (2012)
25. Shakouri, E., Mossayebi, A., Manafi, B.: Designing and fabricating a novel medical insole with universal fluid layer with auto-customizability. In: Proceedings of the Institution of Mechanical Engineers, Part H: Journal of Engineering in Medicine (2020). https://doi.org/10.1177/0954411920926345
26. Shan, S., Kang, S.H., Raney, J.R., Wang, P., Fang, L., Candido, F., Lewis, J.A., Bertoldi, K.: Multistable architected materials for trapping elastic strain energy. Adv. Mater. (2015). https://doi.org/10.1002/adma.201501708
27. Sugiura, Y., Kakehi, G., Withana, A., Lee, C., Sakamoto, D., Sugimoto, M., Inami, M., Igarashi, T.: Detecting shape deformation of soft objects using directional photoreflectivity measurement. In: Proceedings of UIST '11. ACM, pp. 509–516 (2011)
28. Torres, C., Campbell, T., Kumar, N., Paulos, Eric.: HapticPrint: designing feel aesthetics for digital fabrication. In: Proceedings of the 28th Annual ACM Symposium on User Interface

Software and Technology (UIST '15). Association for Computing Machinery. New York, NY, USA, pp. 583–591 (2015)
29. Tymms, C., Zorin, D., Gardner, E.P.: Tactile perception of the roughness of 3D-printed textures. J. Neurophysiol. (2018). https://doi.org/10.1152/jn.00564.2017
30. Tymms, C., Gardner, E.P., Zorin, D.: A quantitative perceptual model for tactile roughness. ACM Trans. Graph. (2018). https://doi.org/10.1145/3186267
31. Tymms, C., Zorin, D., Gardner, E.P.: Tactile perception of the roughness of 3D-printed textures. J. Neurophysiol. **119**(3), 862–876 (2018). https://doi.org/10.1152/jn.00564.2017
32. Uesaki, R., Okazaki, T., Asano, Y., Ueda, Y., Komatsu, S., Ando, Y., Morita, J., Nakatani, M., Tanaka, H.: Haptic feedback provided by 3D printed shoe insoles. IEEE World Haptics Conference (WHC), Work in Progress, WIP.E1.1. Delft, Netherlands (2023)
33. Viseux, F.J.F.: The sensory role of the sole of the foot: Review and update on clinical perspectives. Neurophysiol. Clin. (2020). https://doi.org/10.1016/j.neucli.2019.12.003
34. Watanabe, K., Yamamura, R., Kakehi, Y.: Foamin: a deformable sensor for multimodal inputs based on conductive foam with a single wire. In: Extended Abstracts of CHI EA '21. ACM, vol. 189, pp. 1–4 (2021)
35. Xu, C., He, H., Hauser, S.C., Gerling, G.J.: Tactile exploration strategies with natural compliant objects elicit virtual stiffness cues. IEEE Trans. Haptics **13**(1), 4–10 (2020). https://doi.org/10.1109/TOH.2019.2959767
36. Zeng, J., Deng, H., Zhu,, Y., Wessely, M., Kilian, A., Mueller, S.: Lenticular objects:3d printed objects with lenticular lens surfaces that can change their appearance depending on the viewpoint. In: ACM Symposium on User Interface Software and Technology (UIST '21), pp. 1184–1196 (2021)

Chapter 14
Shitsukan in Industrial Engineering

Takahiko Horiuchi and Maki Sakamoto

Abstract This chapter explores the integration of Shitsukan into industrial engineering, highlighting its significance in product development, user experience, and manufacturing optimization. We review our collaborative research with industries and offer practical insights and methods for implementing Shitsukan-based design. At first, three major industrial applications are presented: halftone image quality enhancement for the printing industry, perceptual modeling in leather design, and star field reproduction in visual entertainment. Each case exemplifies how perceptual qualities influence industrial value and consumer satisfaction. We then expand on practical implementations, such as the quantification of onomatopoeia and the development of the Kansei Material Platform. These initiatives bridge academia and industry, enabling the creation of emotionally resonant products through systematic Shitsukan modeling. This chapter underscores the emerging role of perceptual engineering in fostering innovation and enhancing the value of industrial design.

Keywords Industrial application · Kansei engineering · Onomatopoeia · Material perception · Sensory impression

14.1 Introduction

Industrial engineering, a discipline aimed at optimizing production and service systems, began to spread primarily in the United States around 1910. Specifically, it involves comprehensively adjusting various elements, such as the efficient use of resources, human–machine interfaces, workflow, quality control, time management, and cost reduction, to improve productivity in companies and factories. However, what does Shitsukan entail in industrial engineering? In the context of optimization of

T. Horiuchi (✉)
Chiba University, Inage-Ku, Chiba, Japan
e-mail: horiuchi@faculty.chiba-u.jp

M. Sakamoto
The University of Electro-Communications, Chofu, Tokyo, Japan
e-mail: maki.sakamoto@uec.ac.jp

S. Nishida and K. Nishino (eds.), *Shitsukan—Understanding and Manipulating Material and Quality Perception*, https://doi.org/10.1007/978-981-95-4762-3_14

the manufacturing process, this could mean that Shitsukan should be managed during the production process of physical and sensory characteristics. Shitsukan, encompassing attributes such as glossiness, texture, transparency, and emotional response, contributes significantly to product appeal and user satisfaction. With globalization intensifying market competition, industries must transcend mere functionality and cost-effectiveness, shifting toward emotionally engaging design.

This chapter investigates how Shitsukan can be effectively utilized in industrial contexts. It is structured into two main sections: Sect. 14.2, authored by Takahiko Horiuchi, introduces three collaborative studies between academia and industry that exemplify the practical deployment of Shitsukan technologies. Section 14.3, authored by Maki Sakamoto, details practical implementations including the quantification of onomatopoeia and the development of platforms to support Shitsukan-based material design.

Section 14.2 begins with the printing industry, where conventional digital halftoning techniques often fail to retain textural fidelity. Horiuchi and colleagues developed a texture-aware error diffusion algorithm that improves halftone image quality by incorporating perceptual texture information into the halftoning process. This method successfully reproduces nuanced textures such as gloss and roughness, enhancing the visual richness of printed materials and reducing common artifacts like contouring. Additionally, a glossiness index tailored for halftone color images was proposed, overcoming the limitations of traditional image quality metrics and enabling more accurate assessments of perceived gloss.

The second application focuses on the leather design industry, where Shitsukan plays a vital role in distinguishing between genuine and artificial leather. Through collaboration with an optical equipment manufacturer, the team modeled Shitsukan perception based on impressions such as authenticity, luxury, and quaintness. By collecting a broad set of sensory descriptors and conducting statistical analyses, the authors derived a perceptual model that quantitatively links visual features of leather with emotional impressions. This model empowers designers for crafting artificial leather with perceptual qualities comparable to genuine materials, aligning product design with user expectations and ethical considerations.

The third application addresses the reproduction of starry skies in planetarium systems. As urbanization has diminished opportunities to view natural star fields, accurate and emotionally impactful representations have become increasingly valuable. Horiuchi's team collaborated with a planetarium manufacturer to examine how parameters like luminance, size, and density influence perceptions of the stars' faithfulness, preference, and depth. The psychophysical experiments led to the identification of optimal reproduction strategies for the Milky Way, enhancing the immersive experience in educational and entertainment settings.

Section 14.3 transitions to a broader view of Shitsukan in practice. It discusses the growing importance of onomatopoeia in product communication and the challenge of quantifying these intuitive yet ambiguous expressions. By developing a patented system that links onomatopoeic words with sensory scales, Sakamoto enabled industries to map product impressions in a perceptual space. This technology has been adopted in collaborative projects with various sectors, from electronics to cosmetics.

Furthermore, Sakamoto introduced the Kansei Material Platform, a university startup that extends academic insights into industrial application. The platform quantifies Shitsukan and Kansei values of materials, supporting data-driven product design. By incorporating linguistic, perceptual, and physical data, it facilitates intuitive yet precise material selection, bridging the gap between designer intention and user experience.

Through these examples, this chapter underscores the transformative potential of Shitsukan research in industrial engineering. As consumer preferences evolve, the ability to model and manipulate sensory impressions will become a key differentiator in global markets.

14.2 Industrial Applications

14.2.1 Printing Industry

Texture-Aware Error Diffusion Algorithm

Digital halftoning is an important method for representing grayscale images by using only black and white tones [1]. Error diffusion (ED) belongs to a class of frequency-modulated halftoning techniques [2]. It is widely used because it can retain the details of an image while using a limited number of gray levels to simulate a continuous-tone image. A detailed description and analysis of this algorithm can be found in [2]. Multitoning is a halftoning method that adopts more than two tone levels to improve the similarity between the original and halftone images. The simplest method involves increasing the number of threshold values during the ED process. Recently, the representation of the texture of an image, which includes properties such as glossiness, transparency, and roughness, has become important for reproducing images on display devices. However, the texture of objects is often lost in images reproduced using conventional ED algorithms based on the signal processing theory, and there has been limited discussion regarding the reproduction of texture in printing.

We developed a texture-aware ED algorithm for the industry to improve the quality of texture in multilevel halftone images [3]. In principle, a typical ED algorithm distributes errors regardless of the presence of the pixel of interest in the textured portion. In our texture-aware ED algorithm, the original image is pre-processed to extract textural information. This enables the ED to preserve the texture information that richly captures the Shitsukan. During the execution of the ED algorithm, we quantify how much each pixel carries texture information. To ensure that the error does not spread to pixels belonging to strong texture, we redesigned the structure of the classical ED. Figure 1a and b shows the original image and detected texture information, respectively.

We verified the physical performance of the method by quantizing continuous-tone test images into halftone images and by comparing the results with those of the conventional methods in [2, 4]. Figure 14.2 presents an example of quantized images

(a) (b)

Fig. 14.1 Our texture-aware halftoning method [3] first quantifies the texture information (right) in the image (left)

that illustrate the effect of the algorithm. Figure 14.2a shows a continuous image. Figure 14.2b, c, and d shows the halftone image after halftoning using our algorithm and the conventional methods proposed in [2, 4], respectively. By comparing the Halftone results, we can observe that our algorithm can generate halftone images with good textures. We also applied our method to color-packaging images from websites and confirmed its effectiveness. We also used the current raster image processor (RIP) to print a halftone image and compared it with our algorithm-printing method. Consequently, we produced texture-aware images and reduced the contouring artifacts in the transition region. Our method produces printed images with better texture presentation.

Glossiness Index

Accurate and objective evaluation of halftones remains challenging. The "goodness" of a halftone should go beyond mere sharpness and extend to how well it captures the Shitsukan of the context. We focus on the perceptual gloss as a key Shitsukan characteristic that needs to be reproduced in halftone images. Most image glossiness assessment studies are device-based, that is, they are based on photometer measurements. The structural similarity (SSIM) index [5] is a standard index in the image processing field. Studies in [6–8] used multiple strategies for image quality assessment (IQA). Although these methods simulate the human visual system (HVS) as much as possible, they cannot be directly applied to halftone images.

To the best of our knowledge, the earliest halftone assessment index was proposed by Näsänen [9]. Näsänen's method uses an exponential function for the luminance component to evaluate a dithering halftone image. Subsequently, Lee et al. proposed a new exponential function for evaluating halftone color images [10]. To consider visual color characteristics, they performed a new function for each luminance: red-green and blue-yellow components. Color SSIM was then applied to the reference and distorted images for the localized structural difference assessment. The index color structural similarity (CSIM) [10] is useful for non-gloss images as it captures rich structural information as in SSIM. If there is an object, such as a mirror, the single-strategy index functions well on all parts of the glossy object that reflect the

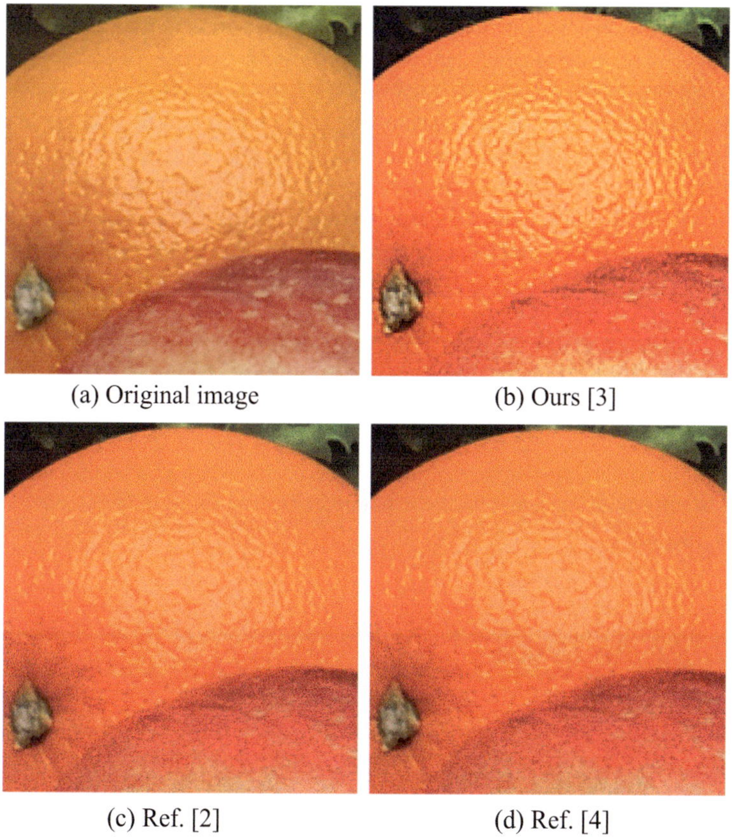

Fig. 14.2 Our halftoning method [3] preserves the texture information of the original image **a** well **b** compared with past methods (**c**, **d**) leading to richer Shitsukan of the scene **a** original image **b** ours [3]. **c** Ref. [2] **d** Ref. [4]

surrounding environment. However, for glossy objects, the proposed methods would fail because glossy parts contain limited structural information.

To objectively realize the correct assessment of an image containing glossy and nonglossy parts, a single assessment strategy cannot meet the demand. In contrast to single-strategy image assessment methods, the methods in [6–8] used a variety of strategies to closely simulate the HVS for image assessment. Inspired by these strategies, we developed an image glossiness index for halftone color images based on structure and appearance distortion [11].

We used a contrast sensitivity function to account for the mechanism of halftone images viewed by the human eye. We estimated the structural distortion for the first strategy using local luminance and contrast masking, whereas local statistical changes in the spatial frequency components for skewness and standard deviation were used to estimate the appearance distortion for the second strategy. The experimental results showed that these two mixed-distortion measurement strategies performed well and were consistent with the subjective ratings of glossiness in the halftone color images. Figure 14.3 shows scatter plots of the signal-to-noise ratio (PSNR), CSIM, the most apparent distortion (MAD) method [6], and the proposed image glossiness metric for 100 images. In all the graphs, each point represents a test image. In Fig. 14.3, the vertical axis represents the subjective ratings of the perceived distortions, and the horizontal axis represents the metrics. The values on each axis range from 0 to 1, with 0 representing poor reproduction and 1 representing the most similar to the original image before halftoning. Thus, if the subjective and index ratings are similar, they will be plotted on a 45° line. To distinguish the effects of the metrics on glossy and nonglossy images, we sorted the subjective data in descending order, and the objective data were sorted accordingly. The first 50 images of the arranged data were classified as nonglossy, and the rest were classified as glossy. The non-glossy images are represented by red points and the glossy ones are represented by blue points. As shown in Fig. 14.3, the proposed index evaluated glossiness more correctly than the other indices. Comparable results were obtained for other halftone methods.

14.2.2 Leather Design

Shitsukan design is essential for increasing the attractiveness of products, which is why product development companies have been qualitatively designing the Shitsukan of a product. To efficiently design Shitsukan, it is important to quantify it. Studies have reported methods for quantifying the perceived impression of materials in terms of the appearance and touch in relation to Shitsukan.

Here, we focus on the visual Shitsukan of leather products. While product designers want to use genuine leather for products such as car interiors and clothing due to their superior quality, the high costs and concerns relating to animal rights compel them to use artificial leather as an alternative. Artificial leather is made of either polyurethane or vinyl chloride. In addition, it is low maintenance, and therefore it is widely used. Furthermore, artificial and genuine leathers use different raw materials and processing methods, which can give a variety of impressions and Shitsukan.

Identifying the Shitsukan perception flow of leather can help in developing artificial leather that is very similar to genuine leather. We specifically aimed at identifying and quantifying representative Shitsukan characteristics of leather perception. We hypothesized that we perceive the components from the identified common representative impressions. Therefore, we focused on some important components of the Shitsukan of leather used in various products. As mentioned above, we focused on perceptual "authenticity" (not a physical classification of genuine and artificial leather) because of the presence of genuine and artificial leathers. We also focused

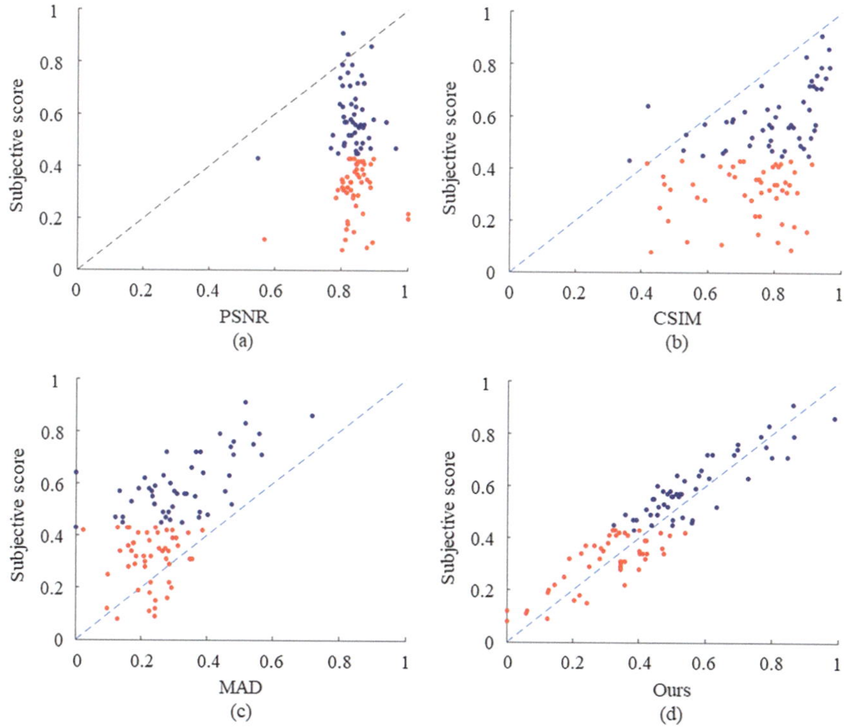

Fig. 14.3 We proposed a novel evaluation metric of glossiness in halftone images. Scatter plots of the PSNR, CSIM, MAD, and proposed metric for test samples halftoned by [3]. **a** PSNR, **b** CSIM, **c** MAD, and **d** Ours. The plot in **d** is closest to the 45° line, confirming that our glossiness index adequately reflects subjective evaluation

on perceptual "luxury" (not the actual price). Finally, consumers prefer leather products whose appearance changes over time. Therefore, we focused on perceptual "quaintness" (not physical old but vintage-like appearance).

The process from stimuli to perception is not a single step, but multiple steps as follows: (1) stimulus, (2) sensory, and (3) perception. Based on these studies, we designed a Shitsukan perception model. In the model, the "Stimulus" step corresponds to the image properties obtained from the measurement experiments. Additionally, the "Sensory" step corresponds to the representative impressions we mainly perceived from leather. The impressions were extracted in several subjective experiments. Finally, the "Perception" step is responsible for recognition based on the information from the previous steps, that is, "authenticity," "luxury," and "quaintness." This model can help designers understand the impression of objects and determine properties that can be controlled to improve Shitsukan.

Related studies that express the perception mechanism using a multi-step model have been reported [12, 13]. However, they prepared, in advance, impression words of the intermediate step. It is possible that there is a low correlation between each step as it is unclear whether the prepared words are appropriate for the Shitsukan of the object. Most of these studies also only apply a single regression analysis for the words included in each step. However, human perception is complex, and some words or stimuli in the previous step become integrated as a single word in the next step. We instead used multiple regression analysis to account for the complex human perception. Additionally, previous studies have reported a method for obtaining words related to perception through subjective evaluation experiments. Some studies [14, 15] obtained words from participants in a subjective experiment and selected them according to their frequency and order. However, this method may not account for words with low frequencies, such as onomatopoeias, despite being important in perception. To address complex human perceptions, such as impressions and Shitsukan, we need more words that express perceptions. We collected impression words from the participants and extracted representative impressions that were perceived from leather in several subjective evaluation experiments. A high correlation can therefore be expected between steps.

We introduced image measurement experiments to obtain physical and psychophysical properties in [16]. Here, we describe the procedure and results of the subjective evaluation experiment conducted to identify the representative impressions that were perceived from the leather from which we obtain Shitsukan scores. We confirmed the correlation between the properties, impressions, and Shitsukan using the proposed model. We confirmed the accuracy of the proposed model through a verification experiment.

Figure 14.4 shows the proposed model using subjective impressions, Shitsukan, and measured leather properties. Image properties were statistically obtained to estimate the representative impressions. Additionally, representative impressions were determined based on the results of factor analysis. As a result, the three components of Shitsukan were calculated using simple equations that used only "surface shape" and "impression of stateliness." These representative impressions in this study may not have been estimated by conventional methods in which the adjectives are prepared in advance, depending on the set of prepared words. Because the words used for perception and sensory perception may differ depending on various factors, such as the age and sex of the participants, we preferred to collect words from diverse participants. We also collected a wide range of words, which differs from previous studies that performed subsequent experiments using duplicate words. We determined that more precise results can be obtained by integrating words through continuous subjective experiments with a wide range of word sets.

The novel findings from our study on this leather Shitsukan perception are summarized as follows: (1) the representative impressions perceived from leather were "surface shape" and "impression of stateliness." According to the related image properties, "surface shape" was related to specular L* and large grains under the condition of diffuse reflection. On the other hand, "impression of stateliness" was related to surface irregularities and kurtosis values under the condition of diffuse reflection. (2) Using only "surface shape" and "impression of stateliness," we could express the three components of Shitsukan using the equations. Their R-squared values were 0.80, 0.65, and 0.62, respectively. (3) The three components of Shitsukan could

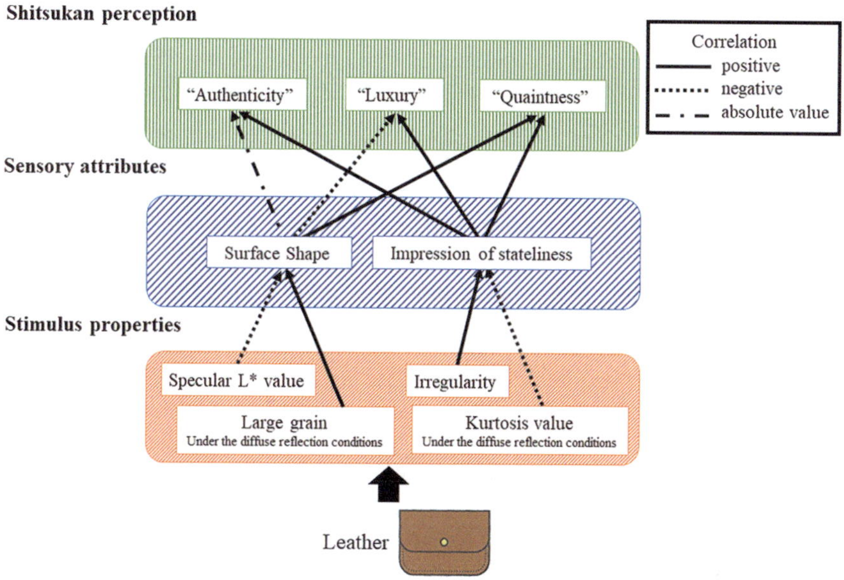

Fig. 14.4 Constructed model using subjective impressions, Shitsukan, and measured leather properties. The representative impressions perceived from leather were "surface shape" and "impression of stateliness." "Surface shape" was related to specular L* and large grains under the condition of diffuse reflection. "Impression of stateliness" was related to surface irregularities and kurtosis values under the condition of diffuse reflection

be identified by the difference in the plus or minus signs of "surface shape" and "impression of stateliness." We also confirmed the robustness of the models through verification experiments.

14.2.3 Visual Entertainment

A sky full of stars has become precious and rare, following the evolution of lighting technology to maintain a comfortable living environment at night. A bright night causes light pollution, and the visible stars in the night sky are limited to bright stars such as planets and first-magnitude stars. In this study, we focused on the most common milky ways. The Milky Way comprises a mass of innumerable stars in the universe. The light of each star is weaker than that of bright stars, such as planets and first-magnitude stars, which can be observed in residential areas. However, they can be viewed as thin clouds in the night sky because of the accumulation of dark stars. In particular, the areas around Scorpius and Sagittarius, where many stars gather, were more observable than in other areas. Therefore, under suitable conditions (extremely dark nights without light pollution and moonlight, no clouds, etc.), it is easier to see the Milky Way in the summer season. However, in urban areas, opportunities to observe the Milky Way are rare because of the bright nighttime skies. To address this issue, the planetarium industry developed an image reproduction system to artificially reproduce starry skies. A planetarium, including the Milky Way, provides a sky full of stars. In fields, such as astronomy, education, and entertainment, it has played an important role in communicating the majority of the universal space.

Studies have reported methods for observing and acquiring images of starlit skies. The use of computer graphics (CG) reproduction methods to generate displays has also been reported. However, discussion on appropriate methods for reproducing star images and assessing such methods in a planetarium that imitates a starry sky has been limited. Therefore, we investigated the relationship between the physical representation factors in a planetarium as well as the perceptual assessment of faithfulness, and preference for represented stars by conducting a psychometric experiment in a real dome with a planetarium [17, 18]. In those studies, the target stars in the experiments were restricted to bright stars with a small magnitude (rating from zero to seven) without darker stars (such as the Milky Way and nebulas), to investigate the effects of color, brightness, and size reproduction in the optical projector of the planetarium. However, to mimic a star field and represent a starry sky more faithfully, reproducing darker stars such as the Milky Way is essential for a planetarium. Moreover, a rendering technique for the Milky Way that considers human perception has not been reported yet in the field of imaging science and technology.

In [19], we investigated the relationship between the reproduction method and assessment of the Milky Way to represent a starry sky by conducting a psychometric experiment using a planetarium with human observers. In our experiment, we analyzed the factors that influence the reproduction of a starry sky with the Milky Way and nebulas by evaluating the three indices (faithfulness, preference, and depth feeling) of the images reproduced in planetarium projections by changing each of the three parameters (luminance, size, and density) of individual stars. Two types of projection systems produce star images in a planetarium: optical and digital. Because of the resolution and tone limitations of the digital projector, it is difficult for the digital system to reproduce a fine milky image with sufficient resolution to evaluate image faithfulness. Therefore, in our experiment, we used a planetarium incorporating an optical system with star plates to reproduce fixed stars, nebulas, and the Milky Way, as shown in Fig. 14.5. Stars were projected onto the dome screen by passing light through star plates installed on a projector.

We selected stars around Scorpius (1/32 of the entire night sky) as experimental stimuli to evaluate star reproduction with the Milky Way because the area around Scorpius has a deeper Milky Way than the other areas. For a faithful reproduction of a starry sky, including the Milky Way, we considered astrophysical factors in a real star observation environment, such as the brightness of the surrounding environment with the effect of light pollution and gradation depending on the zenith angle. Star twinkling is caused by atmospheric extinctions. However, we excluded external factors such as atmospheric extinction in this experiment and determined that it would be preferable to display images of star images with a certain brightness. This was performed because twinkling can produce excessive complexity and uncertainty for observation because of its attractiveness. For similar reasons, the influence

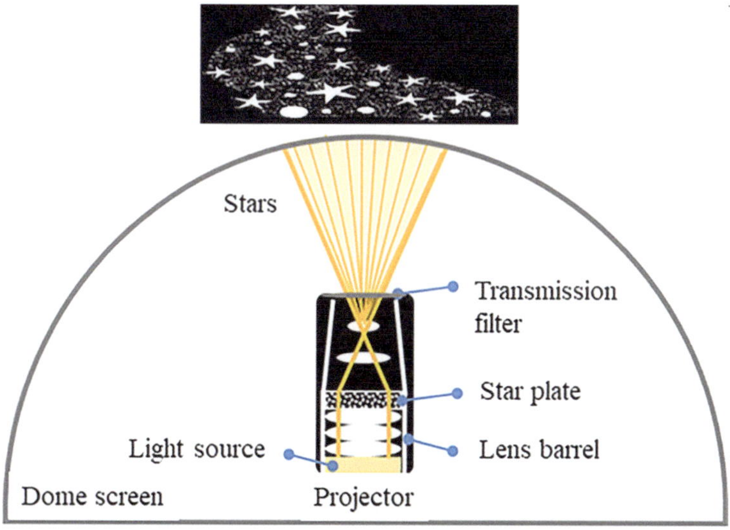

Fig. 14.5 Construction of the optical planetarium. The luminance of the stars was adjusted by inserting transmission filters in front of the light sources. The star size and density were controlled by the hole diameter and number of stars in the star plates

of the solar system (zodiacal light) on the star's perception of air and air light from the Earth's atmosphere (light pollution) must be prevented. The experiments were conducted in complete darkness to reproduce scotopic vision, which is typical of a general planetarium environment.

We prepared 12 experimental patterns by varying the luminance, size, and density relative to the entire star image. Table 14.1 lists the projection patterns used as experimental stimuli. As previously explained, we assumed that the luminance, size, and density of a star in the Milky Way would influence the evaluation of the star image reproduced in a planetarium. Therefore, we determined a standard pattern (Std). This pattern reflects the perceptual faithfulness of the starry sky. Furthermore, for the standard pattern, we prepared additional patterns in which an individual or combined parameter was changed.

The significance of the answered evaluations for each pattern was verified using the Welch's t-test after excluding the outlier data using the Smirnoff–Grubbs test and verifying the distribution equality of evaluations using an F-test. Here, we assumed the normality of the evaluated data. These tests were conducted separately for all 66 pattern combinations ($12 \times 11/2$) for each evaluation index (faithfulness, preference, and feelings of depth).

The projection patterns with the highest rating were Std-$L1$ and S–$L1$ for faithfulness, Std for preference, and Std for feeling depth. We observed a rating tendency for each pattern for all three indices. We focused on the luminance represented by the projected patterns and calculated the total luminance. We confirmed the trend from the peak (high rating) to the valley (low rating) along the luminance order for each

Table 14.1 List of experimental projection patterns to identify factors affecting star image reproduction

Pattern	Changed parameters from Std	Remarks for variable stimulus
Std	N/A	
Std-*L*1	Luminance	Pattern Std but half luminance
Std-*L*2	Luminance	Pattern Std but double luminance
S	Size	Pattern Std but half diameter
S–*L*1	Size and luminance	Pattern *S* but half luminance
S–*L*2	Size and luminance	Pattern *S* but double luminance
*D*1	Density	Pattern Std but 3/2 times density
*D*1–*L*1	Density and luminance	Pattern *D*1 but half luminance
*D*1–*L*2	Density and luminance	Pattern *D*1 but double luminance
*D*2	Density	Pattern Std but 2/3 times density
*D*2–*L*1	Density and luminance	Pattern *D*2 but half luminance
*D*2–*L*2	Density and luminance	Pattern *D*2 but double luminance

evaluation index. In the faithfulness evaluation, a broad peak from Std-*L*1 to S–L^2 and a valley with a brighter pattern, *D*1 existed. The results for the valley were nearly the same for the other two indices of preference and feeling of depth. However, the peak ranges tended to differ. There were two peaks for preference evaluation, and the peak range for the evaluation of the feeling of depth was slightly narrow (–*D*1–*L*1 to *D*2–*L*2). This result indicates that both luminance and other factors affect preference and depth evaluation.

So far, we have reviewed three collaborative studies between academia and industry that exemplify the practical deployment of Shitsukan technologies. Next, introduce practical implementations of Shitsukan in industrial engineering.

14.3 Practical Implementation

In various phases of the manufacturing process, Shitsukan is important. First, Shitsukan is directly linked to the final quality of the product. For example, the finish, appearance, and feel of a product's surface can greatly influence consumer satisfaction. Therefore, Shitsukan management is a critical part of quality control. In reality, Shitsukan can significantly affect a consumer's user experience (UX)—that is, the sensation and operational feel when using the product can greatly influence the user's overall experience. For instance, a good feel or a beautiful appearance can enhance the sense of use and increase user satisfaction. Consequently, in the manufacturing process, the aim is to pursue the Shitsukan that maximizes consumer satisfaction. However, to maximize the product's Shitsukan while maintaining efficient production, it is necessary to optimize the manufacturing process. This involves selecting materials that achieve the desired Shitsukan and optimizing processing techniques. Materials and processing methods directly affect the five senses, such as touch and sight, but Shitsukan also influences higher-level factors like brand image and emotional value. A product with a luxurious Shitsukan can itself become an element that enhances brand value.

Thus, Shitsukan is one of the most important factors in various aspects of industrial engineering. The industry aims to achieve these goals within the manufacturing process. For this, research and development become essential, which is challenging for the industry, as it is often pre-occupied with product production to meet consumer demands. Many companies seek joint research with universities and other research institutions. This section introduces examples of such joint research.

In particular, there are high expectations for patented technology that quantifies onomatopoeia. Onomatopoeia is a type of expression, frequently referred to as "sound-symbolic words," which involves the association between linguistic sounds and sensory experiences [20]. Japanese people use onomatopoeia to describe Shitsukan, such as "sara-sara" (smooth) for touch or "kira-kira" (sparkling) for appearance. It is also often used to describe food Shitsukan, like "saku-saku" (crispy) or "sukkiri" (refreshing), making it useful for expressing the Shitsukan of food and beverages. These expressions are very intuitive but ambiguous, making them difficult to quantify and incorporate into the manufacturing process. However, they are expressions often used by consumers when seeking Shitsukan and are also used among developers in the manufacturing field. Therefore, in our case study, a system that quantifies onomatopoeia was utilized in joint research with companies, which will be introduced in the second half of this section.

From 2015 to 2019, with support from a scientific research grant, the research project titled "Expression of Diverse Social Textures Based on the Correspondence between Physical, Perceptual, and Sensory Aspects" was promoted by our group. The aim was to build a Shitsukan database that links physical, perceptual, and sensory aspects, which is crucial for realizing products that emphasize Shitsukan. A prototype was created over five years, and afterward, a university startup was established to begin industrial application as a consortium under the name "Kansei Material Platform." This section also touches on this endeavor.

In May 2007, the Ministry of Economy, Trade, and Industry (METI) formulated the "Kansei Value Creation Initiative," proposing a new value axis from the perspective of "Kansei value." Kansei corresponds to the English words "sensibility" or "sensitivity." Based on this initiative, METI designated the fiscal years 2008–2010 as the "Kansei Value Creation Years" and launched various measures to realize Kansei value creation. A report from that time [21] summarized the statements made by then-Minister of Economy, Trade, and Industry Amari. In the past, Japan's economy grew by providing products with high performance, safety, and reliability at low prices. However, the conventional value axis (performance, reliability, price) is facing a new phase. Amid intensifying global competition, Japan needs to create new value, not only focusing on high performance and high quality. The keyword in this new value creation is "Kansei," and the "Kansei value" represents satisfaction and economic value realized through "Kansei."

Since the Kansei Value Creation Initiative was launched in 2007, there have been remarkable technological innovations centered around AI. Since 2012, AI-related companies in Europe and the US have rapidly grown by utilizing large-scale virtual data on the internet. In contrast, Japan's strategy focuses on real materials and the Kansei felt through the five senses, with Shitsukan being a crucial factor. Furthermore, against the backdrop of the newly evolved generative AI around 2022, Industrial engineering based on real physical data and Shitsukan and Kansei data must be advanced without delay. To contribute to this direction, academic research is essential, along with actual product development and collaboration with companies that possess physical data of materials. The following section introduces the benefits and challenges of such collaboration, based on a case study of university-industry joint research.

14.3.1 Industry-Academia Collaboration

When introducing the benefits and challenges of industry-academia collaboration, we emphasize that the companies introduced here are those with understanding of academic studies. Actually, there were many joint research projects where it was difficult to obtain the necessary data, making it challenging to publish papers. This is because physical data is so valuable that it is the lifeline for companies. The lessons learned from these experiences are applied in the approach to the "Kansei Material Platform," introduced in the next section.

First, in the process of forming a partnership with a company, it is important to apply for a patent through university, and actively use opportunities to present the university's intellectual property and new technologies. For example, the "System for Quantifying the Sensory Impressions Represented by Onomatopoeia" was patented before the research paper was published. As shown in Fig. 14.6, although it is a simple system that quantifies onomatopoeia into multiple kansei/Shitsukan-related scales, it had a significant impact on industries where kansei/Shitsukan is important, leading to joint research and patent licenses with a wide range of companies.

After applying for the patent, a paper was published in an academic journal, and it received the Best Paper Award from the Japanese Society for Artificial Intelligence [21]. The paper, which focused on Shitsukan, particularly haptics, and specifically highlighted its value, was published in IEEE Transactions on Haptics [22].

During the construction of this system, a vast amount of data was collected from subjects regarding their sensory impressions associated with various onomatopoeias. This data was then analyzed using Quantification Theory Type I, a statistical method that allows for numerical analysis of how each phonetic element affects the impression of an onomatopoeia. For example, the impression of the onomatopoeia "Fuwa-Fuwa" (fluffy) is calculated as follows. "Fuwa-Fuwa" is a repetition of "fuwa," where the first syllable is "*ha*" + "*u*," and the second syllable is "*wa*" + "*a*." Therefore, the impression for the evaluation item "hard-soft" is calculated as $\hat{Y} = X_1$ (1st syllable: consonant "*ha*") + X_2 (1st syllable: no voiced sound or semi-voiced sound) + X_3

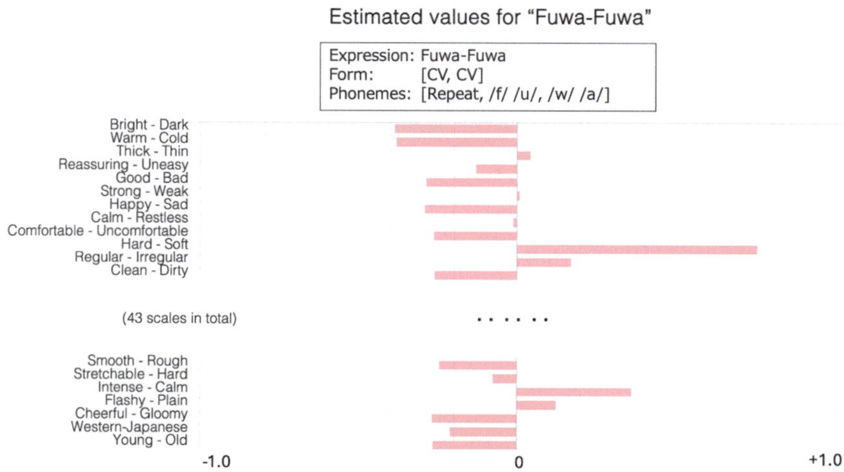

Fig. 14.6 System output of "Fuwa-Fuwa." From the system output, it can be seen that Fuwa-Fuwa represents a texture that is extremely soft, with a bright and gentle impression

(1st syllable: no contracted sound) + X_4 (1st syllable: vowel "*u*") + X_5 (1st syllable: no small vowel) + X_6 (1st syllable: no ending) + X_7 (2nd syllable: consonant "*wa*") + X_8 (2nd syllable: no voiced sound or semi-voiced sound) + X$_9$ (2nd syllable: no contracted sound) + X_{10} (2nd syllable: vowel "*a*") + X_{11} (2nd syllable: no small vowel) + X_{12} (2nd syllable: no ending) + X_{13} (repetition) + constant term = 0.29 + 0.14 + 0.01 + 0.55 + (− 0.02) + (− 0.08) + 0.71 + 0.12 + (− 0.07) + 0.07 + (− 0.02) + (− 0.15) + 0.23 + 4.43 = 6.21.

This predicted impression value is calculated based on impression evaluation values on a scale of 1–7 (with 7 being the highest softness). Therefore, a predicted value of 6.21 indicates a strong impression of softness on the "hard-soft" evaluation scale. When compared to the actual average impression evaluation value of 6.54 given by subjects for the "Fuwa-Fuwa" impression, it is clear that the system's predicted value is close to the actual value. In other words, by investigating the categorical quantity values of each phonetic characteristic that influences the impression of an onomatopoeia, it is possible to determine the impression evaluation value of any onomatopoeia on a specified Shitsukan or sensory scale.

From an academic perspective, we initially recognized only the advantage of being able to quantify the meanings of ambiguous words like onomatopoeia in multiple dimensions. This could potentially eliminate the hassle of the Semantic Differential (SD) method, which requires a lot of responses. However, after hearing from companies that struggled with handling onomatopoeia in product development, we realized that quantifying onomatopoeia holds significant value. This experience gave us the opportunity to learn about the challenges faced in the industry and made us feel that engineering research could have practical value beyond mere theoretical exercises.

The first case study of joint research with a company that we will introduce is a success story that resulted in research being published in an international journal [23] and was also featured on a television program.

Many products such as electronic appliances are made of imitation metals, which are lighter in weight and lower in cost than real metals. However, imitation metals sometimes look and feel cheap. This study proposes that differences in onomatopoeias associated with imitation and real metals can be used in metal Shitsukan design to make imitation materials look and feel like real materials. In this study, we conducted psychological experiments where participants were asked to observe a pair of imitation and real materials without touching them and respond with onomatopoeic words that they felt were associated with them. Participants used significantly more onomatopoeic words for real materials than for imitation materials. Furthermore, we analyzed onomatopoeia obtained for both real metals and imitation metals using the system that quantifies the phonological information of onomatopoeia. The comparison of the onomatopoeia evoked by real metals and those evoked by imitation metals revealed differences in their Shitsukan feelings.

An application example of the system that quantifies onomatopoeia, which has garnered interest from many companies, involved visualizing onomatopoeia on a two-dimensional map, allowing products with the Shitsukan represented by the onomatopoeia to be visualized on the same map. Although the joint research results themselves could not be published in the paper, the ability to quantify onomatopoeia allowed for the principal component analysis of onomatopoeic data and the visualization of this data on a two-dimensional map. This visualization made it possible to position materials based on the degree to which certain onomatopoeic expressions were evoked, allowing customers to clearly see the subtle Shitsukan differences between materials. Many companies recognized the benefits of this approach, leading to joint research with a wide range of industries, including synthetic resin manufacturers, cosmetic brand owners, automotive manufacturers, and food and beverage companies. The specific procedures for quantifying onomatopoeia and positioning materials are detailed in [22].

The process of visualizing onomatopoeias and their associated materials includes firstly collecting onomatopeias frequently used for expressing Shitsukan, and secondly inputting all words into our system to obtain ratings of 26 Shitsukan-related adjective scales for the words. We apply principal component analysis to the outputs of the system, and generate a distribution diagram of the words (see Fig. 14.7 for an example of the diagram). The distribution diagram is a word-based visualization of how the tactile sensation is categorized in the Japanese language. The space could be changed depending on the difference in materials used.

The distribution diagram (word-based visualization) can be used to visualize the relationships among materials. The materials can be placed on the diagram by using the connections between how they are felt with the onomatopoeias. The way in which the onomatopoeias are spatially distributed on the diagram guides people to locate materials precisely and intuitively. People can locate materials directly on the words, or between words referring to impressions of the words. After locating

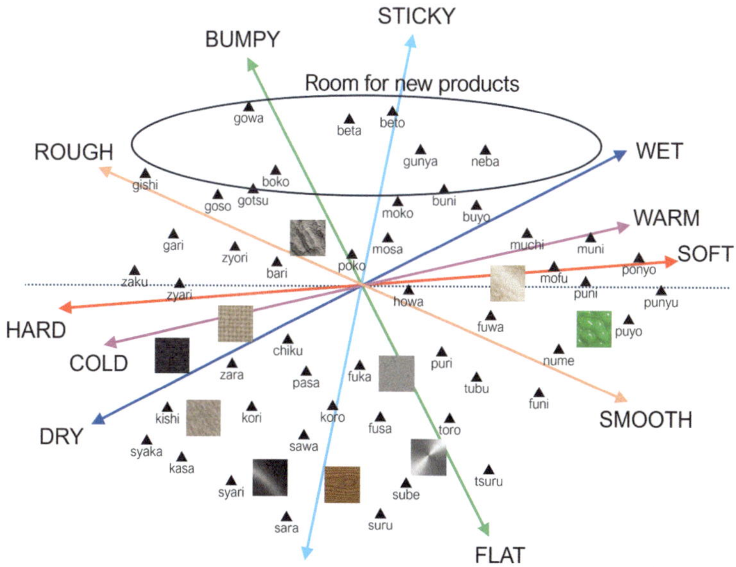

Fig. 14.7 2-D diagram of materials located by referring to onomatopoeias. The category including "gori-gori," "goso-goso," and "gisi-gisi" and the category including "gunya-gunya," "beto-beto," and "beta-beta" are lacking corresponding materials

many materials on the diagram, we can easily grasp the relationships between the diagrammed materials.

For example, when you collect 10 tactile materials that have a wide range of Shitsukan, you can place materials on the diagram and see what kind of Shitsukan is lacking in the market. If your collection of 10 materials are placed as in Fig. 14.7, the diagram indicates that the category including "gori-gori," "goso-goso," and "gisi-gisi" and the category including "gunya-gunya," "beto-beto," and "beta-beta" are lacking corresponding materials. Based on these results, companies may notice the need to develop new materials for the lacking space.

This word-based visualization might be used for product design and communication between designers and customers in the field of product design. If a customer requests tactile feeling by indicating a location on the diagram, a designer can develop a new material/product referring to the location of the onomatopoeia, and/or an existing material/product located nearby on the diagram. If this kind of visualization is used for a specific product, such as cosmetics or fabrics, only one word collection is needed to make a new diagram suitable for the product. After collecting onomatopoeias that are used to express the product, the words are automatically converted into rating scores of 26 adjectives by our system, and a new word-based diagram can be constructed.

One of the challenges in writing papers about the process and outcomes of joint research was that we had to use dummy data because we were unable to obtain the actual physical properties or composition of the materials. This is understandable given the environment of a university research lab where research is conducted with students.

14.3.2 Kansei Material Platform

As we just saw in the previous subsection, there were limitations to what could be achieved through university-industry joint research in a laboratory setting, which led to the establishment of a university startup in 2018. As a company, it became possible to receive confidential information from customers with the responsibility to protect it in case of any information leaks. However, this also meant that publishing papers was generally not possible. This trade-off allowed for the development of a platform that could integrate Kansei value into manufacturing, as required by the Ministry of Economy, Trade, and Industry since 2007.

The prototype of this platform is based on the research outcomes of a project funded by the Grants-in-Aid for Scientific Research, conducted from the 2015 to 2019 academic years. In this project, we constructed Shitsukan database by exploring physical properties, material perceptions obtained by psychophysical experiments, affective evaluations described by language, which can be used as dataset for machine learning to build Shitsukan cognitive model or dataset for Shitsukan engineering. We also attempted to clarify the cognitive mechanisms of Shitsukan perception—that is, how we perceive Shitsukan from materials—and how it can be categorized into onomatopoeic or linguistic expressions by analyzing the relationships among physical properties, material perceptions, and subjective Shitsukan linguistic descriptions. Furthermore, we constructed a system which enables us to convert physical properties to onomatopoeia and vice versa. Finally, we contributed to the development of new materials by generating onomatopoeia appropriate for physical or perceptual properties or discovering new Shitsukan using onomatopoeia. The overview of this project is as shown in Fig. 14.8.

We expanded this academic project and applied it commercially through a university-based venture. One key consideration during this process was the distinction between the data collected under the Grants-in-Aid for Scientific Research and the data used in the commercialized platform.

This platform aims to explore, develop, and create innovations from subjective and ambiguous Kansei needs by quantifying the Kansei value that materials provide and objectively presenting it through quantitative technology. The platform is intended to contribute to solving the challenges of material selection and new material development based on vague concepts and Kansei needs for both material manufacturers and brand owners.

In industries such as automotive, housing, cosmetics, and food, there is a growing practice of creating products that go beyond the traditional evaluation criteria of functionality, reliability, and price by adding "Kansei" as a new added value that evokes empathy, emotion, and resonance. With the aim of improving the speed at which high-quality products that respect Japan's strength in detailed "Kansei" are

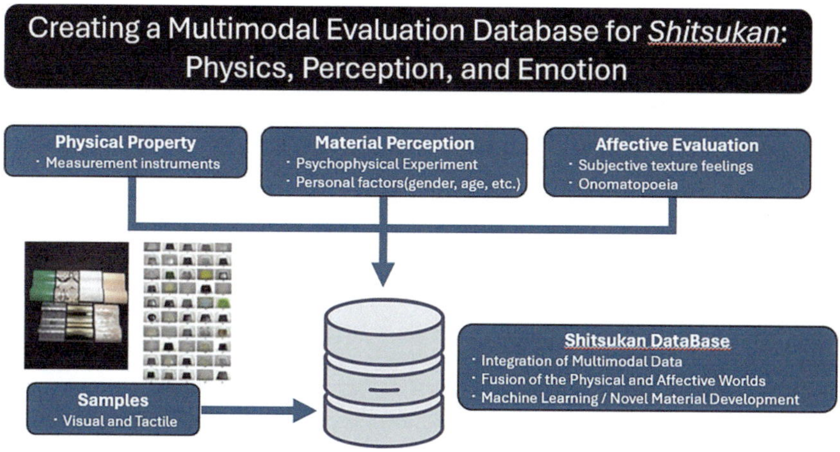

Fig. 14.8 Overview of the project to create a multimodal evaluation database for Shitsukan

brought to market, joint research based on the quantitative technology of Kansei value, as well as extensive interviews with many material manufacturers and brand owners, has led to the launch of the beta version of this platform.

The "Kansei Material Platform" is a cloud platform based on Kansei quantification technology aimed at solving the challenges of material selection and development for material manufacturers and brand owners. Material manufacturers can register their materials on this platform, allowing the Kansei value of the Shitsukan and feel provided by the materials to be quantified and visualized on a positioning map using AI. As a result, both brand owners searching for materials and material manufacturers providing materials can share Kansei value information on the platform, supporting the exploration of materials and the sharing of images based on ambiguous concepts and Kansei needs. In the beta version currently being offered, users can explore materials on the platform based on onomatopoeia that express the Shitsukan of the material, as well as view images that convey the Shitsukan of various materials to enhance design concepts. Materials registered by material manufacturers can be organized into a database on each company's management screen, with their Kansei of Shitsukan quantified. Additionally, the platform includes features that output consumer associations with product concept words by gender and age, as well as features that evaluate the impression given by the patterns and designs of materials.

It is uncertain whether this beta version of the platform will grow in the future, but its success will depend on its ability to become a highly convenient platform that supports product development to realize the desired Shitsukan while protecting the proprietary physical data that material manufacturers wish to safeguard. I am committed to diligently working toward completing one aspect of Industrial Engineering focused on Shitsukan research.

14.4 Conclusion

This chapter has illustrated how the concept of Shitsukan—the perceptual and emotional qualities of materials—can be effectively applied in industrial contexts through interdisciplinary collaboration. We introduced three concrete examples where industrial needs and perceptual science intersect: (1) halftoning techniques that enhance perceived texture in printed images, (2) perceptual modeling of leather appearance for material selection and design, and (3) starry sky reproduction technology that evokes emotional responses through accurate Shitsukan rendering. These studies, conducted collaboratively with industry partners, demonstrate how perceptual attributes can be systematically measured, modeled, and integrated into product development to improve quality, user satisfaction, and brand identity.

Furthermore, we presented practical applications beyond visual design, including onomatopoeia quantification that translates sensory impressions into measurable data, and the development of the Kansei Material Platform, a tool that supports material selection based on perceptual values. These initiatives exemplify how Shitsukan research not only enriches consumer experiences but also facilitates the creation of emotionally resonant products through data-driven design frameworks.

As industries increasingly seek differentiation through sensory appeal, the methodologies and case studies described in this chapter underscore the growing relevance of Shitsukan and Kansei engineering as strategic tools for innovation. By aligning perceptual science with industrial engineering, we can bridge the gap between subjective experience and objective design, fostering the next generation of emotionally intelligent products.

References

1. Ulichney, R.: Digital halftoning. MIT Press (1987)
2. Floyd, R.W., Steinberg, L.: An adaptive algorithm for spatial gray-scale. Proc. Soc. Inf. Disp. **17**, 75–77 (1976)
3. Li, D., Kiyotomo, T., Horiuchi, T.: Texture-aware error diffusion algorithm for multi-level digital halftoning. J. Imaging Sci. Technol. **64**, 050410-1-050410–9 (2020)
4. Shiau, J.-N., Fan, Z.: Set of easily implementable coefficients in error diffusion with reduced worm artifacts. In: Proceedings SPIE, p. 2658 (1996)
5. Wang, Z., Bovik, A.C., Sheikh, H.R., Simoncelli, E.P.: Image quality assessment: from error visibility to structural similarity. IEEE Trans. Image Process. **13**, 600–612 (2004)
6. Larson, E.C., Chandler, D.M.: Most apparent distortion: full-reference image quality assessment and the role of strategy. J. Electron. Imaging **19**, 011006 (2010)
7. Li, S., Zhang, F., Ma, L., Ngan, K.N.: Image quality assessment by separately evaluating detail losses and additive impairments. IEEE Trans. Multimed. **13**, 935–949 (2011)
8. Ding, K., Ma, K., Wang, S., Simoncelli, E.P.: Image quality assessment: unifying structure and texture similarity. arXiv, arXiv:2004.07728 (2020)
9. Násánen, R.: Visibility of halftone dot textures. IEEE Trans. Syst. Man Cybern. **14**, 920–924 (1984)

10. Lee, J., Horiuchi, T.: Image quality assessment for color halftone images based on color structural similarity. IEICE Trans. Fundam. Electron. Commun. Comput. Sci. **91**, 1392–1399 (2008)
11. Li, D., Kiyotomo, T., Horiuchi, T.: Glossiness index of objects in halftone color images based on structure and appearance distortion. J. Imaging **8**, 59 (2022)
12. Okamoto, S., Nagano, H., Kidoma, K., Yamada, Y.: Specification of individuality in causal relationships among texture-related attributes, emotions and preferences. Int. J. Affect. Eng. **15**, 11–19 (2016)
13. Okamoto, S., Kojima, H., Yamagishi, A., Kato, K., Tamada, A.: Layered-modeling of affective and sensory experiences using structural equation modeling: touch experiences of plastic surfaces as an example. IEEE Trans. Affect. Comput. **12**, 429–438 (2018)
14. Hollins, M., Faldowski, R., Rao, S., Young, F.: Perceptual dimensions of tactile surface texture: a multidimensional scaling analysis. Percept. Psychophys. **54**, 697–705 (1993)
15. Delphine, P., Catherine, D., Dominique, V., Agnès, G.: Perceptual dimensions of tactile textures. J. Actpsy. **114**, 165–184 (2003)
16. Watanabe, S., Horiuchi, T.: Modeling perceptions using common impressions: perceptual "authenticity", "luxury", and "quaintness" for leather. Text. Res. J. **91**(1–2), 73–86 (2020)
17. Tanaka, M., Horiuchi, T., Otani, K., Hung, P.: Evaluation for faithful reproduction of star fields in a planetarium. J. Imaging Sci. Technol. **61**, 060401-1–060401-12 (2017)
18. Tanaka, M., Horiuchi, T., Otani, K.: Relationship between faithfulness and preference of stars in a planetarium. J. Percept. Imaging **2**, 010402-1-010402–11 (2019)
19. Tanaka, M., Otani, K., Setoguchi, S., Horiuchi, T.: The reproduction and evaluation of star fields with the milky way in a planetarium. Appl. Sci. **11**, 1413 (2021)
20. Köhler, W.: Gestalt Psychology. Liveright Publishing Corporation, New York (1929)
21. https://www.nopa.or.jp/copc/pdf/kansei-honbun.pdf. Accessed August 20, 2024, in Japanese
22. Shimizu, Y., Doizaki, R., Sakamoto, M.: A system to estimate an impression conveyed by onomatopoeia. Trans. Jpn. Soc. Artif. Intell. **29**, 41–52 (2014)
23. Doizaki, R., Watanabe, J., Sakamoto, M.: Automatic estimation of multidimensional ratings from a single sound-symbolic word and word-based visualization of tactile perceptual space. IEEE Trans. Haptics **10**, 173–182 (2017)

Chapter 15
Depicting Shitsukan

Shin Ishihara, Shota Nakamoto, Hiroyuki Uchiro, Manabu Miki, Yuta Asano, Yuichiro Taira, and Imari Sato

Abstract Paintings are one of the most important objects for understanding Shitsukan, as they reflect the process by which artists perceived and expressed the material and texture of objects. Human skin has long been an object of great interest for artists, who seek to convey Shitsukan, qualities such as softness, glossiness, and transparency, on a two-dimensional canvas. Léonard Foujita, an artist active at the École de Paris in the 1920s, is world-renowned for his original technique of smooth, transparent skin, known as 'milky-white' skin. Destructive analysis has facilitated the identification of several white pigments used by Foujita; however, how he effectively utilized these pigments to achieve his 'milky-white' skin texture expression has remained a secret. Our preliminary investigation revealed that each of the white pigments reported to have been used by Foujita exhibits a unique fluorescent emission. Based on this finding, we measured and analyzed the fluorescent emission of Foujita's paintings under ultraviolet illumination using a hyperspectral camera. Through our analysis, we found that white pigments, which exhibit similar reflective properties under illumination without ultraviolet light, were intentionally arranged according to their fluorescent emission colors. Building on this analysis, we discuss how artists may have exploited the optical properties of pigments to represent the Shitsukan–the optical and perceptual qualities–of human skin.

S. Ishihara · Y. Asano · I. Sato (✉)
National Institute of Informatics, Chiyoda-ku, Tokyo, Japan
e-mail: imarik@nii.ac.jp

S. Nakamoto
The University of Tokyo, Bunkyo-ku, Tokyo, Japan

H. Uchiro
Pola Museum of Art, Kanagawa, Japan

M. Miki
Visionarist Co. Ltd., Ikoma-shi, Nara, Japan

Y. Taira
Tokyo University of the Arts, Taito-ku, Tokyo, Japan

S. Nishida and K. Nishino (eds.), *Shitsukan—Understanding and Manipulating Material and Quality Perception*, https://doi.org/10.1007/978-981-95-4762-3_15

Keywords Art painting analysis · Skin appearance representation · Layered skin structure representation · Hyperspectral imaging · Fluorescence-assisted pigment unmixing

15.1 Introduction

In the field of fine art painting, artists achieve high-quality expressions of materials, even though the objects depicted and the materials used to represent them are completely different. The artists skillfully utilize a variety of traditional and original techniques and materials to express the three-dimensionality, transparency, translucency, glossiness, softness, and vividness, in other words, the Shitsukan of objects on a flat canvas. Therefore, investigating the paintings created by artists and examining their techniques for expressing materials is important for understanding Shitsukan, but this has not been addressed extensively.

The Shitsukan depicted on canvas is also affected by the viewing conditions, particularly the illumination surrounding the painting. In the late 19th century, with the development of tube pigments, painting outdoors ('en plein air') became popular. Impressionist artists recognized the importance of natural light in the creation and appreciation of their work. For example, Claude Monet preferred to paint and exhibit his artworks under natural lighting, believing it revealed a richer, more dynamic range of colors that artificial gaslight could not replicate. His paintings were often displayed in rooms with large windows to maximize exposure to sunlight. Unlike modern museum lighting, sunlight contains a higher proportion of ultraviolet (UV) rays. As a result, artworks created under the sunlight may exhibit unique color characteristics–including pigment reflections and fluorescent emissions stimulated by UV light–that are visible under natural sunlight but may be diminished or absent under artificial illumination.

This fluorescence of pigments seems to have been leveraged by various artists, either unconsciously or deliberately, to express particular colors in their artworks. In such cases, the original color and intention of the artwork may not be conveyed properly without the correct lighting conditions. Fluorescence is the phenomenon of absorbing light and subsequently emitting light at a longer wavelength (lower energy) than the absorbed light. When fluorescence occurs, the human eye perceives both the color emitted by the fluorescent material and the reflected color on an object's surface.

In this chapter, we focus on one painter who turned out to have fully leveraged fluorescence in his paintings. Léonard Foujita (1886–1968) was an artist of the École de Paris (Paris School) active in the early 20th century. Among the painters of the École de Paris, Amedeo Modigliani, Marc Chagall, and Moïse Kisling are notable. While many painters pursued a heavy expression through the use of color, Foujita created a technique for expressing skin mainly in white. His oil paintings of nudes have been called 'Grand Fond Blanc' (Wonderful White) and have attracted attention for their unique expression of skin texture with a soft, milky, transparent feel. Many of Foujita's paintings have attracted widespread interest around the world.

Figure 15.1a shows Foujita's oil painting, "*Nude on Bed with a Dog*," which is focused on this study. The painting is composed mainly of black and white, with almost no vivid color used for expression. Focusing on the white, the tone differs between the nude and the bed sheet areas, and shades of light and dark can be seen within each area. Various materials in the literature suggest that Foujita used multiple white pigments to create his works. An investigation on fragments of Foujita's works from the same period using a microscope [17] confirmed the use of white pigments such as lead white (lead carbonate basic), calcium carbonate, and barium sulfate. A Photograph of Foujita's painting process taken by Ken Domon (in the collection of Ken Domon Museum of Photography) shows that Foujita used baby powder, which primarily consists of talc (magnesium silicate), as a white pigment in his paintings. It is believed that Foujita skillfully combined various white pigments, including these, to create the 'milky-white' skin tones. However, there are still many unresolved aspects regarding how Foujita used multiple white pigments on the canvas to create 'Grand Fond Blanc' and establish the expression of 'milky-white' skin.

We tried a spectral analysis on "*Nude on Bed with a Dog*," which is in the collection of Pola Museum of Art. With the advent of hyperspectral cameras in recent years, it has become possible to capture the reflection spectra as an image and analyze the spatial distribution of reflectance spectra of the painting. In the case of "*Nude on Bed with a Dog*," it is challenging to identify the spatial distribution of pigments by reflectance spectra analysis because most of the areas are painted with white pigments, and their reflectance spectra are all similar. Therefore, we focused on the fluorescence emission properties of the white pigments rather than their reflectance spectra. Our investigation revealed that the difference in colors/spectra between white pigments is much larger under UV light than under visible light, thanks to the unique fluorescence property each white pigment exhibits. This observation is also seen in

(a) Under visible light source (b) Under ultraviolet light source

Fig. 15.1 Léonard Foujita, "Nude on Bed with a Dog" (1921), Oil on canvas, Pola Museum of Art. ©Fondation Foujita/ADAGP, Paris and JASPAR, Tokyo, 2025, C5184

the actual work, where colors due to fluorescence emission appear when the work is irradiated with UV light (Fig. 15.1b). Based on this important observation, we formulated the problem of separating the fluorescence emission spectra of painting materials as a linear mixing model. We applied a spectral unmixing technique to the fluorescence emission excited under UV light. This allows us to clarify the distribution of white pigments, which has been challenging to do in reflectance spectral image analysis under white light sources, and to discuss how the texture of 'milky-white' skin is created through their different uses.

15.2 Painting Analysis Techniques

15.2.1 Conventional Painting Analysis

Conventional analyses of oil paintings rely on photographic techniques–such as infrared, fluorescence, and X-ray imaging–as well as spectroscopic methods, including X-ray and reflectance spectroscopy, to examine the pigments used and the varnish on the painting surface. These techniques are widely used in the investigation of cultural properties, as they allow for nondestructive and noncontact analysis [25]. Infrared photography inspects materials that absorb infrared light, such as underglaze paintings and charcoal, because infrared light penetrates beneath the paint [34]. X-ray photography involves irradiating a painting with X-rays–which have shorter wavelengths than ultraviolet, visible, and infrared light–and capturing the transmitted radiation to reveal internal structures and material composition. Because the transmission of X-rays varies with the density of materials, this technique allows for the visualization of material distribution and hidden structural elements that are not visible on the surface. These methods have been used to investigate the conditions of paintings.

X-ray fluorescence (XRF) analysis is a (semi-)quantitative elemental analysis technique based on the ionization of atoms induced by primary X-ray irradiation. The emitted secondary radiation carries information about the type and concentration of elemental constituents at the observation point [15]. In painting analysis, XRF is often combined with reflectance spectroscopy since elemental composition alone may not always be sufficient to identify specific pigments. Reflectance spectra of pigments captured by reflectance spectroscopy are related to the chemical structure and composition of materials and can thus aid in identifying pigments. For pigments with similar colors, differences in reflectance spectra should not be significant. To address this, techniques such as second-order derivative analysis and multivariate analysis are proposed to enhance spectral distinctions of pigments [9]. However, it is still challenging to find the significant difference between white pigments in this way (see Fig. 15.2e).

Fluorescence photography is commonly used to assess the condition of varnish on a painting's surface and to examine materials that exhibit fluorescent properties [18].

In addition to varnishes, certain lake pigments in oil paintings are known to fluoresce under UV light. Notably, such fluorescence can also be triggered by visible light. Leveraging this property, some researchers have proposed that spectrofluorometric measurements under visible light excitation may be effective for identifying organic synthetic pigments [19].

Early studies on fluorescence spectral unmixing in paintings were based on observations across only a limited number of spectral bands [26]. More recent research suggests that fluorescence emission can be used to distinguish not only various colored pigments but also differences among white pigments–distinctions that are often difficult to discern under visible light alone [28]. These analyses were conducted using prepared pigment samples. However, the applicability of such techniques to more complex, real-world paintings had not yet been fully validated. As we describe later, we overcome this barrier by spectral unmixing of white pigments in actual paintings based on fluorescence emission spectra.

15.2.2 Hyperspectral Imaging

In recent years, advances in hyperspectral camera technology have enabled the capture of high-resolution reflectance spectra through spatio-spectral scanning. Hyperspectral imaging has been applied to painting analysis for pigment mapping and forgery detection [14]. It is also widely used in remote sensing applications, such as satellite imagery, where a technique known as spectral unmixing is employed to decompose hyperspectral images into constituent spectra–referred to as endmembers–and their corresponding abundances. Spectral unmixing allows for the extraction of information at the sub-pixel level. In hyperspectral images, mixed pixels often arise due to the limited spatial resolution of the sensor, photon reflections from multiple objects, or the physical mixing of different materials. Accurately separating these mixed pixels into individual spectral signatures (endmembers) and their associated quantities (abundances) is essential for analyzing the material composition of a scene in the field of remote sensing.

The most basic and widely used spectral mixture model is the linear mixing model [16]. This model assumes that the observed surface is composed of a small number of distinct materials with relatively constant spectral properties and that incident light reflects only once from each material before reaching the camera sensor. Under these conditions, most spectral variation arises from the proportions of these materials (endmembers), and the observed spectrum can be expressed as a linear combination of the endmember spectra weighted by their abundances.

However, when materials overlap or are located at boundaries, light may interact with multiple components through multiple scattering events, resulting in nonlinear mixing. In painting, pigments are often physically mixed, and recovering the original, unmixed pigment spectra requires separating the pure spectral components from the observed mixture. Such nonlinear mixing behavior can be analytically modeled using the Kubelka-Munk theory [3], which relates the reflectance of a pigment layer to its absorption and scattering coefficients.

To apply Kubelka-Munk theory [3] for pigment unmixing, prior knowledge of the absorption and scattering coefficients of each pigment–as well as the reflectance of the underlying surface–is necessary. Moreover, in oil paintings, the situation is further complicated by the translucency of the paint layers, which contain not only pigments but also binding media such as oil. These layers are often stacked in multiple strata, introducing additional complexity into the reflectance behavior. Due to these factors, the non-destructive and non-invasive identification and separation of unknown pigments in oil paintings remain a highly challenging and open research problem.

Studies on spectral unmixing for oil paintings include pigment identification using sparse unmixing via variable splitting and augmented Lagrangian (SUnSAL) [4, 30], as well as pigment unmixing based on deep learning approaches [29]. In [30], the observed spectra are assumed to be linear combinations of known pigment spectra (endmembers) from a predefined spectral dictionary and their corresponding abundances. This assumption limits the method's adaptability, as it cannot be applied effectively to paintings containing pigments not represented in the dictionary.

Conversely, learningâŁ"based unmixing methods support nonlinear mixing models by leveraging deep neural networks to capture complex spectral interactions, such as those described by the Kubelka-Munk theory. However, these methods also require a comprehensive spectral dataset of pigments in advance. Consequently, both approaches face challenges when applied to paintings containing unknown or undocumented pigments, making pigment unmixing difficult when relevant reference spectra are unavailable.

15.3 Previous Analysis on Léonard Foujita's Paintings

As an artist at the École de Paris, Léonard Foujita became known worldwide for his painting technique that incorporated a unique texture expression known as 'milky-white' skin. While there are few documents or research materials on Léonard Foujita's painting techniques, we referred to a research report compiled by Hayashi and Kijima [17], based on several restoration cases of Foujita's works. Here we summarize their report regarding the materials and techniques of Foujita's works. In the restoration case studies in works "Illustration of European Coming to Japan" and "Illustration of Horse," some fragments were collected from the periphery and cracks of the works and analyzed. The analysis reported two ground-coating layers, with barium sulfate in the lower layer and lead carbonate basic, and calcium carbonate in the upper layer, as well as a small amount of silicate. In the restoration case studies in works "Composition" and "Fight," it was reported that while the white in Foujita's work gave a transparent appearance and was different from the classical dense, opaque white, the research showed that the ground-coating layer was the same as that of the Western European tradition (Specifically, it consisted of calcium carbonate, lead carbonate basic, and linseed oil). Foujita's 'milky-white' is not brought about by entirely new materials, but is produced by using these traditional painting materials and layering talc (magnesium silicate), the main ingredient of baby powder, on top of his works. Moreover, records from a survey of Foujita's atelier in Paris, where he spent the last years of his life, report that lead white (lead carbonate basic), calcium carbonate, plaster (calcium sulfate), and talc (magnesium silicate) were found.

Recent analysis has revealed, to some extent, what kind of painting materials Foujita used [17]. Foujita developed a distinctive painting style characterized by soft colors, achieved through the use of traditional white pigments and talc–a material rarely employed in traditional painting. It is thought that he applied glue to a thin linen fabric, then applied calcium carbonate and lead white on top of the glue, kneading dry oil and glue together as a medium and further suppressing the oil with talc (magnesium silicate) so that India ink lines could be drawn to the top surface. It is considered that this method of creating the painting base reproduces the semi-glossy, translucent 'milky-white' texture of the skin [17]. On the other hand, it is considered that Foujita painted the skin texture by replicating the structure of skin on the canvas, intending to have "the material of the canvas itself reproduce the texture of the skin" [12]. This was the opposite of the typical approach of 20th-century artists, who often completed their works with thick layers of bright colors, rather than using skin color.

Previous analyses of Foujita's works have faced challenges in nondestructively and noninvasively identifying multiple white pigments, and little attention has been given to the artist's intentional use of these pigments as a means of pictorial expression. Here, in the following section of this chapter, we focus on the distinct fluorescence emissions produced by different white pigments and propose a method for decomposing and estimating the observed fluorescence emission spectra from the paintings into a set of spectral bases. To explore the role of various white pigments in rendering Foujita's characteristic 'milky-white' skin texture, we estimate the pigment components and their spatial distribution within selected works. Furthermore, through perceptual experiments comparing images with and without fluorescent emission components, we examine how fluorescence influences material perception.

15.4 Fluorescence-Assisted Analysis of Art Works

As an overview, in the following, we show how we conducted a thorough analysis of how Foujita fully leveraged fluorescence. We particularly focused on his use of white pigments and revealed their diverse fluorescent characteristics and his mastery of them. We first captured the fluorescent emission of actual paintings using a hyperspectral camera and UV light. We then estimated the spatial distribution and the fluorescent spectral components of white pigments on the painting surface based on a physical and mathematical model.

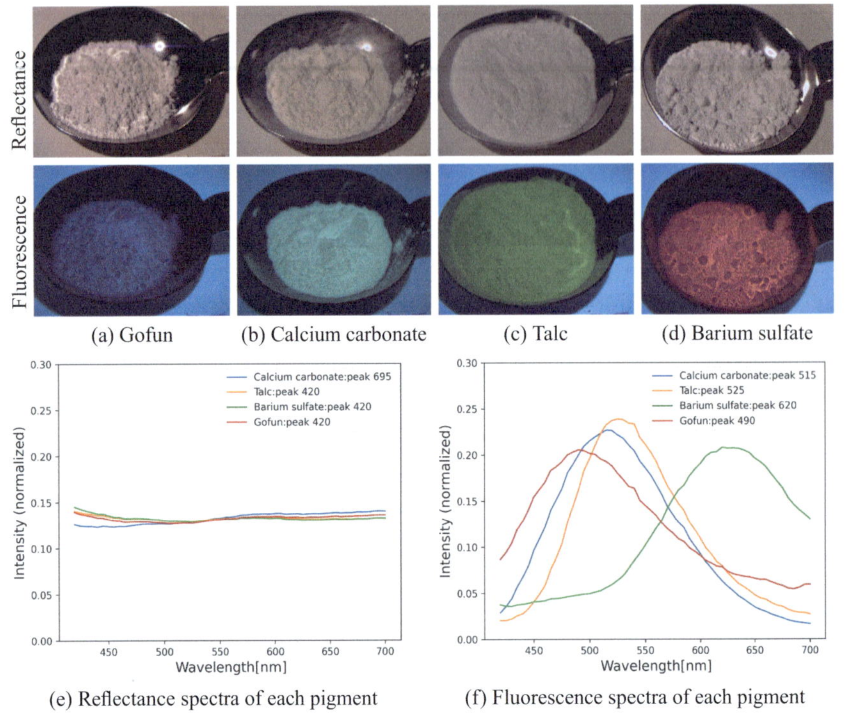

Fig. 15.2 Appearance and spectra of the pigment that was supposedly used by Foujita, as detected by previous destructive studies. In figures (a–d), the upper row shows the appearance of the pigment under a visible light source, and the lower row shows the appearance of the pigment under a UV light source. In figures (e, f), the lines are normalized reflectance and fluorescence emission spectra of each pigment, respectively. Normalization in plots was performed so that the magnitude of the vector is 1 when the spectrum is considered as a vector with the dimension of wavelengths

Previous research has revealed that Foujita used traditional white pigments and talc (magnesium silicate) in creating the ‘milky-white’ base and skin. It should be noted that the pigments used by Foujita are mostly white, and therefore differ only slightly in appearance and reflectance spectra, making the identification of their distribution a very challenging task (see Fig. 15.2a–d (Reflectance) and e). We have measured the fluorescence properties of several white painting materials and found that they exhibit distinctly different appearance and emission spectra when exposed to 365 nm UV light (Fig. 15.2a–d (Fluorescence) and f).

Each painting material exhibits a unique fluorescence emission spectrum, even when its reflected colors appear similar. We assumed that the emission component plays a more dominant role than absorption or reflection. We modeled the composition of fluorescence emission by multiple pigments at a pixel with a linear mixing model and decomposed them using NMF (non-negative matrix factorization). In the following, we discuss the details of this separation method for fluorescence emission spectra.

15.4.1 Fluorescence-Assisted Emission Spectra Mixing Model

In general, when an object including fluorescence is illuminated with light, the observed light includes the fluorescent component and the reflected component of the object. When the wavelength of the illuminating light is λ_i, and the wavelength of the observed light is λ_o, the reflected component is observed only at the same wavelength as the irradiated light ($\lambda_i = \lambda_o$) and the fluorescent component is observed at a longer wavelength than the illuminating light ($\lambda_i < \lambda_o$).

The reflection component in oil painting is often modeled using the Kubelka-Munk theory, which is well-suited for representing the complex optical phenomena observed in the medium. However, this approach is infeasible unless the optical parameters of the individual painting materials are known. In our analysis, we focus on the fluorescence emission component of pigments. We illuminate the target with UV light λ_i, which has a peak wavelength at 365 nm. We capture the fluorescence emission component of the target using a hyperspectral camera to measure the spectrum within the visible light range, where the range of λ_o is set to 400–700 nm. The observed hyperspectral image I_F representing the fluorescence emission component of the target can be expressed as follows:

$$I_F(\lambda_o) = \int \mu(\lambda_i, \lambda_o) L(\lambda_i) d\lambda_i. \tag{15.1}$$

Here, L represents the intensity of the irradiated light, and μ represents the excitation-emission property inherent in fluorescent materials. μ signifies the ratio of light emission at λ_o to light irradiation at λ_i. When multiple pigments exhibiting fluorescence are mixed, in contrast to the reflection, the hyperspectral image I of mixed fluorescent emissions can be modeled as a linear combination of the individual fluorescence emissions as follows:

$$I = I_{F_1} + I_{F_2} + \cdots + I_{F_n}, \tag{15.2}$$

where each I_{F_i} represents the hyperspectral image of individual fluorescence emissions of the i-th component according to Eq. 15.1, and n denotes the number of corresponding components. Thus, the fluorescent emission mixing model for paintings follows Eq. 15.2, and its separation model is consistent with the linear mixing model. Note that for simplicity of our analysis, Eq. 15.2 does not account for the absorption of fluorescent emission by surrounding pigments.

15.4.2 Fluorescence-Assited Pigment Unmixing

From the discussions above, we assume the mixture of fluorescence emission components follows a linear mixing model. Non-negative matrix factorization (NMF), a statistical matrix factorization method, is consistent with the linear mixing model. The NMF aims to decompose the original matrix $\boldsymbol{Y}$ into an abundance matrix $\boldsymbol{A}$ and an endmember matrix $\boldsymbol{M}$, represented by $\boldsymbol{Y} \approx \boldsymbol{A}\boldsymbol{M}$, under the constraint that all elements have non-negative values. The NMF-based spectral unmixing involves decomposing a hyperspectral image $\boldsymbol{Y} \in \mathbb{R}^{P \times N}$, consisting of P spectral band observations and N pixels, into a collection of K individual spectral matrices $\boldsymbol{M} \in \mathbb{R}^{K \times N}$ and their abundances $\boldsymbol{A} \in \mathbb{R}^{P \times K}$. The procedure of the fluorescence-assisted pigment unmixing is shown in Fig. 15.3.

When applying NMF-based spectral unmixing to a fluorescent hyperspectral image of oil paintings, we expect the estimated endmembers to resemble the fluorescence emission spectra of the painting materials. Additionally, since the spectra of painting materials generally exhibit smooth variations along the spectral domain, the resulting endmembers should also exhibit smoothness. Therefore, we chose to utilize palmNMF [10] to extract components that closely resemble the actual spectra and to reduce noise to some extent. The palmNMF employs a convex function minimization method called PALM (Proximal Alternating Linearized Minimization) [6], which incorporates non-differentiable constraints into NMF. The algorithm includes constraints that promote smoothness in the resulting endmembers and sparsity in the abundance proportions. We believe that the fluorescence emission spectra of pigments are expected to be smooth and that their spatial distribution is relatively smooth, making them suitable for our analysis. For a detailed description of the algorithm and further information, interested readers may refer to [10].

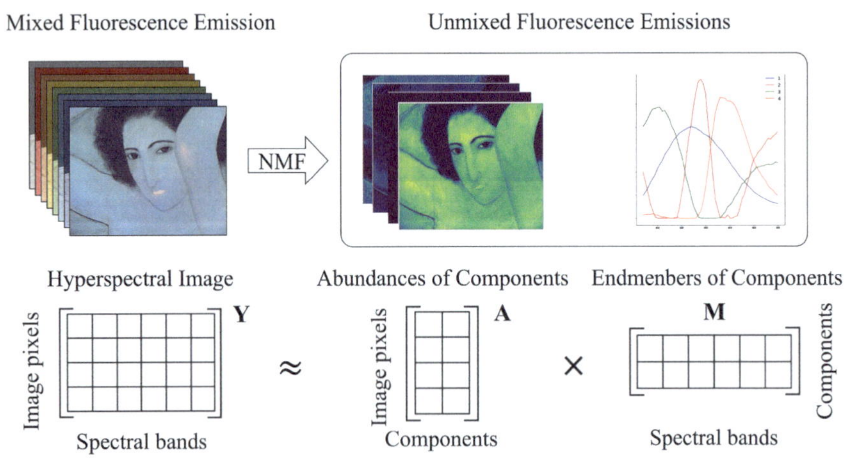

Fig. 15.3 Procedure of our fluorescence-assisted pigment unmixing

15.5 What Our Analysis Revealed of Foujita's Paintings

We attempted to determine the spatial distribution of the specific pigments used by Foujita in his paintings of nudes by performing pigment unmixing based on fluorescence emission spectra. Based on the separation results, we further discuss Foujita's intention to use different types of white pigments. The painting was captured using a hyperspectral camera (EbaJapan NH-8), capable of acquiring images with a spatial resolution of 1024×1200 pixels in 5 nm spectral intervals from 380 to 1000nm. UV light with a peak intensity of 365 nm was used as the light source, and the experiments were conducted using 57 spectral bands ranging from 420 to 700 nm. With the assistance of museum curators, the intensity of the UV light used in the experiments was properly adjusted to minimize damage to the artworks.

The number of endmembers was determined using HySime, a signal subspace identification algorithm [5]. Since HySime estimated that many portions of the target paintings had 3 or 4 subspaces, the number of endmembers for the separation was set to 4. In addition, the values of the abundance and endmember matrices in NMF were initialized using non-negative double singular value decomposition (NNDSVD) [7].

15.5.1 Results of Fluorescence-Assisted Spectral Unmixing

The results of the fluorescence-assisted analysis of Foujita's work are shown in Fig. 15.4. The unmixing of the four parts of Foujita's work revealed a light blue component that is present in both the skin and the bed sheet (C1; Component 1), a red component that is common to the skin and hair (C2; Component 2), a dark blue component that is exclusive to the skin region (C3; Component 3), and a green component that is seen in sheets and some part of face region (C4; Component 4). The light blue C1 component is common to almost all areas except for black areas such as hair and background, and is predicted to be like an underpainting. The red component (C2) and blue component (C3) are primarily found in the skin and appear in complementary areas to each other. This suggests that Foujita intentionally used layered structures in his paintings. The green component (C4) clearly exists mainly in the sheet area and is absent from most of the skin area, except for the upper part of the face. This suggests that Fujita intentionally used this component in the sheet area, or that other components (probably C2 and C3) were used to cover this component in the skin area. C1 is likely to be that of calcium carbonate, as its spectral shape is similar to that of calcium carbonate and the peak positions of the spectra are also similar (Fig. 15.5a). In addition, blue and red fluorescent components were observed in the skin area of all unmixing targets as C2 and C3. For C2 and C3, there was no perfect match with the fluorescence emission spectra of the white pigments we measured. However, when compared based on fluorescence emission color, C2 appeared close to barium sulfate, and C3 tended to resemble gofun (shell lime).

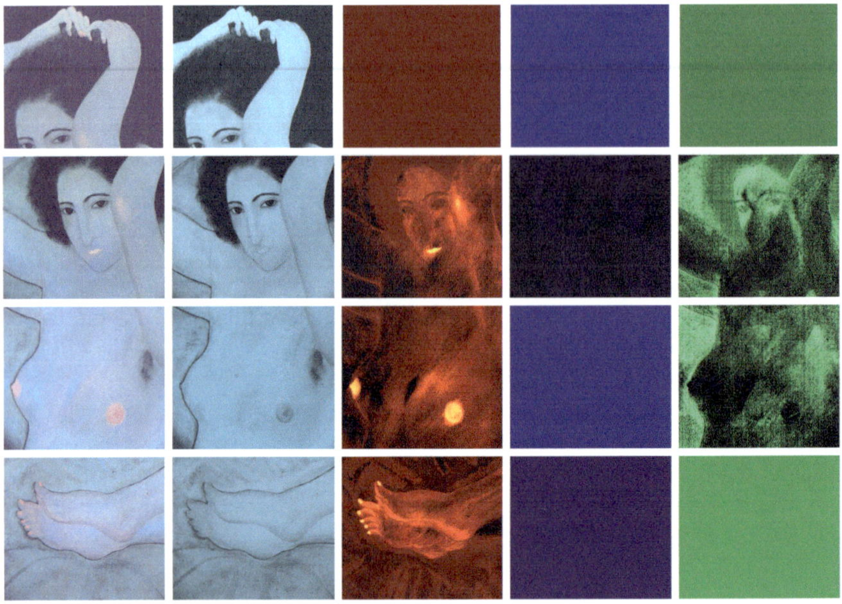

Fig. 15.4 Results of our fluorescence-assisted analysis. From left to right: input image, colorized image of each component, and endmembers plot. From top to bottom: hands, face, chest, and foot parts of *"Nude on Bed with a Dog"*

The spectrum comparison on each pigment and estimated component is shown in Fig. 15.5. C4 exhibits an emission spectrum whose peak position closely aligns with talc, one of the essential materials known to be originally used by Foujita (Fig. 15.5d). While an exact match is not observed in the fluorescence spectrum, it can be inferred that Foujita utilized pigments with blue and red fluorescent properties to depict skin and sheets, respectively, to achieve distinct visual effects.

According to art experts, C4 is likely to be a component of talc used to draw ink outlines, as it is used intensively near the contours of the body, around the eyes, and on the sides of the body. The possibility that talc was applied to draw ink lines has been suggested in the previous analysis [17]. Furthermore, C4 appears to be present in the background as well, which one would expect was probably intended to make the surface semi-glossy or to dry the surface earlier.

15.5.2 Comparison with Subsurface Scattering of the Skin

Here, fluorescence-assisted analysis has raised an intriguing question. Did Foujita use red and blue fluorescent pigments to intricately portray the skin and create a

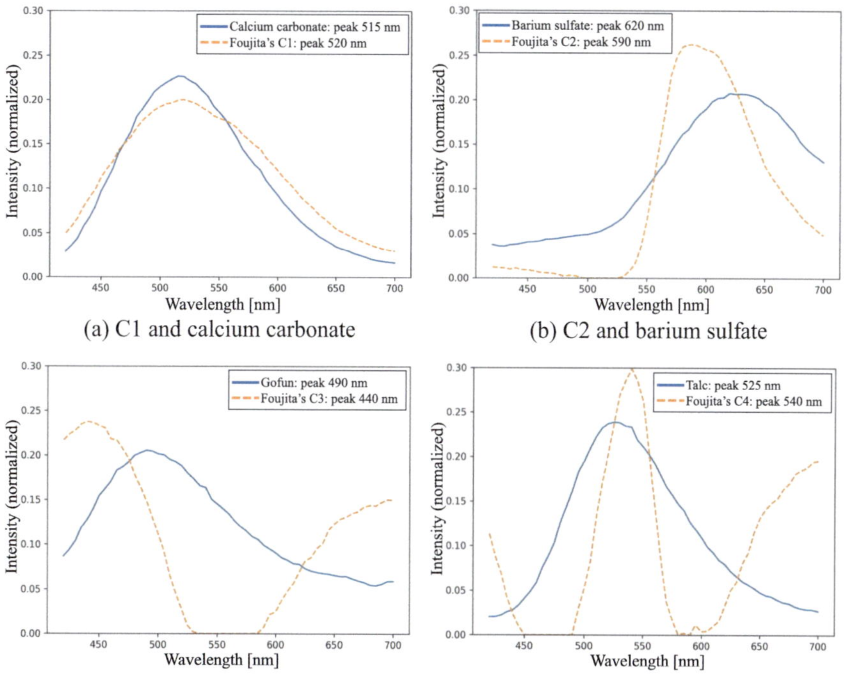

(a) C1 and calcium carbonate
(b) C2 and barium sulfate
(c) C3 and gofun (shell lime)
(d) C4 and talc (magnesium silicate)

Fig. 15.5 Fluorescence spectrum comparison of measured pigments and estimated components from Foujita's work

canvas that resembles actual skin? One of the notable optical properties of skin is its translucence, enabling light to pass through to the underlying layers and resulting in reflection and scattering that contribute to its texture [2]. Hence, we directed our attention to exploring the connection between scattering in real skin and the distribution of pigments in painted skin. We performed high-frequency illumination [24] on real human skin, posed as in the paintings, to separate reflection components such as direct surface reflection and subsurface scattering. We then compared the fluorescence emission in the paintings with these components of real skin to examine whether fluorescence was intentionally applied in relation to the skin's optical properties.

The core idea of the high-frequency illumination method is to separate the direct and global components of illumination in a scene using structured light patterns. Specifically, the technique relies on projecting a high-frequency binary illumination pattern onto the scene and capturing images of how the scene responds. The direct illumination component reacts strongly to changes in the pattern, as it comes straight from the light source to the surface, while the global illumination component–resulting from effects like interreflections, subsurface scattering, and volumetric scattering–changes much less because it is diffused and scattered throughout the scene. By comparing how the intensity at each point varies between the original pattern and its complement, one can isolate the direct component as the part that changes significantly, and the global component as the part that remains relatively constant.

As described above, high-frequency illumination was applied to real human skin, posed as in the paintings, to separate its reflective components, namely direct surface reflection and subsurface scattering. By comparing the color and intensity distributions of the fluorescent emission in the paintings with these components of real skin, we examined Foujita's intention in using different white pigments.

In Fig. 15.6, the top row shows the distribution and colors of the surface reflection and subsurface scattering components of actual human skin, which were acquired using the high-frequency illuminating method. The bottom row shows the separated fluorescent components of the skin depicted by Foujita. Interestingly, compared with the results from Foujita's painting and those of real skin, the red color of the nail and heel and the bluish color of the instep and lateral areas of the foot are similar. This comparison leads to the hypothesis that Foujita may have intentionally used fluorescent pigments to mimic the optical properties of human skin, such as reflection and subsurface scattering.

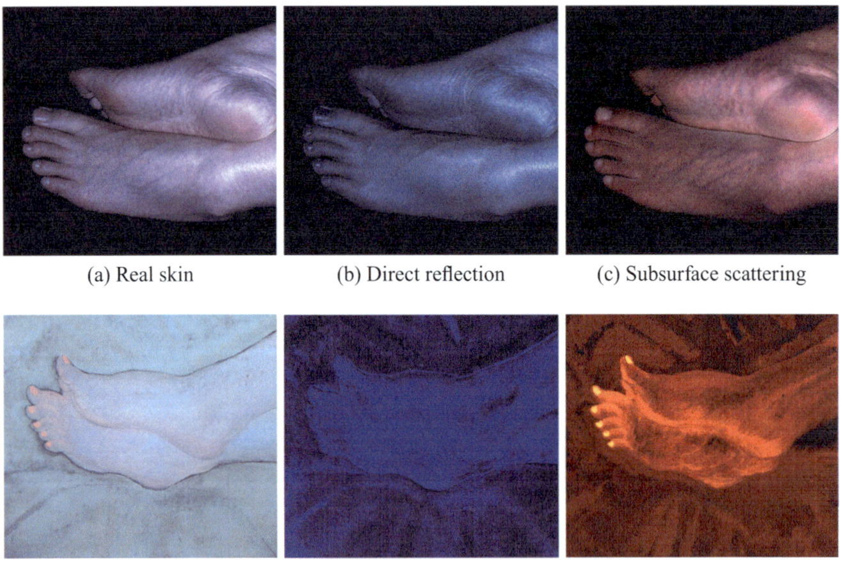

(a) Real skin (b) Direct reflection (c) Subsurface scattering

(d) Fluorescence image (e) Component 3 (C3) (f) Component 2 (C2)

Fig. 15.6 Appearances of actual and painted skin. The top row shows the subsurface scattering and reflection components of actual skin. The bottom row shows colorized images of the components obtained by our method

15.6 Conclusion

Understanding the material expression techniques of artists is one of the important issues in approaching the mechanism of Shitsukan perception [1, 27]. In fine art painting, artists effectively convey material qualities, even though the depicted objects and the materials used are entirely different. Through a range of traditional and innovative techniques, they skillfully evoke three-dimensionality, transparency, translucency, glossiness, softness, and vividness on a flat canvas. Studying these artistic methods offers valuable insights into Shitsukan perception, yet this area remains largely unexplored.

In this chapter, we analyzed the optical characteristics of Foujita's signature "milky-white" skin texture through spectroscopy-based optical analysis. We observed that white pigments, which show almost no differences in spectral reflectance, display distinct fluorescent emission colors under ultraviolet light. Building on this observation, we modeled fluorescence as a linear mixture and applied spectral unmixing to reveal the spatial distribution of different white pigments in Nude on Bed with a Dog. Our method successfully distinguished pigments that conventional reflectance-based techniques could not, highlighting their unique fluorescent properties. Whereas Western painting has traditionally created three-dimensional illusions through linear perspective, Foujita instead emphasized the structure of the skin itself by exploiting the differences in fluorescent emission colors of white pigments. Our analysis suggests that he may have used fluorescent pigments to mimic the optical properties of real skin–such as reflection and subsurface scattering–producing subtle variations in color through fluorescence rather than shading alone.

Our analysis indicates that Foujita's characteristic 'milky-white' skin effect was achieved using different fluorescent pigments to reproduce a glossy texture. Typically, artworks displayed in museums are housed in frames that block ultraviolet (UV) light to prevent deterioration. However, this can diminish the visual impact of pigments with fluorescent properties–such as those used by Foujita-resulting in a loss of radiance. In other words, the quality of Foujita's 'milky-white' skin may not be fully visible under standard museum lighting. Previous studies have discussed how the lighting environment in which a painting is created can influence its visual style [22]. For instance, artists working outdoors under sunlight–as in pleinairisme–may incorporate fluorescent pigments whose full effect depends on UV-rich light. Consequently, when such works are viewed under artificial lighting that lacks UV components, their appearance may differ significantly from the artist's original intent. In future research, we plan to investigate this phenomenon further using replicas of actual paintings, aiming to reconstruct the viewing conditions under natural sunlight. This approach will help clarify how materials contributed to the perception of 'milky-white' skin at the time of creation and may offer museum viewers a more faithful appreciation of the artwork's original appearance, without the need to expose the actual pieces to sunlight.

It would be an intriguing direction to explore the relationship between optical properties–beyond fluorescence–and shitsukan in painting. Previous studies have shown that psychophysical methods link physical stimuli with perception [33], that color and structure support spatial representation [35], and that painting datasets reveal persuasive material depiction and alignment between models and human vision [32]. Research on transparency emphasizes luminance, material, and object properties [31], with Metelli's law [20, 21], gloss [8, 23], and translucency [11, 13] identified as central findings. Collectively, these works suggest promising avenues for advancing our understanding and reproduction of Shitukan in art.

References

1. Adelson, E.H.: On seeing stuff: the perception of materials by humans and machines. In: Human Vision and Electronic Imaging VI, vol. 4299, pp. 1–12. SPIE (2001)
2. Baba, Y., Mashita, T., Mukaigawa, Y., Yagi, Y.: Statistical analysis of human skin based on reflection and scattering characteristics. In: Technical Report 2, Institute of Scientific and Industrial Research, Osaka University (2009). https://cir.nii.ac.jp/crid/1520290884498198528
3. Berns, R., Mohammadi, M.: Evaluating single- and two-constant Kubelka-Munk turbid media theory for instrumental-based inpainting. Stud. Conserv. **52**, 299–314 (2007). https://doi.org/10.1179/sic.2007.52.4.299
4. Bioucas-Dias, J.M., Figueiredo, M.A.: Alternating direction algorithms for constrained sparse regression: application to hyperspectral unmixing. In: 2010 2nd Workshop on Hyperspectral Image and Signal Processing: Evolution in Remote Sensing, pp. 1–4. IEEE (2010)
5. Bioucas-Dias, J.M., Nascimento, J.M.P.: Hyperspectral subspace identification. IEEE Trans. Geosci. Remote Sens. **46**(8), 2435–2445 (2008). https://doi.org/10.1109/TGRS.2008.918089
6. Bolte, J., Sabach, S., Teboulle, M.: Proximal alternating linearized minimization for nonconvex and nonsmooth problems. Math. Program. **146**(1), 459–494 (2014)
7. Boutsidis, C., Gallopoulos, E.: SVD based initialization: a head start for nonnegative matrix factorization. Pattern Recognit. **41**(4), 1350–1362 (2008). https://doi.org/10.1016/j.patcog.2007.09.010. https://www.sciencedirect.com/science/article/pii/S0031320307004359
8. Chadwick, A.C., Kentridge, R.: The perception of gloss: a review. Vision. Res. **109**, 221–235 (2015)
9. Delaney, J., Thoury, M., Zeibel, J., Ricciardi, P., Morales, K., Dooley, K.: Visible and infrared imaging spectroscopy of paintings and improved reflectography. Herit. Sci. **4** (2016). https://doi.org/10.1186/s40494-016-0075-4
10. Fabregat, R., Pustelnik, N., Gonçalves, P., Borgnat, P.: Solving NMF with smoothness and sparsity constraints using palm (2019). ArXiv **abs/1910.14576**
11. Fleming, R.W., Jensen, H.W., Bülthoff, H.H.: Perceiving translucent materials. In: Proceedings of the 1st Symposium on Applied perception in Graphics and Visualization, pp. 127–134 (2004)
12. Fujita, T., Kondo, F.: Bura Ippon: Fujita Tsuguharu Esseisen ; Pari no Yokogao: Fujita Tsuguharu esseisen. Kodansha (2005)
13. Gigilashvili, D., Thomas, J.B., Hardeberg, J.Y., Pedersen, M.: Translucency perception: a review. J. Vis. **21**(8), 4 (2021)
14. Grillini, F., Thomas, J.B., George, S.: Comparison of imaging models for spectral unmixing in oil painting. Sensors **21**(7) (2021). https://doi.org/10.3390/s21072471.https://www.mdpi.com/1424-8220/21/7/2471
15. Janssens, K., Van der Snickt, G., Vanmeert, F., Legrand, S., Nuyts, G., Alfeld, M., Monico, L., Anaf, W., De Nolf, W., Vermeulen, M., et al.: Non-invasive and non-destructive examination of artistic pigments, paints, and paintings by means of X-Ray methods. Anal. Chem. Cult. Herit. 77–128 (2016)
16. Keshava, N., Mustard, J.: Spectral unmixing. IEEE Signal Process. Mag. **19**(1), 44–57 (2002). https://doi.org/10.1109/79.974727

17. Kijima, T., Hayashi, Y.: Fujita Tsuguharu no Kaiga Giho ni Semaru : Shufuku genba kara no hokoku [Understanding Leonard Foujita's painting techniques : Report from the restoration site]. Tokyo Geijutsu Daigaku Shuppankai (2010)
18. Longoni, M., Buttarelli, A., Gargano, M., Bruni, S.: A multiwavelength approach for the study of contemporary painting materials by means of fluorescence imaging techniques: an integration to spectroscopic methods. Appl. Sci. **12**(1) (2022). https://doi.org/10.3390/app12010094.https://www.mdpi.com/2076-3417/12/1/94
19. Longonis, M., Freschi, A., Cicala, N., Bruni, S.: Non-invasive identification of synthetic organic pigments in contemporary art paints by visible-excited spectrofluorimetry and visible reflectance spectroscopy. Spectrochim. Acta Part A Mol. Biomol. Spectrosc. **229**, 117907 (2020)
20. Metelli, F.: An algebraic development of the theory of perceptual transparency. Ergonomics **13**, 59–66 (1970)
21. Metelli, F.: The perception of transparency. Sci. Am. **230**(4), 90–99 (1974)
22. Motoyoshi, I.: Climate, illumination, and the style of western and eastern paintings. Art Percept. **10**(3), 244–256 (2022)
23. Motoyoshi, I., Nishida, S., Sharan, L., Adelson, E.H.: Image statistics and the perception of surface qualities. Nature **447**(7141), 206–209 (2007). https://doi.org/10.1038/nature05724
24. Nayar, S.K., Krishnan, G., Grossberg, M.D., Raskar, R.: Fast separation of direct and global components of a scene using high frequency illumination. In: ACM SIGGRAPH 2006 Papers, pp. 935–944 (2006)
25. Oshita, K.: Scientific investigation methods of oil paintings based on photographic and spectrometric techniques. Oleoscience **19**(9), 387–392 (2019). https://doi.org/10.5650/oleoscience.19.387
26. Pelagotti, A., Pezzati, L., Piva, A., Del Mastio, A.: Multispectral uv fluorescence analysis of painted surfaces. In: 2006 14th European Signal Processing Conference, pp. 1–5. IEEE (2006)
27. Pepperell, R.: The perception of art and the science of perception. In: Proceedings of SPIE—The International Society for Optical Engineering vol. 8291, p. 33 (2012). https://doi.org/10.1117/12.914774
28. Pronti, L., Felici, A.C., Ménager, M., Vieillescazes, C., Piacentini, M.: Spectral behavior of white pigment mixtures using reflectance, ultraviolet—fluorescence spectroscopy, and multispectral imaging. Appl. Spectrosc. **71**(12), 2616–2625 (2017)
29. Rohani, N., Pouyet, E., Walton, M., Cossairt, O., Katsaggelos, A.K.: Pigment unmixing of hyperspectral images of paintings using deep neural networks. In: ICASSP 2019 - 2019 IEEE International Conference on Acoustics, Speech and Signal Processing (ICASSP), pp. 3217–3221 (2019). doi:https://doi.org/10.1109/ICASSP.2019.8682838
30. Rohani, N., Salvant, J., Bahaadini, S., Cossairt, O., Walton, M., Katsaggelos, A.: Automatic pigment identification on roman egyptian paintings by using sparse modeling of hyperspectral images. In: 2016 24th European Signal Processing Conference (EUSIPCO), pp. 2111–2115 (2016). doi:https://doi.org/10.1109/EUSIPCO.2016.7760621
31. Sayim, B., Cavanagh, P.: The art of transparency. I-Perception **2**, 679–96 (2011). https://doi.org/10.1068/i0459aap
32. Van Zuijlen, M.J., Lin, H., Bala, K., Pont, S.C., Wijntjes, M.W.: Materials in paintings (MIP): an interdisciplinary dataset for perception, art history, and computer vision. PLoS ONE **16**(8), e0255109 (2021)
33. Wallraven, C., Kaulard, K., Kürner, C., Pepperell, R., Bülthoff, H.H.: Psychophysics for perception of (in)determinate art. In: Proceedings of the 4th Symposium on Applied Perception in Graphics and Visualization, APGV '07, pp. 115–122. Association for Computing Machinery, New York, NY, USA (2007). https://doi.org/10.1145/1272582.1272605.https://doi.org/10.1145/1272582.1272605
34. Walmsley, E., Metzger, C., Delaney, J.K., Fletcher, C.: Improved visualization of underdrawings with solid-state detectors operating in the infrared. Stud. Conserv. **39**(4), 217–231 (1994). https://doi.org/10.1179/sic.1994.39.4.217
35. Zhao, Y., Lai, S.: Exploring the visual space structure of oil painting based on visual importance. Comput. Intell. Neurosci. **2022**(12) (2022). https://doi.org/10.1155/2022/5112537

MIX
Papier aus verantwortungsvollen Quellen
Paper from responsible sources
FSC® C105338

If you have any concerns about our products,
you can contact us on
ProductSafety@springernature.com

In case Publisher is established outside the EU,
the EU authorized representative is:
Springer Nature Customer Service Center GmbH
Europaplatz 3, 69115 Heidelberg, Germany

Printed by Libri Plureos GmbH
in Hamburg, Germany